THE MIDDLE AGES UNLOCKED

THE MIDDLE AGES UNLOCKED
A GUIDE TO LIFE IN MEDIEVAL ENGLAND, 1050–1300

GILLIAN POLACK & KATRIN KANIA
FOREWORD BY ELIZABETH CHADWICK

AMBERLEY

To Tamara Mazzei, without whom this book
(and others) would not exist.

First published 2015
This edition published 2016

Amberley Publishing
The Hill, Stroud
Gloucestershire, GL5 4EP

www.amberley-books.com

British Library Cataloguing in Publication Data.
A catalogue record for this book is available from the British
Library.

ISBN 978 1 4456 6021 9 (paperback)
ISBN 978 1 4456 4589 6 (ebook)

Typesetting and Origination by Amberley Publishing.
Printed in the UK.

Contents

Acknowledgements

A common truth about a book is that it will make family members suffer, so the very first thank you for unending patience and support goes to Frieder Pfeiffer, without whom this book would not have happened. A big thank you also goes to the other side of the globe, to Sonya Oberman, another long-suffering family member.

This book that their support made possible is a very special creature with its own history, not only because two people from almost opposite sides of the globe got together to make it happen. The idea for the book was born more than a decade ago by Tamara Mazzei, Gillian Polack and a group of writers and readers who felt that a book like this was important. A first outline was written and draft chapters ensued. But a venture of this size and complexity is not an easy one. The first writing team was affected by major life changes, and finally Gillian recruited Katrin to balance specialisations. It took time and several iterations to arrive at the book you hold in your hands today. It also showed us many hidden cultural differences and made two distinctive writing voices merge, which was an interesting experience for both of us.

Therefore our next and very big thank you goes to Tamara, who had a big part in getting this Beast of a book started and who put in a vast amount of work on it before life took her and the book in different directions.

Our second thank you goes to the internet (with a special mention of the residents of LMB, penman-review and other mail lists with a medieval focus), without which this book would also never have happened. When two authors live on different continents, email and online contact make things possible. The internet enabled us to meet online and it provided us with ways to check current research. It also let us find images for the book, thanks to the graciousness of institutions such as the British Library, who make a lot of their pictures available as Creative Commons, or the Rare Breeds Survival Trust and Arche

Warder, who generously provided illustrations from their archives. A special thank you here goes to Andy Chopping from Museum of London Archaeology for his very kind help at the last minute. The internet was also how we could ask for, and receive, the help of people from various places. In particular, Nikolaus Hofbauer, Christina Curreli, Stefan von der Heide, David Lazenby, Ralf Metzner, Indra Starke-Ottich and Sonja Natus from the IG Wolf and Rosemary Watson all put in a lot of effort to help us with pictures, both pretty and informative. Thanks related to pictures also go to Achim Müller, Klaus Biehl, Florian Ottenburg and the crafters mentioned in the picture captions, as well as the few whose names we do not know.

There are other people who need to be thanked. This Beast of a book has been growing for a fair while and quite a few people have helped out with comments or support, thoughts or reality checks during that time. These wonderful people include: Elizabeth Chadwick, Felicity Pulman (who tested several versions for us!), Jenny Polack, Lara Eakins, the late Les Oberman, Mike Mazzei, Nanci Lamb Roider, Nancy Barber, Rania Melhem, Shana Worthen, Sharyn Lilley, Jon Swabey, Suzie Eisfelder, Wendy Zollo, Rita and Peter Kania, Bettina von Stockfleth, Lars Thomsen and Lars Kröger. Thanks also go to the organisers of the International Medieval Congress at Leeds, for that is where Gillian received much encouragement and where the authors met. In fact, Katrin first met the Beast in the conference bar ...

Foreword
by Elizabeth Chadwick

Writing historical fiction set in the Middle Ages has been my career since 1990, but it came about almost by accident. I had told myself stories from early childhood but had never written them down. Always verbal tales, they generally involved my passion of the moment. Horses featured a lot, as did dragons, *Thunderbirds Are Go* and *Star Trek*. However, the mould was eventually made for me when I was fifteen and fell madly in love with a twelfth-century knight in flowing white robes as portrayed in a children's TV series titled *Desert Crusader*. It was a French production, dubbed by the BBC and it aired every Thursday at about 5 p.m. Being at that impressionable age and awash with hormones, I decided the only way to deal with the overload to my system was to write a story loosely based on my hero and let my imagination run wild.

I duly set pen to paper, but swiftly realised that wild imagination would only take me so far if I wanted to create a work of historical fiction that felt satisfyingly authentic. I knew very little about the Middle Ages. I had received a basic grounding in the subject at school, but the operative word was 'basic'. I also knew a little from watching films and the occasional documentary on TV, but it wasn't enough and I had a thirst for knowledge. What did people wear? What fabrics? What colours? How were they made? What did people eat and how? How long did it take to get from England to Jerusalem? How did they tell the time? Did they bathe? How did they go about the matter of prayer? The list was endless, but I was young enough to be undaunted. The only thing to do was visit the library and start researching. I still remember the huge excitement of finding out that a twelfth-century sword only weighed around four pounds and that, contrary to what I'd been taught at school, a warhorse wasn't a hulking great beast of seventeen hands, but a smaller, stocky animal, capable of fast manoeuvre and easy to mount.

The more I found out, the more I wanted to know. Looking back at my research, it was never organised, but rather just one great organic sprawl that grew out of what I needed to know to write whatever happened to be my work in progress at the time – and there were eight unpublished novels before I finally cracked the market with *The Wild Hunt*. I acquired the knowledge in my own idiosyncratic way, but it was decades in the doing. It would have been wonderful to have had *The Middle Ages Unlocked* as a starter volume all those years ago. I might have saved myself a great deal of time. Rather than wandering all over the place like an inebriated spider, I'd have had a route map to follow!

Basically, this book does what it says on the jacket. It unlocks the Middle Ages for everyone – for general readers who want a quick reference work on their shelves or for teachers who need to develop knowledge on the subject for their class. It's for their students to read, it's for re-enactors keen to get a handy overview of their period and it's definitely for writers of historical fiction who need to understand the basics of everyday life in the thirteenth century, but don't want to spend forty years doing it!

Gillian Polack and Katrin Kania are a historian and an archaeologist with forty-two years' worth of experience of all aspects of the culture of the thirteenth century between them, and have an enthusiastic desire to share that knowledge with as wide an audience as possible.

I loved reading the draft when preparing to write this foreword because I discovered all kinds of new things I didn't know, several that will come in very useful for my next novel! For example, in the section on travel, I had no idea that people sometimes carried silver ingots around with them that could be cashed in along the way in foreign countries, somewhat like travellers' cheques. Also on the matter of travelling, I was fascinated to discover that the word 'biscuit' comes from meaning 'twice-cooked' and that biscuits were a staple food for those on long journeys. I also didn't know that the French spoken in the thirteenth century had regional dialects. Someone might speak French with an Anglo-Norman accent or a Poitevin one, but they would still be understood in the Parisian heartlands.

Every conceivable subject is covered under useful headings, so the reader can either use the book in a linear way, or skip from subject to subject as it takes their fancy or requirement. So the section on people is broken down into social groups and circles and personal identity, which includes information on the use of flags, seals and symbols – what people might do to show off their status and place in the world. There's a section on the phases of life with details of the place of children in society, the games they played, how they were perceived and the period when childhood ended. There are the social constructs of marriage with information on how the ceremony itself was conducted. Every conceivable subject you could ask for concerning the life and times of the Middle Ages is addressed in this book. Gardening, town life, textiles and clothing, agriculture, industry of all types, the military, housing and household tasks (how a fire was lit, for example, and how the hearth was arranged) and towns and how they were organised. You begin to realise just how many complexities there were in medieval life, both the obvious and the subtle, and it's all pulled together for you in this work, with notes and very useful suggestions for further reading, as well as some wonderful illustrations.

I found the entire book fascinating. I could have spent the whole foreword quoting pieces and enthusing over every section. For me though, the chapter on religion was especially useful. We live in a secular society and that can lead us to underestimate the role played by religion in medieval life, so to have the basic tenets and premises of the main beliefs and their festivals and ceremonies laid out is invaluable.

What I also like is that the authors are totally honest with the readership. If something is not known in the historical record, they say so; they don't fudge.

As a novelist, one of my mantras is to do the research and then filter it through the narrative, never letting that intensive study show. However, in *The Middle Ages Unlocked*, Gillian Polack and Katrin Kania have truly put their own depth of knowledge on display – and in the process have distilled their painstaking research into a thoroughly informative and enjoyable book that I just know will be of enormous benefit to any reader, whatever the level of expertise. I encourage you to dip in and enjoy!

Introduction

So many people love the Middle Ages. Movies, books, role-playing games and re-enactment: these all help us enjoy – and shape how we see – the period. Tolkien helped create our idea of the Middle Ages, and so have all the writers and movie makers who tell us tales of Arthur and Guinevere. Crafts and cosplay and the Society of Creative Anachronism help interpret medieval life for us. It's complex and diverse, this Middle Ages we share through popular culture.

The Middle Ages of our imagination and of our popular culture is not, however, always close to the Middle Ages that historians and archaeologists know. The most important single difference is that it was not a simpler time than today.

It was a complex time, and medieval states and world views were different enough from their modern counterparts to require effort and understanding in order to interpret and understand them. To our eyes, many medieval concepts look strange. For instance, we tend to think of science and magic as being unrelated: one is rational and the other is irrational. The 'reasoning' used by medieval scholars to interpret a text did not always distinguish between the rational and irrational, and when it did, it was because they were subjects of study, not because they were fundamental distinctions that shaped science and philosophy. Reason was a form of logic in the Middle Ages; it was argument that helped prove or disprove ideas. It was used more in the service of religion than anywhere else, its major advocates being scholars like Abelard and Thomas Aquinas.

Other areas that we think of as separate were closely linked for many medieval English people. They belonged on the same continuum. There was scientific thought, but it fitted within a larger framework of a world that was seen as operating differently from ours. The major force in the universe was not entropy, but deity, and angels and devils were responsible for moving the planets.

Cause and effect were often interpreted differently to today. Metaphysical explanations were just as important as physical, because they fitted science into the universe as it was understood. Demonic magic (whether using demons for good or ill) came from the same cosmological view as saints and miracles. The ability to invoke God, saints, and demons was a powerful tool. And, sometimes, so was mocking any of the above. Some scholars questioned and doubted and made scientific progress; others accepted the official view and taught others to accept it, and their research followed accepted guidelines. Engineering, such as building bridges, was a form of physical manipulation of the world. It could also encompass extraordinary events, such as making an army fly through the air; engineers could potentially achieve magic (as they did in one Old French epic legend), because magic was possible. Magic and miracles were also possible for particularly holy people, for supernatural beings such as fairies and for learned people who knew letter or word magic. Medieval England was a place of contradictions and of exciting intellectual effort.

Documents from popular lore, like recipes and charms, sometimes don't quite make sense to us because we don't instantly understand the reasoning behind them. To use them effectively, we need to understand that reasoning.

It is therefore essential not to assume the Middle Ages shared similar world views and similar concepts to those we have today. Exploring medieval England also means we have to push past our popular constructs and dig down to understand the institutions and languages that shaped people's lives. The relationship of people with the land, religion and the military underpin everything, much more than they do our modern lives.

The influence of religion significantly formed the systems in use for administration and politics as well. Christianity was the governing religion, but not the sole religion. Judaism was practised in some parts of England and throughout most of those parts of France closely linked to England. Many people had contact with Muslims and with heretical groups such as the Cathars through trade and travel. All these religions and belief systems had an impact on people and their lives in different ways.

In a similar way to religion being intertwined with secular government and general structures, the military was also deeply connected to the social and political structure. Medieval military matters were an important part of administration.

Like any other society, that of the Middle Ages is not easy to research or explain. Religion, politics and economy were not independent of each other, and their structures and operations overlapped. This means that many situations had a more complex background than modern minds often expect. England underwent major changes from the eleventh to the early fourteenth century. The shared culture and the broader world view of the period are both very useful paths into the richness and complexity of the English Middle Ages, but they need to be understood; they cannot be assumed.

Some of the concepts that were part of the general worldview were so fundamental and omnipresent that it is misleading to think they are limited to a single area of thought or action. It is important to keep this in mind as you delve into *The Middle Ages Unlocked*.

One very good example of how a single idea permeated many layers of daily life, linking government, social life, religion and economy, is the concept of largesse. Largesse was the liberal giving of money, goods or other values to others, usually equal or inferior in rank. Largesse to poorer people was encouraged by the Christian religion, but it was also a way to show one's own status and affluence, making it an important part of social behaviour.

Generous giving to the poor as demanded by Christianity also helped serve as a sort of social security net. This was especially important as, although the leading families made up a very small percentage of society, they made up a very large percentage of national spending. Their spending habits and customs affected the whole economy: largesse and noblesse went hand in hand.

We discover relationships like that between nobility and the economy through surviving records. They have distinct limitations. The records we have seldom show us daily life and how people structured it, for instance. Records are more common towards the end of our period than at the beginning, but it is only when writing was accessible to a critical proportion of the population and paper manufacture became less unusual (from the fourteenth century) that more consistent data can be amassed for study by historians.

In other words, we have many specific examples for most of the Middle Ages, but we do not know how ordinary or special these examples are. Although we cannot always be certain how typical something was when we only have one instance of a household's finances or any other aspect of daily life, one thing we do know is that wealthier people are more represented in the records and clearly had a wider social interaction than poor people. Through them, we can also see that regions shared some aspects of culture, especially when they shared a language, such as French for speaking and Latin for writing.

Regional differences created distinctive local cultures. For instance, there are many fewer surviving literary manuscripts from northern England than from the south, suggesting that their interest in written stories was far less. These artefacts of high culture reflect differences of the cultures overall. However, it is hard to document the minutiae of everyday life for our period, and therefore many of these regional differences have been lost.

Where our descriptions look generic, therefore, it does not mean society was uniform and that everyone did everything in exactly the same way. Different medieval people viewed the world in different ways. Some concepts were shared; some were not. Some folk ideas spread across cultural groups in the way that trends and fads do today. For example, eggs became popular at Easter for Christians and at Passover for Jews around the same time. The spread of culture and concepts was slower than it tends to be today, because travel was more difficult, but it did happen. International languages such as Latin and Hebrew helped. Some nobles leading their lives in two countries was also a factor, and French culture and society cannot be entirely left out from this book without losing that sense of shared lives that was such a very crucial element of the Middle Ages.

In addition to these differences in the basics of society and government, there are problems comparing or evaluating daily life in all its aspects. Many of the firm standards we are used to in our modern life were neither firm nor standards. There was local and regional variation in weights, measurements, coin and currencies and all forms of law. This means that it is very difficult to get a simple answer to a seemingly simple question, like 'How much did an apple cost?' To answer a question like this, you would need to know place, time, and probably other circumstances. The same holds true for many other questions, like how much income somebody would have, what law would apply to a specific crime or trespass or what a given amount of money would buy.

As trade routes changed, contact was made with hitherto unfamiliar regions, and travellers brought new plants and animals with them, in both directions. However, many species are known in France and England today which were certainly not known in Europe during the Middle Ages. Eucalyptus trees, for instance, were introduced from Australia, and turkeys and raccoons came from the Americas. Exchange of species from both continents with Europe only occurred considerably later.

No matter how it is categorised, the information we are presenting is not cut and dried. It is not just a matter of sources. There is also the question of who reads the sources and what they read into them. Information would have been interpreted by medieval people according to their own frame of reference. This frame of reference was different from ours, and getting to understand that different frame is important to unlock our understanding of medieval England.

Misconceptions

As we have already suggested, modern readers can carry many unwitting misperceptions concerning the Middle Ages due to the importance of this period in popular culture. Some of these are not handled in *The*

Middle Ages Unlocked at all (for instance, whether druids existed – we have absolutely no evidence for druidic survivals), and other core issues are explained in the appropriate places. Some of the most consistent errors made about the Middle Ages in popular culture include: the existence of chastity belts (they did not exist); the belief that the Earth was flat (this was not backed by either medieval scientists or mariners); that medieval clothes were drab and sacklike (when they were often a means of demonstrating wealth); that there was no effective system of law and order (when the robustness of these 'ineffective' systems was demonstrated by England's recovery after the Anarchy, the twelfth-century English civil war); that women had no rights; and that Church rule was absolute and uniform.

A very popular assumption about the Middle Ages is that it was a fairly ungoverned period. This was far from the case. Hundreds of years later, we have medieval records of government and administration for everything from tax to daily administration, and it is clear that only a small part of the medieval records have survived this long. Administration, and especially the justice system, was a complex structure with many different interlinked layers and could also differ from region to region.

The king of England governed England, but also governed (as local ruler) regions such as Normandy and Aquitaine in France, leading to extraordinarily close ties between the two countries. The Church was likewise crucial in social, political and administrative matters. Finally, the structure of society played a big part in social life and interaction.

Unlocking Medieval Sources

What kind of sources help us reach past these popular errors and help readers reach the real Middle Ages for themselves?

Everything that has been preserved since the Middle Ages is a potential source for understanding and discovering the period. There are written sources of all kinds, ranging from romances, such as *Sir Gawain and the Green Knight*, and manuals for physicians or chess players to the rare surviving writing exercises of children. There are legal sources such as laws and the records of court proceedings. There are administrative sources such as records of the Exchequer or the *Domesday Book*, technical treatises and instruction manuals on a wide range of subjects. There are wills, letters, household management treatises and notes in the margins of manuscripts. There is a vast array of religious sources, both Christian and Jewish, including Bibles, sermons, saints' lives, papal bulls, and rabbinical answers to questions. There are also art sources – pictures, carvings, illuminations – and surviving goods of daily life. Archaeology is another discipline that yields a lot of evidence about daily life. All of these potentially help in understanding medieval life.

All these different sources are classified as primary sources in terms of our relationship to them. To understand primary sources, they have to be interpreted; these modern interpretations (usually in the form of scholarly text) are then secondary sources. Since texts were written with specific aims in mind, there is no such thing as a truly objective written report from any time. This does not mean, however, that texts are less useful because they are subjective. Even forgeries are key sources, since they offer a glimpse of what was important to those ordering or making the forgery.

The sources we have seldom show us daily life or the life of the poor, or tell us how people structured it. Identifying an individual over several documents is also only possible in certain cases: there was no uniform use of surnames, and they were often only added when a specific description of a person was needed in a record. Wealthier people are much more often represented in written and pictorial sources, and they clearly had a wider social interaction than poor people as well. Furthermore, more source material from the later Middle Ages has survived than from earlier times, with less written material and artwork the further back in time we go.

To use the different kinds of sources, it is necessary to ask the right questions about their content and their reliability, a process often known as source criticism. For instance, tax records are important sources of aggregate data about medieval communities. There are several instances of surveys done for taxation, which give us amazing data on households, possessions and so forth. While the most famous of these is undoubtedly the English *Domesday* records, there were other surveys done for similar reasons, though none so extensive. While tax records give the most general data on population and wealth, how reliable are they? In 1292, a tax census was made in Paris. From this, we know how many households there were, but can only make estimates of how many people were in each household and hence can make educated deductions concerning how big the population of Paris was at that time. We know the occupation of the head of household, but not necessarily of other household members, which means that the occupations undertaken by women, for instance, are only partly identified. As to how far we can trust tax records, this depends on how honest individuals were when they reported their financial position and how accurate surveys are in assessing this reporting.

Whether you are looking at an old document or a shred of medieval cloth, however, you have to remember that not all sources can be used to answer all questions, and not all sources are equally reliable.

It is seldom enough to look at a text; you also have to look at the date of the earliest manuscript in which it is preserved. There is always the chance that either the text or parts of the text is not authentic, and tests such as language checking and verifying information in other sources become very important. Most medievalists have formal training in skills such as codicology (study of the codex, that is, books) and palaeography (study of ancient handwriting) to help them work through the problems thrown up by manuscripts themselves.

In the age of the internet, research has become much easier. During the last years, many databases have become available – usually freely accessible to everybody – and have made it possible to look at digital copies of original manuscripts and illuminations, small finds and transcriptions of texts. Many of these databases can be found via the websites of larger museums, such as the British Museum or the Metropolitan Museum. For scientific articles, specialised search engines like Google Scholar (scholar.google.com) or article databases such as JSTOR assist discovery. Some of the databases offer free access to some of their content as well. Larger libraries, especially university libraries, may offer access to some of the journals online if you have a library card.

The ready availability of more and more sources makes it easier to get an overview of variations and possibilities, provided one does not stop looking after the first few finds. A wealth of material is still not available (and much of it has not been published in any way yet), so there is hope of an even greater number of accessible sources in the future.

Reading primary sources is one thing. Interpreting them is another. There is a vast scholarship that covers so many aspects of the Middle Ages. This scholarship is the giant on whose shoulders this book rests. At the end of the book some of it is discussed, offering paths into specific subjects and some of the key works on critical subjects. A complete bibliography would be many volumes long, so we are providing guidance and an introduction rather than everything the heart could desire.

Definitions and Terms Used in This Book

This book is an introduction to the Middle Ages of England and English-linked France, based on scholarly research but taking a broad view. The sheer variety of rules, laws, customs, and aspects of human life mean that any deeper look at them needs far lengthier discussion than is possible in a volume of this size.

Unless otherwise stated, 'European' in this work refers to Western Europe alone, not including the Iberian Peninsula.

Political history is not a focus. There are excellent introductory and specialist volumes on this subject.

This book is your starting point. It provides the understanding you need and the links to explore the Middle Ages further, and we hope you will come across many fascinating aspects of this time in our history.

Common Abbreviations

CE: Common Era
BCE: Before Common Era
fl.: *floruit* – active time of an artist or writer
r.: reigned – the dates of reign of a king or pope
c.: *circa* – around the date
b.: born – date of birth
d.: died – date of death
s: shilling (*s* being the medieval convention)
d: pence or penny (*d* being the medieval convention)

Rich and Poor, High and Low
The People of Medieval England

Any society is made up of the people living in it. In the case of medieval England, this was a hierarchically structured, complex society that was influenced both by parts of the population that were stable over generations and by a fluidity caused by movement of people to and around the country and across different hierarchical levels. England was not simply the Anglo-Saxon versus Norman stereotype; it included people from these two backgrounds, from mixed backgrounds and from other backgrounds entirely. The shape of society also varied from region to region, reflecting regional history, trading patterns and religious practices.

England offered different types of status to different foreigners, depending often on their links with locals and whether or not they held land in England or any of its close neighbours. Skin colour was not a major issue in the Middle Ages. It was mentioned in the literature, but darkness of hue had different connotations to today, and modern US cultural assumptions (including those regarding slavery) attached to those with dark skin did not apply. Religion, however, was a major source of difference and even of prejudice. Nationalism and regionalism also brought bias, for instance with jokes concerning the reputation of people from various regions being quite popular.

In a hierarchical society, gender roles and social interactions were often expressed through complex social customs. There were many social customs and specific pieces of etiquette that marked the Middle Ages, some of which can be reconstructed from surviving sources. Just like today, modes of address, greetings, even choice of language depended upon social status, the region, and the current situation of those present.

Reputation was a fundamental part of society at all levels. Needing to be seen as a knight of virtue may not have stopped corruption, but it made many people very aware of public repute and its effect on them.

The reputations of your family, of yourself or of your country were all important. A story most people would have knowledge of was that of Roland's defeat in the pass at Roncesvalles in the Pyrenees. Roland did not want to sound his horn for help, partly because he did not want to lose his good name. The fear of losing reputation and good name was a very important motivator in medieval society.

Social Groups and Circles

Social behaviour and social life were governed by definitions of one's own group or social circles and distinguishing one's own circle from others. This demarcation of 'them versus us' was made visible by many different means such as names, clothing, language, food or behaviour; it is also very visible in stereotypes and stereotypical slurs.

Life in the Middle Ages was more defined by the complex relationships between people than by written law. Individuals and the relationships between them were key to the secular system of government, armies and warfare and the whole of society. The system of government, for instance, was often based on exchange of loyalties to establish and re-affirm relationships, frequently accompanied by goods or grants of land and land usage.

Family influence was a key factor in this society. While inheritance came from one's parents (inheritance by the eldest son was the norm for land inheritance in England), an uncle might step in to establish social and political links. Medieval society, therefore, comprised individuals who acted for themselves, but also as part of their families and friendship groups. It was close-knit and complex. It was also dynamic; it changed significantly over time and had a propensity to instability. The saddest illustration of the dynamism and the instability is during the reign of Stephen, often called the Anarchy (1135–54), when Stephen and Matilda's argument over kingship led to a disastrous time for the country as a whole.

Political patronage is another example of the importance of personal connections. From above, it ensured that friends were rewarded and it reduced the number of potential enemies. It could be used as a tool to prevent certain families from becoming too powerful and to find a place for very talented individuals from families of lesser importance. From below, it worked to obtain political and financial gain, and also to provide security. Patronage might involve land, the right to determine who married one's heirs, but it could also be expressed as assistance in finding a good marriage for oneself or one's friends and family. It ranged from the acquisition of big estates right down to local exemption from a specific tax. Many acts of patronage consisted of small exemptions from taxes or similar burdens.

The titular head of this system of social and political loyalties was the king as first among peers, with the senior members of the leading families (magnates) also possessing a large amount of power.

The chief powers were the royal family and the leading families. These leading families dominated medieval society and had the most potential to deliver benefits from patronage. Many of them were, in practice, as powerful as the monarch in their own region. In England, around 250 families dominated politics and government. They could be royal, be magnates (with titles and wealth but not royal), belong to the upper clergy or have land holdings concentrated in a specific area or spread out over the whole of England and into France. This upper layer of society included a changing proportion of lesser nobility and new men (those heading rapidly towards nobility). It could have mining links and merchant links, town bases or great agricultural strengths. It could be Norman or Anglo-Saxon, or mixed. It could be very military, or deeply religious, or both. Each of these 250 families had its own characteristic profile comprising its own mix of these components and was linked to other families through marriage and shared responsibilities and interests.

Within this group of influential families and individuals, ranks changed depending on place, on religious status and on secular status. Earls and archbishops were senior to all other secular and religious ranks apart from royalty.

Together, those people who held a significant amount of land and were entitled to bear their own coat of arms are referred to as gentry by some modern authors. This reflects their general status rather than the state of their vassalage. These people could be earls, barons, knights or untitled. There is a strong argument that an actual gentry class was formed from around 1180. However, the description of a man as a gentleman or something similar really only dates from the fourteenth century.

Below this gentry class were those with mixed tenure; people who may have held property in fief themselves or rented it. They may have leased it under a sharecropping arrangement or might farm it as part of a lord's terrain. It was also possible for them to have parcels of lands from different lords, or have a mixture of land they held in fief and land they rented.

This hierarchical group below the gentry included town and village dwellers, rural dwellers, craftspeople, business people, peasants and probably large groups of the Jewish community. Since there was a less consistent hierarchy within this part of society, personal wealth played an especially important role in determining the status of individuals. Wealth and status could differ greatly – rich peasants could have had more land and more wealth than poor gentry. Status was also influenced by the sort of work a person did, by ties to the lord or the Church, by the amount of livestock a person owned and most probably other, less traceable factors. Near the bottom of the hierarchy were people who had little or no independence, such as apprentices, serfs and slaves.

Serfs were basically farmers without private landholdings, with high levels of reporting or accounting to their lords and with limited movement. Serfs did not necessarily farm less land than the free, but they paid higher rents and were subject to more dues. They also had other restrictions. For instance, they had to obtain permission to marry or to migrate. These restrictions varied from region to region – it might be better to be a serf in one region than a free man in another. Robert Fossier has estimated that up to 10 per cent of the population in Normandy and Picardy were serfs; 12–25 per cent in Aquitaine, Ile-de-France, the Rhone Valley and Burgundy; and over 50 per cent in the Basse-Loire, Poitou, Berry, Champagne and Haute-Lorraine.

In some ways they were descendants of the Roman slaves and were defined as not free in legal systems. Even when freedom was granted en masse – as Louis IX of France (1214–70) did – it generally had to be paid for. They could often buy their freedom, and they shared the popular negative feelings about servitude. If a serf escaped the lord's estate and lived for a year and a day without being taken back, then technically they were free. Towns became associated with this freedom, but they were not the only place to run to.

Throughout our period, serfs were gradually given more freedom, but it was a slow and, for the serfs, arduous process. Serfs had stringent limitations on how much they could own and potentially enormous limitations on what they could do with their lives and on their rights in the justice system. Serfs were bound to the land and technically unfree, but they could not be bought and sold, and they had well-defined rights: they were not slaves.

The poorest rural dwellers were labourers and cottars, some of whom were serfs but others of whom were technically free; freedom did not always bring financial security. In an economy that was not cash dependent, labourers often lived from hand to mouth, and cottars had insufficient land to make a living without external help or work as a labourer. In a difficult year, these labourers would be the first to founder within mainstream society.

At the bottom of the social hierarchy were people who were outside mainstream society. Two key groups in this category were outlaws and beggars. Prostitutes, lepers, executioners and other occupations regarded as dishonest or undesirable were also in this category, as were slaves.

Slavery was not common in Western Europe in the Middle Ages; however, it was definitely in existence. Information about slavery, though, is very scarce. Both England and parts of France sold non-Christian slaves in the twelfth century. For example, Aïssa, a female Saracen slave bought in Marseilles in 1248, cost 9 livres and 15 sous. Slaves had very few rights; for example, they were not allowed to own property.

Children were sometimes regarded as property. An example of this mentality was demonstrated by French theologians, who regarded Jewish children as the property of slaves and hence removable. This view was not shared by all Christians. In Jewish law, children were never considered property. Canon law also said that if priests had children, they were to be confiscated and were to become slaves of the Church. Children of slaves were not generally considered slaves.

Slaves were really not fully entitled to marriage until the middle of the twelfth century, when the Church took a clear position in favour of marriage for Christian slaves. Adrian IV (the only pope to be born in England, r. 1154–9) described slave marriages as valid because they shared the sacramental nature of marriages made by the free.

Most slaves were probably owned by Christians, due to Christian sensitivities about Jews owning Christian slaves and Jewish sensitivities about enslaved Jews. However, both Christians and Jews (presumably less sensitive ones) sold slaves in France. Girls aged twelve to twenty-five and boys aged nine to thirteen were prized, but people over thirty were not. All enslaved Jews were entitled to be free if they converted to Christianity.

The Church tried to diminish the numbers of slaves and made statements condemning slavery. This may have had some effect. For instance, Philip II of France (r. 1180–1223) made it easier for slaves to gain their freedom by declaring that they were free if they could reach the borders of his property. Slaves were, by the thirteenth century, a disappearing luxury.

The Jewish population's demographic profile was quite different to the Christian. Due to restrictions in England, Jews were mainly confined to towns and were thus under-represented in the lowest classes. However, like Christian society, a very small group of the eminent led Jewish communities. They were equivalent to the magnate families in many ways. The titles used for this group in government records were equivalent to those of lord and bishop in Christian society.

Beneath this small group were the moderately well-off Jews, who worked in trade or craft and who do not seem to have been community leaders and dignitaries. The final group of Jews was everyone else, covering a wide range of town occupations.

Though serfs, slaves and possibly Jews were the hierarchical groups considered unfree, the medieval concept of freedom is not comparable to our modern understanding of freedom. Most households kept at least a few animals and a small garden plot, which always meant an obligation (being not-quite-free in medieval terms). Freedom and obligations in the Middle Ages were thus more along a continuum than absolutes, and there were limits in both directions; while even small landholdings implied a limit to freedom, even a serf could not be denied tenure or separated from his or her family.

One possible way of seeing how groups defined themselves and distinguished between 'us' and 'them' is by looking at prejudices against other people or groups. The lower classes were largely distrusted by the upper classes. Even the words *villain* and *churl*, which began as simple labels referring to social position, took on negative qualities eventually. Those in power considered that giving serfs too much power was a bad move because they were innately worthy of distrust. Many English Christians felt similarly about English Jews.

The writer Richard of Devizes wrote a scathing report of most of England in the very early thirteenth century. The only city that he praised was Winchester as it was peace-loving, prosperous and good to its Jewish community. London was a collection of the bad habits and vices of all the different ethnic groups living there, for instance; Canterbury left its people to die on the streets because of its preoccupation with the worship of Becket; Ely was putrefied and all people in Bristol were soap makers.

The first generation after the Conquest held negative views of the Norman newcomers, but by the second generation these had mellowed somewhat. The newly arrived Normans returned the distrust; Orderic Vitalis reported that Thurston of Glastonbury ordered monks shot if they sang an Anglo-Saxon chant instead of the Norman one he had ordered.

The Christian French and English thought that their fellow Jews had a different smell. So had saints, however, who smelled sweet after death.

The British Isles were full of different reputations. Englishmen were changeable. Scots were full of guile and Welsh were treacherous. There once was someone from Norfolk who was so sorry for the load his horse bore that he picked it up himself ... then climbed on his horse. This anecdote is part of a late twelfth-century satire from Cambridgeshire, where Norfolkers were lambasted severely.

The English were, by the French, mainly considered to be happy drunks. If they weren't happy drunks, they were at least drunks. The French also claimed that the English were not serious enough and had a tendency to dream. The English, in turn, considered themselves very quick of mind and castigated Germans for being slow thinking. The French and Gaulish, according to the English, had a tendency towards levity and games of love. People in England also mocked the Bretons as self-deluding with their 'Breton Hope', the belief that King Arthur was still alive and would return, and the fact that those who didn't think King Arthur was still alive were still grieving for him.

Relationships and Modes of Address

One way of tracing the relationship of people toward each other is
by looking at the modes of address between them. What was polite is
not easy to define, however, not least because we have few records of
interaction between people. Some social situations would have been
handled very strictly and according to etiquette, and others would have
been more flexible.

Titles indicated a person's rank in the social hierarchy. Both inherited
and courtesy titles were used to show respect. Medieval society was
also a society based strongly on precedence, the relative seniority of
people in different circumstances, so a large range of generic forms of
politeness was used. It is hard to reconstruct these nuances from the
written texts that are all the records we have. It is possible, however,
to understand some of the forms and, in particular, to interpret the
use of them (for instance, if a word is used as an insult) as related to
reputation. Reputation (*fama*) was very important in the Middle Ages.

One important detail that can be confusing is the language the
speaker or writer used. When the language was Latin, Latin titles were
used. Titles in France were given in French. Titles in England were
given in French and in English. In fact, many French titles were used in
English, by English speakers (*dame*, for instance, is a French word that
was used by English speakers and is frequently translated into modern
English as 'lady'). The nobility in England and the wealthier merchants
also used French titles. The key to actual usage probably lay in who
was speaking to whom and when. For instance, when talking to learned
men or in a conversation between professionals, *maistre* could be used,
while a student talking to a teacher would use *domine*. Most people
were known by their first names or an honorific. Formal titles in front
of personal names appear to be unusual until the thirteenth century.
Personal status might have been shown by indicating their household
office, however.

One of the reasons this is so tangled was because formalised titles
were in many ways only just developing during our period, and they
were not consistent. For instance, the term 'prince' generally described
a senior male member of the royal family, but could also be used to
describe an important leader. Jewish leaders, for example, might be
known as 'princes of the Jews'.

Similarly, the title *ber* (Old French) or baron (English), which denoted
the rank immediately below an earl or count, could also be used as a
euphemism for a prostitute. It could also mean good, or courteous
when describing someone, so it referred to both a birth status and the
personal qualities of someone. The word technically meant a warrior,
someone noble and brave. Abstractly, it referred to magnates, but in

practice could also refer to more junior nobles with those qualities (such as when referring to them or commanding them; instead of using their name, the speaker might say '*ber*'). In address, surviving examples suggest that the word was often used alone, that is, not followed by a proper name; for example, as an order from a king to a baron: 'Ride, *ber*, and conquer'. Perhaps a good way of thinking of it is baron as a status (one of the magnates), but also baron as a noble and brave man, for instance the leader in a battle.

During our period, the only title used formally in England was earl (of Anglo-Scandinavian origins), which is translated as *comes* in Latin, and is equivalent to the French *comte*, which became count in English (French speakers in England used the French term). In French, and especially in France itself, the big vassals – those who owed fealty to the king – were usually *comtes*. Earls/counts could be addressed as 'lord', but could also be called by their title and then their proper name (for example, 'Earl Henry'). There was no substantive difference between count and earl. There were only seven under Henry I in England and eleven in 1300.

The huge variation in who held the titles was based on an equally huge variation in powers. The courtesy of the title was extended to all, but they were not equal.

Anyone addressing someone senior to them (such as a baron if they were not themselves noble) would use lord, sire, or *dan* (lord being the English, sire and *dan* being French); the Latin version was *senior*. The word was also a general respectful address for men (for example to a lord or the elderly). It was also the correct address for someone who held a fief or was married to someone who held one, and could even be used as a term of endearment for a lover or husband. These terms could also be used when addressing the head of a household or a property owner until around the end of the twelfth century. After that, they were mainly used when addressing knights.

The most frequent form in English was simply lord, without using the personal name in addition to the title. The equivalent sign of respect to a woman was to call her *dame* (in Latin, *domina*), and *ma dame* was the most common form of polite address for a lady of rank in England for both French and English speakers. The use of *dan*, sire and dame as signs of respect was very widespread in French-speaking countries (which included England) by the twelfth century. *Demoiselle*, which literally means 'little dame', was a term of respect that could refer to an unmarried lady, young women (or even adolescent girls) or women who might be junior in rank to a dame.

Many vassals were called *homme*, as a generic term. Generally, someone who worked on things to do with war was an *homme* (man) if he were not quite senior enough to be a *ber*. Those who took oaths of vassalage were men (*hommes*) to their lords (sires). Men at the same level (such as knights together) could call each other companion. Cousin was used by the upper classes when addressing all relatives other than next of kin. People close to each other may also have greeted each other with a kiss.

Some terms, such as vassal, were more likely to be used when talking about someone than as a direct address, even though it had a formal meaning in address.

Anyone even halfway well brought up would greet people before doing anything else, however urgent, and would say farewell to them properly when leaving. A knight or lady never simply walked into a room or entered a household, nor did they simply leave a place without blessing someone in the name of God. If everyone present was inferior in status, then at least some of them still had to be greeted. Greeting superiors was undoubtedly more arduous, requiring (in the case of great lords and kings) a bend at the knee. The reason for this was technically to call blessings upon them. Without greetings, there was no courtesy, and without courtesy, any claim to status was not backed by the actions appropriate to status.

Informal modes of address included terms of affection as well as insults. Terms of affection were, for instance, *dous* or *doux* (literally meaning 'sweet'). The use of these terms was not limited to close friends or family, such as a mother or brother, as even a lord could be addressed as *doux sire* or even *beau doux sire*, and God could be referred to as *doux Dieu*.

'Sweet heart' and 'dear' could be used to indicate a close relationship, as with your lover or your child. Another affectionate term (although maybe less indicative of closeness) was *beau* ('handsome'), which could be used to indicate respect or to flatter a man of rank. For instance, *beau sire neveu* ('handsome lord nephew'), is how Charlemagne addressed his nephew Roland in the *Song of Roland*.

Using these terms together indicated much closer affection, such as between brother and sister, lovers and husband and wife. Men might be called *beau doux ami* ('beautiful sweet friend') or *beau doux compagnon* ('friend') or *beau doux frere* ('brother'). Women may be called *ma douce amie* or simply *amie*.

The most used words at the opposite ends of the spectrum reflect the qualities expected in the less well bred: churlishness and villainy. These words do not have the same meaning as today, however. A *churl* and a *villain* were Old English and Old French words, respectively, describing a person of low station. A *villain* was not automatically evil, just not noble; a *churl* was not necessarily intentionally rude and coarse, just untutored and lowly.

As both French and English nobility spoke Old French, insults in Old French would have been understood even by many speakers of English.

They would have been the most common insults, not only among French native speakers and nobles, but also among those with any sort of pretension to nobility or good breeding, unless the individual was strongly anti-Norman.

For the mildest insults of all, from warrior to warrior, probably calling them a coward or a liar would suffice. The most useful all-purpose mild insult is *fals* or *faus*, which has come down to modern English in the word 'false', but had a wider range of meanings in the Middle Ages. Some insults referred to region or nation, such as the French claiming that the English had tails and English men menstruated.

More vulgar insults, such as *longoigne* or *coille*, can be found in the scatological literature of the time and have retained a part of their meanings in modern French. There were also more subtle insults that could be insinuated into a conversation. Those with forked tongues were liars, clever with rhetoric and sought rewards such as money and expensive cloth, for instance. If you called someone a Cluniac (Benedictine), you might be suggesting that they were a glutton, or if you referred to them as a white monk (Cistercian), you might be hinting at possible avarice.

Some gestures were also obviously insulting, although it is harder to locate evidence of these. A closed fist with a thumb between two fingers was not only considered rude, it also helped ward off demons.

Inside households, hierarchies and etiquette influenced the way individual members were addressed and treated. In the rules he wrote down for the Countess of Lincoln around 1240, Robert Grosseteste divided staff into three groups in terms of courtesy due. At the top were the knights of highest status, the gentlemen, the valets and similar people. Then came the knights of lower status, the chaplains and the heads of household divisions. This group was the *fraunche maynee* (literally, the 'free household'). Finally came the inside servants, the outside servants and the grooms.

Within the big divisions of rank, there were different levels of precedence. In addition, whether the person was of gentle birth or not affected their status. The senior person (of highest social status) in a given place at a given time was given preferential treatment (the best chair) whether that person was a peasant or a lord.

Similar hierarchies existed in other communities that were not households, such as religious communities or occupational groups.

Names, Colours and Seals: Identifying Oneself

Whatever one's role in life, identification of oneself and one's allegiances were important. People showed their allegiances and class through a variety of means, such as names, clothing or heraldic devices.

Naming practices in the Middle Ages were not the same as present ones. Surnames were not used uniformly during our period, for instance. Some of them were place names, some indicated family of origin, some female surnames reflected their husband (but not always the current husband!) and many indicated profession. Hereditary surnames were not common during our period. Names followed cultural norms; for instance, Anglo-Saxon names diminished very quickly in the higher echelons of English society after 1066. An important exception to this may have been London – a high percentage of Londoners had English names in the early twelfth century. What kind of names people found attractive and used is likely to have been quite regional.

Male Jews had a religious name as well as a secular name: they needed the religious name for ceremonial reasons in the synagogue, and these names may or may not have been used in everyday life. Jewish women only had a secular name. Boys' names were given as part of the circumcision ceremony, while girls were generally named on the first Sabbath after their birth.

In writing, the names would follow the style of the language that was being written. Latin documents would have the Latin version of the name, for instance.

In some situations, it was necessary to clearly mark one's identity in ways that went beyond the use of a name. One of these circumstances was on a battlefield, which eventually resulted in the rise of heraldry.

Heraldry is a system of badges, colours and coats of arms so that retainers and adherents and people who are otherwise linked can be recognised. These coats of arms can be found in many places, for example on flags, on shields, represented on tombs or on stained glass. When they appear in public buildings, such as cathedrals, it is likely that the family described by the arms played an important role locally. This could have been as simple as making a donation for the building's foundation or being buried there, or it could be more political.

Heraldry really began to form in the eleventh century, with the *gonfanons* (banners) attached to lances reflecting the colours of allegiance. Shields might be painted with personal motifs at this stage, but they were not formal heraldic devices and there was little inheritance of devices.

By the thirteenth century, shields were marked, as were horse caparisons. Seals and rolls bore blazons, and so did horse harnesses, buckles, belts, and even domestic objects such as plate and furniture. Expensive items donated to a church might bear the insignia of the donor, from vestments to floor tiles and windows.

Heraldry was not an exact system during our period. It became more consistent as it became more widespread, but it lacked the formalisation that characterises it today. Additionally, even during the thirteenth century, with this massive proliferation of devices and their use, heraldry was not universal. During our period the most important element in identifying allegiances were the colours. Blue and gold, for instance, generally showed that the family was linked to the French royal family. The fleur-de-lys was first recorded in 1147, but was not generally associated with the French monarchy until the early thirteenth century.

The oldest known pattern is checked, adopted probably during the crusades and referring to a chessboard pattern. The most common beasts were the lion and the eagle. The leopard was used by the Count of Anjou around 1127, leading to its use in England by the Angevin dynasty.

Decorations on shields seem to have been inconsistent in the eleventh century, but by the middle of the twelfth century, they copied the devices on banners. In the early twelfth century, men fighting in the same unit would paint their shields, lances and possibly their helmets. Family symbols, therefore, predated formal heraldry. By the middle of the thirteenth century, so many devices were being used that lists were made to sort them out (heraldic rolls).

Arms from the twelfth century might include religious devices. For example, William I was given a flag by Pope Alexander II, which had a cross on a white field, and Geoffrey of Monmouth described king Arthur's shield as showing an image of the Virgin Mary.

The standards and flags representing families were used as rallying points during a fight and also to indicate where attacks were coming from. Standard-bearers were generally too busy to fight and were discouraged severely from doing so. Some of them wore clothing that matched the banner's colours, to heighten the visual effect.

More mundane needs for identifying oneself were needed for everyday tasks such as authenticating documents. In a society that was not defined by universal literacy, a seal was a common way of authenticating documents. Seals were thus an important demonstration of identity. Knights and lords had seals, as did many other individuals. Towns also had seals. The authentication of documents was done by pressing the seal into a mixture largely comprising beeswax and resin, sometimes reinforced with fine hair. Autographs tended to be used as confirmation of the seal, not instead of it. Best known are the signatures of monarchs; most common among these were probably the first initial of their name followed by an R, for Rex.

In theory at least, no deed was valid without a seal's impression attached. Contracts under seal were considered legally binding. This led to an increase in seal use during our period to cover all those who could sell land, as it was important to have binding transfers of free land to have a clear title to it. In the eleventh century, many documents (especially church documents) didn't require seals, and until the early twelfth century at least, seals were really only used by armour-bearing people such as knights and the upper nobility. Their use did not become common at more levels of the hierarchy until around 1200, but by the end of the thirteenth century even some *villains* used seals. In fact, in the Statute of Exeter in 1285, it stated that insufficient freemen were to be found to hold a grand inquest, *villains* with seals and decent landholdings could serve.

Seals were engraved by goldsmiths and often had legends showing important information about the bearer such as his or her name, titles, possessions and functions. They could be precious items in themselves: Henry III's first Great Seal cost £5 6s 8d, which was, coincidentally, around the price of a rather nice illuminated manuscript. A clockwise legend in Roman capitals was typical until around 1200, when Lombardic script often replaced the Roman. While most legends were in Latin (or, for Jewish seals, Hebrew), some also used the vernacular.

Another way of showing one's identity was by the use of objects that symbolised, for example, power and status. Prime examples of this are the sceptres and crowns of kings. As a sign of honour, the king could allow a favoured individual to carry his sceptre at a big event, thus publicly giving importance and status to the bearer.

A good example for a ritual connected to social identity is the entrance into knighthood. While becoming a knight was purely secular in its origins, the Church increasingly appropriated parts of the knighting, and religious acts such as vigils, blessings and ritual baths were added. Originally, knighting probably started with sword girding or being given the equipment necessary to practice as a knight. The concept of belted knights refers to this. There was no standard practice, however, and we have no evidence of a formal ritual before around 1100. References to dubbing in this time refer to the receiving of equipment. *Adoube* in Old French (the language of the knightly class) actually meant equipped: the man who was being dubbed might already be a knight and just receive a new set of equipment. By around 1130, dubbing had turned into a small ceremony where girding the knight with a sword belt was the centrepiece.

By the late twelfth century, performing a ritual to create a knight was quite common. The exact form of the ceremony, however, differed from place to place. It could include the girding of sword or spurs, a ritual bath, a vigil, Mass, confession, Communion, a sermon on knightly duties and some form of a blow. The vigil was probably a common aspect of the ceremony from about 1160–80.

One instance of this type of knighthood ceremony is described in the Pontifical of Guillaume Durand. The sword was blessed after Mass, and sanctified specifically to defend the Church, orphans and widows, to fight against heretics and infidels. There was then a suitably military reading from the Old Testament. The sword was placed in the knight's right hand with the words 'Take in the name of the Father, the Son and the Holy Ghost'. The knight brandished his sword three times before he returned it to its scabbard. The bishop gave the kiss of peace then blessed the knight's banner.

Symbols and ritual were just one aspect of showing one's identity and one's status. Public performances of symbolic acts, such as a surrender or giving a kiss of peace, served to show relationships between magnates, kings and vassals. Symbolic behaviour of this kind could also include violent acts to send specific messages, such as killing a man to avenge a grievance.

Showing Off and Showing Respect: Social Status

Displaying one's social status was crucial to keeping and affirming one's position in society. This was done through several different means: dress, conspicuous spending (including generous acts towards others), and general manners.

Showing appropriate behaviour was also very important for confirming and keeping one's place in society. Good manners were important enough to warrant their own literature: one of the earliest books of manners (the *Liber Faceti*, from the first half of the thirteenth century) is by an English scholar, John of Garland. Courtly literature was also full of good and bad examples for behaviour and manners.

Despite the existence of some written guides to etiquette, good manners were mostly taught privately and from person to person – it was not a subject that most people looked for in books, although they would expect their favourite hero, for instance, to demonstrate all the social graces. These graces would have been particularly demanded of the gentry and nobility.

A person's behaviour signalled innate qualities and the quality of their upbringing. Suitable dress, proper behaviour and actions considered positive – for example demonstrating virtue and generosity – were all part of a declaration by individuals about who they were and where they fitted. What was seen as good or proper manners in speech and behaviour would have varied according to the language, social status, the circles a person moved in, and from region to region. In some instances, what was seen as proper behaviour was different from modern associations; for example, tears were not seen as unmanly but considered appropriate, especially when it concerned the death of someone who owed their loyalty or the death of a loved one. Another difference was the close association of inner beauty (character and behaviour) and outer beauty with high status. Accordingly, rich and well-born people were supposed to be happy and look happy, regardless of their inner state, as happiness was considered attractive. If they could not look happy, then they should at least control their unhappiness very well.

Good manners were manners that made a person fit for court: our modern use of the word 'courteous' still hints at this. The terms or words used to denote good manners or behaviour, however, have changed a lot in meaning since the Middle Ages. 'Courtesy' (Old French *courtoisie*) did not really relate to being courteous in the modern sense, but to being courtly as in having the skill and knowledge to move inside court circles. This implied loyalty and faithfulness as well as proper behaviour and a thorough social education. All the qualities of someone noble were usually described in Old French, and while the words used have obvious modern descendants, the meanings used during our period seldom survive. The fact that Old French words were generally used (even in English and by English speakers) demonstrates clearly that in both England and France courtly virtues were associated mainly with the French-speaking aristocracy.

Personal qualities were described in quite particular ways in the Middle Ages. For instance, a true knight was *deboner* ('debonair'), but natty dressing and nonchalant poses had very little to do with this. He was kind to the needy and unfortunate; he was generous. Being *deboner* was almost a virtue in terms of its importance, and it could be learned. One of the reasons boys were fostered into great households was to obtain personal qualities such as this.

Gentilesse likewise reflected the attributes of gentility: good manners, gentleness (except in war) and honour. It meant 'noble' rather than 'gentle', generally speaking. However, nobles were ideally condescending and generous. Largesse referred especially to generosity, often specifically relating to presents and food. This was a particularly important term; largesse demonstrated status to the world – a mean king or noble was one lacking in *gentilesse*, largesse and other noble qualities. It was the idealised end of a society that rested on a system of bribes and favours. In contrast, churlishness and villainy pointed to a lack of social graces.

Showing respect where proper was also a part of good behaviour. That could mean that those of inferior rank might walk behind their superiors, or that the person of superior rank or with precedence might walk on the right of two people or in the middle of a group of three. It could also mean removing a cloak or hat when in the company of a superior who did not wear them.

Table manners were seen as very important, and some descriptions of medieval table manners survive. A particularly well-known manual of etiquette was by Robert Grosseteste for young boys (written *c.* 1240), where he discussed estate management, household management and discipline, as well as basic courtesy.

Most dishes were served in bite-sized pieces, as soups, pottages or pies. This is because the three main implements used at table were a spoon, knife and fingers. Since people ate with their fingers, it was customary for them to wash their hands before and after eating. It was considered very barbaric to clean fingers on clothes, which meant that any table with pretensions of gentility would also include water to wash hands with, and cloth napkins – it was also bad manners to wipe one's fingers on the tablecloth. If two people shared a table setting, special courtesy toward one's meal partner was expected, for instance cutting a shared fruit into pieces fit for eating. Fingers were supposed to stay as dry as possible and most definitely not to be dipped up to the knuckles in any wet substance. Lips were to be wiped regularly, partly because people shared goblets, but also out of general courtesy. Solid food was picked up with the fingertips only, and sauces and anything else wet should not be allowed to drip or spill on clothes or on the tablecloth. Talking with a mouthful of food or drink was not considered nice. Not having cut fingernails, eating greedily, dipping food into the salt cellar, having elbows on the table, having an unclean nose (or blowing your nose noisily at table), not washing fruit before you ate it and eating your bread before the rest of the food served; all were considered somewhat uncouth. Good table manners were seen as the habits of elegant society, and many people would have copied them.

Providing food, drink and general hospitality to travellers was also a part of good manners. Hospitality was an indicator of generosity, and generosity was a very important indicator of rank and nobility. Hospitality therefore was not just a sign of the social graces, but also a sign of rank. The treatment of a visitor again depended on his or her rank; particularly important visitors might even be met on the roadway, given presents, compliments and led into the accommodation.

Welcoming guests was the first step in providing hospitality. Ideally, this included helping them descend from horses if necessary, providing them with fresh clothing and an opportunity to bathe or wash themselves and taking care of their animals, baggage and staff. Extra courtesy could include being met quite a way from the building and being accompanied a way down the road upon leaving. In literary texts, the host's daughter was often the guest's main assistant, which may, however, reflect an ideal or be a plot device.

Feeding your guests was crucially important to show both your hospitality and your generosity. At the least, the guest should be given bowls, a table and linen, bread and wine so that he or she could wash their hands and sit down to immediate nourishment.

Proper behaviour for a good Jew was in many ways similar to the behaviour described above. In addition, though, it included the study of Torah for as many hours as possible, and following *halakha* (religious law), which guided manners in everyday life. Support to the poor should be given without showing off; this support included making books available to children from poor backgrounds and paying teachers so that more people could fulfil the supreme requirement of Judaism: to study Torah.

The proper use of language is another aspect of good manners. Language was just as contextual in the Middle Ages as it is now: one was not supposed to use certain words in front of certain people. Swearing was colourful and multilingual as well, as we have already seen. People had a choice between English words, French words and religious-based oaths. The use of language has undergone a lot of change since the Middle Ages, and today's readers may have difficulties in understanding the double-entendres or in estimating the intensity of an insult. For example, *coille* can be translated as stupid, but was quite a vulgar insult, since the underlying reference is to testicles. Even royalty were reported as having favourite swearwords. For example, William the Conqueror used the mild 'By the splendour of God' and his son, William II, preferred the more obscure 'By the Holy Face of Lucca'.

Many oaths that have come down to us come through literature. Simple oaths included 'By faith' and its equivalents, or swearing by the parts of one's body or by the soul. 'Damn it' and its equivalent are attested in the late thirteenth century, but probably go back further than this. Many oaths are related to God. The simplest is, of course, 'God' (*Deus*, the Old French word, was used as much by English speakers as by French) but *Goddoth* and *God it wite* were used in England in the thirteenth century. A popular oath in Norman England and in Normandy was *datheit* (possibly originally from the words 'God's hate'). Many parts of God's body could also be used, including the arms, bone, teeth, heart and nails. Even his passion or wounds could be used as bad language, as could Mary or saints' names. Shock and horror and distress were likely to be expressed with 'Christ shield me' or a similar phrase.

Wealth and Poverty

There was a strong connection between one's status in society and the wealth one had. The main source of wealth in the Middle Ages was the land, and especially farming. This makes it quite difficult to assess wealth in comparison to modern wealth, for income was often not translatable into cash equivalents and landholdings were often not disposable. Poverty, likewise, is difficult to assess, although recent work by scholars such as Samuel K. Cohn Jr. is developing new methods and sources of information that will change this.

One key piece of data established from measuring skeletons is that people in the Middle Ages may not have been much shorter than we are. This suggests that basic nutrition was good and that assessable wealth is not a good indicator of basic quality of life in the Middle Ages. Additionally, from around 1050 to 1200, there were significant improvements in the overall standard of living due to the favourable climactic conditions of the Medieval Warm Period and to agricultural innovation. The standard of living fell off with the poor harvests in the beginning of the thirteenth century. This provides a backdrop to specific problems caused by political and social unrest (notably during the Anarchy) and due to specific crop failures. The bad years were part of a long cycle of gradual improvement. This must be taken into account when considering what wealth and poverty meant in the Middle Ages.

While land was the main source of income and food, trade and income from crafts and industrial work were also sources of wealth. More gained their wealth through land than these other sources, and land wealth could include such useful things as mineral exploitation and taxes on trade. It also possessed great political advantages, being linked to political and military power. Around 90 per cent of the population, however, lacked disposable income and did not own property, and thus their wealth is hard to assess. Those who were able to maintain their relationship with the land were more prosperous in good years and better able to survive bad. These peasants (whether serf or free) comprised the single largest demographic group in medieval society.

Besides loss of that link with the land, the main causes of poverty included fire, famine, discrimination, bad weather, war, injustice, and the poverty of choice (Christian religious poverty).

The kind of poverty most people associate with the Middle Ages includes beggars clustering at the gates and the reluctant provision of alms. Some scholars suggest that this was not nearly as prevalent as many people think and that the real poverty in the Middle Ages concerned lack of power and control over life. Most poor were not free to leave their land without permission, to marry and so forth. These rural poor were largely labourers and cottars. They tended to marry less frequently than the comfortably off and to marry younger. They were the first hit by problems: they had fewer reserves to see them through failed crops. In the north of France and in England in 1196, for instance, there was a famine that forced many peasants to vagabondage. Some survived by turning to theft – if they were caught they were usually hanged or mutilated in punishment.

Groups who were liable to poverty (either temporarily or long term) included all sorts of travellers (especially those like pilgrims who might take vows of poverty), or vagabonds, serfs, those hiding in forests (outlaws and those fleeing the land) and, in thirteenth-century England, Jews.

There were many who were poor, such as day labourers and those with insufficient land to feed the family. Many peasants, for instance, had lives that were bordering on extreme poverty in bad years. They were instantly in dire straits when they lost their lands, but had sufficient resources most of the time. In 1069, when the northern counties were harried by William, an enormous number of families were pushed over the brink and did not survive, and in 1073 there was a famine so bad that the sick were not taken care of and the dead were not buried. There were also famines recorded in England in 1087, 1093, 1096 and 1099. While few of these covered vast terrains, they were all disastrous for the lowest levels of society in those regions.

Responses to poverty varied. One possible action was getting support from others by means of loans or by obtaining help from a religious community through alms, medical assistance or as the live-in poor. Another possibility was turning to illegal actions – stealing and poaching.

Famine was an ever-present threat, since both storage possibilities and food import possibilities were limited. Where regional records are available, they can give information about bad harvests; for example, in England in 1224–5, 1283–4 and 1290–1 for all grains, with 1246–8, 1256–8, 1274–5 and 1293–6 being bad for wheat and barley in particular. The most frequent cause for famines was adverse weather, causing bad growing seasons (either too wet or too dry) or bad harvesting seasons (too wet). Very cold winters could also lead to famine, due to the higher need for food.

Famine often led to a general weakening of both the human and the animal population, which heightened the danger of epidemics. Depending on the size of the affected region, famines could be more or less localised; the worst famines were of course those where a large area was strongly affected. In times of famine, people would be forced to make bread of anything that could be ground into flour, such as tree bark.

Rural monasteries, Jewish communities and many wealthy households automatically allocated provisions for the poor into their daily running costs. Wealthy households, for example, had a specific budget and allocated it to a certain number of people only. This didn't stop the needy from clustering at doors in the hope of food, but it certainly meant that food could be hard to get for some. How far that provision for the poor served in any given instance is difficult to evaluate, so we do not know whether it was a stopgap measure or genuinely assisted long term. For instance, in 1244 Henry III made provision for 20,000 meals at Westminster and 15,000 at St Paul's. We do not know how many poor people benefited by this and over what period of time.

In daily life, peasants often sought ways of adding to and varying their food sources and of obtaining extra income. One of these means was poaching. Since it was illegal, it appears most frequently in the written record and was often judged under forest law. This means we know more about poaching than about wild harvesting or income supplementation through craft. The most common species poached were deer or smaller game, often using traps or snares. Some poached deer were not trapped at all: they were simply scavenged. When the hunt failed to collect its wounded or dead prey, locals might spirit it away. Foresters were known to turn all the sacks on a suspect's land inside out to check for this.

Poaching was usually punished severely, though the fate of poachers who were caught was not predictable. Some were pardoned because of their poverty and many more turned to outlawry. Some bribed potential witnesses with cash or even a share of venison so that they would get off scot free, and even some foresters were bribed. But when they were caught and tried and witnesses testified, fines could be very heavy.

Gender Roles

Getting a good grasp of the gender roles and gender-specific social interactions for the Middle Ages is not easy. Different sources allow for many conflicting interpretations regarding influence, status and opportunities for women. Some sources highlight women as successful workers, guild members or holders of office; other sources seem to emphasise that women were seen as inferior to men and were granted less rights and fewer opportunities.

Medieval society and culture was, in its general lines, both patriarchal and misogynistic. However, there was no monolithic definition of masculinity or man or femininity or woman, even though efforts were made to create and promote rigid definitions, both in literary as well as in theological and didactic texts. This fluid and inconsistent gender definition can be seen when studying characters in medieval texts. For example, women are given their own titles in many medieval tales. In the eleventh and twelfth centuries a *conteresse* or *countasse* (*comitissa* in Latin) was a wife, widow or daughter of a count, unless she was a female ruler at the same level as a count. The female equivalent of *duc* was *duchesse* (*ducissa* in Latin – note, though, that *dux* could also be used as a female title).

On the other hand, there were some things very closely associated with women. An example for this is the spindle as a symbol of the productive, working woman on many images from our period.

In books on manners that appeared towards the end of our period, the proper behaviour of women was discussed. Literature such as Old French romances also gave some guidance on how ladies should behave and what skills they should possess. Women were expected to keep their gaze meek and certainly not let it rove and to neither stride nor wave their arms when walking. If the skirt had to be carried, then it was usually with the help of the left arm, though the girdle could be used to truss it if both arms were needed. They did not show their legs, and women in religious orders automatically covered their feet when sitting.

2

From Cradle to Grave
Life Phases

Much of the basic data necessary to describe life cycles, such as average age or level of infant mortality, is difficult to determine for the Middle Ages. For instance, without being able to accurately calculate child mortality, which is impossible given the nature of records in our period, we cannot know what life expectancy people had in the Middle Ages. Nor do we know the ratios of children to adults and to the elderly. We know that the child mortality was higher than in the same regions today, as was mortality from childbirth and from illness. However, there were old people in medieval society: we have records of bishops, for instance, who were in office for over forty years. Though records for daily life are patchy, they are improving as archaeologists add their data to the work of historians in the field.

Childhood

Detailed evidence concerning how children lived in the Middle Ages is surprisingly scanty. There have recently been revisions in how childhood is regarded, notably by Shulamith Shahar and Nicholas Orme. The older view that there was no real childhood in the Middle Ages is no longer widely followed.

Childhood was divided by medieval scholars into several stages. These stages varied from writer to writer, but a common classification was:

infantia – to seven years
pueritia – ages seven to twelve in girls and seven to fourteen in boys
adolescentia – from twelve/fourteen until early adulthood
juventus – post adolescent youth

The later stages of life were not described as often as these early stages. Children started their life influenced by wealth and status of the parents. One of the defining factors for the future of the child was the legitimacy of its birth. If the parents were married when the child was born, then even if the marriage was annulled, the child was generally considered legitimate.

Care of the child started before birth. For example, pregnant women may have tried to avoid salt, as it was considered to be bad for the development of the child's nails and hair. It was also recommended that they eat little and often and of the highest quality food available. Birth defects were attributed generally to the expectant mother eating the wrong food, or the couple having sex at the wrong time of year or in the wrong position. Popular tales suggest that there was a belief among some that multiple births were due to infidelity, which could make life rather difficult for twins.

Pregnant women were supposed to avoid anger, exercise, sex, beatings, fear, physical labour, too many baths and too much sunshine. It was recommended that they wear clean clothes and eat pears. From about two to three weeks before delivery, some doctors also recommended a daily herbal bath.

There are quite a few pictures of childbirth, including some showing women being operated on for caesareans and being attended on while in labour, though most are from after our period. Women attending an expectant mother would probably have included the midwife and female friends and neighbours. In a difficult birth, a doctor might also be called upon. Although medical treatises about gynaecological matters were largely written by men, vaginal explorations before the birth would be done by a woman.

Very small children are often shown swaddled in cloths or cloth strips. The exception in most cases is Jesus Christ, who is depicted either naked or clothed in adult garments due to symbolic reasons. In the earliest years of life, many infants slept in cradles. Others also shared a bed with the mother or wet nurse.

The infants were integrated into a religious group by baptism or circumcision. Baptism generally took place several days after birth. It is covered in more detail in the section on religion.

In Jewish communities, there was often a celebration the first Friday night after the birth of a child. A baby boy was circumcised eight days after birth, and a girl was named in synagogue the first Saturday after birth. The new mother was not allowed out alone until after the circumcision.

Some of the best sources for care of infants are medical recommendations that tell us about what was seen as ideal and hint at actual practices. For example, medical experts of the day recommended breast milk and were concerned about the effects of the milk of cows, goats and sheep on an unweaned infant. Through this we know that some women did not breastfeed. Medical experts also recommended that infants be fed on demand, not to a predetermined timetable, and bathed at least once daily in clean water.

Babies of the very aristocratic were usually nursed by someone other than their mother. Bernard of Clairvaux was impressed that his own mother breastfed him, pointing to the practice of employing wet nurses. Scholars recommended that a wet nurse be healthy, clean, have a clear complexion and large breasts. The whole onion family, spicy or sour food was not recommended for her. To increase the levels of milk, a health drink was suggested, comprising legumes, rice flour, milk, sugar and fennel. However, we do not know to what extent wet nurses were used even in the ruling classes. Breastfeeding by the mother may well have been considered positively, as the babies fed at their mother's breast in the Swan Knight series of epics grew up to be better, stronger and more heroic than their counterparts.

According to recommendations, breastfed children should be weaned when their first words and steps came. From age five, proper speech was considered possible.

Children were not simply considered miniature adults. We have records of special games, toys and songs for children. Children's toys included dolls, spinning tops, toy horses and wooden models of various kinds. Known toys from the Middle Ages (with most evidence dating from after our period) include rattles, hobby-horses, rocking horses, blocks, hoops, dolls, bones, spinning tops, balls, little boats, whistles, puppets and drums. Children also played games, ranging from marbles to competitive games. Some of these games were mimicking adult activities, but others included hide and seek, follow the leader and other informal group games.

We have little evidence for nursery rhymes and children's songs, as they were just not written down from the eleventh to the thirteenth century. There is some evidence that words such as *lulla* and *lullay* were associated with them. The term 'nursery rhyme' is modern and most of our rhymes clearly date from long after our period: 'Twinkle Twinkle Little Star' was penned in 1806. However, some seem to have originated back in the Middle Ages, and a very, very few can possibly be traced to our period. The main rhymes that date to the Middle Ages in general (and the evidence is seldom sufficient to date them more precisely) are a riddle-song, a way of counting the months and a bed-rhyme.

The only rhyme that can be clearly dated as far back as the thirteenth century is a variant of 'How Many Miles to Babylon' because it was written into a late thirteenth-century sermon as a children's game. It is a catching game, and in the example that was given in the sermon, the catcher obviously missed the target.

'How many leagues do I have to Beverleyham?' 'Eight.' 'Can I come by daylight?' (and child runs) 'Yes you can' (and curses). The first child runs quickly and ends up in the same place saying 'Ha ha slow coach, I'm back where I was.'

Medieval scholars such as Guibert of Nogent realised the value of loving care of children, and deplored when it could not be given. Children were not excluded from adult company as a rule, but would have helped with chores and work at a younger age than modern children. This also served as part of their education. Some children, especially noble children, were also fostered away. We know from the young boys who were destined to become knights that service to elders began around age five. From age seven, many boys of noble rank became pages and were no longer in the women's domain.

Hebrew texts talk about early character development (before school age), where children were to be treated kindly, as being afraid was considered bad for their development. These texts show a clear recognition of the special attention needed for small children, including the basics such as teaching them to walk and to speak and making sure they sleep at night. One rabbi gave a caveat: too much time spent babbling with unweaned infants could wreak havoc on the learning time an adult needs. There had to be a balance between the parents' needs and the child's.

Not all children were wanted or welcome, and especially poor parents may have had trouble caring for and feeding their children, particularly during famines or other times of disaster. The killing of infants, therefore, is not unknown. Some babies, for instance, were just thrown into a river. A less drastic solution was abandoning the infant. The steps to abandoning a child must seldom have been taken lightly. For many people, it was a choice between abandoning the child at a monastery and watching the child starve.

Not all abandoned babies were found. But those that were found were taken care of as best as a system with little organised public social welfare could. There is very little evidence that children born to Jewish parents were abandoned at all. However, babies born to them or to parents with mixed parentage (where the mother was Jewish) were liable to be confiscated, which would also prevent them being brought up Jewish.

Babies to be abandoned were generally wrapped carefully in swaddling clothes, sometimes with a token tucked in, then placed somewhere presumably safe, such as in a tree, to protect them from wild animals. Some babies were hung in sacks. Exposed children were often found with salt. The salt was to indicate that they had been baptised. To be on the safe side, however, many priests would baptise the child again. Some were laid on the door of parish churches, as they had prime responsibility for dealing with unwanted children. Some monasteries also took children in. We have little evidence for what happened to them if they were not oblates (taken into the monastery to take orders and lead the life of a religious) or adopted by someone.

Those who made it into a monastery might be bound to a religious life as infants, or be permitted to wait until they were six to seven years old, or even ten to twelve years old, before making their final choice. Their life would have been very strict and frequently with strong limits on physical affection from the monks, for fear of paedophilia. It would have been rather like a very austere boarding school, with dormitories, caning for misbehaviour and compulsory lessons.

Childhood ended with the coming of age. This age depended at least on the gender of the person and the region he or she lived in. Before coming of age, legal statutes did not give a person responsibility under law. The earliest ages stated as age of legal maturity, according to customary and canon law in many places, are twelve years for a girl and fourteen years for a boy. In Judaism, children became adults in all religious matters at twelve years plus one day (girls) and thirteen years (boys).

Around that time, formal training for a profession would also have started. This also includes training for the fighting aspect of knighthood: it started around age twelve, and from that time took up most of a boy's day. Boys were often trained with their peers, to help develop the team experience they would later need in war. Most knights would also have received some education so they could be functionally literate (able to read very simple Latin and, in England, to use French) and be at least somewhat familiar with vernacular literature. Many fewer of them would be versed in philosophy or know advanced arithmetic. Training and education for knighthood generally lasted until around age twenty-two, in which case the young man might be formally dubbed a knight or not, depending on his individual circumstances.

Menarche may or may not have been linked to a girls' coming of age, but was considered to be around the same time for many girls. As a general rule, medieval medicine placed menarche from twelve to fifteen and menopause around fifty.

Menstruation, known in Old French as the *privee maladie*, translated by Michael Camille as 'secret sickness', was analysed from a medical angle by physicians. Basically, the blood was seen as important in the body for the foetus but was seen as toxic to women. Menstruation was therefore cleansing to the women (men eliminated their toxicities with beards and with bigger veins). Cures for amenorrhea were important. But, for the same reasons, some learned doctors saw menstruating women as dangerous. They could endanger inanimate objects, their husband and their children. The blood could prevent crops from germinating, turn wine sour and even cause rabies.

Adulthood

Adult life differed according to a person's social situation, prosperity, cultural background and region. Some factors, however, linked adult experience across England. These are the major formative rites that marked key stages of peoples' lives.

Marriage was an important event in a person's life and led to significant changes in social status. In many regions, marriages (in any religion) were private affairs, just for the family, with the clergy playing an increasingly prominent role as time progressed. Eventually it became standard to have a priest present for the wedding. Peasant couples might live together for a considerable time without marrying. There are some indications that many weddings featured love songs, obscene gestures, feasts, dancing and lewd jokes.

In Christianity, marriage may have been preceded by a formal betrothal. In Judaism, this was almost always the case. The Jewish betrothal has changed little since the Middle Ages; however, it is now generally part of the formal marriage ceremony. The key words are 'You are betrothed to me in accordance with the laws of Moses and Israel.' Until these words are spoken, the bride has several opportunities to cancel the engagement.

When a ring was used in Christian betrothal, it was probably plain silver or gold with no gems or inscriptions. In Judaism, the ring may have had a house as decoration. The Jewish marriage ceremony consisted chiefly of seven blessings and the breaking of a glass in remembrance of the loss of the Temple. Anything else (including processions or parties) was additional. The ring given at the wedding was plain, although some had inscriptions.

A Christian marriage basically consisted of the exchange of promises or vows followed by bed (the consummation). The promise did not have standardised wording in the Middle Ages, as far as we know, nor was there a standardised ritual. Marriage in a church was not a necessity, even though many marriages took place at the church door from around the twelfth century.

In 1072, the Council of Rouen declared that marriage should be celebrated in public before midday. It should include a genealogical check, a blessing and a very simple vow; for instance, 'I take you as wife/husband'. The main component was the exchange of the ring and the promises. However, this was only in theory. Apparently, some couples knocked on the church door, and when the priest opened, asked for a blessing and recited their vows so quickly that he could not prevent it.

More formal marriages were also possible. By the eleventh and twelfth centuries, in Normandy, Brittany and Anglo-Norman England, the most formal version of a Christian marriage consisted of the following parts:

legal preliminaries, the giving away of the bride, formal confirmation of the dowry by the groom, exchange of promises, blessing of the ring, placing of the ring on the bride's third finger, nuptial Mass and blessing of the bridal chamber. These proceedings would have frequently begun at the church door and finished in the home.

From around the beginning of the thirteenth century, the Church recognised secret marriages, or marriages performed without witnesses or priests. There was quite a bit of abuse of this recognition, and several scams have been recorded which were formulated to take advantage of the fact that the Church would generally uphold an earlier secret marriage above a later, public one. While public marriages were not necessary, they could be very useful, especially legally.

Within the Church, marriage was different. Until the early twelfth century, married priests had illicit but valid relationships, which meant that the marriages were binding once they were made. From 1223, priests, deacons and subdeacons could not marry at all, and their marriages had no legal protection. They were also forbidden mistresses (at least in theory). There were many protests about this development – some of them were very violent. Even reformers tolerated marriage of the lower orders, however. From the mid-twelfth century, the higher the member of the clergy was in the Church hierarchy, the less likely they were to be married. Wives of clerics might be respected members of society, or they might be regarded as social and religious outcasts.

The rulings were far less strict towards the sons of priests than towards the wives, as the priesthood was still open to them in many cases. In many communities, wives of clergy enjoyed some social status. The factors that determined which end of this spectrum any given wife belonged on included the region, how late in the period the marriage took place and how close that district was to the papacy and how far it accepted those official rulings.

Marriage was prohibited at some times of the year in both Christianity and Judaism. For instance, many Christian marriages took place the second Sunday after Epiphany because it came after a long period of prohibition. From the end of the twelfth century, in fact, teachings about marriage were put into many sermons on that day, in readiness. No Jewish weddings were permitted between Passover and Pentecost except on the feast day of Lag b'Omer.

Cross-religion marriages were strongly disapproved of, and if children resulted from a cross-religion marriage, Christians regarded all the offspring as Christian, while Jews regarded the children as Jewish if the mother was Jewish.

Tenants (and serfs in general) needed to obtain their lord's permission to marry. Slaves and serfs could theoretically marry even to those working for different masters. It could, however, affect the status of their children. If the marriage was between people who owed loyalty to two lords, then the one losing a worker had the right to demand a replacement tenant.

Vincent de Beauvais wrote that a wife was, in relation to her husband, neither lady, nor servant, but an equal companion. A woman's financial interests after marriage were protected to a certain extent.

Medieval theorists were sharply divided between the wish for chastity and the need for children. Therefore, sometimes the ideal marriage was seen as a chaste one (with Joseph and Mary given as an example) and sometimes people were told marriage was there for carnality: 'Go forth and procreate!' There were also many views in between these two extremes. Thus, an individual's notion of marriage would depend more on the specific teaching and advice they received than on any single view of what marriage was.

What was this like in practice? An English peasant woman married mostly around age eighteen to twenty-two, with richer peasant girls often marrying earlier. Late marriage often happened if the couple needed to collect the wherewithal to live on once they left home. If the couple was too poor, they could not get married; these were the people who often became junior servants, for example at the manor, if they were lucky. This does not mean that they were grateful for the opportunity. Unmarried Christian women were subject to the *leyrwrite*, a fine for sleeping around; they would be told off by a court, but no stigma appears to have been attached, as many women who paid this fine married afterwards.

Technically, Christian marriage was for life and could not be undone or divorced. Most references to divorce in Christian marriage actually referred to a separation. The partner seldom had the right to remarry in these cases. This is quite different to Jewish divorce, where the divorce was easier to obtain, and was also a complete cancelling of the marriage contract after consideration by the Beth Din (Jewish law court). Remarriage was possible in Judaism (albeit with a short waiting period for the woman).

However, Christian marriages could be dissolved if they were considered invalid. This usually resulted in separation or annulment. In the twelfth century, grounds for annulment could include lack of mutual consent, a contract with a non-Christian, a religious profession (one of the couple in orders), a public vow of chastity, and consanguinity. Consanguinity meant that the couple in question were too closely related to each other, although the definition of this could vary. Sometimes presumption of death was also allowed as a reason for annulment. Any impediment had to exist prior to the marriage for annulment to take place. These marriages were not legally valid in Christianity and were the closest that medieval Christianity had to a modern divorce. New factors such as adultery, cruelty or desertion after the marriage did not count.

Severe marital problems that did not fall into these categories were grounds for separation only, and even that was hard to achieve. Some clerics held that adultery was sufficient reason, while others argued that consanguinity or impotence were necessary. James Brundage lists as reasons for dissolution: impotence, entry into a different religion, a long absence, intractable illness, a bad crime, rape, adultery or a second (consummated) marriage. If a wife believed her husband dead, then most authorities believed that she could remarry. If he reappeared, though, she had to return to him.

For most people, however, a Christian marriage was almost impossible to dissolve. Holding a large amount of personal power was an aid to gaining divorce, if so desired.

In theory, at least, the Church insisted on free consent to marriage. Likewise some secular laws (for instance the laws of King Cnut, r. 1016–35) said that a woman should not have to marry a man she disliked. If a girl was forced into marriage, a sympathetic church court might annul the marriage. Likewise, there was some room for manoeuvre if the marriage was contracted by parents or guardians between children who were too young to consent.

Other impediments to marriage existed. Even sex before marriage could be regarded as an impediment, though in itself was not severe enough grounds to dissolve a marriage. Insane people could not marry and neither could nuns, since they were pledged to God.

Adultery was strongly stigmatised in both Christian and Jewish society. Women could be banished from the home, separated from their children and have their dowry confiscated by their husband. With little in the way of public welfare available, adultery could lead to destitution for women. Adulterous women might have their heads shaved and be marched through the streets, with jeers and even physical abuse following them. The husband was not allowed to kill an adulterous wife, although he might get away with killing her lover. Bastards born out of pre-marital sex could be made legitimate through a simple procedure, but those born to adulterous relationships could not.

In Jewish law, adult daughters were able to arrange their own marriage, while minors had marriages arranged by their fathers. The maternal uncle played a special role in many families. This often meant in practice that the child's father's family provided land and the mother's brother was useful for patronage and influence.

Jews had divorce readily available to them in the form of a *gett*, a document of about ninety words. The husband could divorce the wife on many grounds, although in most cases there would be a community-enforced attempt at reconciliation. From the eleventh century, most rabbis refused to preside over a divorce unless it had the wife's consent. The wife could divorce for very specific reasons: the husband had newly developed physical defects, he didn't have sex with her, he worked in a smelly trade (for example as a tanner), he had bad breath, he could not have children and so on.

This divorce was known as a *kitance* or *akitement* in Old French, and the term was based on the language of legal contracts. This is because Jewish marriage was considered a contract between the two parties rather than a sacrament. In an ideal situation, the couple would receive marriage guidance before divorcing and would not divorce on trivial grounds.

The community had to approve of the divorce, and once accomplished, the dowry had to be repaid. Divorces were also available where they would avoid a greater evil, for instance in cases of adultery, murder and even acute marital breakdown. There was an assumption in Judaism that marriages were intended to be happy.

In England and northern France in particular, most communities would have followed the tenth-century ruling of Rabbi Gershom that women could not be divorced against their will. Likewise, *levirate* marriages (a widow marrying her deceased husband's brother) followed the rule of Rabbi Gershom, who limited a husband to one single wife, and were not practised after the eleventh century.

Until around 1200, if a Jew (either male or female) could not obtain a *gett*, they were able to convert to Christianity and have the marriage dissolved. Christianity did not allow for relapse into Judaism, so this was not a step to be taken lightly. After 1200, even this became more difficult, as the Church required that the spouse who remained Jewish insult Christianity before granting the dissolution.

Canon law had problems with the relative ease of obtaining a divorce under Jewish law, possibly because it made Christianity look less desirable. Canonists spent a lot of effort trying to get Jewish divorce covered by canon law, but were only able to do so when the Jewish couple contravened canon law.

Heathen (non-Christian) marriages were generally considered valid in the twelfth century, just like mixed marriages were considered valid. If, however, the mixed marriage ended in a divorce (possible for both Muslim and Jewish marriages) then, following a ruling by Pope Innocent III (r. 1198–1216), the Christian was permitted to remarry. This means that, while these marriages were considered legally valid, they did not have the sacramental qualities of a Christian marriage and were therefore not binding to the same degree.

Heathens were permitted more than one wife if their own law allowed it. Christians were never allowed this latitude (again, according to a ruling by Innocent III).

Marriages also ended through the death of one partner. For women, widowhood entailed a significant change in status to that enjoyed during marriage. Some women had alternatives for the first time. Widows of rank often retained their dower right, for instance, which comprised a significant portion of her husband's property upon his death (subject to her not remarrying). This was not always available, however, as it was legal for the wife to agree to its alienation during her husband's lifetime.

Widows could choose remarriage, reprising the role of a wife, or they could remain widows. They had the possibility to continue or start running a business or farm, or they could take religious vows. Widows (and unmarried women) who went to monasteries but did not take vows generally lived in their own houses outside the monastery. By 1200 and especially from 1215 in England, widows of higher rank were permitted to seek their rights in court if they were denied their dower or maintenance.

In Judaism, too, widows were more independent with a higher level of property control, although Jewish widows had a special position in relation to the Crown. Like the Christian widows to whom this applied, they could pay money to buy freedom of choice, such as the choice to either stay single or to remarry whom they liked. King John, especially, made money from this. In 1175–6 the widow of Ralph de Cornhill paid the king 200 marks, three palfreys and two goshawks to get out of marrying Godfrey of Louvain. She was allowed to keep her lands and marry where she liked.

Sex and Sexuality

Medieval views of sexuality went hand in hand with medieval views of love. Since the nineteenth century, when the concept of courtly love became associated with the Middle Ages, the nature of love as seen by medieval people has been hotly debated. Literature on love ranges from romantic texts to bawdy ones. Much of the love life of individuals remains hidden from us, however. Marriage, childbirth and death appear in formal records, but emotions are not equally well recorded. Ideals of beauty, such as the white skin of a woman or the shapely legs of a man, are mostly mentioned in literature. Generally, sexuality and lust are much easier to grasp than the medieval concept of love, as they were frequent topics in all kinds of texts, including literary, judicial and medicinal ones.

Thomas Aquinas claimed that women existed only for procreation and to give men food and drink. While this view was not universal in the Middle Ages, it was sufficiently common among scholars to affect the way women's sexuality was technically discussed. Women were considered to have higher levels of sexual desire than men, with many reasons given for women's lust. Albertus Magnus said that women could never be satisfied.

This view of women's sexuality came from two main sources. The first was Galen's writings, claiming that women also produced seed which needed to be released for reproduction. Followers of Galen suggested that women had to find sex pleasurable to get with child. The second, Aristotelian school, claimed that the pleasure was irrelevant because there was no seed to be released by it. Both views saw women as soft, carnal and very sexual. Open mouths (even mouths open through talkativeness) were seen by medical writers as indicating desire.

Men, on the other hand, needed to protect their masculinity and were typified by careful control. At least one medieval writer suggested that women became stronger with intercourse, and men weaker and liable to early ageing if they performed too often. Additionally, according to some medical authorities, men were not permitted masturbation because they needed to protect their valuable semen, which was central to their masculinity. This masculine nature was why they were able to think rationally, which gave them their social authority and spiritual power. However, this idea of conservation of masculinity does not seem to have restricted the development of medicine to reduce impotence, or to discourage some men from seeking prostitutes. It also did not prevent aphrodisiac cures being recommended for some male illnesses.

Lovesickness was seen as a legitimate illness for men. When a man demonstrated a huge desire for a particular woman, it was seen as a form of melancholia and therefore an illness according to some doctors. The cure depended on the man's need. It could be treated with wine, by sending the man away from the object of desire, by encouraging his proximity to the person or even by having sex with another woman. An alternate cure was to be forced to listen to misogynistic tales.

Medical writers advised their specialist readers on abortion, contraception and even how to enhance sexual pleasure, since female orgasms were considered necessary to produce male children. Most of the written record about both contraception and childbirth concerns formal applications of theory, whether in religious texts or in records of births or criminal behaviour. The written record, therefore, focusses on the extraordinary far more than the everyday. Research into motherhood in the Middle Ages demonstrates that, like childhood, it has more in common with modern attitudes than stereotyping about the period suggests.

Many herbs were available which could have been used as contraceptives or abortifacients, but knowledge of these herbs and their properties would have varied, and knowledge of doses and side effects would also have varied.

Some herbs that could have been used included celery and celery seeds, ginger, parsley (which was considered to stimulate menstruation), rue, myrrh (probably the most expensive option), tansy, pennyroyal and Queen Anne's lace.

Christian theologians were often strongly against contraceptives and abortion. They repeated their concerns with both techniques frequently, which suggests that they were arguing against current practice rather than stating a theoretical position. Due to the strong Church influence on medieval medicine, it is unlikely that doctors officially prescribed any contraceptive and abortive herbs, and much knowledge might have been obtained by word of mouth. Contraceptive techniques seem to have been mostly tacitly accepted when used within marriage, however. Judaism also did not approve of contraception as a general rule, with nursing mothers being an important exception. The Talmud recommended two years of *coitus interruptus* as the main contraceptive technique, while the Church recommended complete abstinence from sex. The Church argument for complete chastity was stronger later in our period, even though it often contradicted reality. Even within some of the religious orders, chastity was often breached.

Most medieval Christian scholars thought sex a sin, meaning that it was an intrinsically evil act. Despite this, the Church had very mixed views of human sexuality, and there were even important scholars such as Peter Abelard who disagreed with sex being a sin. Chastity was increasingly promulgated as a virtue as our period progressed. Sex outside marriage was a problem, of course, but so was having sex when being married less than three days, when the woman was pregnant, menstruating or nursing, it being Lent or Advent or Whitsun week or Easter week. Feasts and fasts in general were not approved days for intercourse, as were any Sunday, Wednesday, Friday, Saturday and any day at all if it was still daylight. In the most extreme view, couples could not be naked, had to be working for a child and not for pleasure, had to use the missionary position and so on. On the other hand, sex was necessary for the conception of children and these were desirable in the eyes of the Church.

Clerical celibacy was introduced during the eleventh century, but was not instantly followed, nor even much liked. The Bishop of Paris was driven from his cathedral by his angry clerical staff when he announced they had to be celibate. Worse, a supporter of celibacy for clerics was burned alive by furious clergy in Cambrai in 1077. Gradually, however, it took hold, although it only really became normal from around the middle of the thirteenth century. Even when priests were forbidden to marry, they could keep concubines, although this was far from encouraged. The emphasis on celibacy had an immediate effect on the children of priests. Clerical celibacy was far more enforced than secular, and, as a result, children of clergy lost many of the rights to inherit and to potential careers that they had previously enjoyed.

Homosexuality was a subsection of sodomy. Sodomy was defined as sex with someone of the same sex, with an animal or sex in anything other than the missionary position – it did not relate solely to homosexuality. Having sex simply for pleasure (that is without the possibility of producing a child) was also classified as sodomy by some writers. Some scholars, in fact, even argued that sex with adults of different religions counted as sodomy. From around 1250, homosexual sex was given tougher penalties than the other varieties of sodomy. This largely refers to gay sex; lesbian sex is almost impossible to document. Because there is no simple medieval definition of homosexuality, modern understanding of it has had to be gleaned from indirect evidence. In the Latin version of the medical text by Avicenna, homosexuality was considered as an illness.

The first documented Western European execution of a homosexual was in 1277. There is some evidence for active homosexual behaviour being progressively more condemned as time passed. The lowest punishment in most cases appears to have been a fine, with castration for a repeat offence, followed by exile or death. The negative discussion comes from scholars and from legal practice. In everyday life, many people may well have fought against these restrictions. Priests were warned not to explain it, so that no one would be tempted by it, which must have made it very difficult to reconcile religious theory with sexual reality. That the Church was formally intolerant and even persecuted homosexuals, however, is without a doubt. Several major Church writers advocated greater punishment of sodomites from the thirteenth century. The punishment during the time of Edward I of England (r. 1272–1307) was death by burning, but we do not know how far this was enforced. Judaism, likewise, was at best ambivalent towards homosexuality in men, but possibly had a less negative attitude to that in women.

Sodomy was considered the worst sexual deviation for Christians, together with incest. These were, in canon law, equivalent to murder, forgery and heresy. Masturbation was a lesser problem in canon law and fornication (sex outside marriage by those who were not married) was the least in legal terms. Some of its more standard opinions included punishing adulterers and fornicators heavily, and the Church took a stance against infanticide as well as against abortion and contraception. It was also not in favour of women entering a church during menstruation or for forty days after the birth of a child. People who committed adultery with someone could not marry them later. There was also a popular belief among Christians that premarital sex was proscribed by the Church and was a sin, even if it was not considered as very serious compared with adultery or incest. In this instance, the more educated the priest, the less severe the penalty may have been. However, to a certain degree, all sex outside marriage was sinful and required penitence. This included masturbation as well as sexual dreams and even rape. In theory, both men and women were culpable, but in practice, it appears that women were punished more often. Muslims were believed by the Church to be generally guilty of sodomy, while Jews were guilty only of simple lust.

During the eleventh and twelfth centuries, Church reformers sought to reduce intercourse even within non-clerical marriages. The Church re-emphasised during this period that sexual activity was only for the purposes of procreation and that there should be no sexual activity whatsoever outside marriage. In some areas, they had more success than others. In fact, chastity occurred at several levels according to the Church, with the lowest and easiest being avoidance of sex and the highest being chaste even in dreams. Given that the regulation of dreams was almost impossible, there were some sexual ideals where the Church failed outright in the vast majority of cases. There was a great deal of social resistance to these reforms, some for political reasons, some for social and some for personal ones. Nevertheless, it appears that the reforms achieved a reasonable level of outward compliance. Some modern scholars suggest that the twelfth-century romance ideals were a way of dealing with these restrictions emotionally.

Jewish scholars, on the other hand, did not see sex as evil but, like Abelard, a natural part of life, especially if part of a marriage. Sex was considered mainly for procreation, but one was permitted to enjoy it. In fact, in Judaism, the wife had clear sexual rights, including sex to meet her needs and no sex without her consent: marital rape was forbidden.

Sexuality was also used to make money in the form of prostitution. Prostitution increased during our period, despite the increasingly judgmental attitude of the Church towards intercourse. This increase may have been due at least in part to the number of women without other marketable skills and the number of men prepared to take advantage of this.

During our period, prostitutes were largely regarded as not quite inside ordinary society. Prostitutes were often associated with heavy make-up, especially with the application of much powder and rouge. There were various limitations on what they could do and how far they could be a part of the wider community, though these limitations varied according to place and time and the views of specific authorities. Frequently they were not permitted to bear witness, that is to say, to testify before a court. In some towns, there were attempts to force them to wear distinctive clothing. They might also be forced to live and practice their trade outside town walls, although some places – mainly large towns – seem to have had the equivalent of a red light district; for instance, in the mid-thirteenth century, Smithfield had Cock Lane and London had Southwark. There were no municipal brothels until after our period.

Brothels during our period are generally hard to trace. After our period, bath houses became increasingly associated with brothels, but there appears to be no evidence of this until around the fifteenth century. Bernard of Clairvaux, however, deplored prostitutes taking advantage of long queues at mills to tout for trade as people waited to have their grain ground.

Some preachers actively worked to rehabilitate prostitutes, even to the extent of having their followers marry these women. For instance, Henry the Monk bade his followers marry prostitutes in the early twelfth century. Fulk of Neuilly encouraged prostitutes to join a special Cistercian convent he founded for them in the 1190s, and he also married them off. He collected money from Parisians for dowries.

Old Age, Death and Burial

A good death was important to people. This entailed being prepared for death, preferably after a long life. It wasn't good to die young, violently or without confessing and receiving absolution for one's sins. Pain was often considered an essential part of Christian death because it was thought to be the deserved punishment for sins. Having foreknowledge of one's time of death enabled a person to take the actions necessary for a good death.

Throughout the Middle Ages, the Church had fixed ideal rites for the death of a person. These rites began with confession and penance. Since someone who was dying was usually not able to do the prescribed penance, someone else was required to do it instead, unless the sick one recovered and then had to do it in person. The sick one was then washed, dressed in clean clothes and brought into church if possible. For the actual death, the person should ideally rest upon straw and ashes. Priests brought the cross, spoke the peace rite and sprinkled blessed water and blessed ashes on the dying. They then spoke a set of prayers, followed by anointment with blessed oil (Extreme Unction). Finally, everybody present recited the Credo and the Lord's Prayer, followed by Communion for the sick (the Viaticum). Of course, the ideal rites were not always what really happened. During the High Middle Ages, the cleric performing the Extreme Unction usually demanded the items necessary for the rite as donation: the linen cloth used as bedding, the necessary candles and so on. Later, the priest might demand money or the best garment or best animal for his services, a practice that must have made Extreme Unction a rite that was disliked or even hated by the public.

While Extreme Unction was always administered by a priest, the Viaticum was quite frequently given to the dying by a family member in the house. This was allowed because of the common wish of Christians to die with the Viaticum Host still on the tongue.

The common belief was that either angels (or occasionally Christ himself) or demons would accompany the soul of the deceased into either heaven or hell, depending on whether the soul was deemed good or evil.

Taking vows just before death was considered a certain method to save a person considered sinful from purgatory or hell, according to several medieval accounts. This was due to the inherent holiness of the monks' habit, covering up the sins of the person inside. Last-minute vows could be so popular that some convents had one monk whose work was rushing to the dying with a habit and witnessing the vows. This practice, seen as taking an easy way out, was criticised sharply. Once taken, the vow of any order could not be revoked, and should the sick person recover, he or she then had to spend the rest of life in the monastery. These last-minute vows could also be abused: it was possible to 'gently remove' a person by sedating them, claiming to a member of a holy order that that person was dying, dressing them in the habit of the holy order and thus making him or her spend the rest of their life in the monastery.

Deceased people were still very much a part of life. They still existed in the other world, albeit with a changed status. Saints were, in some cases, able to rise and interact with the living. Speaking somebody's name meant invoking that person who was then considered to be present. This mindset was the reason for the medieval cult of the dead. The dead were witnesses for the acts of the living, and their spiritual welfare could be influenced by the acts of those alive, for instance by others doing penance for them. This led many people to try and buy salvation for their soul by giving gifts to the Church in exchange for prayers and pardons. Naturally, the clergy did not discourage this practice: occasionally clergymen were known to actively seek lands and money when attending a deathbed.

The dead were considered to have some rights, among them the right to a wake and an undisturbed grave. From the eighth century, burials for Christians were only allowed in the vicinity of a church. This churchyard did not only serve as a graveyard, but also for congregations, as asylum and for diversions. The place in which a person was buried often depended upon the person's wealth or status. For example, the average person would be buried in the churchyard of the parish church, while noble patrons might be buried in the churchyard of an abbey they had supported. To be buried inside the church itself was a sign of high status. This was quite restricted and only granted to nobles and people considered worthy, usually bishops, abbots, priests and very rarely non-noble lay people. The highest honour was to be buried inside the church before the high altar.

Burial rites developed considerably during the Middle Ages. The most important acts were washing of the deceased and dressing the body, then carrying it from the house to the church on a pallet. If the body stayed in the home overnight, there may have been a watch kept over the body. Sometimes the body might be embalmed with ingredients such as musk, myrrh and laudanum, although evidence suggests this was very unusual. Prayers for the dead were spoken before the burial itself, and Mass was performed.

Early in our period, the body was shown uncovered on a bier, at home and en route to burial. By the thirteenth century it was sewn in a shroud and placed in a coffin. If the person was wealthy, they might be buried in the coffin, but most coffins were used only for transport.

While the burial garment was usually white, the actual nature of the garment seems to have varied considerably. Although most people were wrapped in a shroud only, sometimes hair shirts or other penitential garments have been found in medieval graves. If a shroud was used, the body was either wrapped in it or sewn into it. When a coffin was used for the actual burial, it was usually wooden, although more expensive stone sarcophagi are known. If a wooden coffin was used, it might have been nailed shut. Examples of coffin nails have frequently been unearthed in cemetery excavations.

Senior clerics were usually buried with chalices and other religious equipment; this equipment could be made especially for the burial. Kings were also buried with insignia, but everyone else had no grave goods, except for some pilgrims being buried with boots, coat, staff and an indication of their pilgrimage.

The funeral procession could be small or be a large crowd. If the deceased was wealthy enough, the procession could include poor people at the tail end. These were given money to attend the funeral and demonstrate to the world how important the deceased had been. The procession bearing the body traditionally halted three times on the way to the church. There was no prescribed funeral or mourning clothing for these attending the funeral, and ordinary clothing seems to have been worn in many cases. Wearing black only became de rigueur for Christians towards the end of our period. At the church, a bell was sounded, and the Office of the Dead was said. For an important funeral, there would be a sermon, and for a wealthy deceased person, a feast may have been prescribed in the will.

The night before the funeral Mass, those who wished to would keep a vigil in the church praying for the soul of the deceased person in hopes of speeding them through purgatory and on to heaven. Sometimes, if they could afford it, family members or friends would give money to the church to pay for additional Masses to be said for the dead person's soul.

Some bodies were not allowed into churches by clerics. These included the bodies of women who died in childbirth and those of people who died violent deaths. The argument was that their blood polluted the church. Peasant infant burials have been found on peasant land as well as in the churchyard. This is probably because canon law forbids the burial of an unbaptised infant in consecrated ground. Those excommunicated were also not allowed a Christian burial on consecrated ground, and no prayers were spoken for them. In addition to the unbaptised dead and excommunicated people, heretics and non-Christians were also denied Christian burial. In theory this also applied to suicides and women who died in childbirth, although enormous numbers of exceptions seem to have been made for these two groups.

The practice of burying different parts of the body in different locations was not a common practice in general, though it seems to have been more common among the high nobility. This was usually done when someone died a long way away from the place of burial, for instance when dying on a crusade. The intestines or other organs could be removed if the body was to be transported over a long distance. For even longer transports, the bones could be extracted and boiled and sent to the place of burial; this is known at least for the thirteenth century. The practice of moving the dead to a spot of burial far away was at its height during the middle of the twelfth century.

In some cases, it was a hotly contested honour to receive part of a king or of a particularly saintly person for burial. This was the case with the burial of Henry the Young King (1155–83), whose body was kidnapped by the people of Le Mans and buried in their cathedral. The citizens of Rouen, where Henry had pledged to be buried, threatened to raze Le Mans if the body was not returned to them. Their threat was successful. Separate burial of the heart had a particular symbolism, as was illustrated by the burial of Richard I's heart in Rouen, the principal city of Normandy, while his body was interred at the abbey of Fontevrault with his parents. With the exception of Henry I (r. 1100–35), it should be noted that the kings of England were buried on the side of the Channel on which they died.

Remembering the deceased and helping them in the afterlife was an important ongoing task after the burial. While the Masses were supposed to help shorten the dead person's stay in purgatory, they were also important in helping the living grieve. From the ninth century, a liturgy of the dead was introduced as part of the mourning procedure. It is interesting to note that with the rise in popularity of this liturgy came an increase in the number of ghosts reported. Masses were said three, seven and thirty days after death, and offerings were often given to the poor in memory of the deceased. Frequently these offerings were through donations given to the Church. Most people had sections of the Office of the Dead recited at weekly, monthly and finally annual intervals after burial. A requiem Mass might also be held. Worthy Christian dead were remembered through memorial books and the use of anniversary Masses.

Other aspects of remembrance were grave markers or tombstones. Most of these, however, would have been rather simple. During our period, effigies were not common except among the highest nobility, mostly kings and queens or prelates of the Church. The high nobility were sometimes buried in elaborate stone tombs, carved for decoration. Until the twelfth century, however, there were few elaborate tombs or memorials, even for kings. Fancy tombs could be seen as a way to ensure that people would remember them and pray at their grave, but also as a means to shore up a dynasty. Of course, personal vanity may have played a role, too. Altar tombs were probably the most common type for those who merited expensive burials, gradually shifting to a picture of the deceased on a coffin and then to an incised slab. The transition from one to another was not consistent, so all three types could be found in the late twelfth century. Brasses were slowly added to this mix from the beginning of the thirteenth century. By the late thirteenth century, most of the more elaborate tombs featured either incised slabs or brasses.

Brasses were made of an alloy of copper and zinc (often called latten). The chief places of manufacture were Cologne or Flanders. Many brasses were probably coloured with enamels, for example showing heraldic shields in appropriate colours. Very few brasses survive in either France or England as they were targeted during later religious disputes. Brasses were most likely to be found in the east of England and the part of France nearest Flanders. Generally, however, incised slabs were the most common choice.

In the thirteenth century, increasing numbers of visits to famous tombs was part of a change in behaviour towards the dead that led to an increase in fancy monuments. Pilgrims wanting cures went to the tombs of saints. They were well known for wanting to get as close to the body as possible, for instance by placing their heads or body parts inside carved features such as those decorating the main tomb of St Hugh, in Lincoln Cathedral. Some pilgrims even slept on the tombs.

Jewish burial practices were distinctly different from the Christian ones. Jewish deathbed penitence was common during our period, although not codified until the thirteenth century. From the thirteenth century, it consisted in saying the *Shema Yisrael* ('Hear, O Israel') before ten men, including at least one rabbi. Prior to then, it was probably a more private arrangement. Christian influence may well be responsible for the move towards a formal confession.

Jewish burials required a *minyan* (ten adult Jewish men) present. It was standard to ask for forgiveness of any wrong done to the dead. The corpse, eyes closed, arms along the body, was draped with material, leaving the head and feet uncovered. Mourners followed the body to the place of burial, walking with heads covered and lowered, their hands hidden under their robes, which were dark-coloured or black. Chief mourners were parents, spouses, siblings and children.

At Jewish funerals it was customary to throw a clod of earth over one's shoulder after the funeral was finished. This was regarded as sorcerous by Christians in Paris in the early thirteenth century. After leaving the cemetery, it was important to wash one's hands before entering any home. While washing hands, extracts from psalms 90 (verse 17) and 91 were recited three times.

Mourners sat *shiva*, a ritual seven days of mourning following burial. They sat close to the ground and wore torn garments as a sign of their grief. During *shiva*, a special meal was given to the chief mourners by their neighbours and friends. The mourners were permitted no greetings for three days and social intercourse was restricted until after the seven days. The water containers kept outside homes were emptied to signify bereavement. A candle was kept alight for the whole seven days. There was a lesser mourning period of thirty days following this, and the mourning was finally finished after a year.

The Jewish custom of a prayer of remembrance and candle lighting every year to honour the dead may have been practiced in the Middle Ages.

Cemeteries were often planted with trees and shrubs. Tombs generally had tombstones. Excavations of the Jewbury cemetery in England have revealed that wooden coffins, usually pine or oak, were used for burials. Many Jews made cemetery visits annually, often on days of mourning such as the ninth day of the month of Av or the evening before Day of Atonement. If a Jewish cemetery was not available, then many visited a Christian one, despite the concerns some rabbis had.

A very big difference was the stance on suicide. Jewish suicide, especially where the person was faced with murder or compulsory conversion by a crowd and chose to die instead, was known as *Kiddush ha-Shem* ('sanctification of the name'). It was not undertaken lightly, and it was not seen as a negative act.

After Death

While the formal religious concepts of the afterlife were widely believed, there existed alongside these a rich set of popular beliefs which embroidered and modified the formal notions of death and afterlife. Connections between the living and the dead were seen as perfectly possible. In twelfth-century London, oaths were often taken over a dead person's tomb. Keith Thomas suggests this was so that the ghost would avenge any perjury, although it is also possible that the ghost was a kind of supernatural witness, that is to say, a link between the oath-takers and God. Ghosts and spirits were particularly associated with cemeteries and were capable of transforming them into places of peril. William of Newburgh commented that the bodies of the dead left their tombs, wandering around the living and terrifying them. They could be combated with holy water and other religious items.

The popular belief in ghosts was strong, evidenced by different types of reports of ghostly appearances. The main reports of ghosts we have are normally of ghosts of Christians or are unspecified demons, 'demon' being the standard way to refer to an extraordinary creature. There appears to have been a wide range of views of ghosts.

The types of ghost stories that are more than just a mention in passing fall into two basic categories. The first are tales transcribed by clerics which refer to the visionary experience of someone other than themselves. Sometimes the experience was a dream, but, more frequently, it was a waking vision. The ghosts in these tales were described as like a living person – some could even be touched. The second type of story can be found in biographies, more frequently in the form of dreams, but with waking visions still important. Sometimes these ghosts were invisible presences.

Ghosts were capable of communication: Gervase of Tilbury reported ghostly appearances in Arles in 1211, where secrets were told to the living. Ghosts of ordinary people could not intercede with God-like saints (who were never considered ghosts), but were capable of giving useful advice (such as telling living relatives where a lost item was), announcing imminent deaths or even providing suitably instructional religious messages. Oddly enough, most surviving accounts of ghosts refer to male ghosts.

Jewish ghost reports included ghostly synagogue services. If a living person saw their ghost in that service, it foretold their death. Live people could witness these services, but some who saw them thought they were bad omens. Possibly to prevent this, people knocked on synagogue doors before entering. Special meetings of ghosts in prayer were on the evening of new moons and on the festival of Hoshanah Rabbah. These special prayers by the ghosts were undertaken to help the living.

The Christian Church suggested that ghosts were souls of people in purgatory, unable to rest until their sins were accounted for. This accounts for so many ghost stories appearing in clerical didactic works, and it also gives a learned framework for the suffering of those who appear in Hellequin's Hunt.

Hellequin's Hunt is one of the most important tales linking the afterlife with ordinary people. It was described with quite a few variations, but the most detailed as well as the earliest appears to have been that of Orderic Vitalis (1075–1142), telling of a man who was caught out at night and saw things that were not really for human eyes. He saw a parade of the dead, already being punished for their sins. In the Jewish version, the dead were punished by having to pull carts, but the Christian versions were more varied and the punishments more exotic. Hellequin's Hunt appears to initially have been believed mostly in Anglo-Saxon England and areas settled by Scandinavians, in Brittany, the Welsh borders and the area around Hereford. By the thirteenth century, it had spread to the east of France.

3

Death and Taxes You Cannot Avoid
Government

In contrast to the present, where most societies have a very pronounced distance between Church and State, both national and regional governance were closely linked to Church governance in the Middle Ages. According to medieval belief, kings ruled through the power given to them by God.

There was also no separation of powers as we know it in the Middle Ages. Judicial, executive and legislative functions were not seen as separate functions of government, but as extensions of each other. For instance, much of the legislative function (making new laws) was undertaken by the executive (the king) who was also technically responsible for the judicial function at its highest level.

Both secular and Church governing structures relied on administrative districts. As is still the case today, even small changes in government meant changes for the whole populace: a ruler helps shape the country.

Secular Administration

Individuals and the relationships between them were key to the secular system of government. This system was based on exchange of loyalties, often accompanied by goods or grants of land and land usage. The titular head of this system of social and political loyalties was the king (as first among peers), with the senior members of the leading families (magnates) also possessing a large amount of power. All rulers depended on the support of their high-ranking vassals and local lords.

Showing one's influence and power was a vital aspect of secular administration and government. This was achieved by the use of ceremonies, insignia and titles, in addition to the displays of wealth and status that showed social status.

A king's coronation ceremony is a prime example of a demonstration of power. In England, coronations appear to have been formalised towards the end of the twelfth century. At their coronation, English kings swore a tripartite oath. They swore to maintain the peace of the Church, to banish iniquity and to give just judgment. The French coronation ceremony followed a precise order, the key aspect of which was the anointing of the new king with holy oil. This again shows the connection between Crown and Church. In France and Britain (but not in Brittany), crowns were part of the royal regalia.

A formal assembly of important people at the royal court, with the king wearing the crown, was also called a coronation. These crown-wearings were held in different numbers by different kings. For instance, Henry III (r. 1216–72) called up to sixteen a year.

Rulers in the Middle Ages were never anonymous and seldom figureheads. Each ruler was very individual. To understand their laws and their government, therefore, we need to look at their lives and at the important events that shaped them. The rulers of England had blood and marriage ties across Europe as well as within England. In many ways, they were at the heart of the networks of families that made up the ruling classes and shaped the country; where senior ecclesiastical and secular appointments came from depended largely on the king.

Kings, and to a lesser degree, barons, exercised certain powers and rights that sometimes make it difficult to distinguish between actions that could be considered public as opposed to actions that seem more private in nature to us. The exact nature of these rights depended on time and place and could, for instance, include the right to levy a tax to pay for a daughter's wedding. This was a prerogative of lords and not limited to kings.

From the twelfth century, the increasing amount of public life kings had to fulfil led to changes in administration, but it also led to changes in their public appearances and finally a more kingly burial and an elevation of the king's perceived spiritual status.

The lords were crucial to secular leadership in both England and France. Lords who swore an oath of fealty directly to the Crown, regardless of their title, are also known as the great vassals. All of these people could have vassals in their turn, as well as other people who owed them loyalty. Professions of loyalty might be accompanied by acts of homage, for example kneeling before the lord and putting the hands into the lord's hands for the oath. These acts were an open demonstration of relative status. Vassals may have been obligated to provide a certain amount of military assistance. While technically the word vassal had a formal meaning, it could also be used to describe a young noble. In addition, vassal could mean someone senior in civil service, as opposed to a fighting man.

In late thirteenth-century England, the relationships between lords and their men began to take the form of indenture of retinue, with annuities and the wearing of livery. The indenture text was written out twice on the same parchment and the two copies were then cut apart with sawteeth edges, hence the term 'indentured'. Basically, the indenture was an agreement of service for the man and, in exchange, remuneration by the lord. Indentures could be for life or for a specified period of time like a specific military campaign. The service and the remuneration or provisions varied from agreement to agreement.

The relationship between the king and the leading families was not always amicable – witness the 'Mad' Parliament of Oxford, 1258, where Simon of Montfort and his peers forced the king to accept some radical changes to government.

Land was divided into districts to enable administration. Specific terms were used to describe these districts. The basic unit of land for administrative purposes in England was usually called a *hide*, a *carucate* or a *wapentake*. The amount of land in a district varied depending on the richness of the soil and the region under discussion.

The hundred was the basic unit for administration relating to the manor and its court, as well as for tax collection and military matters. It was a fiscal region that technically consisted of 100 *hides*, so the size of the hundred again depended on the wealth of the region. While boundaries were not constant, the court functions ensured the continuation of the hundred itself.

For further administrative purposes, land was divided into territorial units usually called counties or shires. For accounting purposes in England, twelve hundreds were considered to make up a shire. The boundaries for these units were somewhat fluid and several new counties were created in the twelfth century. A few counties (Kent and Sussex, for example) were based on earlier Anglo-Saxon kingdoms, and others were created around 1066, when William I became king. The *Domesday Book* lists thirty-three counties, while the final number was thirty-nine, indicating that the remaining six came into existence later.

As with all the other aspects of ruling the country, the work of administration was not done by the king alone. Administrative districts were governed by officers who often had quite specific roles. These offices could be rather profitable occupations. They were known by different names, depending on the time and the region, even though their functions – for example delivering the king's proclamations in country courts or public places – may have stayed the same.

Court officers handled matters near the king; for instance, the offices of the Exchequer handled matters to do with taxation and finance. Outside the court, a sheriff ('shire-reeve') appointed by the king presided over both the judicial and financial issues of each region under the king's direct rule. This included presiding over the county or shire court and receiving payment of all the fines that had been imposed.

Sheriffs were often quite independent and could have a rather high income.

A sheriff did not hold the office for life, although it could be held for many years. The duties of a sheriff could be very broad, ranging from financial, legal and administrative to peace enforcement. Some of these duties were constant (mainly the financial obligations) and some were in response to circumstances or to royal instructions. The role, importance and specific tasks varied according to region and over time.

Another example of an administrative official is the bailiff. Bailiffs were administrators in the districts below shire or county level. While the term was later linked specifically to legal matters (issuing writs, for instance, or finding juries), in the Middle Ages the term was less specific. Bailiffs carried white rods or staffs to indicate their role. They might also act as the king's representative in the region and govern in the king's absence.

Local administration was heavily male. For example, male aletasters regulated the ale industry, even while ale making was largely done by women. It was not exclusively so, however; sources also tell us of female sheriffs.

Some towns had their own administration. Throughout the Middle Ages, more and more towns became burghs. They ceased to be administered by the lord of the district and his representatives, and began to administer themselves. However, throughout our period, most towns and villages were still under a lordship.

Parliament

Neither England nor France were absolute monarchies. The ruler did not operate alone. He consulted with the senior members of society through assemblies and tribunals (including, in France, the English king through his French holdings). Assemblies were a part of the government from at least the ninth century. However, these assemblies did not act or fulfil the same function as a modern parliament.

The word 'parliament' was seldom used in the Middle Ages. The major meaning of the Old French word *parlement* was 'meeting'. The rough English equivalent is *folkmoot* ('a meeting of citizens'). It does not imply any special or ongoing status for the meeting. This was the primary meaning of the word until the end of the twelfth century.

The king's advisory council in England was called the *witenagemot* (also known as the *witan*), a council of bishops, abbots and the upper military. This group of the king's peers, relatives and friends had no fixed membership. It was capable of being very influential but did not make decisions. In legal terms, it helped the king with great land grants through witnessing them. In practice, like the French advisors of the same period, the wise men probably gave their counsel mostly as individuals.

In Norman England, this became the Curia Regis. From the 1150s, this council became more established, and the word 'parliament' began to be used. The work the council did was still mainly consultative. However, members of the Curia Regis gradually built up an expectation that the king would obtain their consent for major decisions. During the reign of Stephen (1141–54), the senior lords held that if the king made a decision without the consent of the barons, then that decision would only be valid for the lifetime of the king.

Around the thirteenth century, other meanings of parliament became increasingly important. A parliament could be a formal meeting to talk, as it was, for example, in 1188 when Philip II of France, Henry II and Richard met at Bonmoulins to discuss government. This was an extension of the earlier idea of meeting, to include a specific political or governmental agenda.

From the second half of the thirteenth century, the English Parliament was summoned to meet on a regular basis, two or three times a year. How regularly individuals were called upon depended on their position. It was still largely a meeting of the 'great and good' of the realm. Only about 120 people (including ecclesiastics) met the very high income level of this group and were otherwise eligible. Of these, most would have been barons.

By the end of the thirteenth century, England's Parliament met regularly and was an important factor in the king's decisions. It included a limited form of representation and consultation with the commons as well as with the great magnates. It did not, however, fill a direct legislative role.

In both England and France, legal administration was closely tied up with general governance, so judges and those who were active in the legal system would have worked alongside the ruler in seeking clarification and, if necessary, changing legislation as events unfolded. It is important to note here that the law acted as a far more effective check on the power of the king than did the role of Parliament.

Law and Justice

Law is never an easy subject, and in the case of the Middle Ages, it is particularly complicated. It is also particularly important. In both England and France, law and administration were intertwined. Much like coins, weights and measurements, law would change not only over time, but also from region to region: law and justice were usually local. This makes it very difficult to get an answer to a question regarding law, since it is necessary to know place, year and jurisdiction.

Even though it is complicated to understand, some basic knowledge of medieval law is important, as the shape of the law had an enormous effect on everyone who lived with it.

Making and Administering Law

How was law devised? Firstly, the chief legislators were the king and justices of the king's court. Courts were also the places where legal innovation happened. These courts were not like a formalised modern court of law. They consisted of the region's ruler or his representative and administrative officers, and interpreting and administering law was only one of its functions. For their legal function, courts could be further supplemented by law experts, officers, witnesses and jurors if necessary.

Most law changed through interpretation in the courts and through practice in everyday life. Many government documents, while not legal documents, influenced the law: we often see charters by kings stating what principles they feel should underlie decisions on certain matters during their reign. For example, Henry I's coronation charter reinforced Edward's legal decisions and demolished those of William Rufus, while the various charters concerning the Jews reinforced the basic attitude that the English kings held towards their Jewish subjects. This kind of document gradually shaped and changed law by establishing new general patterns of behaviour.

Multiple systems of law applied in England. Justice operated at different levels within these systems, with different authorities taking responsibility for the different levels. And there was more than one legal system in operation at a given time. How those multiple systems played together was also not fixed. England can also be divided into two regions, based on its historic settlement in the early Middle Ages. One region was the north-east and east of England (the old Danelaw), centred on York, Stamford, Lincoln, Derby, Leicester and Nottingham; the other region was south-west England.

Law itself was not always put into writing. In the eleventh century, civil law was almost purely unwritten. By the end of the thirteenth century, large chunks of law were starting to be written down.

Those administering the law looked for stability, but changes in society, culture and even the substance of daily life – such as harvest size or access to material goods – can lead to changes in how things are done. This, and the nature of evidence of medieval law, makes the subject very complicated. There was no differentiation between civil and criminal trials, for instance. Systems of civil law included customary law and Roman law; religious law included canon law and *halakha*.

Another important gradual change was that more legal practitioners underwent formal training, which meant that they were trained within the Christian education system. Jewish law diminished in importance as anti-Semitism increased in both England and France and as the writing down of laws excluded Jewish jurisdiction from some traditional areas.

While changes in law did not necessarily have an immediate effect on local people, it meant important political changes and very important changes in how society was run. Law was very closely linked to both political and socio-cultural change and never operated alone.

Types of Law

Civil law was the law of everyday life for everyone not part of a specific religious body. Forms of civil law in the Middle Ages included customary law, forest law and regulations for inheritance.

Customary law is a generic term for a very ungeneric set of laws. It applied to the regional and local oral customs which helped courts decide cases. They were not formalised.

The knowledge of customary law lay mostly with lay people; it was not the province of clerics. Customary law was not based on Roman law or canon law, but a combination of the older law system of the region plus the case law that evolved within the memory of those living. It underlay Western Europe's legal systems, being the standard law of the land. Even Gratian (see canon law, below) said that when there was no authoritative legal precedent in canon law, customary law should be referred to. However, as Roman law became better known, it was often cited by jurists even where customary law was in force, because Roman law was seen to be more prestigious and learned.

The place where customary law was enunciated – the court – was where it was maintained and where change of laws, if necessary, happened. One important aspect of customary law is that a lot of the change happened in such a way as to go unnoticed. There was a feeling that traditions went back into the distant past even when they were of quite recent making.

Even though customary law was so important, most of it was never written down and has thus been lost. In the instances when customary law was recorded in writing, the documents were not generally for wide distribution, but for use by individuals, for example for teaching or reference. When English customary law was written down (the most important document being the twelfth-century *Tractatus de legibus et consuetudinibus regni Angliae*, attributed to Glanvill), Roman and canonical law tended to be used as guidance to set up a written framework, even though they may not have been actually used much in the everyday pursuance of justice.

In this everyday pursuit of justice, the king's authority was technically ultimate, but lords had jurisdiction within their own terrain. These used customary law in a way that is sometimes called feudal law since it operated within and upheld the feudal system. Some definitions of feudal law see it as primarily covering obligations between vassals and their lords, including military service. According to others, it overlapped with customary law.

In many cases, local authority was upheld even if it contradicted higher courts, unless there was some sort of formal appeal against it. This means that despite the move to a more centralised legal system, local variants of customary law still dominated in most local legal proceedings.

Forest law was generally seen as a separate set of laws in England and Normandy. It had its own administrative arm, including a chief justice of the forest and local forestry officials. In the thirteenth century, around 25 per cent of England was technically forest. How far forest law was applied differed quite strongly from reign to reign. Under the stronger rulers, forest laws were applied more stringently, whereas under rulers such as Stephen of England, they almost fell into disuse.

Rulings particular to the forest included limitations on killing animals (especially deer because they were technically owned by the king) but also regulations that required landowners to obtain special permission from the royal officials before cutting down wood. People sought to have land exempt from the royal forest whenever they could to avoid application of these laws. It became a big issue in England around the time of the *Magna Carta*.

Inheritance regulations were sometimes seen as part of customary law, sometimes not. They were not consistent across regions. They were very important, though. Inheritance was key to the functioning of medieval life because it meant inheriting not only goods but rights and a place in the network of people.

Generally, when a man died, the first in line to inherit were his children and family, followed by his widow. Bastard children who had been recognised were not necessarily excluded.

This could lead to the widow ending up with very little or nothing, since she had no more claim on her original family. To prevent the widow from falling into poverty, a dower right was often fixed for her. This gave the wife the right to a part of the husband's property (usually between half and a third of his lands) as long as she did not remarry. The dower could not be alienated without her permission during the husband's lifetime. However, the dower was not always granted to widows without their insistence or even legal struggle, even after the *Magna Carta* affirmed the dower right.

If a death left property without heirs, the land was transferred to the next person up the line in feudal hierarchy. When a noble tenant died and the heirs were not fit to rule by themselves (for example minors, idiots or felons), someone else took wardship. The guardian was often either a family member or the Crown, depending on local law and circumstances. For the Crown, it was also possible to pass on the wardship to someone else. Guardianship entailed custody of the lands, ability to arrange the marriage of the heir, control of the military obligations attached to the land, sale of non-essential goods, control of unfree tenants and the collection of feudal dues. It was an important part of wardship that the lands be kept intact and not be degraded. The heir to the lands had to be supported, and widows and heiresses were not supposed to be pressured into marriages they did not want. Wardship could be abused, though, as well as used for strategic political or military purposes.

Inheritance regulations also applied to the Crown. The French throne passed from father to son throughout our period. In England, the succession followed an unsteady pattern in the eleventh and twelfth centuries. William I, for example, passed over his eldest son, Robert, Duke of Normandy, and left the English throne to his second son, William Rufus. Or rather, he left it to God, but he hoped God would give it to Rufus. Salic Law, forbidding women succession to the crown, did not apply during this time in France and England, as far as we can ascertain.

The basic inheritance regulations could be modified by giving away parts of the property before death or by making a will. Only a small percentage of medieval wills were recorded in writing, with the number increasing into the thirteenth century. Oral testaments in front of witnesses were the rule and equally valid in law as written testaments. Wills could be made by women as well as by men and even by serfs, though specific regulations might have limited their rights in some locations.

Another part of the legal system was Roman law, which is the codification of the decrees of the Roman Emperors, undertaken under Justinian (*c.* 483–565). By the eleventh century, Roman law had largely fallen into disuse. Knowledge and understanding of Roman law then grew again until, in the thirteenth century, it became an important part of the legal world once more.

The formal study of Roman law in the new universities gradually undermined the importance of customary law, so there is a strong link between the early history of universities and the changes in local legal systems in the thirteenth century. There is an even stronger link between the centralisation of government and the regularisation of legal systems.

Most importantly, by the thirteenth century many civil and ecclesiastical legal principles and constitutional matters were decided based on Roman law. While this did not necessarily have an immediate effect on local people, it meant important changes in politics and society. The biggest impact, of course, was on the Jewish population, as Roman law was very unfavourable towards Jews. The legal changes in the thirteenth century added to other social and cultural changes, leading to Jewish expulsion in 1290. It must be noted, however, that law was not the only factor.

The parts of the law governing the Jewish population, including edicts, charters and other legal documents, are called Jewry law. This was not a legal code so much as specific provisions relating to Jewish issues that were legislated on by non-Jewish legal bodies.

Jews were governed, by and large, by the same legal system as the rest of the population, save for their general rights and obligations, which were the subject of special royal charters. These charters specified their differences from the general population and brought Jews directly under the governance of the Crown. This was important in terms of separating the Jewish population from the non-Jewish population where a dispute brought the Crown into conflict with the local authorities, for instance.

Jews were also limited in some important legal aspects: they could not act as *frankpledge*, and, in cases where Roman law prevailed over customary law, they could not accuse Christians or testify against them in secular courts. Jews could, however, make proof by oaths, which enabled them to provide evidence against Christians less directly. Jews were permitted to object to Christian testimony against themselves, unless equivalent testimony was provided by someone Jewish. Another major source of difference was the very limited jurisdiction the Church held over the Jewish population compared with the non-Jewish population.

Where Jews interacted legally with the State and with the Church, *halakha* or self-government were often compromised. What happened legally then depended very heavily on how far Jews were integrated into the wider community and with how much respect they were treated. Possible developments were the matter going to trial, the Crown being called in to arbitrate (as happened, for example, in thirteenth-century Oxford), or the secular lord determining the legal outcome.

In practice, Jews appear to have been, by and large, slightly apart from the normal legal system and could be at a disadvantage when it was called into play.

Set apart from the secular law, but as important in governing, was religious law. Canon law, also called ecclesiastical law or church law, is the law of the Christian Church. It was not the legal system of any secular state. It was a body of laws and regulations, some of which operated solely in an ecclesiastical setting and some of which ran parallel with secular law. Canon law primarily handled matters involving clerics, Church matters and legal matters regarding marriage.

The term 'canon' comes from the Greek word used to describe the rulings of the early Church councils and was only used to name the legal system from about the twelfth century. It was often contrasted with civil law, especially since both systems borrowed elements from Roman law.

Historically, canon law can be divided into two periods: before Gratian's *Decretum* (*c.* 1140s) and from the *Decretum* to the Council of Trent (1545–63).

Canon law in the eleventh century basically meant collections of the decisions of the Church councils, letters of popes and statutes by bishops. These varied from region to region. Popes continually modified canon law and had the powers both of interpreting the law and of making new laws.

Gratian rationalised collections of legal documents in the twelfth century. He wrote a thesis that collated the laws actually in force, quoting relevant sections. It is this document, the *Decretum*, which provided the systematic basis for canon law from then onward. It was used as a textbook for teaching canon law until at least 1234, when the *Decretals* of Pope Gregory IX were promulgated to replace former collections.

The eleventh to the thirteenth century was a period of dynamic development in the codification of canon law. This was partly due to inconsistencies in the ways legal specialists were trained. Although the work of Gratian and, towards the end of the thirteenth century, that of Gregory were widely used, many other collections of legal texts existed.

England was particularly important in the formulation of canon law from the twelfth century, especially due to such scholars as Bartholomew of Exeter (d. 1184) and Roger of Worcester (d. 1179). In France, the teaching of canon law took centre stage, with the most notable teacher being also one of the most notable international scholars in the field, Hostiensis (b. *c.* 1200).

Integral to how canon law worked was its interpretation and modification. For example, canon law interpreted current theological views of Judaism and attempted to bring them into reality in medieval society: the provisions from the Third Lateran Council (1179) were the core of canon Jewry law in the thirteenth century. The interpretation and modification was done by the pope and the bishops (who had legal jurisdiction in terms of religious law over their diocese), but also by Church councils and other bodies.

While canon law collections were important legal sources, they were not the whole of canon law. Canon law was regional and thus variable in practice, although basic principles remained constant. Access to law manuscripts also differed, and not even Gratian's collection was available everywhere. Finally, regional secular laws could affect local church law. To confuse matters still further, the canonists who codified canon law in the twelfth century used Roman law as a tool, so parts of canon law were very similar to aspects of secular law in the twelfth century.

Religious law was, of course, not limited to Christianity. Jewish people were also ruled by their own religious laws. However, a basic tenet in Jewish law is that the law of the land (whether customary or common law) held precedence over Jewish law.

Jewish law, also called *halakha*, is based on Jewish religious texts. Technically, it is a path to be followed using the rules expressed in the Five Books of Moses (the Torah) and the later explanations and expansions of them. In the Middle Ages, it was followed by most Jews. This must not be confused with legislation regarding the Jewish population in other legal systems.

Jewish law was more a system of ethics and anecdotal instructions than a formal legal system. It relied heavily on interpretation by the knowledgeable (either individual scholars or local synods of rabbis) and on practical implementation. While *halakha* was religious in nature, it governed many facets of everyday life, ranging from prayer to dress and behaviour and even eating habits.

Halakha can be divided into three segments: Torah law, Rabbinic law and *minhag*. Torah law was derived directly from commandments and prohibitions in written or oral Torah (Torah or Talmud). Rabbinic law derived from the interpretation of the Torah and its commentaries by key rabbis. *Minhag* comprised customs and traditional practices, including local traditions that did not necessarily have a firm basis in *halakha*.

An important facet of medieval Judaism was the fences principle: key commandments in the Torah were often protected by fences to ensure that there was no chance of them being broken. For example, the prohibition of stewing a kid in its mother's milk had as its fence the general rule to not mix milk dishes and meat dishes, in case the milk came from the mother of the animal in the meat dish. Some commandments were given a whole series of fences, like the use of separate tableware for milk and meat dishes, and that ordinary bread should not be cooked in an oven at the same time as meat dishes in case the bread becomes part of a milk meal.

Just like all the other types of law, Jewish law was not the same everywhere. While it was all based on Talmudic sources and interpretation of these sources by rabbis, key experts of *halakha* interpreted the law for the wider Jewish community, and major rabbinical centres offered their own interpretation when called on for opinions. Centres communicated with each other, but local variations in law existed which reflected regional variations in Jewish life and its relationship with the external environment. This could lead to major differences in some cases. For instance, the Jews of France appear to have followed rulings by the German rabbi Gershom of Mainz (b. 960) which limited men to one wife and which gave women the right to refuse divorce. The Jews of Spain, however, did not follow those rulings.

Most Jewish communities had limited authority to settle legal matters which related solely to the community, and where outside authority was not called in. As a general rule, Jewish communities avoided non-Jewish tribunals wherever possible. This would have been reinforced by the limited rights Jews had in relation to those tribunals. Jews went to non-Jewish courts, however, when the outside government required it, or when it was technically impossible to resolve the matter in a Jewish court.

Jurisdiction

In an ideal situation, each type of law dealt with different cases or different aspects of cases (mostly different authorities for trial as opposed to punishment), or people chose between them. When it was possible to choose between jurisdictions, people could often opt for the court that supported their case better. In practice, though, nothing was ever so simple.

Anyone in religious orders was under the legal governance of the Church except where they held land from a secular lord, in which case the jurisdiction belonged to the secular lord. Other people who fell under canon law jurisdiction were crusaders and Christian widows (who also had access to secular courts if necessary). Sorcery and witchcraft were tried in religious courts, but once the culprit was condemned, they were handed over to the secular courts.

Marriage was religious and everything relating to marriage technically belonged to canon law or *halakha*. Property disputes as a result of marriage, however, could spill over into civil courts. Church property was technically under canon law, but was also the property of the king and his vassals, as the king held the land on behalf of God. Quite often this was resolved by the king's vassals holding land on behalf of the Church or its religious houses, or by the Church being forced to sell the land to someone who could hold it within a certain time period. This means that in practice, most legal matters concerning land were under secular law.

The land tenure problem also applied to Jews and explains why some modern authors declare that Jews couldn't own land. Jews could and did own land, but whether they were able to hold land as a fief and be vassals of a lord was a very difficult issue. One of the very few regions where this issue was resolved in the favour of individual Jews (with them entering fully into the normal social and legal system) was in the region around Toulouse, in France.

In many ways, the different jurisdictions were quite separate. With political and social changes or upheavals, however, areas of law tried to move in on one another. For instance, the assertion of canon law over customary law by Thomas Becket in England was linked to the events leading to his murder. Another example is the treatment of Jews in Blois outside the normal jurisdictions in 1171, leading to the death of around thirty-one innocents.

For both jurisdiction and its enforcement, knights played a key role. They formed the backbone of the military side of government and also played important roles in running the administration and local rule, especially in the courts. Work undertaken by knights in the late twelfth century included judicial as well as military responsibilities. For instance, it was a knight's responsibility in England to check that people who gave the excuse of sickness to avoid court appearances were genuinely ill. Knights also undertook some prestigious administrative and judicial tasks such as valuing property. Most importantly, the sheriff would ask four knights from a given place to elect twelve men to form a jury, a procedure described by Glanvill.

Other important tasks undertaken by knights in the thirteenth century included electing grand juries and grand assize jurors, bringing county court records to the king and a range of judicial tasks, including those that knights undertook earlier, such as checking out claims of illness as a reason not to appear at court. This made knights an intrinsic part of the system of government.

Jurisdiction was mostly handled through courts. Most courts were linked to land tenure or religious administration, but some industries also had their own courts, for example the Derbyshire lead miners. In both England and France, courts ranged from national to local. At the top of the English and northern French legal hierarchy was the king and his court. Then came the county courts, followed by the regional courts. Finally, courts operated by nobles on their own land (manorial courts) could also administer law. Generally, the pettier and more local the case, the more local the court. Courts had a dual role: they settled disputes and they maintained social order. The more important a person was, the more influence that person had in court.

The king's courts generally only handled certain types of cases. For example, legal quarrels between barons were ideally decided in the royal court. Other cases were handled centrally when written authorisations (writs) were given. From the twelfth to the thirteenth century, the increasing prevalence of writs shows a gradually increasing influence of the king's courts.

In the king's absence, he was represented by the justiciar. The first justiciar was appointed by the king in the early part of the twelfth century. His job was to oversee the judicial organisation on the king's behalf. Though there were occasionally two justiciars in England at the same time, there was frequently only one and, in the thirteenth century, sometimes not even that. It was a very important office and was usually occupied by only those of the highest nobility.

Most cases were handled by courts operating at the local level, generally manor courts. Manors served as administration centres for the district as well as courts, collecting rents, services and dues. However, the village also had some legal jurisdiction, especially through the role of village constable. Quarrels between those subject to the same lord were decided in the court of that lord. If it was between those who owed duty to different lords, the county court ruled.

Courts all existed as a means to interpret laws and carry out legal decisions. Their structure, however, could vary. The actual workings of courts were also different according to regional culture, law and practice. Thus they operated within the cultural constraints of their specific region and society. Some things remained the same for all courts, though, such as torture not being legally sanctioned in England.

Different roles within the legal system served different needs and purposes. The most important roles were carried out by sheriffs, coroners, justiciars, bailiffs and notaries. Notaries were responsible for writing connected with the courts and with legal documents. They learned sufficient law to undertake these roles either directly or indirectly from the teaching of Bologna, but there were not many of them and they were banned from courts of common law. Bailiffs were administrators that also acted as chief judges in courts, although few would have formal training in law. They also arrested people if necessary. Experts in legal matters often represented lords in the county courts. These professionals were frequently the stewards and bailiffs of the lords. The senior manor representatives were natural allies of the lords in the county and even the manor courts.

Courts were presided over by gentry (normally the lord's steward), but everyone else who held important roles were normally tenants. Where there was no regular court in England, itinerant royal justices served to establish temporary ones. Court officers such as the sergeants handled administrative matters. Professional lawyers in these courts were lawyers by profession and practice, and, unlike canon lawyers, did not necessarily have specialist training.

For problematic cases where it was not possible to determine an outcome, courts could also hold a trial by ordeal or by combat as a last resort to solve the case. Fundamental to the effectiveness of this method was the belief that God would aid the innocent or the person that was right and thus decide the case. The ritual included a mutual oath (basically, both sides stating, 'I am right'), often with the combatants holding hands.

The ordeal was supervised by the Church and varied depending on the offence, region, gender of the accused and other circumstances. People of appropriate background could also claim trial by combat. The use of ordeals faded during the thirteenth century, with Innocent III banning the obligatory ecclesiastical involvement in 1215. Even earlier, Church officials and Jews were generally exempt.

A system of *frankpledges* (sometimes called tithings) was used to get people to their local court and to testify. Adult men were required to be members of a group of ten to twelve who were responsible for each other's good behaviour. The other members of the group could be fined if one of the members didn't appear when summoned to court, and a village could be fined if it was found to have men living there who were not members of a *frankpledge* group and who had not been granted exemption.

There were many exemptions to *frankpledge*. For example, lords were exempt, as were members of their households because it was the lord's responsibility to produce them in court if their presence was required. Men holding freehold land were exempt because their land was considered their pledge. Women were seldom allowed to act as *frankpledges*, and the system of *frankpledging* did not apply to Jews.

Just like specific court structure, enforcement of the law also varied according to the region, and also according to whether the place was a town, a village or a rural community. In rural districts and in most villages, the law was often enforced by officers who also served in the courts, such as the catchpole who made arrests. Other policing tasks were carried out by bailiffs and their representatives or, in the case of towns, municipal officers.

Criminals or alleged criminals could postpone their arrest or their punishment by claiming sanctuary, most often provided by consecrated Christian churches. While only very few places would provide sanctuary for an unlimited time, sanctuary always offered the alleged offender a choice of later trial or expatriation.

Forms of punishment can generally be divided into two groups: social and bodily. The severity of the punishment depended on the severity of the crime, which could again vary from region to region for the same offence.

Fashions in punishment also changed over time, though 'speaking punishments' – such as taking a hand for theft – were often reported. Small offences could also be settled by payment of a fine. Capital offences were punished by death throughout the Middle Ages, though methods again varied between regions and over time. Prior to the thirteenth century, for instance, hanging was used only for those convicted of homicide, while it became a more common capital punishment later. As an alternative to capital punishment, the combination of blinding and castration may have been used.

Punishments and their enforcement were also somewhat related to the social and political status of the offender. From about the middle of the twelfth to the start of the fourteenth century, no high nobility in England suffered corporal or capital punishment. This was for political reasons – most of the English nobility had land in both England and France and could thus flee to France if threatened by the English king.

Methods of social punishment usually included public shaming of the offender, using tools such as pillory, stocks or tumbril. Depending on local law or custom, humiliation could be augmented by pelting the criminal with rotten fruit, rotten eggs, mud or even stones, adding an aspect of corporal punishment. The stocks, or the pillory, were not only a spectacle, but a real punishment even without added corporal punishment. The offender's social contacts (neighbours, business partners, friends and relatives) would all remember this person for the crime. A social punishment was thus no small punishment.

Another punishment given by courts was outlawry. This was not limited to the lower classes. For instance, outlaw status was declared in county courts in England. Outlawry meant that the person was considered outside the law and thus had no legal protection from others. When someone did not appear in court four successive times and no one was prepared to pledge his appearance for the next session, he was declared an outlaw. This was usually for a limited time. Women and children under twelve could not be declared outlaw. Women were given substitute punishments.

Outlaws are documented as hiding in forests until the period of their outlawry was past and they could return home. For example, in Feckenham Forest in England, in the 1280s, up to 100 men lived there in one band led by Geoffrey du Park. This band was documented, however, because of its notoriety. It was particularly violent and brutal, not even sparing the poor.

Some famous criminals acted according to modern perceptions of outlaws, but were not actually outlaws. They were merely too powerful for their criminal activity to be easily addressed. Thomas (II) de Marle, Seigneur de Coucy, for instance, who died around 1130, was a notorious robber baron. He was predatory and dangerous. He sacked Laon and Amiens, and pillaged the countryside. He was of such ill-fame that on 6 December 1114, anathema was declared against him in Reims.

Taxes and Tithes

No government or administration can work without money. Funds for public administration were raised, like today, by levying taxes and tithes from the population. There is evidence for working tax systems, but it is very hard to fully document medieval taxation: records often did not survive or, in some cases, were not created in the first place.

Medieval taxation was not like the centralised tax systems of today, which tend to distinguish clearly between public, business and personal wealth. It grew, sometimes with planning and sometimes more organically, from the needs of a given ruler and the exploration of ways to meet those needs. To describe it in modern terms, this resulted in a series of mechanisms that met government income needs on local, regional, religious and national levels. One of the reasons for the complexity of systems governing taxation was the diversity of sources of income for the government, reflecting the nature of society itself. Taxation also seldom had legislation underpinning it. Only in some cases was it due to a law; in others it was by custom and in still others by a decree. Payments were made on different levels: to the lords, to the Church, to the king and to the community. Just as with other administrative things, regions could differ widely from each other, and some regions had more systematic tax systems than others.

In contrast to the modern money-based tax systems, medieval government at all levels received these payments in form of a mixture of money, service and goods. The proportion of these three streams of income could vary considerably. Taxes could also shift from one of the streams into another; for example, it was possible to give *scutage*, a monetary payment, in lieu of giving military service.

Government income can be roughly divided into regular income from taxes and tariffs, such as tolls and customs, and special taxes that were raised upon need. Regular taxes were payments in money, service or kind that were expected and may have been due on a certain date, although they were not always taken. However, taxes could change over time from special to regular, and sometimes the sources recording a given tax do not make it clear whether it was levied upon need or a regular tax. One good example for this is the Danegeld, a tax raised in the eleventh century. This tax was not always levied at the same rate: it was higher in 1084 and 1096, for instance. The Church was normally not liable for it, but paid in 1096. Technically, it was emergency funding, but Henry I (r. 1100–35) managed to transform it into a kind of annual levy. He and Stephen (r. 1135–41) both conferred a range of exemptions to magnate families and barons to make its annual levying stick. The Danegeld transmuted to dues linked to vassalage, and their use became more clearly defined and, in some cases, expanded over time. It was finally abandoned in 1162.

The backbones of the system were dues, taxes or payments connected to the use of land. Land tenure varied according to the region, impacting on land management and people's lives. For example, someone living in the north of England might have held land under *cornage*. This meant he had to accompany the king in wars or raids on Scottish territory. Two months of service for one's lord was the standard until about 1066, when in many cases forty days of service became the standard. Property held on behalf of a lord could be inherited, or could be given directly by the lord: it was not a simple system. Service for fiefs was typically military, as opposed to service for peasant holdings, which were non-military and given in money and in kind. Payments also could change over time – in the late thirteenth century, for example, there was a movement towards cash payments in many places.

One of the earliest examples of a type of a land tax was documented in the *Domesday Book*, which was the survey made by William I (r. 1066–87) of all his English lands. This tax, called *geld*, was assessed on land units (*hides* or *carucates*). The king could, and did, grant exceptions to the *geld* for those he favoured. In 1130, for example, around 40 per cent of the total amount due was never received because of exemptions. During Henry II's reign, *geld* taxes were not levied after 1162, but Richard I restored them in 1194. They were levied again several times until being discontinued in 1224.

Set dues were usually paid on fixed days. In England, Michaelmas was one of the four main dates for settling of accounts, the other three being 25 March (the Annunciation or Lady Day, which was the beginning of the financial year); 25 December (Christmas); and 24 June (the Nativity of St John the Baptist). Northern France settled accounts at Easter. English taxes were recorded by the Exchequer; the main source for studies today are the *Pipe Rolls*, which are unfortunately not complete. Each Exchequer roll contains one year's worth of material, divided into four terms.

The most numerous class of people paying dues in both England and France was peasants, and they mostly owed them to their local lord. While the dates above applied, other days for peasants to pay dues included the Nativity of the Virgin, when one pig in eight went in dues; St Denis' Day, when the normal manorial dues were paid; and Palm Sunday, when the sheep aspect of dues was paid. Other dues included, for instance, an obligation for peasants to help the mason if the lord was building; if they sold their land then the lord gained part of the profit; if their daughter married outside the seigneury they paid a fine; and most of them were obligated to use their lord's mill and oven and pay for this use.

Taxes on an on-demand basis were levied in addition to regularly scheduled payments. This could be both small-scale or regional taxation and large-scale, national raising of money. Special taxes were a useful method to raise money for extra expenses in case of wars, emergencies or big events. One example for this was the so-called 'Saladin tithe', levied by Richard I in 1188 to finance a crusade. This was set at a rate of 10 per cent for all income and moveable goods. Another tax was levied at the stunning rate of 25 per cent on income and personal property when funding was needed to pay Richard I's ransom in 1194. In 1207, John levied a similar tax referred to as a 'thirteenth' on both income and moveable goods. Taxes on personal property generally started out as a special tax when Henry II instituted this in 1166, but it is hard to find solid documentary evidence before taxation of personal property was brought under the Exchequer in 1290. Until 1334, individual taxpayers paid taxes of fixed proportions on individual assessments. These percentages could be a ninth, a tenth or a fifteenth of the amount assessed.

Feudal dues ('aids') were payable to the king or lord on certain specified occasions, for example the marriage of a daughter or the knighting of a son. The king asked his vassals for it when it became due. Aids were not only levied by the king, but could also be levied by a lord on his vassals. A lord could, for example, levy a tax on one of his vassals for knighting the vassal's son or for helping finance the marriage of his daughter.

It was not necessary for the king to seek advice from advisors or a parliament before demanding aids, though it could lead to trouble if he wanted money above and beyond the amounts advised or demanded unreasonable amounts of money without consulting them first. Aids due to the king included 'relief' (a sum paid by the new holder of a fief acknowledging the lord's continuing rights to the property) and *scutage* (payment of money or goods instead of military service), as well as funds for ransoming the king's body. Kings and lords both were quite capable of abusing the system and demanding extra dues when they could enforce them. This could lead to friction or even outright conflict.

Regarding special taxes, different rulers used different means to raise more money. Richard I, for instance, exploited the circuits made by itinerant judges, with a special 'forest eyre' (circuit) in 1198 and 1207, while John (r. 1199–1216) used feudal obligations and fines as well as forced loans.

Additional payments were also demanded of the Jewish population. This led to corruption at many levels of government, but particularly, in England, in the Exchequer of the Jews. In 1234, the Archbishop of Canterbury was sufficiently shocked by the level of corruption to accuse those officials. But by this time, the large finances in England had begun to move out of Jewish hands to the Cahorsins or Lombards – Italian financiers.

Taxes on Jews were, in fact, often especially harsh. English taxes were usually levied on the Jewish community as a whole, which reflects its unusual legal position: the Jewish population was often treated as the king's personal property and considered as a single body for taxation purposes. In 1194, an important record of the status of English Jewry was created. It is known as the Northampton Donum and was a result of the leaders of the Jewish community trying to work out how they could raise their 5,000 mark share of Richard I's ransom. With this sum, the Jewish community was forced to pay three times the amount of the wealthy independent body that was the City of London. However, even trying its best, the community only raised half of what was demanded. It had already spent a large part of its goods on funding Richard's crusade initially. Jews also paid within their specific communities to fund communal needs.

While fiscal demands of Jews were often higher than those made of non-Jews, those made in the twelfth century were unusual. More typical taxes for the Jews of Champagne, for instance, included a tax on settling there, one on seals when debts were registered, a toll for cleaning causeways, an inheritance tax and a tax on leaving the county. Under Henry II of England (r. 1154–89), however, the exceptional became the ordinary, resulting in a great deal of destitution.

Governments also received some income from the legal system. A further stream of income was formed from tolls, duties and similar payments. Such fees and charges were levied at borders, which included the borders of market towns or fairs, not only national or regional borders. Examples of this were tolls on people and goods using roads, bridges or entering a market or town. In Montpellier for example, in the second half of the twelfth century, all Saracens entering the city were charged three *sous* per person (this was listed next to pigs in the tariffs).

Various customs taxes were levied on incoming or outgoing goods such as wine or woollen cloth. The first surviving evidence of a comprehensive tax on foreign trade in England was in 1195, although certain goods (such as wine) had been subject to various taxes earlier than that. The tax was 1/10 levied on all overseas trade, but we do not know if it was a one-off, or levied over a certain period. It was the precursor of a taxation by 1/15 levied by John around 1202–4 on imports and exports. Just as was the case with taxes, special arrangements could be made, or dues could be paid in other ways than handing over money. For example, the Cinque Ports (Hastings, New Romney, Hythe, Dover and Sandwich) enjoyed toll exemption. In return, they provided ships where military fiefs would provide knights. Taxes on foreign trade brought in by the international merchants who traded through these ports were negotiated directly with them until 1340.

Government income and king's income were two different things, though they are sometimes hard to keep apart, and payment for expenses concerning the court may have come from either. The king's income was composed mainly of income from the royal demesne (lands), overlordship, taxation, and the rendering of justice. For example, 40 per cent of the royal income was from the royal demesne.

Medieval systems of taxation lacked the full bureaucracy of the modern system, making them more flexible but also often more arbitrary. Those working in administrative positions in England or France did not always receive a regular salary. A common custom was to siphon off some of the money raised through taxes or to use the privileges of the office to generate income. For instance, the position of sheriff could be very profitable for its holders and they were often willing to pay for it. Richard I (r. 1189–99), for example, was said to have auctioned off the positions to the highest bidder in order to obtain money to help finance his crusade. This siphoning procedure instead of regular pay did not always work out well, however. In 1170, Henry II had an inquest performed into how much the sheriffs were making from their positions. He then dismissed twenty-two out of twenty-nine sheriffs.

Finally, religious administration also required money to cover costs. The Church had an income stream from tithes as well as profits from offerings, donations, bequests, income from legal fines and payment for services, and so on.

Tithes to the Church were regular payments based on the Biblical notion of giving a tenth of income to the Church, while taxes to the Church could be levied in addition to this. For example, there were two major tax assessments by the papacy in the thirteenth century. One was the 1254 English Valuation of Norwich and the other was the 1299 Taxation of Pope Nicholas. They demonstrate that the Church taxed at a national level, as they provide a near-complete list of every parish in England.

There was a great deal of friction and potential friction because of the amount that was levied by the Church (which could be quite high) and because the situation of the person paying was not always taken into account. This could lead to revolts or protests: in the Exeter region, the farmers were so incensed by the tithe in cheese demanded by the local parson that they 'paid' by pouring milk onto the altar. Some priests even tried to tithe Jews in their parish, disregarding the fact that Jews were exempt.

These many facets and regional differences mean that taxes are a complicated topic, and there are not always enough surviving sources for in-depth research. During the civil war in England (*c.* 1135–53), many records were destroyed. Henry II and his officials rebuilt the system after 1154, carefully documenting it. Due to this, a good account of the ideal operations of the Exchequer office exist from this time, notably in the *Dialogus de Scaccario* (1176–9). The real transformation of varied taxes into a system of taxation was in the thirteenth century.

At its best, taxation was linked to ownership of land, to life events (such as paying a *heriot*, a kind of tax to be paid when someone died) and to service. At its worst, it could be arbitrary and cruel, such as everyone in England paying the Saladin tithe towards Richard I's crusading goals just two years after the initial crusade tax, with the Jews taxed at a much higher rate. The system ran into constant problems largely because it lacked a strong formal underpinning which would have enabled taxpayers to know where they stood, and the scope for bad decisions was huge. The innate sense of justice of those in power could make an enormous difference to how much was demanded in taxation. This operated as much at the level of the manor as it did at the level of princes. An unjust lord could demand harsh additional labour or dues and leave his peasants and serfs starving; a good one demanded his dues and no more. But whether taxation was moderate or high, just as today, death and taxes seemed inevitable and both equally worthy of complaint.

4

God is Everywhere
Religion

Religion permeated daily life. For both England and France, the two main religions were Christianity and Judaism, with Christianity strongly predominant. While the existence of Islam was known, it did not have a significant following in, or a strong influence on, these two countries.

Religion provided the basic fabric for interpreting and explaining the world, both for Christians and Jews. Though there was significant overlap in some of their basic assumptions of the operation of the world, they were largely separate.

Religions had to handle the influence of daily life on their practices and rules, and thus changed over time. In Christianity, with the growth of the institution of the Church, this adaptation to social developments became slower and more difficult, leading in some cases to protest movements that split off from the main Church.

There were major changes to western Christian religious teaching and practices during the Middle Ages. Religious practice became more standardised, priests became more celibate, and the Church became more and more political. It also became richer in land and in material goods. Nevertheless, overall, the practice of Christianity in the Middle Ages remained considerably varied. Some medieval Christians led austere lives, while others favoured an over-the-top version of Christianity, full of pomp and panoply. Abbot Suger, for instance, favoured the splendid approach when he was in charge of the abbey at Saint-Denis (from *c.* 1122). This range gave ordinary people considerable choices in how they saw their religion. It was not always austere and restrictive: it could be splendid and full of rich tales and miracles.

Finally, not all worship was related to Christianity or Judaism, or approved of by the Church. For instance, the Anglo-Saxon Church was against the worship of wells and trees, regarding them as continuance of sacrifice to non-Christian gods.

Christianity

Religious Knowledge

As Christianity was a strong part of daily life, the average person would have known at least a few Bible stories, the Ten Commandments, the Seven Deadly Sins and the Virtues opposing them, the Sacraments and participative texts that appeared over and over again in services. The core biblical stories are the Nativity, the Crucifixion and the Resurrection. While Christianity technically revolves around the Bible, it is hard to estimate how much knowledge of the complete text medieval people had.

During the High Middle Ages, as today, there were four gospels (Matthew, Mark, Luke and John) as key texts for Christianity, along with such works as Paul's Letters. However, those four gospels were not the only ones. Others, such as the Gospel of Thomas, had been deemed apocryphal by Church councils, but were nevertheless used in the community as a whole: as a source of Christian understanding, as a source of teachings and as a source of glamorous stories. For instance, the depiction of the hellmouth with Jesus emerging, having liberated the Ancients who had died before the redemption of Christians, comes from the apocryphal Gospel of Nicodemus.

The Seven Deadly Sins were *accidia* (sloth), *gula* (gluttony), *avaritia* (greed), *superbia* (pride), *luxuria* (lust), *ira* (wrath) and *invidia* (envy). They were regarded as especially severe. Their counterparts were the Seven Virtues, which could include, among others, charity, patience, kindness, faith and temperance. Neither list was standardised for a long time, with the Virtues taking longer to become a fixed set.

Saints and angels were very popular in medieval iconography and would also have been part of many people's general knowledge. There were nine orders of angels: cherubim, seraphim, thrones, dominations, powers, virtues, principalities, archangels and angels. The archangels most often mentioned were Gabriel, Raphael, Michael and Uriel, all of whom came into Christianity from Jewish tradition.

Angels in medieval Christian pictures were generally depicted as robed human beings with light around them: they might be carrying a diadem or sceptre to indicate their importance. Angels were important in Church preaching because they could act as spiritual guides – as links between God and man. They are even more important in popular tradition, however, with an English view suggesting that good angels were responsible for good dreams and bad angels for nightmares.

Saints and Relics

Saints and their relics were an important part of Christian belief. While the term 'saint' was used from the early eleventh century, it was not a standard term until the middle of the twelfth century. The cult of saints became very extensive already during the early Middle Ages, and early saints were usually established through popular belief in the person's sanctity.

From the tenth century, it became common practice to require an official sanctification before venerating a saint. This official sanctification was first performed by the bishop, but became the exclusive right of the pope at some point in the twelfth century. An official sanctification (canonisation) usually included a process to verify that the deceased had led a saintly life and performed one or several miracles before or after death, preferably edifying miracles specifically linked to the virtues that had illuminated the living person. These virtues were also of primary importance to sainthood: Innocent III (r. 1198–1216) declared that sainthood rested on merits and miracles both.

Canonisation was a long, complex and costly process that required a sufficiently large group of applicants (who also had to foot the bill). Political influence at the Curia, the council around the pope, did no harm either. This led to a relatively small number of canonised, official saints. There were more southern French saints than northern French, for instance, and relatively few English saints approved of by Rome. In fact, only three English saints were formally approved during the thirteenth century (although some thirteenth-century saints obtained later approval): Gilbert of Sempringham, 1202; Edmund of Abingdon, 1246; and Richard of Chichester, 1262. Rome added all canonised saints to the religious calendar, setting a date for each saint and developing special liturgical variations of Mass for each one.

Those canonised as saints by the Curia, however, were not the only ones to be venerated as saints. The majority of saints were of local or regional origin and not officially sanctified by the Church. Some local cults of saints or local traditions were not even very Christian in origin or practice, such as the local veneration of St Kunefort in Neuville chez Lyon in the thirteenth century: St Kunefort was a dog that lost its life while saving a child. Local differences in saints also led to a varied saints' calendar in different places.

Mary (the mother of Jesus) was at the top of the hierarchy of the saints, followed by the apostles and the evangelists and then by other saints. At the very bottom were those not approved by Rome, who had only a local cult.

Mary was the centre of a very real religious focus. This resulted in a passionate belief in, and reliance on, her particular holiness and powers (known as the Marian cult). During the twelfth century there was real growth and diffusion in the Marian cult. Mary was dealt with differently in art than in previous centuries, churches were dedicated to her, miracle stories were attributed to her, and theological debate focussed on related issues (for instance, the Immaculate Conception). She was often portrayed as reading a book when the Annunciation came, showing her to be literate.

Mary's help in interceding for souls was considered important, but her capacity to bring about miracles on earth was also key to her cult. She was considered to have a special position among the saints, being capable of potent intercessions. An additional religious ritual was added to the rites for many communities from the twelfth century, in honour of Mary. It was often said daily, and known as the 'Little Office of the Virgin.' Once a week (generally on a Saturday) the office of the day was replaced by the Commemorative Office of the Virgin. In addition, several feast days were linked to Mary.

Saints were usually associated with a region, social group, certain events or issues and were called upon in prayer to help with problems regarding these. St Anne, for example, was patron saint for women in childbirth and seafarers and associated with wells, springs and healing water in France. Hugh of Lincoln (1135/40–1200) prayed to her in thanks after he was rescued from a storm. Fever was obviously a common woe, as there were no fewer than 108 saints who could be approached to help cure it. Men of all classes sought help from the saints with their illnesses, while lower-class women were far more likely than the more prosperous classes to seek this avenue of relief. Saints could also enjoy their own reputation. St Gilles, for example, had a reputation for being especially quick to answer prayers.

Many towns also regarded one saint as their patron saint; for example, Narbonne's patron was St Paul. Larger cities, like Paris, might also have several patron saints; in this case, they were St Genevieve and St Marcel. Finally, professions had their patrons as well, such as St Sebastian for archers. 1 November was All Saints' Day, on which all saints were honoured.

Saints were especially venerated on their anniversary day, often including feasts in their honour. For example, St Nicholas had his special day on 6 December; he was venerated from the eleventh century onward. His cult in the Middle Ages was, however, very different to the modern cult of Santa Claus.

In addition to praying, people made votive offerings to saints. These offerings could take many forms, such as candles or money. Special votive gifts were frequently wax images that represented the problem or the nature of the aid being asked, such as a wax arm for arm problems.

Alas, saints were not always sweetness and light when it came to helping those in need. A poor, sick boy visited Canterbury and fell asleep at the shrine of Thomas Becket: it was said that this so incensed the saint that he refused to heal the boy. Other saints could be stricter and even turn people blind or cripple them for inappropriate behaviour.

Saints could be reached by praying, but they could also be physically touched through relics. Relics are body parts or items connected to Jesus, his family and saints. Today they are often classed into primary relics, which are pieces of a saint's body, or secondary relics, which are items that had touched the saint's body in life or death. Opening of saints' graves was very rarely done until the eighth century. The bones of saints were often housed in sumptuous reliquaries for veneration. Mary was considered to have left no relics of her body, because she went straight to heaven (the Ascension). Despite this, there were a number of relics relating to her, ranging from bits of her veil and drops of breast milk, to the garment she wore when she gave birth, held in Chartres.

Relics offered contact with the numinous and, through this, not just help in the afterlife, but very concrete assistance in this life. The monks of St Cuthbert's in Durham would bring the relics from the cathedral to fires in the city to seek God's aid in putting out the fire. Litigants often swore on saints' bones rather than on the gospels. Relics were also placed into an altar when it was consecrated. The altar was then in honour of the saint or saints whose relics it contained. This made relics an even more important part of Christian religious practice. Relics were in high demand, and considerable sums were paid for them. The Church tried to keep the craze in check, which was one of the reasons for saints requiring an official declaration of sanctity from the tenth century onward.

Possession of relics meant notable prestige as well, also a factor in the handling of them. Relics could be stolen, for example 'because we can do better by it', or with a theft justified by the belief that the saint's bones belonged in a different place. Relics could also be sold, especially when hardship hit. They were a very portable form of piety.

The power of a relic was dependent on the power of the saint; the most potent relics were those of Christ himself. Power was not related to physical size, so splitting them up into smaller pieces to get more relics was an accepted practice. In 1199, Hugh, Bishop of Lincoln – later St Hugh – visited Fécamp in Normandy. Fécamp owned a bone of Mary Magdalen. Hugh tried to break off a bit of the bone to take back with him, but was unable to, so he bit two pieces off and asked the chaplain to mind them for him. The people of Fécamp were very distressed by this, but Hugh's reputation was so great that they could do nothing.

The practice of splitting relics led to an increase in their number, helped along by misinterpretations, misunderstandings or even blatant invention of relics. There are many girdles of the Virgin Mary, several heads of John the Baptist (he apparently had between four and ten heads), innumerable pieces of the True Cross and many nails, also from the True Cross. Sometimes the multiplication of relics could be followed. A classic example of this is the case of St Albans in around 1069–70. The community of St Albans left the body of their saint with the abbot of Ely for safekeeping. When Ely delivered the saint back, it was actually a substitute body: they kept the one they were sent. Odense also had a body of St Albans, claiming that it was the original and that the one sent to Ely was a substitute ...

Even copies of holy objects that pilgrims had purchased could become relics when the next generation forgot they were souvenirs. Given this, it is not surprising that some people were quite sceptical about many relics. Their importance and general veneration were not diminished by that.

Religious Books

Religious books, especially the Bible, were key to Christian services; however, books, in particular illuminated ones, were expensive items. In theory, every church possessed a Bible, but there are only a few complete Bibles surviving from our period. Many parish churches probably had at least a psalter or partial Bible, though some may have done without: evidence suggests that at least some priests were completely illiterate. In northern France, many vernacular illustrated Bibles were produced as exemplified by the *Bible Historiale* by Guiart Desmoulins, dean of Saint Pierre d'Aire-sur-Lys in Artois, in the late thirteenth century. This Bible was a translation and paraphrase of the Latin Bible with an interpolated commentary.

Though a poor church might find itself with only one or two books apart from a Bible, a wide range of other books were also used for religious services. These books contained material to help with the running of Masses and offices; for instance, a missal contained the detail of the Mass. The psalms were an important aspect of religious books, and all literate people would have been familiar with them.

Religious Calendar

The Christian Church used a religious calendar as a firm structure for the religious offices. This was also the main calendar for secular life. Market days, hiring days, due dates and other fixed dates were usually not recorded as day and month, but as a saint's day or similar. The calendar's dates were also used to mark season changes or the start and end of work periods in agriculture. The calendar was developed partly from the Jewish calendar. The terms 'liturgical calendar' or 'liturgical year' that are commonly used for the Church calendar today only came into use in the nineteenth century.

The Church year consisted of four separate but interacting cycles. Each year was marked by several seasons, the Temporale, of which Lent and Advent were the most important. In addition, feast days, held on saint's days, were observed – that was the cycle of Sanctorale. In addition to these, a week structure was observed. Sunday was the first day of the week, celebrated with Mass in memory of death and resurrection of Christ. The other days could also have a special theme; for instance, Friday was marked for devotion to the cross, and Saturdays were dedicated to Mary. Finally, Mass was observing a yearly cycle of Bible readings and topics for preaching.

What makes the Christian year a bit complicated in terms of dates is the fact that it comprises a moveable feast date, Easter (which can fall between 22 March and 25 April), which in turn determines several other dates.

The date of Easter Sunday is preceded by a penitential period of nine weeks in preparation of the feast. Ash Wednesday, forty-six days before Easter, is a day for confession and marks the beginning of Lent, a period of fasting with severe food restrictions in preparation for Easter. During Lent, there was only a single meal a day in most households. This was served late in the afternoon until the thirteenth century, when the meal moved to the middle of the day. The meal was generally supposed to be based on bread, legumes, salt and water, but milk, eggs, fish, cheese and wine were allowed.

The last week before Easter is called Holy Week and starts with Palm Sunday. Maundy Thursday and Good Friday were celebrated at the end of this Holy Week. Maundy Thursday included the bishop washing the feet of twelve poor people. On Saturday, a night vigil (the Vigil of Easter) was held. Easter day was then celebrated on Sunday as the principal feast of the year. We have some evidence that eggs were considered appropriate for the Easter celebrations during our period. For instance, Edward I's household received 400 eggs on Easter Sunday. Most of these were coloured with vegetable dyes, but a few were decorated with gold leaf. There are also records of hard-boiled eggs brought in for blessing on Easter Sunday; for instance, at Wycombe in 1221, a vicar was permitted to keep one tenth of all eggs and cheeses so presented. After Easter, two or three more feast days followed: the Thursday four weeks after Easter was Ascension Day, and fifty days after Easter, the celebration of Pentecost took place. From 1264 on, the Thursday after Pentecost was the festival of Corpus Christi.

Advent is the four-week period of penitence marked by the four Sundays before Christmas (according to the practice of Rome). While there were food restrictions during Advent, it was not as severe a time of penitence as Lent, since harvest festivals still occurred in this time. Advent was also the beginning of the Church year. It was marked by several feast days in succession after Christmas Day on 25 December, turning Christmas into a twelve-day celebration. The word 'Yule' may already have been in use in northern England.

Feast days included processions, a regular part of Church procedure. Most of them consisted of walking from one part of the church to another, and were part of the ordinary services, but could also be held outside the church. Processions were also held to avert plague, to avoid bad harvests, to stave off bad weather and so on. Worshippers walked in a set order, most often led by a processional cross, candle bearers and a thurifer. They aimed to show repentance and piety in the hopes of encouraging God to help. These were not surreptitious superstitions: they were encouraged officially. In 1289, for instance, the Bishop of Chichester told all the priests in his diocese to set about with prayers and processions because there was a storm brewing.

Rituals

Ritual acts were an immensely important part of Christian religious life, and were also used to legitimate secular rulers (for example through the anointing of kings), to support and secure good rulership through prayer, and to elevate and legitimate political acts. Correct and precise completion of religious rituals was very important. This included the proper use of certain implements, such as the Communion chalice (for wine) and *paten* (a dish for the consecrated Host), precious containers to hold the consecrated Host and other items such as cloths for covering, cleaning and preventing direct touching.

A very small and immensely common ritual was making the sign of the cross. This was a typical gesture for Christians and well known; it was used on people and things to bless them or to ban evil influences. Performed on one's own body, it was a gesture meant to ask for God's blessing, to consecrate oneself or to keep oneself safe. The sign of the cross could be performed anywhere and at any time. Simultaneous prayer or the addition of items such as holy water could strengthen its influence.

The most important rituals of the Christian Church are the sacraments. These are specific sacred rites involving a material element. A sacrament, according to the definition developed during the twelfth and thirteenth centuries, is a material element representing and bestowing an invisible spiritual benefit. Once administered, the new status of the recipient could not be revoked, whether the recipient had accepted the sacrament willingly or not.

Sacraments were always influences on the body as well as on the soul, and there exists a multitude of reports of spontaneous healing due to the administration of a sacrament, such as baptism washing off an illness. The exact number of sacraments was still not standardised in the twelfth century. Only after the listing by Peter Lombard in the twelfth century and through the influence of his works did the seven sacraments known today become the common definition.

Baptism, or christening, was the first of the sacraments and a key part of identification with Christianity. The christening turned the person into one of God's children, and it was believed to cleanse the soul of all sins, including original sin (the sin committed by Adam and Eve, which was considered hereditary). Infants were baptised as soon as possible after they were born, generally within eight days of birth, or in some cases on the same day. The consequences to an unbaptised infant who died were dire: theoretical exclusion from heaven and actual exclusion from burial in consecrated ground. Because of this, a priest was not needed to perform the ritual; anyone could do it in an emergency, even a pagan or heretic, so long as their intention was to perform the ritual in accordance with the wishes of the Church. Midwives were expected to know the proper form of the words and keep clean water available so that they could immediately baptise the infant if its survival seemed unlikely. They might even be called upon to baptise a protruding limb in a difficult birth. In case of the death of the mother, the midwife would sometimes perform a post-mortem caesarean so that she could deliver and baptise the infant before its own death.

In most cases, water was sprinkled onto the infant, but the person performing the baptism might sometimes prefer complete immersion. Medical experts commented that this practice was not good for so young a child.

The mother was encouraged not to enter the church until after a formal churching or purification ceremony, which usually took place about a month after the birth, so she may not have been present at a baptism ceremony in the church. For a baptism, at least one godparent was necessary. Godparents answered for the child at the baptism and promised to bring the child up in Christianity. Godparents were seen as spiritual relatives and on a par with blood relatives; they were also expected to stand in for the parents if these died prematurely. It was thus not possible to marry a godparent or a godparents' close relative. The spiritual relationship was also used to found political pacts or similar secular relationships, so the choice of godparents could be politically motivated.

Confirmation is when a Christian is anointed with chrism (a special blessed oil) to confirm their relationship with God and with the Church. In the original Roman rites, this anointing was performed by the bishop directly after baptism. Confirmation was practiced already in Anglo-Saxon England. The size of dioceses at that time made it impossible to administer it immediately after the baptism ceremony in most cases, and it thus turned into a separate sacrament administered to juveniles.

It was, as prescribed, administered by a bishop, usually during an annual circuit through his diocese. Though confirmation is treated in the scholastic works about sacraments, in practice it was often not administered at all during the Middle Ages.

Communion means consuming the consecrated Host (a form of unleavened bread or wafer) and sometimes also consecrated wine. This is a central element of Christian religious life and a central part of every full Mass. According to Christian belief, bread and wine is transformed into Christ's flesh and blood during the ritual act. There was considerable dispute on the exact details of this transformation or transubstantiation by Christian scholars from the eleventh to the sixteenth century.

From about the twelfth century, it became increasingly common to lift the transformed Host for viewing after the transformation. According to an instruction in York in the twelfth century, lay people were supposed to be on their knees for the Elevation of the Host and to lift their eyes to look at it. In the thirteenth century, however, Pope Honorius III (1216–27) instructed that heads should be bowed.

For receiving the sacrament, the Communion wafer was placed directly into the mouth of the recipients. Taking it into the hands first was forbidden, since hands were not regarded as pure enough: only those living in total celibacy had pure hands in this sense. From the twelfth century on, it became increasingly common for lay people to only receive the bread and to forego the wine. This was probably mostly due to fear of spilling the wine. It was possible to receive full Communion by only taking the bread according to a common theory in the twelfth century, as Christ was fully present in both bread and wine.

Though Masses were celebrated very frequently, Communion was not received as often by everybody. The recommendation for lay people was to receive Communion three times a year, at Christmas, Easter and Pentecost. In 1215, the Fourth Lateran Council insisted on Communion at least once a year, at Easter, for laity. On the whole, many Christians may not have been taking Communion even that regularly. There was no insistence on more frequent Communion, and even in monasteries, it was probably taken about once a month and only in a few instances once a week. This was not due to low levels of interest in this sacrament, but to very strong religious awe: it was believed that receiving it too often was disrespectful of its great significance.

Not all Christians were eligible to receive Communion, for instance because they had committed a sin. Taking Communion while not eligible – not in a state of grace – meant a crime against God instead of the redemption otherwise promised by the consumption.

Confession has been regarded as a sacrament since about the eleventh century. Medieval Christianity stressed that confession and penance were necessary to cleanse the soul of sins, and confession and penance were thus central to Christian spiritual life. The earliest form of penance, public confession before the whole congregation, was only used in very rare cases up until the thirteenth century; the most common form of confession since the ninth century was the private confession of penitent to priest.

The sinner first made contrition, which was regarded as a very important part of confession, and then confessed. The appropriate penance was determined by the priest after hearing the confession and could range from repeating a set number of prayers to physical chastisement (usually beating). The priest granted absolution of the sins directly after confession; the acts of penance were performed afterwards. Serious penance often included some manner of public shaming. For his involvement in the murder of Thomas Becket, Henry II was forced to walk barefoot through Canterbury to Becket's tomb, where he was whipped by monks and required to spend the night in fasting and prayer.

From about the fourth century, durations of penances began to be standardised. The most common penance given was fasting for a set amount of time. Other forms of penance included prayer, almsgiving or paying for Mass; these could be substituted for fasting. It was even possible to have somebody else do the penance, for instance for a lord to send someone else on a pilgrimage. This was quite common practice in spite of criticism by the Church.

More educated priests had written guidance on appropriate penances. Confessional manuals were used until the twelfth century, when at least some were incorporated (more or less) into canon law provisions. These manuals were more of a handbook than an encyclopaedia. It is hard to say how many priests had access to them and how rigorously they were used.

Many penances concerned matters sexual. The rules of the Church state that intercourse is only allowed for married couples and only for the purpose of conceiving a child. Sexual intercourse was further restricted by calendar rules. Thus contraception, extra-marital affairs or sexual acts not permitted by the Church, such as sodomy, mis-timed intercourse and even simple lust, were all liable to confession and penance. The worst sexual deviations for Christians were sodomy and incest, which were, in canon law, equivalent to murder, forgery and heresy.

Regular confession and absolution was one of the requirements to be eligible for receiving the other sacraments. The Fourth Lateran Council in 1215 made confession once a year obligatory.

Indulgences are sometimes considered related to confession and absolution. Technically, indulgences were offered to pilgrims when they visited a shrine. The indulgence itself did not grant forgiveness of guilt or permission to sin, and did not promise salvation (though the ignorant might well believe it did some or all of these) but simply remitted some of the penance once absolution had been given. From the eleventh century onward, indulgences – or paying money to the Church instead of doing the other forms of penance, including payments to support the crusades – became more and more acceptable and common. All indulgences were considered to operate best when the individual receiving them was in a state of grace (that is, had confessed, repented and been absolved). This was certainly not the same as the most popular modern and reasonably popular late medieval misconception of an indulgence: buying an exit from purgatory.

The next of the sacraments is Extreme Unction, one of the fixed rites to assist the dying. This was a ritual anointment of the dying person with blessed oil, sometimes also called 'Last Rites'. The oil was applied in form of multiple signs of the cross to the back, neck, head, breast, hands and feet. Only priests were allowed to perform it, and it was considered obligatory for any dying person, including unconscious people.

Another of the sacraments was the taking of orders, a requirement for attaining any kind of rank in the Church. Orders were not only considered a sacrament, but were also clerical ranks, divided into major and minor. Technically, the highest of these orders was the priest, but some acts were reserved for bishops, who were priests with an additional higher administrative status. Priests were able to celebrate Mass and grant absolution from sins; they were in charge of the cure of souls, which is day-to-day work at the parish level. Many of these were trained through a kind of apprenticeship with a local priest. The rank below the priest was the deacon, who was able to baptise people. The minimum age for priesthood and deaconhood was generally twenty-five.

In rank below the deacon was the sub-deacon. This was a minor order until 1207, when the rank was shifted to a major order. The other minor orders, descending in rank, were acolytes (assisted at Mass), exorcists (the lowest level permitted to undertake the rite of exorcism), lectors (technically one who read) and porters (technically a door keeper). Often those in minor orders were generically called clerks. They did not have to be celibate.

When men moved into higher orders, they retained the capacity to do all that those in lower orders could do; for example, everyone above the rank of a deacon could baptise.

Women were not permitted into any of these ranks. Priests were generally imported to perform the sacraments for communities of nuns, although the nuns were permitted to take part in Divine Office (the prayers such as *matins*, *prime* and *terce* that were to be recited at certain hours of the day).

Marriage was not considered a sacrament in the earlier parts of the Middle Ages, only from about 1250. The simplest binding form of

Christian marriage from the late twelfth century was a verbal declaration such as 'I take you as my legitimate wife/husband'. It needed the agreement of both parties, but it did not need consummation. Christian marriage rites were not completely formalised at this time. For example, the announcement of intent to marry and holding the marriage in a public place were not required until after the Fourth Lateran Council – but even after this, secret marriages were still regarded as valid.

It was next to impossible for Christians to divorce after marriage became a sacrament, since sacraments are lasting and cannot be revoked. It was easier to get an annulment than a divorce, although even then, this was difficult.

While the sacraments were the most important ritual acts of the Christian Church, other rituals were common as well. For example, Christian women might expect to be churched after childbirth. From the time of churching, the new mother was permitted to go to church and, once she was no longer breast-feeding the child, to have sex. Churching was supposed to let a woman be purified by the priest. Thus women who had not been churched (especially, for instance, those who were guilty of having children through non-approved practices such as adultery or outside marriage, or whose husbands were excommunicants) were not eligible for the purification of Mass. Bishop Nicholas Gellent of Angers officially informed his parish clergy in 1270 that some women came to church without proper churching. He made it clear that it should be up to the priest who was eligible and when.

Smaller rituals such as prayers, benedictions and blessings were part of daily life for lay people as well as for clerics. Together with the protection of the saints, they were believed to save people from dangers such as illnesses and bad weather. Benediction rituals served to prevent crop failure and livestock illnesses, enhance fertility of the soil or protect a person during a voyage. Benedictions were also spoken during church rituals for key moments of life, such as birth, death and marriage, where they became part of the ceremony of the sacraments.

A certain form of prayer is also pleading to a saint, especially a martyr, for forgiveness of sins. Martyrs were considered to be freed of all sin and all sinfulness by their death, seen as blood baptism.

Although prayer beads (paternosters) were used to count Our Fathers earlier, the recitations of the Ave Maria which became the rosary (with the beads used to mark repetitions) did not begin until the thirteenth century.

Church Services

Church services are formal gatherings for worship; the best known and most important Church service is the Mass. The rites of Mass were not the same everywhere: while the Roman rite of Mass was used very widely, it was used fairly idiosyncratically. The Sarum rite, a variant of the Roman rite as performed in Salisbury, was arguably the most famous of our period and was copied by many churches in France and England.

Mass consisted of a fixed set of prayers and hymns, blessings, canticles (such as the *Magnificat*) and readings from important texts. The readings were usually very short, except for the ones during *matins*. The order and length of the offices as well as hymns, texts and sermon topics varied according to the time of year and day, and also according to the day of the week. The first section of Mass (like much else in the Christian liturgy) was originally Jewish. The second section of Mass was more recent and purely Christian, commemorating the Last Supper with the sacrament of Communion. This part in medieval Christian liturgy overshadowed the first section.

Material for the sermons came from three main sources: the Scriptures, collections of *exempla* and encyclopaedias, and concordances and lists of how to locate suitable tales. Some priests also had access to written collections of sermons, which were a very popular form of literature during our period. There were also preaching manuals, to help with the construction of a sermon.

Sermons often included entertaining tales and parables. They were not simply scary stories about hellfire and damnation, but taught a great deal about the religious culture most people needed to handle everyday life. A lot of fundamental explanations concerning how to interpret the world around them came to the general populace through sermons, reinforced by Church art.

Items that were proper to a specific day were used in a religious service on only this day. Some items were proper to Sundays, for instance, but other items would only be used once in a year. Common items were used on more than one day. Readings came from the Bible or texts by Church fathers or other notable figures. For special occasions, saints' lives could have been read, especially towards the end of our period.

Mass would have been a different experience for a medieval person than for a modern person. Masses were not held in vernacular, but in Latin. Mass was thus not as accessible to most lay people as modern Masses are. In addition, the priest was distant from the congregation in terms of space as well. Mass was thus mostly heard, not seen. Because of this effective blinding of the congregation, much of the service had to be clearly indicated by sound. For example, commencement of Mass was signalled by a bell.

The priest faced the altar in the east, turning his back to the church nave. Most people in a church would have been listening and praying, and occasionally offering responses or singing. During the eleventh and twelfth centuries, Mass was run by the priest with the laity in attendance but only participating in certain parts. From about the twelfth century, the Host could be raised (the Elevation) so that people could see it.

Attending weekly Mass was probably the norm during most of our period, with up to three Masses said daily for the benefit of particularly religious individuals, such as Henry III (r. 1216–72).

Parish churches were expected to hold one Mass a day, but secondary chapels in large parishes might have several a week instead. In cathedrals and other places with large communities of religious, Masses would be arranged to suit community needs. Private Masses could also be arranged. For instance, institutions could have benefactors who demanded Mass for their souls in return for gifts of money or land. There were, in addition, special Masses for special needs, for example to avert plague, or to encourage good weather for crops. This led to several Masses being held each day in convents or more important churches and possibly also in smaller churches.

The main church services were *matins* (at night), then *lauds*, then six more services between dawn and dusk, following a weekly cycle. High Mass was generally celebrated between *prime* and *vespers*. Church offices were mainly recitation of psalms framed in items that progressed the service. Public prayers in a cathedral were usually held five times on a weekday (*matins*, *lauds*, High Mass, *vespers* and *compline*) and nine times on Sundays, with additional services for the most important feasts.

Monasticism

Religious communities for Christians were an important influence on both religious and secular life. The best-known sort of religious community is that found at monasteries. They could be quite small, with only a handful of people, or be as large as Gloucester Abbey around 1100, with around 100 monks. The more residents, the more functions were taken care of in a specialised manner within the monastery.

Monasteries were at least partly closed off from the secular world. There was, however, not always a strong divide between the cloister and the outside world. When a monastery was newly established, and when an order was new, the groups of monks were often very zealous in excluding the outside world and focussing on their religious goals. Over time, many monasteries softened their attitudes and became centres of craft as well as functioning as merchants, landlords and political influences. Personal lives were also not necessarily always austere: nuns in England were known to have kept pet dogs and cats, and we have evidence of birds being kept at the Holy Trinity in Caen.

The religious consisted of monks, nuns, regular canons, regular canonesses and friars. Regular canons were men attached to cathedrals who had taken religious vows. The term 'monk' was used a lot more loosely in the Middle Ages than now: it could mean someone in a monastery, but it could also refer to a canon or a friar.

Monks or nuns took vows binding them permanently to the monastery and its rule. Most monasteries housed either monks or nuns, but in some cases, double monasteries existed that accommodated both males and females. It was easier for males to become monks than for females to become nuns, although there was considerable growth in the numbers of both during our period. Taking vows was technically not reversible, though sometimes a monk or nun might run away from religious life. In addition to administering vows to a mortally sick person to save him or her from purgatory or hell, it was even possible to use this rite of taking vows as part of penitence in politics: forced entry into a monastery was used to disempower and disinherit rivals.

The most important orders until the thirteenth century were the Benedictines, Cluniacs (those following the Cluniac reforms) and Cistercians. From the thirteenth century, the Dominicans and Franciscans need to be added to this. The Templars and Hospitallers were specifically associated with protecting pilgrims, although in reality their roles were more varied than this.

The general requirement for an order was the papal permission to establish it. Each order had its own rule and its own government. The Benedictine order was different in kind to others, as it was not really a formal order. Benedict was considered the founder largely because he was copied by his successors, and that copying resulted in various formalised newer orders. Successors of Benedict, such as Augustine, founder of the Augustinian order, are therefore themselves considered to be Benedictine.

A key facet of some types of monasticism was religious asceticism. This related to food and to lifestyle in general. It also related to cleanliness, such as washing hands before every meal. The most famous example of religious asceticism was the Cistercian order. The Cistercian, regarded as one of the least intellectual of orders and originally very ascetic, sought out depopulated regions to set up monasteries. The notion of asceticism also led to an increasing focus on celibacy and a decline in the number of priests with concubines or spouses. In general, celibacy was more observed by the more senior clergy than parochial clergy, who often had mistresses and children.

The mendicant orders (the Dominicans and the Franciscans, the chief preaching orders) were a thirteenth-century development. In 1216, Pope Honorius III established the Order of Friars Preachers (Dominicans) while the Friars Minor (Franciscans) were already formed in 1209. The Franciscans did not arrive in England until 1224, however. These two orders were not just evangelical religious groups;

they also comprised a kind of intellectual elite, with many of their number being very committed to education. They worked outside the cloisters, especially as pastors and teachers. Their pastoral mission was particularly important. The chief orders (Franciscans were Friars Minor or 'Grey Friars'; Dominicans were Friars Preachers or 'Black Friars'; Carmelites were from Our Lady of Mt Carmel or 'White Friars'; and Augustinians were Austin Friars) had strong links with the papacy and, during our period, a very strict commitment to poverty. Their mobility and their dedication to teaching were major factors in the thirteenth-century dissemination of Church material and growing uniformity in Christian religious practice. As a result, many members of these orders (but especially the Dominicans) were active in working against heresy in the Church.

The influence monasteries wielded varied considerably, depending on their composition (male or female), their links with the outside world and their connection to places and people of power. Some male monasteries wielded enormous temporal power, while others were focussed solely on how to find enough bread to eat. Most of the female foundations had only limited influence, and some had less than that, especially small and poor monasteries. A few – very few – had power as great as that of a bishopric, with the abbess consulted about important issues. Of these, Fontevrault was the chief, because of its link with both English and French royal families. In almost all other cases, women in orders were subordinate to men. Innocent III pointed out bluntly, in 1210, that Mary may have been better than the Apostles, but the Apostles had been given the keys to the kingdom: that is, men had the temporal power. This meant that even in many fairly powerful institutions, most women were accountable to a man.

While there were differences between monasteries as buildings, especially between orders, there was a certain level of uniformity due to common requirements. The physical church was the most important section of the monastery. It was the focal point of monastic life. When there was not enough money to build the whole monastery in stone, the church was built first, while the rest of the complex was built of wood, at least temporarily. Other core components of a monastery were the cloisters, chapter house, dormitory, refectory and parlours. In addition, every monastery needed the buildings and areas necessary for daily life such as storage rooms for goods ranging from grain to gold, kitchen, latrines, gardens and animal housing. Cloisters comprised the *garth* (a garden open to the sky) and the cloister walks (covered passages on all sides of the *garth*). The north cloister walk might have desks for reading and study (*carrels*) with a book cupboard built into the nearby wall. If the monastery was a centre of manuscript production, there would also be a *scriptorium*.

Larger foundations had much more than this core and could include large barns, a brew-house, a wine press, a kiln and a mill. Most of them would have had a wide range of components, each working together under careful managers to keep the system functioning. The novices had their own area in the monastery. Gardeners and animal keepers may have had separate rooms. Various animals lived in a monastery, usually including sheep, goats, cows and pigs, though the number would vary considerably according to the type of monastery and its prosperity. Some monasteries had their own fishponds and tanning pits. Many places also had a guest house and extra kitchen for their visitors, a school, separate accommodation and kitchen for the abbot and a place for bathing.

Monastery gardens are reasonably well known from documents and plans, though not in every case or for every monastery. The monastic garden at Canterbury in the middle of the twelfth century, for instance, was placed between the dormitory and the infirmary, being about half the side of the cloisters. Durham Cathedral Priory garden was next to the *reredorter* and was around 3 by 23 metres. A monastery might also have had separate orchards and a vineyard outside the walls.

Many gardens were kept to assist infirmaries by making medicinal herbs available. For instance, there was a triangular one at the abbey of St Peter in Gloucester that was bounded by the infirmary itself, the infirmary chapel and an external wall.

An almonry could be set aside especially for managing alms. Monastic obligations to the poor included giving them the kiss of peace and reading the Bible to them as well as feeding them. Ideally, their feet were washed and they were given clothes as well. In reality, many monasteries simply gave handouts, often through a dedicated officer (almoner), and remained at a distance from the poor. But monasteries could also have live-in poor. One particular Cluniac monastery had provisions for eighteen poor people. Each received food (including daily bread, and meat twenty-five times a year), an annual gift of wool for clothes, and a pair of shoes every Christmas. In return, they performed some services at the monastery. Monastic help also extended to the ill, the old, widows and orphans, but the numbers who could be helped were always limited.

In England around the eleventh century, most monasteries were found south of the Humber and were linked to the king with local disciplinary control by the diocese or by another bishop. At that stage, English monasteries were not linked to the nobility and none were directly subject to Rome. In France, however, this was not the case and from the twelfth century, especially with the linking of twelfth-century English foundations with Normandy, the two countries began to be more similar, with each influencing the other.

Not all people who led religious lives entered fully into a monastery and took oaths. At every monastery, there were lay members who worked and participated in prayer but were not fully part of the religious life. The numbers of lay members diminished in the twelfth century.

Other women (and some men) chose lay religious lives that were outside formally sanctioned religion. Some took vows of chastity, or pursued lives of personal holiness. Others chose a form of worship that was outside the sanctioned Church entirely, while still being very Christian. The best known of these were an informal group operating largely in the very north of France and in Belgium: the beguines and beghards. They took no vows, but lived in group houses and devoted themselves to leading holy lives. Individuals could leave when they wished, and the group sustained itself by its labours rather than by taxes or gifts or land ownership.

Additionally, there were many ways for people to practice popular piety, such as participating in pilgrimages and processions. Men could also be attached to cathedrals as canons and still live in a secular fashion. While these secular canons could have wives, children, separate houses, and separate incomes, some also lived in a religious community.

There were also the choices made by hermits and mystics. Mysticism was seen as more appropriate to women than to men, as women were sometimes considered to have more prophecy and mystic vision in them to make up for their deficiencies in other religious matters. A very particular expression of religious mysticism was to cut oneself off from the world almost entirely. Anchorites, anchoresses, hermits and recluses were those who wished to dedicate themselves to a solitary life of prayer and contemplation. More people became hermits in the twelfth century than in the preceding centuries. This choice was particularly common around 1050–1150, with more people choosing the life of a hermit in Brittany and central France than elsewhere. Becoming a hermit could mean a life somewhere remote from other people or settlements, or another form of seclusion: many spent the remainder of their lives without freedom of movement, enclosed in small chambers or cells connected to churches. It isn't clear, however, how solitary these mystics truly were, as they still had to receive food and drink from carers through a window or other opening in their cell. And this partial or almost total seclusion was not necessarily how most hermits in France and England existed. Some of them were very sociable and could act as the wise person of the village, for instance Wulfric of Haselbury (*c.* 1080 – *c.* 1154). Some lived in hermitages, while many wandered and begged. Some hermits made a living by accepting payments from people to go on pilgrimages on their behalf. So, far from being cut off from the world, a few hermits even became spiritual directors for others!

Most hermits were lay, and their spiritual knowledge could consist of as little as knowledge of some of the psalms, the Credo, the Ave, and the Lord's Prayer. Most undertook physical labour to gain a living. But no one hermit was typical of all the others: hermit life was unregulated and probably very individualistic. Many were linked to religious orders or houses such as St Godfric of Finchale (d. 1179), who was attached to Durham. This linkage may not have been without consequences: some of the functions of hermits were subsumed into monastic orders during the twelfth century.

Buildings

Designated places for worship were an important part of medieval Christianity. Church or chapel buildings could come in different sizes and shapes, and churches are the most famous and best-known examples of medieval architecture, apart from the occasional castle or palace. Church buildings were places for worship that were in many cases also intended to be spectacular. They were a visual and material means to praise God and were lavishly decorated with wall paintings and furnishings that are mostly lost to us today. Christian religious architecture, which survives much more often than secular buildings, is also the basis for definition of the two styles in our era: the Romanesque and the Gothic style. These architectural terms have become associated since with other kinds of art and even with time periods.

There were several types of churches. Of these, the most common was the parish church. These smaller churches would not necessarily have been made of stone. In fact, the majority would have been made of less permanent and cheaper substances, such as wood. These less robust churches were the ones the vast majority of the populace was familiar with and frequented. There were probably several hundred in each diocese, with perhaps two staff members for each (a priest and someone in a minor order). More important churches were usually larger and constructed from more expensive materials.

During the eleventh and twelfth centuries, there was an ecclesiastical building boom in both England and France. From towards the end of the thirteenth century, construction of major cathedrals was waning, and small parish churches became the vehicles for stylistic innovation. However, even during the period when monumental cathedrals *were* being built, not all church buildings were large, followed the current style or were made of stone; smaller parish churches or private and semi-private chapels would have been much more prevalent than the large, dominating cathedrals.

Chantries were usually not independent foundations, but part of a church (such as a side chapel). They were often endowed by an individual or family sponsoring them to read Mass daily for the benefit of the sponsors. If the donation was sufficient and the chantry was wealthy enough, it could operate as an independent church, along collegiate lines.

Household chapels were integrated into larger buildings, such as castles or large mansions, and served as a sort of private church for the household.

There were also shrines that were regarded as places of healing, often built at the site where a miracle (such as the vision of a saint) had taken place. Shrines were visited by people with particular illnesses. Healing saints to whom prayers, offerings or pilgrimage could be made included St Roch (against plague), St Blaise (against goitre), and St Fiacre (against gangrene).

No matter whether large or small, cathedrals and churches also served important social and communal functions. They were often used as meeting places, for example for guilds or for communal organisations. While this was not a right (the priest could refuse access) it was very common. This would have led to a different association of a church building compared to the modern one, where churches are mostly reserved for worship or Church-related events. This can be seen, for example, from a letter by Robert Grosseteste in 1238, where he complained about artists grinding their pigments for painting on the stone altar instead of using their own stone slabs.

Church Administration

The immense importance of the Christian Church in daily life, and the sheer numbers of those employed by the Church or connected to it, also meant that there was a need for administrative structures. Church administration and its hierarchy worked not only alongside the secular system, but were intertwined with it. In simple terms, the pope held the highest rank in the Christian Church. From the time of Innocent III, the pope was also the vicar (the earthly representative) of Christ.

Bishops were priests in charge of dioceses, which could be regions or towns. The diocese was the main regional administrative unit of the Church, while individual churches administered religious matters at the parish level. The cathedral was the administrative seat of the diocese and it had its own staff, usually consisting of monks, canons or men in minor orders. Many of these staff were regarded as clerics or clerks. The canons could be regular (having taken religious oaths) or secular. A very, very few bishops were also secular, although the vast majority were not. There were sixteen to twenty episcopal sees in England and Wales, with most bishops having previously been royal clerks, monks or cathedral clergy. Canons formed the council of the bishop and assisted him in the ruling of his diocese. Canons also formed the non-monastic communities of collegiate churches. These, though similar to a cathedral in their religious observances, were not the seat of a bishop and thus did not have administrative responsibilities for the diocese.

In practice, the bishops were responsible for most interpretation and everyday local development of Church matters. In England there were fifteen bishops in addition to the two archbishops, and in Normandy there were six bishops plus the one archbishop. Archbishops oversaw bishops for a specific region. Bishops could also be cardinals, which gave them the right to help elect popes.

Abbots and archdeacons were often roughly equivalent to bishops in the hierarchy, but varied considerably in terms of power outside the Church. While theoretically this hierarchy was independent from worldly hierarchies, members of powerful families could also be found in influential positions in the Church. Many Norman bishops were from noble and military families, the classic example being Odo of Bayeux (*c.* 1036 – *c.* 1097), half brother to William I of England; many English bishops, on the other hand, were monks and learned men. To attain any kind of rank in the Church, one had to take orders, which was one of the Christian sacraments. Despite this hierarchy, the Church was not particularly centralised. While technically everyone answered to Rome, and the pope was the one capable of changing belief and canon law, administration and actual legal practice was local.

Popes frequently communicated with bishops on specific issues through papal letters. These letters were usually standardised. They opened with the name of the addressee and a formal greeting, and included a statement on the pope's special competence on the question. The middle section discussed the subject of the letter; it described the problem, presented a legal or speculative reflection and included the papal judgment on the issue. The last section of the letter gave the date and information of any penalties for those disregarding the letter.

Not all letters from the pope were bulls. A papal bull was a formal letter having particular status from the pope, often framed in exactly this way. The word arose from the seal used to authenticate papal documents, which was described in Latin by its shape, *bulla*, meaning rounded or raised.

A common penalty for not acting in accordance with a papal bull was excommunication. Technically, being excommunicated meant being separated from the Communion of the faithful in Christ. This meant not being able to participate in Mass, not being able to be married or buried as a Christian, and was a quite powerful penalty. It also included the capacity to bring in secular authorities. In thirteenth-century England, for instance, the secular arm helped enforce good behaviour after forty days. This meant that excommunication was used by the Church in some ways that look strange at first glance. For instance, in 1275, Bishop Giffard in Bristol excommunicated Jews for insulting, blaspheming and for injury when a chaplain gave a sick Jew Communion. Other Jews were excommunicated for not paying debts. Since Jews were not permitted Christian burial or to attend Mass, the purpose of the excommunication must have been to draw the secular arm into Church dealings with non-Christians. It also suggests that excommunication was used quite widely.

The central hierarchy and local administration of the Church led to many tensions between rulers and the papacy. The Investiture Controversy of England (in the twelfth century), which led to the murder of Thomas Becket, is the most famous instance of such tensions. Tensions also existed between the papacy and its local representatives. Some places (such as Reims) had particularly strong relationships with the papacy, while other regions fought for their autonomy every inch of the way.

The Church was further divided into secular clergy (those who had the cure of souls, responsibility for sacraments and lived in the outside world) and regular clergy or religious. The religious followed monastic rule and belonged to an order. In the eleventh and early twelfth centuries, the difference between these two was more marked than in the thirteenth century, as quite a few secular clergy were married or had mistresses.

Married clergy and those with concubines also might have had children. Numbers of marriages may be difficult to determine because many discussions of them refer to marriage and de facto relationships equally as concubinage. The percentage of married canons probably varied considerably over place and time, but at least 30 per cent of the canons working at St Paul's, in London, around the turn of the eleventh and twelfth century, were married. There is evidence of a large percentage of clergy that were sons of priests until the early twelfth century and even evidence of sons of canons inheriting their father's canonries. This practice, though, seems to disappear around the middle of the twelfth century. There was increased discrimination against the children of clerics as time passed, including fewer career options for them. Illegitimate children of the clergy were given a particularly rough time.

There was considerable difference between a clerk and a cleric, the cleric being within the Church and the clerk operating in any part of the community requiring the capacity to read and write. Originally all clerks (those who worked in jobs that required Latin, such as account keepers) worked through the Church. Over time it became less and less necessary to take minor orders to produce books or work in keeping records for a non-Church organisation, and a difference between clerics and clerks developed.

Judaism

Judaism was the second important and influential religion in medieval England and France. The religious practices of Judaism have not changed very much since the Middle Ages. The Jewish religion was (and still is) structured around several key books: the Torah, the Talmud and the *takkanot* or *responsa*. Many aspects of modern Judaism were, in fact, developed by medieval scholars and commentators using media such as the *takkanot*, so French and English Jewish communities had access to these books assisted by the explanations of some of the most learned scholars in Jewish history.

Christianity and Judaism have certain sections of their holy books in common, since the Old Testament of the Christians largely corresponds to the Tenakh of the Jews. For Christians, however, the New Testament is much more important than the Old Testament. One of the rare instances where knowledge and importance was very similar in Judaism and in Christianity is the psalms; those who prayed in Latin knew the Latin psalms, and those who prayed in Hebrew knew the (older) Hebrew version. All 150 psalms were shared by the two religions, with the only difference apart from language being a variation in the numbering.

The Christian Church assumed that it had moral right over Judaism and that the Rabbinical Judaism that had developed since the fall of the Temple (CE 70) was to be trusted less than Ancient Judaism. The Christian Church tolerated Judaism, but Jews were seen with suspicion nevertheless. Jews had little choice but to accept the Church's predominance in England and France. Judaism in Western Europe in the Middle Ages was closely intertwined with special regulations, laws and treatment different from those experienced by Christians. Practising Judaism was also not always easily possible.

Religious Knowledge

While Judaism can be summarised as resting on a legal and ethical system and a belief in God, it is a complex religion, with much emphasis on the gradual accretion of documents and the legal interpretation of the Torah. It is technically a law-based religion, with *halakha* and rabbinic interpretation underpinning its complexity with systems of interpretation and explanation. Because of this, Judaism has many specialist terms.

Judaism relied on textual knowledge. Medieval Jews heard the whole of the Torah and Haphtarah (related texts) and also the texts related to special festivals through synagogue prayer, but only those learned in religion were familiar with other documents. Generally, the practice of Judaism was very ritualised and formalised. Hebrew and Aramaic language was used for all ritual purposes. Many special rules applied for ritual implements and festivities. Religious practice, just as for Christians, was strongly integrated into daily life through a number of rules and mechanisms.

Popular Jewish symbols that were also used in religious rituals during our period included the seven branch candlestick, a ram's horn, the Ark where the Torah was kept and Hebrew inscriptions. Some modern Jewish symbols were not much known, especially the Star of David.

Religious Books

The most important book in Jewish religious practice was the Torah, containing the Five Books of Moses: Bereshit, Shemot, Vayikra, Bamidbar and Devarim (Genesis, Exodus, Leviticus, Numbers and Deuteronomy). The Torah was not only the most important document for the Jewish religion and source and centrepiece of ritual practice, but also the basis for Jewish law and a record of Jewish early historical tradition. The Torah is only a segment of the Christian Old Testament. The remaining books were known within Judaism, but not as significant. Judaism also had books that were regarded as apocryphal. These included III Ezra, Tobit, Judith, some of the Book of Esther, Ben Sira, Susanna and I and II Maccabees. These books had little religious status.

The Torah was preserved in unillustrated scrolls, much as they are today. However, non-ritual versions of the Torah, especially those with commentaries by scholars, were written in codices, or bound books as we know them. Thus the older scroll form, standard for most Jewish writings until the ninth century, was preferred mainly for religious purposes from the eleventh to the thirteenth century.

Jewish religious literature beyond the equivalent of the Christian Bible was complex. At its heart was the Mishnah, the first collection of rabbinic teaching, first written down around 200 CE. A full sixth of it concerned women, giving women a range of roles from being fully legally autonomous to being dependent. The most autonomous women in Judaism are single adult women, married women, widowed or divorced women. Also important was the Tosefta, first written down around 250 CE, which complemented the Mishnah. Following the Mishnah was the Gemara (or the Addition), which provided more explanations and tales that illuminated key principles. The Gemara thus comprised important interpretative texts written down after the Mishnah. Together they made up the Talmud.

The Talmud takes the rules listed in the Torah and provides instruction about them and analysis of them. It is not a formal legal code like Gratian's *Decretum*, but was used in the Middle Ages (and is still used) as a source for interpreting *halakha*. Important segments are in tale form and record key oral traditions while providing essential teaching texts. It is often called the 'Oral Law' due to its origins. The Talmud and its interpretation were crucial to both religious and legal practice in Jewish communities. It had two branches, one known as the Babylonian Talmud (written down in exile) and one which was known as the Palestinian or Jerusalem Talmud, which was much shorter. The Babylonian Talmud was the one used by the vast majority of Jewish England and France.

There was also rabbinic exegesis, or explanations of these religious writings, and aggadic literature. The aggadic literature taught religious fundamentals through narrative and folklore.

These books were interpreted through *takkanot*: ordinances, glosses, rabbinic commentaries and responses by rabbis. The most famous and possibly the most complete series of glosses and commentary on the Torah is by a twelfth-century French rabbi, Rashi (Solomon b. Isaac, 1040–1105), who lived mainly in Troyes.

Of all the Jewish religious teachings, the Talmud was the most disliked by medieval Christian theologians. An extreme example of this dislike was when the burning of the Talmud in 1242 and 1248 was supervised by William of Auvergne, Bishop of Paris.

The chief work of Jewish mystic literature was the Zohar, written by Spanish and possibly southern French Jews in the twelfth century. The Zohar reflected the philosophy of Kabbalah. Kabbalah (from the Hebrew word for receiving or tradition) developed in the south of France during our period. It described the world in terms of ten primary manifestations of deity (the ten *sefirot*). These *sefirot* were usually drawn on a tree-like diagram, which was borrowed by learned magic traditions very quickly. Concepts like *binah* (understanding), *tiferet* (beauty) and *chesed* (love) served a religious function in mystical Judaism, as well as a magic function, especially in fields such as alchemy. For Judaism in our period, however, the religious function was pre-eminent, and Kabbalists such as Isaac the Blind (*c.* 1160–1235) were known for their thoughts on interpreting and understanding the world.

The only prayerbook in our period was the Siddur Tefillah (the order of prayer). Other books like the special prayerbooks used on festivals developed in the fourteenth century. The exception to this is the Haggadah. The Haggadah was the book used to guide the family service for Passover. In most cases, it was incorporated into the Siddur Tefillah, but we have some surviving thirteenth-century manuscripts (which could have glorious illuminations), which wealthy Jews may have used for their festive celebrations. French Haggadot appear to have been decorated in the margins, with the pictures describing what was happening in the nearby text. The actual material in the Haggadah was very similar to modern Orthodox Haggadot.

Religious Calendar

The Jewish religious year used a lunar calendar with solar adjustments. It had a nineteen-year astronomical cycle and was established around 360 CE by Hillel II. Unlike the Christian calendar, it has not changed significantly between the Middle Ages and today.

An adjustment scheme that adds or subtracts whole months and additional days meant that the individual festivals always stayed in the same season, comparable to the Christian Easter. The first month of the year was Tishrei. The first day of Tishrei was known, therefore, as Rosh HaShanah, or 'head of the year'. This day fell on dates between early September and early October. Yom Kippur or Day of Atonement on 10 Tishrei was the most sombre day of the year. The Makhzor Vitry, a medieval prayer book, stated that a ram's horn was blown at the end of the service concluding Yom Kippur. This also signalled the end of the Yom Kippur fast.

Sukkot was a very agricultural festival, occurring in the European spring. Festive picnics were a feature of it, especially eating in outdoor huts built for the festival.

Purim was a festival including the giving of gifts and often marked by a certain degree of mayhem, possibly even to the extent of burning effigies. More normal practices included dancing and parties. The main ritual requirement of Purim was the Book of Esther being read aloud, with the congregation drowning out the villain's name, Haman, during the reading, so that it could not be heard. This festival was quite specifically a children's festival and children were encouraged to be very boisterous in drowning out Haman's name. This was also an occasion when Jews gave presents to non-Jewish servants. Servants may also have accompanied the children of the family on their house-to-house visit to collect Purim gifts. It was also traditional to give gifts to the Jewish poor on Purim.

Chanukah was another festival often associated with children. It celebrated winning back the Temple by the Maccabees. Special lamps used for the eight days to commemorate this still exist. Twelfth-century lamps appear to have sat on bench tops with eight lights on one level. One found in Lyons was made of local stone, with a row of oil and wick containers set in horseshoe arches. From the thirteenth century onward, lamps were often made for hanging on a wall, such as a bronze

lamp from northern France, with a backplate that was decorated like a
Norman building.

The reading of the Torah also followed an annual, calendrical cycle.
In one cycle (one year) the whole of the Five Books of Moses were
read aloud in prayer in the synagogue. From the twelfth century,
communities celebrated the end of the Torah-reading year when this
cycle was completed.

The Jewish holiday days can be grouped according to their religious
importance (Passover and Yom Kippur, for instance, are predominantly
religious festivals), their agricultural origins (Shavuot is one of these),
their normal calendrical operation (each new moon is a festival) and,
finally, whether they commemorate historical occasions, such as Tisha
b'Av.

Services

As in the Christian Church, ritual was an important part of the religious
life. For synagogue service as well as for certain formal rituals, a
minyan (prayer quorum) was a requirement. The *minyan* was a group
of ten adult male Jews that stood witness to the acts. Judaism is and
was, however, quite flexible in some regards to rules, and if it was not
possible to gather a full *minyan*, compromises may have been made.

As Judaism in general was centred around books, they were also a
key point of rituals. While the Torah was by far the most important,
prayer books were in use as well. With this emphasis on the written
word in the religion, Jews were more likely to know how to read than
Christians. It is thus possible that reading of texts and prayers was done
by a larger part of the congregation.

In general, liturgical services were structured around a reading from
the Torah, with psalms and other prayers used to frame it. The standard
order of prayer in services for France can be found in the Makhzor
Vitry, an eleventh-century compilation by Rabbi Simkha of Vitry. It is
similar to the order of service in England, but places such as Burgundy
had some differences. Jewish religious practices, then, differed from
place to place, with England ignoring Continental practice when it did
not suit.

In the services held on every Sabbath and festival, a passage from the
Torah was read aloud, followed by a passage from other books of the
Old Testament (Haftorah) that reflected the ideas in the more-important
Torah passage. Services in synagogues were generally led by a *khazan*
(cantor) who often sang the whole service so that not all members of
the congregation needed to own the expensive books. Evidence seems to
suggest that there were many small synagogues rather than a few large
ones in any given community, but the picture may change as more work

is done on the subject. In France, it is probable that many religious services were held in private homes; similar services in homes may have happened in England.

Services were held three times a day: Shakharit (morning), Minkha (afternoon) and Ma'ariv (evening). Ma'ariv was regarded as optional. Although in Palestine a ram's horn was sounded to announce when a service was going to begin, the greater difficulties of being Jewish in England and France meant a more unobtrusive announcement: the *shamash* (a synagogue official) announced services by knocking on doors.

The chief part of the daily services was the Shemoneh Esrei (the eighteen blessings, although in reality there were nineteen blessings, often known today as the Amidah). The Shemoneh Esrei was a collection of biblical quotes composed into a prayer. It may not have been repeated at Ma'ariv to shorten that service.

The blessing by the priests or *kohenim* was in three parts. The priests lifted up their hands to bless the congregation. Since priests were born and not ordained, the number of priests present depended on the number of adult males present whose fathers had the right fathers.

The *Shema* ('Hear, O Israel') was a very well-known prayer and belonged in all services; the words would have been known to any Jew with even a little religious background.

The Torah reading was the highlight of the service in religious terms, because of its importance in Judaism. It was read from a large scroll, which was held up by the wooden posts it was wound round. Ideally it was held high, so that everyone in the congregation could see it. In some congregations, the Torah was raised after the reading (for example in northern France and most of England), and in some before the reading (for example in any place with a strong Spanish influence, and possibly southern France).

Services ended with a *kaddish* (a common prayer) read by one person. These days the full version is often called the Mourner's Kaddish, but the earliest reference to it as a specific prayer for mourners appears to be in the thirteenth century. The full version was used in our period, along with a shorter, earlier version.

Additional services were held on Sabbath and festivals, for example the Musaf service was added to the morning service on Sabbath. The High Holy Days (especially the Day of Atonement) were very prayer-intensive. They used the daily service schedule to structure the praying of the day and then added the prayers specific to the occasion. As in Christianity, some prayers were proper and some common, although these terms were not used. Musaf, for instance, was significantly different on Rosh Hashanah to its equivalent on other days of the year. At the end of Sabbath, there was a short service called Havdalah, to mark the end of the time of rest and prayer, although this service might have been held in homes.

Married men wore a *tallit* (a prayer shawl) for certain services. The *tallit katan* ('little *tallit*' – a garment worn as part of everyday clothing) was introduced in the Middle Ages, but its actual use in France and England during our period is uncertain. It may have been introduced after our period.

Religious Ceremonies

Circumcision – the removal of the male foreskin – was a key ritual for Judaism. It was part of the covenant between Jews and God. Jewish boys were circumcised on the eighth day after birth during a ceremony in the synagogue. The circumcision was a community occasion and involved a *minyan* in addition to the person performing the operation.

The boy was carried into the synagogue and held throughout the operation. From the thirteenth century, there was a move to bar mothers from the ceremony because of a distaste of women taking an active part in the service. In these cases, a male sponsor carried and held the child.

The actual circumcision was preceded by blessings and the recitation of Numbers 25: 10–13. It was followed by blessings by the father, blessings spoken over wine and a prayer for the child's good future by everyone present.

From the thirteenth century, the night before the circumcision developed a special role. It was sometimes feared that evil spirits would try to prevent the circumcision happening, so friends met at the newborn's house for a prayer vigil. Some communities also had celebrations on the seventh day. Another development from the eleventh to the thirteenth century was a trend towards paid professionals running the occasion, a change that displeased many rabbis.

Formal introduction of Jewish boys into their religious adulthood was marked by the bar mitzvah. The earliest documented bar mitzvahs were not before the thirteenth century, and primarily comprised a Torah reading and special blessing by the father in the synagogue. However, education towards religious adulthood, that is participation in synagogue services and rituals, was a key requirement for leaving childhood, even before the development of a formal ceremony.

According to Jewish rules, there were circumstances when a person was considered unclean. Judaism used ritual bathing to restore ritual cleanliness. The best-known causes for uncleanliness are menstruation or childbirth in women, but men could also become unclean, for example through contact with dead bodies. During the bath, the person was fully immersed, including the hair. The ritual bath required living water, such as water from rivers or ground water. Access to ground water could be obtained by building a shaft deep enough with a basin at the bottom. These *mikvahs* are sometimes found during archaeological excavations.

Just like in Christianity, marriage was an important ritual in a person's life, and closely connected to changes in social status. Judaism encouraged a betrothal before marriage accompanied by a pre-nuptial agreement, usually signed well before the wedding. It included financial commitments by parents, the date of the wedding and the penalties for breaches. It was a formal contract rather than a religious agreement, though it included a ceremony with blessings for bride and groom and possibly a betrothal ring for the bride. This procedure followed the Talmudic prescriptions: the declaration of intention to marry (normally one year before the wedding, although this delay does not seem to have been obligatory) and the wedding itself.

The Jewish marriage ceremony itself had much in common with its modern counterpart. It depended on the consent of both parties to the marriage contract, which was read aloud during the ceremony. The wedding was held under a canopy, in public, and included the bride walking around the groom seven times, seven blessings and the groom smashing a glass with his foot. A wedding ring was given by the groom to the bride and placed on the forefinger of the bride's right hand. It had no gem, but was sometimes inscribed with 'Mazel Tov' (a standard saying for wishing someone well). The bride wore a garland, preferably with olive leaves in it to remind everyone of Jerusalem.

The whole occasion was a great festivity, and framed in a great deal of activity such as a wedding procession. During the week after the wedding, the blessings were said again at festive meals in honour of the bride and groom. It was traditional to have an adult male at each dinner who had not been to the previous one.

Jewish weddings were forbidden on Sabbath and during several other periods of the year, ranging from single days to several weeks. Jewish marriages in England in the thirteenth century had to include special provision for the very heavy taxes that the Crown imposed on Jews.

As in Christianity, many more ritual acts apart from the ones stated here were usual. For example, when Jewish children were born, the men prayed psalms in the house for the woman in labour. Some communities placed the Torah and phylacteries on the woman's bed or at the door of the room, lit candles and so forth to ensure a safe birth.

Buildings

Jewish communities had several physical requirements in order to fulfil their religious obligations. Places to pray were important, although given the very few remains of synagogues it appears that private homes may have been considered satisfactory for many communities. In some cases (especially in England), they had to suffice, because many of their Christian neighbours did not want Jewish houses of prayer in their midst and communities could be punished if noise from prayer was audible outside.

Like baths, clean wells were very important for ritual purposes. The unleavened bread for Passover, for instance, had to be made with very pure water.

Jewish law demands quick burial, so acquiring a cemetery was one of the major obligations of any Jewish community. It came before the obligation to build a synagogue, because any room would do for prayers in a pinch. However, when the laws of the land were unsupportive, this could be a major difficulty. For example, all English Jews had to be buried in London until 1177. There was sufficient hearse traffic for it to appear on toll-lists as a separate item. It also created problems: there is at least one account of dogs howling as corpses rolled by on their carts. After 1177, some communities were allowed to purchase or rent a local burying ground outside the city walls. The Northampton Jewish community paid an annual rent for a burial ground (outside the north gate of the city) to the Priory of St Andrew. Although the new cemeteries could be outside the town walls, they were more often on the edge of the Jewish quarter, about fifty feet past the last house and often walled to prevent desecration. It was also possible for several Jewish communities to share a cemetery, and each cemetery had a small building for ritual purposes.

Troubles: Heresy, Dissent and Persecution

Religious practice was not uniform within the Middle Ages. Some of the differences in worship or belief were not accepted by the authorities, though, which could lead to trouble.

Heresy is a complicated issue, and all that can be given here is the briefest of overviews. To be a heretic means to refuse to confirm to standard belief. However, standard belief and interpretations of it changed over time, as did popular religious beliefs.

Heretics were given opportunities to recant and reform. If they accepted this, and then relapsed, they were liable to receive the worst punishment. The use of burning as the ultimate secular punishment for heretics in England seems to rest on a common law precedent: the burning of a deacon who converted to Judaism in 1222 in Osney. Jews who converted to Christianity then Judaicised (returned to Judaism) were also prosecuted as heretics.

Although the modern popular view of heretics is that they were all burned, in reality only a small percentage were likely to have suffered this fate. While medieval heresy has attracted a lot of attention by modern writers, there is little on record from 1050 to 1100. Until the twelfth century, a standard punishment for heresy was confiscation of goods. However, with the ecclesiastical reform in the twelfth century, interest in disciplining heretics rose. In 1116, Henry of Lausanne, a renegade cleric in the Le Mans region, was accused of heresy, as was a priest called Peter of Bruys in the 1120s and 1130s. Both were at liberty for many years. Eventually, however, Peter was burned and Henry died in prison.

In the thirteenth century, starting with Innocent III's *Vergentis in sernium* (March 1199), penalties became much tougher. In fact, the thirteenth century in general demonstrated a stronger interest in heresy and in expunging heretics than earlier. The Church's main reason for harsh action was fear of moral contagion. In 1229, the Council of Toulouse ordered that repentant heretics should wear two yellow crosses on their clothing to warn others. In 1252, Innocent IV said that heretics were thieves and murderers of souls and should therefore be punished as other thieves and murderers. From this time, torture was permissible in dealing with heretics. In fact, the penalties became the same as punishment for treason, because heresy was seen as treasonable. Innocent III even applied penalties to those who helped heretics, starting with excommunication for a first offence, and moving to punishments such as being banned from holding public office or inheriting. Men were punished more severely than women by and large. In all cases, there was a series of procedures to be followed before punishment.

Heretics could plead in their defence, of course. The strongest argument in their defence was denying that they did it at all. There were other possible defences, including being under the influence of a demonic power, being too young (under fourteen), being too old (medically attested senility), being asleep or illiterate, having been taught badly or being under emotional strain. Making heretical statements when under threat of one's life, however, was not considered to be as strong an argument.

The best-known heretics of our period are the Albigensians, also known as the Cathars. Their particular variant of Christianity was unique to the south of France and was tolerated by the counts of Toulouse who ruled the region. Their persecution and the crusade that led to their murder were partly politically motivated in order to reduce the power of the count of Toulouse. The Albigensian Crusade caused death and hardship for other populations of the south of France as well as the Albigensians, including the Jewish community. It also involved military and religious people from other regions of Western Europe, including England. The only other major heretics of our period were the Waldensians, who practiced in the very north of France and in Belgium.

Not all heretics belonged to large groups or had spectacular histories. Some were sceptics (denying, for example, the literal transformation of the bread and the wine in the Eucharist), and some were simply in the wrong place at the wrong time, or said the wrong thing to sensitive ears. In the thirteenth century, for instance, in Sesairol in southern France, a woman in childbirth was suspected of heresy because she called on the Holy Spirit for help instead of Christ or the Virgin Mary. This had nothing to do with Church teaching, but a great deal to do with popular belief!

In 1184, inquisitors were first appointed by the pope to work against heresy. They were not very active initially. In 1234, Gregory IX established the Inquisition proper, to deal with the Cathar heresy in Languedoc. Once people confessed to heresy and persisted, they were dealt with by the secular authorities. Those who did not persist simply undertook penances such as wearing yellow crosses on their clothing, undergoing imprisonment or restricting their diet. Over time, these penalties became harsher towards the Cathars.

Apart from heresy, another reason for religious persecution was apostasy, the rejection of God. Medieval Christians believed that the first apostates were fallen angels. According to the influential theologian Hostiensis (c. 1250), there were three forms of apostasy. The first was converting to another faith and was considered traitorous and worse than never having been Christian in the first place; it could bring confiscation of property and even the death penalty. The second form of apostasy was breaking major commandments (such as 'you shall not kill'), and the third form was the breaking of holy vows for those who had taken religious orders. Culprits were expelled from home and imprisoned.

Judaism was much more lenient. Converts away from Judaism were regarded as sinning but still Jewish, according to Maimonides in the twelfth century. Forced converts were called *anusim* and attracted special prayers. Rashi, the Jewish sage, specifically rebuked people who insulted and humiliated those who had undergone compulsory conversion. In his eyes they were still Jewish, and therefore worthy of respect.

There was considerable tension between Christianity and Judaism, and due to the more powerful position of the Christian Church, Jews had to cope with a number of difficulties and discrimination. Anti-Semitism in the Middle Ages was very real, but it was not uniform; it changed over time and operated differently in different places. It was also not solely due to religious differences. Some activity that looked anti-Semitic was really a nasty form of political expediency. However, a vast number of egregiously cruel deeds were perpetrated in the name of Christianity, ranging from compulsory conversion or expulsion from a particular place to mass murder. And there were many small intolerances also, including local priests forbidding congregants to visit the households of their Jewish neighbours and the imposition of laws that impacted only the Jewish population. These intolerances were reinforced by the increasingly anti-Jewish slant of canon law.

Until the eleventh century, Jews and Christians were roughly equal in standing in most of Europe. The biggest changes to this happened from around the First Crusade (1096) to the Black Death (1348). When the First Crusade was launched, Jewish people were seen with more suspicion, and the amount of violence against Jews started to grow.

With this changing view of Jews came accusations of committing acts supposedly linked to Jewish rituals or to hatred of Jews for Christians. These accusations have been uniformly proven to be unfounded, which has not stopped their proliferation even to the present day. One of the earliest of these was made in 1144 by a Norwich monk named Thomas of Monmouth. He claimed that the Jews had tortured and killed a young apprentice named William and then disposed of the body in the woods. According to the monk, the boy's family was unable to proceed with charges against the Jews because they were under the protection of the sheriff and the king. The story of Little St Hugh was another infamous accusation of ritual murder, which supposedly occurred in the city of Lincoln in 1255. A large number of Jews were arrested and imprisoned in the Tower of London for this. According to one account, eighteen of these Jews were hanged, and another seventy-one were saved by Richard of Cornwall, the king's brother.

During and shortly after the coronation of the famous crusader king, Richard I, in 1189, violence against the Jews began to grow alarmingly. The first incidence of this shocking violence took place during the coronation itself; the citizens of London turned on Jews bringing gifts to the king and as the chronicler Richard of Devizes said, 'the Jews in the city of London began to be sacrificed to their father, the devil'.

Similar attacks on the Jews occurred in other English towns following Richard's coronation. For example, Jews were murdered and their houses burned in the towns of Lynn and Stamford in Lincolnshire. A planned attack on the Jews of Lincoln was apparently prevented by the intervention of Bishop Hugh and the castellan of Lincoln Castle, who allowed the Jews to shelter within the castle.

The most violent of these incidents took place in York, where some nobles who owed money to Jewish financiers forced their way into the home of a recently deceased Jewish lender named Benedict and killed everyone inside, including his wife and children. Other Jews took refuge in the castle, though any who were caught were offered the choice of baptism or death. Unlike Lincoln, the castellan of York did not wish to offer refuge to the Jews. Instead, he fetched the sheriff and a band of local knights to remove them from the castle. They failed; however, there weren't enough supplies in the castle for a prolonged siege, and when this was realised, some of the Jews committed suicide. Others who were promised baptism and life if they surrendered were killed as soon as they exited the castle.

The coronation of Richard I was not in itself a turning point for anti-Semitism in England, but symbolically it can be regarded as such, because from that time on, being Jewish in England became increasingly dangerous and hard.

The images of Jews most Christians carried with them were from Church teachings, both formal and informal. These images included visions of Jews as at worst deicides and heretics, and at best witnesses to the truth. Jews were linked in many Christian minds to the Antichrist and to the devil. It is not surprising, therefore, that it was considered a crime for a Christian to sleep with a Jew, and that Jews were considered not quite human until they converted to Christianity.

How people reacted to this view of Jews depended on who they were as individuals, how they related to their society, how they felt about the values they were presented and on the nature of their personal religious convictions. It was perfectly possible for Christians and Jews to be friends, to work for each other and even to have love affairs, though in the thirteenth century it became increasingly difficult.

At the beginning of the thirteenth century, Innocent III tried to place limits on Jews in customary law and to use some customary laws against Jews. For example, when Thomas Aquinas spoke against the compulsory baptism of Jewish children, Innocent claimed that custom permitted it. This may have been part anti-Jewish, but also part of his strong attempts to unify the Church and make it look to Rome. At the same time, the reign of John reduced most English Jews to destitution by impossible tax rules. Their situation was made even worse by the civil war against John. These changes were so great and the mistreatment of Jews so horrendous that many of the surviving Jews were forced to migrate out of Western Europe entirely.

Forced conversion to Christianity also increased, in particular from the twelfth century onward. Up until 1140, Jewish parents were allowed to determine the religion of their child; forced baptism of Jewish children, although often done, was discouraged by secular authorities. After baptism, all minors were considered Christian in popular theology, regardless of whether the baptism was undertaken without the parent's and the child's consent. If the parents of a child took the case to a high enough level of ecclesiastical court, then this popular theology might be overturned, as parental rights were part of canon law. This might have restricted the level of abuse in some areas. Canon law said that baptism of adults was invalid if coerced, unless the person had agreed, for instance in order to save their own life. Crusaders threatened death or conversion quite frequently.

When Edward I took power in 1274, the Jews who remained in England formed a near-destitute community. They had been banned from most activities that would allow them to rescue themselves from destitution. In the late 1270s and 1280s, poor Jews in England starved due to the effects of public policies towards them. Most normal means of earning an income were closed to them. For instance, in 1283 a statute was passed excluding Jews from the protection normally given to merchants. Some turned to the open road and became highwaymen, some converted to Christianity to find a measure of safety. None were allowed to leave the country without a permit, and permits took money and influence. After fifteen years of increasing poverty and humiliation for English Jews, their property and outstanding loans were seized to pay taxes and the Jews were expelled from England in 1290.

The Church often condoned certain customs because of the alleged Jewish role in crucifixion, even during the best of times, when the two religions lived happily together. These customs were generally at their worst during Lent and reached a peak in Holy Week. They included the stoning of individuals and houses and slapping Jews on Good Friday. This practice also may have led to the frenzies of massacre and of blood libel when society was less stable.

Attacks on Jews were also quite common during crusades. Preachers preached against Jews, and Peter of Cluny even demanded that Jewish property be confiscated to finance everything. Ironically, Jews were also forced to pay for crusades which included the murder of Jewish civilians. The anti-Semitism in England increased during the Second Crusade and again in the Third Crusade.

The impact of the crusades on the Jewish community is indicated by changes in the religious rituals; after the crusades, an extra prayer was added at Passover for this reason – the only vengeful prayer in the regular canon. For the circumcision ceremony, a special chair for Elijah the Prophet was added to the right of the sponsor's chair, perhaps in the hope that peace and an end to suffering would come soon. These were great changes in an otherwise very static ritual set.

5

Fighters Will Fight
Military

Medieval England rested as much on a military base as on a religious outlook. War was not incessant, though a list of years in which wars were fought might give that impression. It punctuated peace rather than the other way round.

Military aspects of life were intertwined closely with daily life and with governance. War could have a legal basis, which would have been argued by those with legal backgrounds and churchmen. The Church argued (at least in theory) for a just war or holy war. Lay law experts argued more about who could wage war on whom. The most important time for these arguments was the fourteenth century; however, they did exist during our period and instances of how such arguments might have worked can be found in compilations of customary law. Military aspects were also connected to religion in other ways, as prayers and blessings were seen as an important support for the fighting. A good example for this is the use of flags that had been blessed, which was increasing in the eleventh and twelfth centuries.

Military matters, therefore, did not stand independently, but need to be seen in relation to normal daily life, religion and government.

Medieval Warfare

In many modern minds, military, warfare and the concept of knights are closely connected to each other. Medieval warfare, however, was as diverse as the people doing the fighting and did not consist of cavalry charges only. There were artillery fights and fighting on foot as well as sieges, guerrilla warfare and ambush and manoeuvres that would be called special operations in modern warfare. It did not always rely on knights, and most of the fighters were neither knights nor nobles. Different regions also had different fighting traditions. This often served as a brake on escalating violence. For instance, in

1055, Ralph, an English earl of Continental origin and nephew of Edward the Confessor, was frustrated in his attempt to get his levies from the English marches to fight like his French soldiers. The modern image of honourable fighting is also far from medieval reality: ruses, concealments, subterfuges, betrayals and other dirty tricks were part and parcel of medieval warfare. For example, commanders – a primary target for the enemy fighters, crucial as rallying points for their own fighters and often the only thing holding the army together – might disguise themselves by wearing no arms at all, or by using decoys. Destruction of the countryside as well as of towns and cities by fire was a typical part of war; robbing food and cattle while moving through a territory also served to feed the army. Ravaging the enemy's territory could even be central to the concept of warfare, with the avoidance of open battles against an opposing army as far as possible.

War was a negative thing for many whose everyday life came into contact with it, such as the residents of a region touched by war. Even those who were on the winning side might find their lives devastated, such as peasants having their land and buildings ravaged or destroyed. Some people buried their valuables to keep them safe, and many suffered loss of income, food and support.

The overall picture of battle and war in reality was usually one of many little independent armies or individuals with the right to fight. They grouped together under a leader, for instance a king or another lord. However, once they had finished the mandatory fighting time that was due to their lord, individuals could either leave the army or continue fighting, usually for some sort of reimbursement. A lot of small military action was the inevitable result, with larger armies mainly being pulled together to meet major crises. The kings and major lords maintained a small core unit that allowed them to act quickly when necessary. The royal retinue of fighters was especially important: they could even be considered a small army in some cases, capable of going into battle without need for additional troops or equipment support.

While military matters were a standard part of medieval life, larger military campaigns were often seasonal, running during the spring to autumn months. This was partly due to the logistical challenge of keeping men and beasts fed. Another reason was the limited amount of fighting service that most vassals were due their lord – usually a period of forty days. There were, however, also campaigns running into or through winter. Actual battles were usually short and seldom lasted more than a day. Longer conflicts were often punctuated by truces, and the length of a conflict or of a war may have been less important than the length and amount of individual campaigns during this war. Sieges, however, commonly took several weeks or months.

Besieging a castle or a town was not simply a matter of surrounding it and waiting. The besiegers used various strategies to bring their opponents to their knees. They might use machines to throw things into the castle or the town, for instance. The material thrown might be incendiary or might consist of rotting animals (in the hope of inducing infection and lowering morale). The besiegers could break down walls using simple picks and iron bars, battering rams and stones thrown from artillery machines. They might fill in ditches and moats with whatever material was available. Besiegers might undermine walls using the skills of miners and sappers. A very famous example of this is the fall of Chateau Gaillard in Normandy, where the mining made a big enough breach to allow for successful attacks using ladders.

While all this was happening, the besiegers had to be protected against the people they were attacking. Trenches helped, and so did banks and palisades. Engines could be used as well, including approach engines such as wooden castles and sentry-boxes. Approach engines were many and varied, and each functioned slightly differently. Which ones were actually used in a given situation depended on the knowledge of the engineers and the needs of the besiegers.

The besieged had several options. They could sit and wait, dealing with the inevitable running down of supplies as best they could. They could send out for help. Making sorties, counter-mining or using siege engines on the besiegers were all options – sieges did not have to be passive. In fact, some sieges even had jousts between the besieged and the besiegers, to while away the tediously long day. Psychological warfare was at least as important as the physical mechanics in determining a siege's outcome.

Most soldiers served limited campaigns only before returning to their everyday lives. Only a few of the fighters had warfare as their main and only profession; even knights usually had many diverse tasks, not all of them related to fighting.

It is not always easy to tell how frequent wars or skirmishes were throughout our period or how many fighters were taking part and who they were. The military action in fights and battles is also not easy to grasp or evaluate through the sources available. For instance, accounts of battles in chronicles and other documents are not always reliable: in many cases the number of men fighting is overstated to demonstrate how outstandingly important the melee was. Accounts may also be influenced by the author, and thus end up very biased towards one side.

Descriptions of medieval warfare range from the thoroughly glamorised, describing the splendour of silks and satins, shining armour and beautiful tents, to the thoroughly miserable army slugging through rain and mud with no shelter, no provisions and with horses and men starving. Most campaigns were probably somewhere in the middle, and individual comfort of the armies' members depending on circumstances as well as on personal wealth and ingenuity. During military campaigns, access to grain or other fodder and water could be a significant problem for a mounted army: the logistics of supply played a crucial role in medieval warfare.

The importance of having a well-coordinated force, including having troops advancing in good order and good timing for alliances in battles, was well known. Brotherhood or companionhood in arms were formal partnerships between soldiers and a common practice. Such an agreement could encompass sharing of winnings and losses and be of mutual aid to each other. These agreements were usually done between those of equal rank.

The individual fighters who made up groups, armies or garrisons were recruited by various methods. For a lord in need of fighters, an obvious source was his own family; other fighters would come from his tenants, especially those with a knight's fee. In addition, there were the permanent household staff, household knights and retainers held for military or other services. There seems to be a shift towards the recruitment of paid retainers instead of calling in the services of tenants between the twelfth and the fourteenth century. However, this might be a result of changing forms of evidence and not an actual change in the composition of forces. The lure of personal glory gained through combat, or of grants of conquered territory and ransom, could also draw men to fighting. This was supported by the cultural expectation of men to be fighters – unless they were clerics, who were not supposed to be fighting at all. Canon lawyers, however, allowed bishops to provide soldiers, exhort men for fighting in a just war and travel with the army – and some bishops might even have fought themselves in spite of the prohibition.

William's army in 1066 included volunteers from Brittany, Flanders, Champagne and even the south of Italy. The number, and probably also the motivation, of volunteers would depend on the cause: a cause that seemed appealing and worthy would draw more volunteer fighters than one not considered as important. For those that had not volunteered and did not wish to fight, desertion was a possible way out, particularly when fighting within the country. This could lead to very significant shrinkage of the recruited forces between leaving the place where the men where mustered and arriving at the actual site of battle.

There was a clear division between foot soldiers and cavalry until the fourteenth century, reflecting the social differences between those who were mounted and those who were not. Otherwise, there were not many distinctions of rank in a medieval army. A distinction of ranks among the knights and other mounted fighters seems to have developed gradually during the course of the later twelfth century. By 1300, there were knights banneret – usually leaders of smaller troupes – followed by normal knights, followed by sergeants, squires and valets. The bannerets were distinguished by a rectangular banner, as opposed to a normal pennant. While it is clear that the bannerets had responsibility for cavalry forces and received more pay than ordinary knights, the sources do not reveal details about their work.

Members of fighting forces below the level of knights are less well described by our sources, often with shifting and not very precise terminology. For instance, sergeant could mean an ordinary foot soldier, but also a mounted fighter equipped in much the same way as a knight.

Supplementing a group of fighters with mercenaries was also an option, particularly towards the end of our period. Mercenaries were professional soldiers without fixed political masters. In essence, they were stateless. They were much more flexibly employed than regular knights. Mercenaries could be mounted fighters, foot soldiers or specialists.

Some mercenaries had a shocking reputation. Particularly notorious mercenaries and mercenary groups were banned by the Third Lateran Council in 1179 because they did not respect religious institutions, widows, orphans, the very young or the very old. The ban effectively slowed down the use of mercenaries until the late Middle Ages. The banned groups included German mercenaries from Brabant, as well as mercenaries from places like Aragon and Navarre. Mercenaries in England were very popular in the eleventh and early twelfth centuries; the thirteenth century, however, saw a decline in the number of mercenaries, and the *Magna Carta* version of 1215 promised that all foreign knights, crossbowmen, sergeants and paid soldiers would be removed from England. Very few mercenaries were used after the end of the civil war in 1217.

Cavalry

Cavalry was critical to medieval warfare, and the image of armoured riders with couched lances approaching each other is still an iconic one.

From about the eighth century, cavalry usually was the deciding factor in winning a battle; this stayed unchanged until the rise of firearms and new tactics from the fourteenth century. From the late eleventh century, shock tactics using cavalry were very important. The body of men on horseback, with their lances couched under their arms, would have been very imposing. Cavalry was also well suited for swift raids.

Today, medieval fighting is often imagined to be chivalric knights fighting on horseback, using lances or swords. For the knights' contemporaries, too, there was a knightly ideal in courtly literature, especially the Arthurian romances, conjuring images of strength, courage, obedience and virtue. However, reality was rarely like the literary ideal. While knightly virtues were held in high esteem and were certainly seen as aims worth striving for, contemporary documents show that knights could also be greedy, violent and not terribly virtuous at all. In both texts and illustrations, armour – the hallmark of the professional warrior – was in some instances also used as a metaphor for ferocious, brutal and fearsome fighters.

In addition to this very different reality of knighthood, medieval cavalry was not as closely connected to knighthood as often supposed. In the eleventh century, all mounted fighters were termed *milites*, and these ranged from men of high standing to those of lower status, and possibly even included unfree men. In 1193, the Tower of London garrison numbered twenty knights and eighteen mounted sergeants. In 1267, eight knights and thirty sergeants were taken to Nottingham by William of Leyburn, where the local garrison consisted of two knights with their squires and twenty sergeants plus archers and other fighters. Generally, only about 20–30 per cent of the cavalry were knights during the late thirteenth century until well into the fourteenth century.

The word *miles* started to shift towards a description of noble or near-noble soldiers from about 1050 to 1100. This was probably linked to the development of cavalry as a prestige aspect of fighting. The change was gradual: non-noble knights were found in both England and France in the eleventh century, with several scholars arguing that their status was much lower than that of knights later in the period. In fact, they were not homogenous as a group, with many more being simple soldiers than is the case in, say, the late thirteenth century. Knighthood was not purely hereditary in England. After the first quarter of the thirteenth century, 'knight' was used as an honorific with increasing frequency, showing the importance of these members of society. The less wealthy landed knights often had smaller parcels of land supporting them and so were more closely tied to the land: they were often partly farmers.

By the late twelfth century, however, an increasing number of knights had forbears who had been knights. The development of a formal ritual for knighting coincides with the clearer differentiation of knights and mounted sergeants in the later twelfth century. From about 1270 on, knighthood was associated mainly with nobility. This does not mean that all nobles were knights, however. In both England and France, most knights were dependent on a lord, owing him duty and loyalty. How that duty was expressed and what it entailed changed over time and circumstance.

It also seems that an ability to fight or command did not influence whether somebody would become a knight. Men were supposed to become knights if they held a knight's fee, which meant that any man holding land worth more than a certain amount would be compelled to knighthood; the criterion was primarily financial in the thirteenth century. Thus some men had the title of knight although they did not actually fight. Around 1192, Nigel de Longchamp scornfully called these men Holy Mary's Knights.

A knight would be expected to play his part in war, however. By 1241, if a piece of land in England was worth £20 per annum, then the owner was expected to either be a knight or pay the *scutage* to the king instead. In practice, many people probably fudged whenever possible and some lords may not even have known how many knights' fees they owed in service to their lord. There may have been between 1,200 and 1,500 knights in England at a given time, with numbers declining significantly from the middle of the thirteenth century. Coss suggests that around the middle of the twelfth century, English knights may have numbered as many as 4,000–5,000, including knights of lower social status and wealth.

In 1277, Edward I had 228 knights and 294 sergeants (some people sent two mounted sergeants instead of one knight). One reason for these diminishing numbers was the cost.

The average income of the lesser knights around the time of the *Domesday Book* was around 30s to £2 a year. They were therefore richer than a moderately well-off peasant in the eleventh century, but not significantly richer. This balances information available from Normandy at the same time, where the average Norman knight had a *fief de haubert* – enough to maintain himself, his horses and his equipment. Compare this to a minimum income for knights for the majority of the thirteenth century of £20 to £30 a year. From 1292, the minimum income expected of an English knight was £40 a year. £5 was the minimum for social respectability, so knights had moved significantly higher in their social and income status. There were, however, considerable expenses connected to knighthood as well: knights needed enough money to pay for equipment including horses, which meant a warhorse and at least one additional horse for riding outside of battle, plus a horse as beast of burden. Around 1250, the equipment of an English knight was about equal in value to one year's average knightly revenue. They also needed enough funds to pay for training.

Training for the fighting aspect of knighthood included horsemanship, fighting with several weapons and wrestling, as well as training for good general fitness, for instance through weightlifting. Hunting gave experience in scouting and in working with different types of terrain. Archery was an important part of this education, as was tilting at the quintain. The actual activities done as part of their drill or training done by knights are not easy to trace, and the closest thing to a drill manual for knights is the Rule of the Templars.

Being a knight became more expensive as time passed and armour became more extensive and costly. However, it was not only more expensive to dress and arm as a knight, it was also more expensive to act as a knight. Administrative duties increased and possibly ceremonial duties as well. In the thirteenth century, even more skills were added to the list of knightly essentials, meaning more expenses for training. Some of these skills included castle management and management and training of hunting dogs.

With the advent of special tournament armour, a separate set was needed for entertainment and jousts to actual fighting. These expenses were a reason for many potential candidates to not take up knighthood.

Because it was harder to be a knight, thirteenth-century rulers occasionally fined instead of giving someone a knighthood, especially in England in the 1250s. These fines helped maintain the numbers of men available to fight through using the funds to support recruitment. This added recruitment, however, may not have reversed the loss of fighters overall.

Regarding the actual number of mounted fighters, these are hard to calculate from records, which mostly begin from the thirteenth century. Chronicle estimates can be used as an indication, though their reliability may vary, and the numbers given or calculated vary between several hundred to almost 2,000.

The most important piece of equipment for a cavalry fighter was, obviously, the horse itself. Warhorses were bred for the task, and from the end of the thirteenth century, the warhorse was often described as the 'great horse'. The terms *magnus equus* or *grant chival* can be found in France by 1302 and in England from around 1313. This indicates a change in horse size through breeding: the size of military horses grew considerably from the eleventh to the thirteenth century. The smallest eleventh-century horses are depicted with the feet of the riders almost touching the ground, while the later horses are closer to modern riding horses in size. This increase in size reflected the military needs of the day, including the increase in weight of equipment the knight used.

Since horses are, in their basic nature, prone to running away from danger and conflicts, a warhorse also needed to be specially trained. A good warhorse was expensive to buy, to train and to maintain. Warhorses were stallions, never geldings or mares. This was probably partly due to stallions being more aggressive, but there was also a social implication to the sort of horse ridden: riding mares or geldings could be seen as odd, undignified or demeaning for a military man.

When a horse was killed on campaign for a lord, compensation was demanded. An average of thirty livres tournois was paid by Louis IX of France (r. 1226–70) on his crusade for each of 264 horses lost. Even though attacking or killing a horse was seen as unchivalrous in theory, practice was much different, and loss of horses in battle and even in tournaments was common.

Warhorses were equipped with a high saddle with supports and stirrups to keep the horseman stable. Riders rode with straight legs, according to illustrations, a very different style to the modern English rider's position. From about the twelfth century onward, warhorses were also equipped with armour. Equipment for saddlehorses included a saddle, bridle, saddlecloth and maybe additional cloth.

The saddle and other equipment used with horses could vary quite a bit. Harsh curbs, for instance, were used by the military as tools for battle and for tourney, while milder restraints could be used in other situations. The shapes of spurs were quite varied, including lozenge-shaped ones. The rowel spur was not introduced until the thirteenth century.

Foot Soldiers

Mounted fighting was not the be-all and end-all of medieval warfare. Soldiers on foot would, in most cases, have been considerably more numerous than the mounted part of an army. In some cases, even knights fought on foot, such as in the battles in Normandy in the early twelfth century. Knights also fought on foot during naval battles or in defence of castles, when the terrain was tough for horses.

Overall, however, foot soldiers of different kinds, including long-range fighters, made up substantial parts of medieval armies. As with cavalry, exact numbers are very hard to establish. Accounts from the late twelfth century mention non-mounted forces of about 300 to 2,000 men. While there are no accounts that can be depended upon as accurate totals of available, or employed, forces on foot, it seems that their numbers were rather small from the Norman period to about the middle of the thirteenth century.

Recruitment of foot soldiers from the middle of the thirteenth century through the reign of Edward I (1272–1307) took place on a much larger scale, although it still did not reach the number of modern infantry. Foot soldiers were also not deployed in the same manner as modern infantry. Calculations from the war accounts hint at numbers in the higher thousands for the non-mounted parts of the army. For instance, a recruitment drive in January 1283 brought about 5,000 men to the royal army. Within the army, the men were organised into smaller units of twenties and hundreds, with an officer for each twenty and a constable for each hundred.

The concept of a very large component of foot soldiers in armies was not completely abandoned later on, though numbers seem to have declined again towards the end of our period.

How and where the fighters were recruited is harder to tell than the recruitment of knights, as there was not as much formal obligation involved. There was the basic obligation for every man to help defend against enemy attack, though this was probably used to raise men for local defence in times of need. Recruitment for armies might have been local as well, but Henry II also experimented with several recruiting methods during his reign, including a system parallel to the knight service.

An important element in the recruitment was the payment. While men might fight under obligation to help defend against enemy incursions, they did not have to serve without receiving some payment to cover their costs. This was not a reward or a payment large enough to draw a lot of men voluntarily into fighting, but enough to provide the fighters with their subsistence needs. Payment for a normal foot soldier in the thirteenth century, for example, was probably higher than payment for a common agricultural labourer, but lower than that usual for a skilled craftsperson.

In addition, fighters could be offered a share of the proceeds of war, and men in prisons could be offered pardon in exchange for fighting. Ransom for captured enemies was another possibility to profit from war. It could include money, precious metals, property, arms, armour, prisoners or livestock.

How exactly the non-mounted fighters were equipped, regarding both their armour and their weapons, is hard to tell. The typical weapon of foot soldiers in Norman times seems to have been the bow, but detailed recruitment evidence from Norfolk in 1295 shows that men were provided with knives and swords. Armour and weapons had to be provided either by the fighters themselves or their local communities, and this could lead to very ill-equipped armies indeed. Cudgels, mallets or axes may also have served instead of swords or spears, and some sort of second weapon for close combat was part of an archer's war equipment, too.

Archers and Other Long-Range Fighters

Archers (both with longbow and crossbow) were a key aspect of medieval long-range fighting. A noble might fight using mainly lances, swords and other up-close equipment, but they knew something of archery through hunting. William I and his sons were all notable archers, even William II (r. 1087–1100), who died hunting. However, archery in a war situation belonged mostly to the foot soldiers, citizen militias, mercenaries and peasants. As time progressed, it slowly became more prestigious. In the thirteenth century, crossbowmen were given tax exemptions for training and were even able to compete for prizes in competition.

Archers could both be foot archers and mounted archers, and some of the accounts of warfare distinguish these groups from each other very clearly. The heyday of the mounted archer, though, was after our period. Archers were used to soften the enemy for an attack, and were often employed to cover both attacks and retreats, or to spring an ambush. Their placement depended on the tactics and the terrain and did not always mean they were well-protected: Orderic Vitalis noted that forty bowmen in the front rank of the English army brought down many of the enemy horses in the Battle of Bourgthéroulde. When archers defended a castle, they were generally posted on battlements and walls, sheltered by loops where possible.

Archers could inflict telling defeats on an enemy army, including killing the enemy leader. This, for instance, happened in 1066 to Harold Godwinson, in 1106 to Geoffrey Martel (the count of Anjou) and in 1199 to Richard I. Despite this usefulness, they were also more liable to be killed than knights, not being noble and therefore not being ransomable. In fact, they were not necessarily treated with much respect during our period: the bow was not considered a heroic weapon.

A typical bow was made from a stave of suitable wood with enough strength and flexibility. Yew is famous for being used for bows, but many other kinds of wood are also suitable. The bow was worked so that its arms bent equally under stress and fitted with a bowstring. To shoot, an arrow was fitted to the string, pulled back and released. Medieval bows were usually much heavier to draw than modern sport-shooting bows, with a draw weight of probably 100 lbs to up to 175 lbs; they were not held drawn. Archers could loose arrows in rapid succession. Pictures of archers show them neatly arranged in lines and ranks, and such a troupe could be easily directed to shoot in unison, achieving a rate of at least ten arrows per minute. The result was a cloud of arrows that was very visible and very audible, with a terrible and terrifying impact. When aiming for long-range, arrows could fly distances of several hundred metres, making the bowmen a very dangerous target to approach. Wooden bows tire out when left strung and also lose some of their shooting power over time; if mistreated, they may also break.

Crossbows had worse reputations than longbows. Norman archers used crossbows in the wars of 1066, for instance, which may be how this weapon reached England. The crossbow was a short mechanical bow mounted on a stock with a trigger release. Contrary to the longbow, it had to be tensioned with more strength than a normal person had in the arms; cocking the crossbow was thus typically done with help of a stirrup to employ one foot as well as both arms. Its short, thick, iron-tipped bolts could reach as far as 300 metres and had strong punching power. The crossbow was often associated with mercenaries (such as the Gascons employed by Edward I of England). Use of the crossbow against Christians was condemned at the Second Lateran Council in 1139. Until the end of the twelfth century, its use was more typical in southern Europe than in the north. Its use in England only became widespread in the late twelfth century. However, in the thirteenth century it was used in most places, with a larger variety used to defend fortifications.

Its main limitation was that preparation to shoot took time – much more time than taking another arrow to the bowstring with an ordinary bow. However, once the crossbow was cocked, it could be held ready to shoot for much longer than a longbow. From around 1200, it was used mounted as well as on foot in both England and France.

Finally, there was a bow often known as the short bow. It was small and was made of wood, horn and sinew. Typically, it was very powerful. It was probably rare in our places and period, although it appears in some manuscript illustrations. It was mainly used in the Middle East, especially by archers on horseback. In opposition to the Western longbow, this was a recurve bow that had a different balance between arm length and throwing power.

Much smaller than a bow or crossbow, but also an effective weapon and very easily concealed, was the sling. Fighters who used slings were employed, for example, in the siege of Exeter in 1136, brought in from distant parts according to the accounts. Slings could be used to throw small stones or metal pellets, delivering them with considerable force, easily able to kill a person when hit in the head. In contrast to bows and crossbows, slings were cheap and easy to make, easily repaired or replaced, much more robust in bad (wet and cold) weather, and could be used with one hand, enabling the fighter to carry a shield for his protection. However, using the sling accurately enough to make it as deadly as a bow or crossbow needs a lot more practice.

The use of projectiles in battle, however, was not limited to individual sling users, archers and crossbowmen, but also included larger artillery weapons. Medieval artillery can be roughly divided into three different groups, according to their source of power. One group, descended from the Roman ballista, used tension as source of power. These machines often looked like crossbows mounted on stands. Tension was built up in the throwing arms, much like in regular-sized crossbows.

The second group used torsion to accumulate energy for the shot. This group had a throwing arm that could be used to throw different objects, such as stones or pots filled with flaming liquids or quicklime. The third group also had a throwing arm, but this one was powered by a counterweight. Prime example for machines in this group is the trebuchet. The trebuchet had a range from around 80 metres to around 120 metres, with larger machines giving a bigger range. These machines became particularly popular as the period progressed, with great development happening from about 1180 to 1220. All of the various kinds of artillery machines were large or very large (modern reconstructions stand up to 18 metres tall) and needed considerable expertise to use with accuracy. There was actually a professional known as an *artillier* in the latter half of the thirteenth century. This was someone who made the machinery of war, especially bows and other weapons. The most widely used technology around 1300 included trebuchets. Their sophistication made specialist knowledge of increasing importance.

Weapons and Armour

As always in the history of warfare, the development of weapons and armour are closely related to each other. New materials or new styles of weapon are needed to counter the gradual improvement of armour, and better armour is developed to protect against the new weapons. Changes in fighting style, in their turn, are also interconnected with these developments.

Weapons and armour could mean a significant expense for a fighter, and the individual equipment was thus depending on several factors, including the wealth of the individual. To give an example, the basic equipment for a knight, apart from the necessary horses, included a lance, sword, spurs, helmet and some form of armour, such as a mail hauberk. The Assize of Arms, set out in 1181, laid down the duties of free men to have military equipment available in case of need; the most basic requirement for ordinary free men were a gambeson (a quilted protective garment for the body), a simple helmet and a spear.

Quilted and padded garments would also have been worn under the mail shirts. Mail hauberks, put together from rings riveted closed and solid rings, were a good protection against cutting weapons. They were, however, not necessarily a full protection against arrows. Hauberks were also an expensive item; the cheaper alternatives were cloth or leather armour. Cloth or leather armour could also be lighter than ring mail, which may have been helpful in some circumstances.

Ring mail could be used to protect the torso, arms and legs. Attached to a helmet or worn as a coif, it could also protect the neck. Gradually, from about 1250 onward, the mail hauberk got additions of plate pieces to protect knees, elbows, arms and legs as well as the chest. This started the development of full plate armour, which ended well after our period.

Protection of the head was achieved by using helmets. As they limited vision and communication, and more closed versions also possibly air supply, helmets were put on at the very last moment before an actual fight: in 1217 a squire reminded William Marshal at the battle in

Lincoln that he had yet to put on his helmet. There is discussion by modern experts about whether helmets could be decorated with paint, but evidence is rather patchy.

Finally, shields could offer flexible protection for the head, body and limbs – though they could also be used to hit the opponent. The shape of the shield changed from the Norman long, kite-shaped shield to a smaller, more triangular shield used by the mounted knight.

Weapons can chiefly be divided into whether they were used for thrusting, cutting, hitting and fighting from a distance. Typical weapons associated with medieval fighting were the sword and the lance, the main weapons of the knight. Swords were the prestige weapon. In the twelfth century, swords were relatively uniform in size and shape, and were used for cutting more than for thrusting. In the thirteenth century, new forms developed, and by the middle of the century there were specialised cutting and thrusting weapons as well as specialised cutting weapons, which were significantly bigger. Most swords were around 1.25 to 1.5 kilograms in weight.

Scabbards were made to suit the form of the sword or knife inside them, so they varied in form mostly with the swords contained. There are few archaeological finds of scabbards, and those date mostly from before our period, but similar scabbard types can be supposed for our time. Scabbards typically consisted of a leather outer hull around a wooden core that was itself lined with (lightly oiled) fur. Some were made of one piece of leather, stitched together with flaxen thread, while some had thongs which could then be tied in quite complex knots. Some were engraved, some stamped, some incised and some embossed. Since a sword was an expensive item, a proper sheath should not have added too much to the cost.

Lances were another major piece of weaponry. They were usually made from the wood of the ash tree and developed from lighter forms, suitable for thrusting or throwing, into more substantial versions that were used couched under the arm. The main strength of a couched lance was against other cavalry. Although there was mighty force behind it and high danger in using it, its main aim was actually to unseat the opponent and get them to yield (resulting in both ransom and victory). Lances were easily broken, however, and they depended on the combined momentum of horse and rider for their best effect. Swords and other weapons were more often used when killing was the aim. Despite this, our period was marked by the importance of heavy lanced cavalry and the concomitant importance of the knight carrying the lance.

Many other weapons existed and were in use, from maces and war axes, or long pike-like weapons, to knives and cudgels, and probably also regular tools such as hammers and axes. The latter especially, when employed by men that used these tools on a daily basis as part of their regular work in crafting or farming, should not be underestimated. Another weapon was the caltrop, used to hurt and hamper both foot soldiers and cavalry. An especially effective way of deploying them was throwing pots filled with iron caltrops and caustic lime.

There was also more than one type of explosive in the Middle Ages. For example, Greek fire was a petroleum-based explosive, a Byzantine invention, which reached England by the late twelfth century. It was used well into the thirteenth century.

Gunpowder was also known in France and England during our period, but seldom used. By the middle of the thirteenth century, it was known in both explosive and rocket formulae. Handguns may possibly have been known in the late thirteenth century, but the evidence is very unreliable. Even in the fourteenth century, they were rare. Cannon were not used until the fourteenth century.

Holy War

One of the common modern popular associations between war and the Middle Ages was the notion of 'holy' war. The reality is that there were wars that were backed by the Church and that had religious imprimatur. There were other wars, also regarded as holy by the populace, which the Church did not approve of.

For those who sought holy war, the desire to make Christianity the paramount religion was key. Also important (in the case of the Albigensian Crusade, for instance) was the desire to change local politics and to push for one single branch of Christianity. However, even wars that were proclaimed as holy, such as the First Crusade, were not necessarily considered as such even by participants. On the other hand, the People's Crusade, where Peter the Hermit, or Little Peter, raised around 15,000 would-be crusaders in central and northern France and the Rhineland, is an example of a holy war that was not considered such by the Church.

To understand the very mixed character of holy wars it is necessary, in fact, to study each war extensively.

War abroad, as most of the crusades and holy wars were, also led to problems for those at home. When John went to war in 1202–4, he levied 1/15 in imports and exports, and forbade the exports of weapons or of most foodstuffs. His brother's infamous 1195 Saladin Tithe (to fund a crusade) was more demanding still.

For those inclined to fight for their religious beliefs independent of holy wars, it was possible to take oaths to become a member of a fighting order. The Order of the Temple and that of the Knights Hospitaller were the most important of the military orders operating in England and France. Their aim was to preserve Christianity and to protect Christians (mainly through military means).

The Church militant did not only engage in religious wars, however. Members of the Church fought in normal wars as well. For example, in the late twelfth century, the Bishop of Auxerre (Hugh de Noyers) was part of the army and even fought against his king.

6

Nature and Culture
Living with the Land

The vast majority of medieval people lived in very close proximity to the land: landscape, climate and resources all had immediate effects on how they lived their lives.

People and their environment – both natural and human-made – always influence each other. When a society is strongly based on agriculture, this is even more the case. While government and religion gave the cultural and administrative frameworks for the Middle Ages, the land gave shape and rhythm to everyday life.

The following sections will give an overview of the environment in medieval England, from the shaped and unshaped landscape to exploiting the resources available. They will also explain the main environments built by people: villages and towns.

Landscape, Climate and Weather

Landscape, climate and weather naturally had a great influence on agriculture and harvests. But buildings, clothing and many aspects of daily life also reflected the general climate of the area.

What people saw when they looked out their doors or over the land from a hilltop varied according to region and even within regions. For instance, Sussex can be geographically divided into weald, down and coastal plain. These different landscapes have an influence on the climate and prevalent weather patterns that in turn help determine flora, fauna and cultural land use. Regional wind patterns, likewise, had a strong effect on local inhabitants and helped form their lifestyles.

At the very least, it should be understood that there were big differences between one area and another, such as the difference between highland regions and lowlands. Highland regions tended to be more isolated in terms of habitation and less rich in terms of farming than the lowlands. Highland regions are, among others, the north and east of England, the Pennines, Lake District, Northumbria, Dartmoor and Exmoor.

While the position of mountains or highlands as well as lowlands is usually the same today as in the Middle Ages, not all aspects of the land are as stable. Water levels, for example, can change significantly over time. This means that medieval wetlands, marshes, lakes and rivers were not always identical to their modern equivalents. River beds might have shifted and there may have been changes in river flow. For example, the Thames around London was quite different to today's Thames, as was the course and size of the River Rother in Kent and Sussex.

General climatic conditions can be reconstructed by pollen analysis made from samples taken during archaeological digs. This provides information about the different species of plants growing in the given region and thus indicates climatic conditions as well as the use of the land through indicator species.

Climatic conditions and thus the prevalent weather patterns during seasons can change over time. Since most weather, like most minor natural occurrences, goes unchronicled, it is not always possible to reconstruct climate and weather conditions for a given time and region. Written records are usually only available for extremes, when someone was interested enough to record the occurrences – provided that the records have survived. For some regions, individual calendars of wet/ dry/hot/cold weather, floods and famine can be reconstructed by using specific sources, such as monastic records. Records with the level of data needed for this are only available for very few specific places and times.

Chronicles and other sources, however, do allow an approximate reconstruction of the climate and typical as well as atypical weather of Continental Europe. From the ninth to the twelfth century, the climate was generally rather dry and sunny, enabling, for instance, grapes to be grown as far north as London and possibly even farther. The 1190s were very wet indeed, but there was also a series of soaking summers in the two decades from the 1140s to the 1160s.

Adverse weather had direct repercussions on daily life, much more so than it has today. Floods at Berwick in 1294 made the bridge across the Tweed collapse. The bridge was replaced by a ferry. Likewise, in 1282, great frosts in England caused many problems in stone structures. London Bridge was one of the more spectacular collapses, due to the lack of upkeep by Henry III's wife, with five arches collapsing in February. Even more dramatic was the collapse of Rochester Bridge, as the entire bridge fell. The great fire in London in 1133, however, had nothing to do with the weather.

Agriculture, Farming and Sustenance

Both climate and weather directly influenced the life and work of most people in the Middle Ages. It is therefore not surprising that many works of art celebrate the agricultural seasons, including numerous manuscript illuminations. It is in these works of art, through the archaeological records and in very occasional administrative texts that we find much of our knowledge about peasant and rural life.

By the start of the Middle Ages, humans had already been changing the land they live in for thousands of years. Land use and agriculture had left their traces on the landscape, ranging from small changes in plant and animal occurrences to significant changes in the shape of the land itself. Thus there was not much really wild, untouched land left in Europe. In England in particular, genuine wild land was hard to find.

Landscape shaping was not restricted to farming or improving arable lands. Distinctive shaping also took place where mining (for ore or salt), quarrying stone, digging for peat or similar activities took place. Land was also reclaimed for extension or building of ports. In England, for instance, the standard technique was to build a wooden revetment on the foreshore a bit out from the existing bank, and then dump rubbish in it until it was full.

Other landscaping involved parks and forests. There was upheaval when William I created the New Forest as a hunting ground. While research has shown they mainly comprised infertile soil, there was sufficient upheaval for chroniclers to report on royal forest very negatively. They wrote of villages being laid waste and families driven from their homes. Some even saw the death of William II in the New Forest as divine justice.

Most of the land, however, was formed and shaped for agricultural purposes. Managed rural land can be classified as arable land (good farming land), meadow (not as valuable as arable, but important for animal husbandry), pasture (more marginal than meadows, not very valuable) and wood.

Arable land could either be farmed permanently or intermittently. New arable land could be gained by *assarting*, which is transforming other land such as wooded or marshy areas into arable land or pasture. *Assarted* land was usually put into cultivation almost immediately and was a very important source of arable land.

Much fenland gave way to farming land in our period, with considerable drainage taking place. Dyke-reeves and voluntary cooperation between villages were a feature of this reclaimed land along the coast. Notable drainage in England took place in Romney Marsh (Kent), the Essex Marshes, the Somerset Levels and the East Anglia Fens (especially in south Lincolnshire and east Norfolk). All this land was colonised as new agricultural land, with new towns such as Emneth and Tilney in Lincolnshire built on it.

Woodland was important for timber, but also because its underwood offered a multitude of herbs and plants as long as it was not over-harvested. Woodland could be used for wild-harvesting and foraging.

There are certain key words which help explain how forest was defined: outwood, woodland, forest, chase, park and warren. Outwood was terrain reserved for the landlord's use, while woodland was accessible to tenants for the collection of dead wood to use as firewood and for grazing animals. Forest in general meant terrain where hunting happened and forest law applied. Forests were not necessarily virgin woodland, nor were they all, in fact, woodland. The entire county of Essex was technically forest, including its villages and farms. A chase was essentially a private forest, reserved for hunting and on a noble estate. Forest law generally did not apply to chases, which came under customary law. Despite this, the rights of chase often parallel those set up under forest law.

Parks were secure areas with mixed grassland and woodland, usually reasonably small and specially stocked for hunting (and possibly pleasure). Formal parks may have been introduced into England by the Normans, although there were at least thirty-six in England before 1066. The number of parks grew over time. The park's main purpose appears to be supplying the manor with venison and to act as an enclosed hunting ground. Many were also farmed as coppiced woodland. They had boundaries that were clearly marked, for example with cleft oak stakes in an earth bank alongside a ditch, a hedge or even a stone wall. This boundary was also important for keeping deer and other animals inside the park.

Most parks were around 100–200 acres, although a few could be considerably larger. Woodstock in Oxfordshire, for instance, was just over 11 kilometres around. It also sported a stone wall instead of the more typical bank and ditch. Parks had their own overseer, generally known as a parker in England. Some parks were established with the help of the Crown: Richard Montfitchet was given 100 deer from Windsor Forest in 1202 to help establish his park at Langley Marsh.

Warrens were special areas where rabbits and sometimes hares were stocked. Free warren, on the other hand, was when the lord of the manor was given the right by the Crown to hunt small game on their own estate.

Woods were carefully managed. Underwood was used for fuel and for making wattles, tools and hurdles. Tall trees in coppices (called 'standards') were often branchless for 3 or 4 metres, to create timber that was good for building. Big-branched trees were, in fact, mostly found outside woods and were not as useful as timber for building. Coppices with standards could be an important source of manorial income.

Woodland was very regional in terms of tree varieties. English native trees were primarily alder, ash, crab apple, elm, hawthorn, hazel and oak (with oak and ash the most common). A typical Essex forest would have mainly oak, hornbeam and ash, while the most important trees in northern France and the London basin were hawthorn and oak. Beech was the most common tree in the Chilterns, with birch also growing extensively there. Sherwood Forest was mainly oak or birch.

The greatest piece of woodland in England was probably the Weald, with its most important trees being oak and birch. In the late eleventh century, the Weald was over 50 per cent wood, according to recent estimates. This wood delivered timber and fuel for salt farming and charcoal production, and the charcoal was used locally to produce iron. Much of the Weald had tracks and swine pastures. Other great woodlands in England were in the Chilterns and some areas of the west Midlands.

Forests were also important sources of other produce in many areas. Careful management of them could lead to an immense richness and variety of harvest. Birds were hunted for sport or food, while pastureland supported horses, cattle and sheep, and pigs foraged for acorns in autumn. Other animals were hunted (both illegally and legally). Forests thus produced meat (for example from wild boar, deer, rabbit and hare), furs (from foxes, otters, martens, stoats and weasels) and bone and antlers. Fish could be obtained from streams. Almost any foodstuff, in fact, could be wild harvested. Coppices and woodlands provided wood for burning, for building, for fencing, for making clogs and tools, for reinforcing roads, for charcoal and to produce wood ash for soap. Wild fruit and nuts as well as fungi were foraged seasonally. Fern, moss and bracken served domestic uses and were also gathered. Wild honey could also be foraged, and, for industries such as the leather trades, bark could be obtained for tannin.

Finally, even wastelands were used for common pasture and were sources of turf, reeds, rushes, sedge, fish and fowl or drained to serve as permanent pasture, so it is understandable that truly wild lands were not easily found anymore.

Cultivated and managed lands – such as fields, grazing pasture, gardens and orchards – were marked and separated by boundaries. These boundaries varied (mostly regionally) from hedges and ditches, to streams, wooden fences and cob or drystone walling. Temporary hedges of cut thornbush were especially popular in England and north-west France.

There were several different types of field systems in use. The best-known field systems, which are also most often described in

English works on the subject, were the open field systems in use in the Midlands. These were usually farmed by the community, with good and bad land being ploughed communally and divided into strip fields for the actual crop growing. The strip fields were then allocated to families by lot, and thus good and bad land was shared fairly. There was at least one open field for each major village.

Both flora and fauna, especially in wooded areas, were much more diverse and rich than we are used to today, and included quite a few animals that are extinct today, such as the aurochs in France. Different species were found in different regions, depending on the climate, landscape and intensity of settlement. For cultivated or farmed species, it also depended on which plants and animals were preferred by the population. As forests diminished and wet areas were drained to add to farmland, and as human population increased, species diversity in areas such as forest and fen diminished. This applied in particular to the population of migratory species, such as birds, which was constantly changing. Due to England being an island, extinction of certain species was technically easier to achieve than on the Continent. However, this did not mean that species were extinct in England earlier than in France or in regions of the Continent.

Wild and Cultured Plants

Plants provided the bulk of foodstuff as well as building material, fodder for animals, raw materials for textiles and much more. There are several sources for learning about plants grown or available in the Middle Ages. Plants and their uses are documented in herbals and medicinal tracts, for example. Under good conditions, plant remains can also be preserved in the soil and evaluated after an archaeological excavation. Finally, pollen analysis can give some indication of what was growing in a given region and time.

Surviving herbals from the eleventh to the thirteenth century add up to over fifty different manuscripts in England alone. Most of these documents were used as references by physicians, apothecaries and scholars. The major sources of this theoretical knowledge included Pedanius Dioscorides (fl. 40–65), whose medicinal knowledge of plants was particularly important. Adaptations of his work included plants indigenous to Europe and those known only through trade or travel, seldom distinguishing between them. In fact, his work provided essential background for Western herbals, with an important new translation (known as *Dioscorides alphabeticus*) made around 1100. Herbals were nevertheless not the main source of knowledge in the Middle Ages. Most knowledge about plants and their uses would have been passed from person to person verbally.

Listings of general herbs in herbals included sage, parsley, dittany, fennel, hyssop, cumin, anise, pellitory, rose, lily and violet, while medicinal plants included mallow, agrimony, nightshade and chicory. Also named as plants for eating were cereals, beans, kale, borage, beet, leek, garlic, mustard, spinach, onions, peas and others, as well as fruit such as cherries, strawberries, grapes, figs and quinces. Species for wild harvesting included oak, beech, pine nuts, raspberries, wild strawberries, mulberries and blackberries, cornel, sloes, hazelnuts, hawthorn, box, buckthorn, bullace, poplar, willow and lime tree (linden). All of these could be cultivated as well. It is important to keep in mind, though, that medieval plant varieties were not necessarily the same as modern.

Some herbs and spices used commonly in the Middle Ages are considered toxic today, such as pennyroyal (*Mentha pulegium*) or mandrake (*Mandragora officinarium* or *Atropa mandragora*). Herbs and spices may also prove dangerous in certain conditions, especially during pregnancy. Plants that are very toxic, however, were known and of course not used for food purposes.

Trees cultivated in orchards in England included plum, damson, bullace, medlar, mulberry, quince, walnut, chestnut, hazel, hawthorn, blackthorn, briar rose and cornel cherry. Apple trees and pear trees would have been particularly numerous in England and Normandy. Some stone fruits were also grown, depending on climate. Peaches were available around the early thirteenth century, but only as a great luxury. Cherries were known in the north of France and probably in England from around the twelfth century.

The cultivated varieties were by no means the same as those on the market today and included fruits that were not intended for raw consumption. For instance, the warden pear needed cooking before it could be eaten. Different cultivated varieties spread into other countries, such as the pesse-pucelle, a type of pear introduced into England from France under Edward I. Popular apples around 1200 included the pearmain and the costard.

Trees also provided wood as a raw material for uncounted uses beyond timber for houses, furniture and ships, such as shoots for basketry work. Tree bast (an inner fibrous layer of bark) could be used to make ropes. Different properties of wood species were well known and the wood was selected accordingly. This also included the selection of wood types for use as fuel, with soft woods typically providing a fast-burning fire and hard woods burning longer and often also hotter. When the heat from a wood fire was not enough, the wood could be turned into charcoal with help of a charcoal kiln. Charcoal was also produced from different kinds of wood, depending on the intended use and the regional availability. It burned much hotter and with much less smoke than the original wood and was thus often used in industry.

Oak, birch and alder were particularly important trees in England and the north-east of France, with ash, lime and maple also making an appearance. Beech was mainly to be found in the south of England. These were not the only trees in these regions, but the ones with clearest modern evidence.

Ash was often found with oak, but was not usually harvested as heavily, as it was not as good a load-bearing tree for building. Ash wood is hard, heavy, yet tough and elastic, and was mostly used for tool handles and the frames and shafts of vehicles. Elm, also a tough and elastic wood, was probably more widely used than ash though still not as extensively as oak. Ash and beech were the cooper's preferred woods for making cups and bowls. Hazel was used extensively for wattle work and for thatching. Hornbeam and beech were also harvested for fuel, especially in London.

Other plants also found various uses; for example moss was used as insulation material, and a large variety of plants contained dyes used for textiles.

Most plants that were used were grown locally. Plants and foods that were imported had to store well to survive the transport or had to be conserved beforehand.

Wild and Domesticated Animals

Just like plants, animals are listed in books like encyclopaedias, but information about them can also be gained by animal remains found in archaeological excavations. It is sometimes possible to determine which kinds of animal lived in a place at a certain time using archaeozoological analysis of bones, but appropriate source material for this is only rarely available.

Medieval encyclopaedists divided the animal world into different groups. *Quadrupedia* were four-footed mammals. Anything that flew was grouped under *aves*, aquatic species under *pisces*. *Serpentes* were reptiles and amphibians, while *vermes* comprised insects and their larvae, worms, spiders and animals that didn't fit elsewhere. *Vermes* would thus also include common and often present parasites like lice, bugs or intestinal worms. Finally, there was a group for monsters and fabulous animals, including beasts such as dragons, unicorns and griffins in the bestiaries.

Animals were used as a source of food and raw materials for products, but also as farm or production animals in a wider sense – they were employed as working animals in farming, as beasts of burden, used for hunting other animals and for herding or keeping vermin in check or as pets for the amusement of adults and children. They were even used in the execution of criminals, for instance by tying them to a horse and dragging them. Animal manure was spread on fields as a fertiliser and their hair or wool was shorn and used for making textiles. The carcasses of slaughtered animals were almost entirely utilised: their skin turned into fur, leather, rawhide or parchment; their bones used for items like combs, awls, dice or paternosters; horn could be turned into semi-translucent plates, or it could be made into glue, as could the hooves. Animals and humans were in contact continuously, not only in rural areas. Domesticated animals were also kept in towns and cities: this included not only small animals such as poultry, but also larger animals such as pigs.

Animal husbandry was an important part of farming: animal products such as meat, skin, leather, milk, bones and horn were essential to daily life, and farm animals provided an important and controlled source. Domesticated animals also were the source of most of the meat consumed in the diet.

Compared with domesticated animals from twenty-first century breeds, most medieval animals were smaller. They also gave lower yields of meat, fleece and milk. Modern estimates regarding live weight of animals, fleece weight of sheep and milk output of milk animals, however, can differ quite widely. On the other hand, medieval domesticated animals were more resilient than modern overbred specimens. In addition, they were not bred to high specialisation, but did deliver for example meat, milk and fleece in the case of sheep, or meat and milk in the case of cattle.

Animal husbandry was seasonal, much more so than today. For instance, pigs or cattle were mostly slaughtered in November or December, supplying meat for the winter season and reducing the number of animals to feed. Dairy cows, breeding and working animals or those needed for meat in the future were not slaughtered unless the family was suffering great hardship.

Large numbers of sheep and cattle denoted wealth, as did the increased amounts of fertiliser available because of the animal numbers. Breeding of animals was done after rules gained through experience, and neutering of horses, cattle, pigs and birds was also possible.

Small animals, such as poultry, were kept in towns and cities as well as in rural settlements. Birds provided a source of fresh meat throughout the year, as well as eggs. Eggs were also seasonal. Hens needed very little space and could thus be kept easily in towns; geese and ducks required more ground. Dovecotes were more likely to be found on land owned by the more prosperous in society, including well-off peasants. Generally, the numbers of managed poultry increased continually throughout the Middle Ages.

Farming of larger animals was often migratory. This usually meant grazing or foraging in higher grounds such as hills or mountains in the summer, and returning to the warmer valleys for winter. A common migration phenomenon was transhumance, which is the long-distance migration of herds. The animals and their herders could cross political borders during this migration. In rural areas with no strong migration, it was common practice to let animals forage in the wider area and on common ground. Often they were taken quite far from their home to preserve nearby fodder for the harsher weather. Herders – such as shepherds and swineherds – supervised the foraging animals. They were fed on the fallow land, but were also allowed to graze on the stubble left after harvesting, and their manure provided fertiliser.

With the great role of foraging in animal husbandry, herding was an important job. Shepherds had special customary rights in many places. For instance, many shepherds had the right to a bowl of whey throughout summer and ewe's milk on Sunday, a lamb at weaning time and a fleece at shearing. Often, they were permitted to graze some of their own sheep with the lord's, thus getting access to better pasture. Another customary right was to keep the lord's flock on their own land for the two weeks near Christmas, which fertilised their land.

The number of beasts on the land was often controlled locally according to the capacity of the land, which means it was seldom controlled by individual farmers. In Cold Ashby in 1231, for example, the local abbot and then lord of the manor agreed that for every 60 *virgates*, there would be no more than four oxen or cows, four pigs and twenty-four sheep.

Milk animals in England were mostly sheep and cows. Cattle were also a source of meat and labour, but quite expensive to keep. In winter, cattle ate hay, straw and sometimes peas and vetches. Other animals that were less demanding were given less attention in terms of fodder, due to its expense. Cows were generally not added to the breeding stock until they were four years old.

There was a change of main dairy animal from sheep in the eleventh century to cows in the thirteenth century. In the thirteenth century, sheep were used mainly for growing wool for the wool trade, especially in regions such as Lincolnshire, Yorkshire and the Midlands. Sheep could be farmed for large-scale wool production for international markets, or could be farmed on a small scale for cloth for local use. Short wool sheep were farmed on the poorer pasture, as a rule, especially near the borders of Wales and Scotland, on the Yorkshire moors or in the chalk downlands. Sheep with longer wool were farmed on rich grasslands, fens and marshes, with the best quality wool produced in Lincolnshire, followed by Yorkshire, Shropshire and Hertfordshire. There have been no finds yet that would be classified as modern long wool, that is, none have a fibre length of 160 mm or more. Archaeologically, it can be very difficult to distinguish between sheep and goat since their bone material is extremely similar. Goats were hardy creatures that delivered meat, milk and hair for textile production, so a substantial goat population can also be expected.

Pigs were common, although their numbers went down as the woodland was progressively *assarted*, since they were often herded into woodlands for foraging. With the diminishing number of pigs, more cattle were husbanded from the high Middle Ages onward.

The horse was a special case in animal husbandry. Though horseflesh could be eaten, horses were generally bred for other reasons, most importantly for use as a means of transport. Horses were not common until the eleventh century, but breeding efforts ensured that they grew in numbers from the eleventh to the thirteenth century. Most medieval horses were noticeably smaller than modern types of horse.

Horses were carefully bred, and import or export of horses was often restricted. There is considerable discussion as to which modern types of horse are closest to the medieval breeds.

Different breeds of horses were suited for various lines of work. The great variety of uses for horses can be seen from the many different names: sommeliers (packhorses), rounceys, palfreys, sumpters, hackneys, pads, hobbies and the well-known destriers used for battle. Cavalry horses were part of most military endeavours. Draught horses were used in farming, partly replacing oxen in the thirteenth century; they were better able to plough heavy soils. Horses were also used for pulling carts or wagons. Lighter riding horses were needed for travel, leisure and messenger services. Horses underwrote civilised life and could be very valuable animals. A good horse did not only make work or travel easier, but was also a status symbol. The disadvantage of horses is their high maintenance cost: good quality feed is needed for horses, and grooms were often employed to care for them. Donkeys and mules were less prestigious and less expensive than most horses. However, using mules for riding and transport did not necessarily indicate low status.

Pets were also not unknown, from singing birds to lapdogs for the entertainment of nobles. Cats were kept to kill vermin and for their fur, while dogs were bred for specific purposes, especially for hunting or to keep them chained as watchdogs. Some pets were quite exotic to our views today: an abbess in Romsey kept monkeys, renowned for their nuisance value. However, images of pets shown in illustrations might be misleading: small furry animals depicted with ladies were symbolic of sexual lust, and squirrels especially were used as a euphemism for the penis. Likewise, men could be shown with animals to hint at their lust.

Between the truly domestic animals and the truly wild animals were many different levels of control by humans. Animals such as deer species or rabbits could be farmed by keeping them in enclosures. This method was especially used with non-native species such as the fallow deer (*Dama dama*), which were introduced by either by the Normans or the Romans and kept in deer parks, or with rabbits, probably introduced sometimes in the twelfth century and kept in rabbit warrens. Farming of animals was not restricted to land creatures, but was also done with birds such as swans, peacocks, partridges and pheasants. Millponds and artificial ponds were used for fish production and weirs could be used to trap fish. Monasteries often had their own ponds to ensure fish supply. In towns, ditches could be an important part of the rights of charter for boroughs because of the fish in them. Finally, managed bees provided honey and beeswax, both important products.

Many wild animals were hunted: this was both a means of provisioning and, for the nobility, a leisure activity. Wild boars were mainly found in remote and dense woods and were a prestigious, but dangerous, quarry for hunters. Evidence is less clear on whether some other wild species, such as wild cat varieties, were hunted or not.

Seafood and wild fish were also very popular as food, especially (for obvious reasons) in regions where it was readily available. Whales, porpoises and sturgeon were generally regarded as royal fish, though fishermen who found a beached whale were usually permitted to have the carcass minus its head or tongue. In addition to nets, fishing rods, fish traps and fishing spears were used. The fishing industry was particularly busy in summer when the herring run started in the North Sea and moved south down the coasts of England and France.

Overfishing was already a danger in the Middle Ages, and people were aware of it. For instance, Philippe IV of France ruled in 1289 that certain types of nets were forbidden or only allowed during certain seasons; he also regulated the mesh width to prevent overfishing.

Animals were considered differently according to their rank in a perceived hierarchy. Hunting birds, for instance, were the most valued of birds, while species caught for food were at the bottom end of the hierarchy. Similarly, a warhorse would be prized much more than a packhorse or a mule. Possession of animals – hunting birds, caged birds, valuable dogs and horses and exotic animals – could be a status symbol as well.

The close contact between animals and humans everywhere brought with it animal-related problems and accidents. For example, deer could use crops as a ready food source, thus endangering the livelihood of peasants. Predators such as wolves could kill both livestock and people; they were thus often feared and hated. Wolves were numerous and in frequent contact with humans. They turned especially dangerous when they were hungry, for instance during a hard winter. Wolves were hunted down with all possible means: wolf traps, poison and special hooks baited with meat (*hamecon de loup*) that tore the animal up from the inside. In England, exiled nobles were allowed to return if they were able to kill a certain number of wolves. This all led to the wolf being close to extinction in England by 1281. Peter Corbet was hired to kill all remaining wolves in the western counties in that year.

Despite this, wild predators were not the only – and often not the greatest – danger to humans. Even non-predatory domestic animals could be a direct danger. For instance, several cases of children being killed by pigs were reported in medieval texts. Sometimes, especially from the thirteenth century on, those animals were then put to trial and formally sentenced to death.

The trials against animals that are documented from the thirteenth century and later hint at a slowly changing view of the fauna, seeing them as more akin to humans. This changing view was, however, still very far from our modern stance. The concept of animal rights or the protection of animals, as is quite widespread today, was not common at all. Some scholars argued that charity and love were only meant for human beings and were wrong towards animals. Applying the rules for interaction between humans to animals was a sin according to Church rulings. The saints who interacted with animals and refused to kill them or even healed them did so because they saw the animals as parts of God's creation which should not be disturbed, or as symbols for a higher truth, such as the lamb as symbol for Jesus. Animals were generally believed to be without a soul, which permitted treatment that would be unacceptable today. For example, tethered birds were held as toys for small children or as practice targets for shooters, and a boy whipping a horse for fun was seen as normal. Laws that protected animals were not introduced for the animals, but to protect the interest of their owners or of humans in general. However, not all animals were treated badly, and there is also evidence for loving relationships between animals and their owners.

Farming

Farming and farming tasks were very typical, and the bulk of the population was at least partly occupied with farming work. Thus farming provided the backbone of the society: it formed settlements and was of key importance to the economy. Even town dwellers lived closer to the land than many modern Westerners, since the seasons could be seen in what food and which materials were available and in what work could be done. Many also had some access to land for farming or gardening.

Arable lands were measured in units based on the use of the land. The basic unit was the *diurnale* or *hide*, defined according to different sources as either how much could be ploughed in a day or how much land was necessary to feed a family for one year. Larger units were also used for description: a *carrucate* was how much a single team could cultivate in a season, and a *bovate* was what a single ox could plough in twelve months (which was around seven to sixteen hectares generally). The actual amount of territory this covered depended on factors such as terrain, fertility of the soil, soil structure and climate.

The wealth of farmers depended very much on the amount and quality of the land. Depending on local or regional custom, inheritance rules could lead to a farm and its fields being divided between several people, thus changing the look of the land and the value of individual farms. Cottars in the late thirteenth century generally farmed less than 4 acres, while the more prosperous farmed 5–20 acres. The wealthy, who farmed a full *virgate* (two *bovates*) as a minimum, often had properties of 20–40 acres.

In addition to the crops needed for subsistence, those who could manage to do so grew cash crops as well. These were mostly to pay rents, but also to buy household goods, farm equipment and other items that were not made on the farm.

While farmers in most regions of England would be able to grow enough for a living and maybe a little extra, very small farms, especially with poor soil, did not always yield enough for living. These very poor farmers often hired themselves to those who were richest for additional income. Other additional income to help make ends meet could come from industry (such as brewing, textile work or carpentry) and charity. Farmers with and without these additional industries made up the bulk of population in a village.

Crops were farmed using a cycle of rotation, with the crops used in the rotation depending on the region. Rotation was either biennial, with a field planted one year and left fallow the next, or, more frequently, a three-field rotation. The three-field rotation cycles went from winter cereals (wheat and rye) planted in autumn, to spring cereals (barley and oats) and legumes, both planted around March or April, to leaving the ground fallow. Crop rotation was important in ensuring good crops.

The land was prepared by opening the soil. This could either be done by ploughing or by turning the soil with a spade and, if necessary, breaking earth clods. Ploughs could be drawn by humans or with the help of animals. By the late eleventh century, most heavy work on the land was done by oxen where possible, that is where there was sufficient wealth to keep an ox or an ox team. In the thirteenth century, horses started being commonly used and might have taken over a large part of this work by the late thirteenth century.

Fertilisers were also used. We know about several different types, including chalk, sea sand, seaweed, animal dung (which could be bought or produced locally), straw (either ploughed in or buried), lime, marl and compost. Fields were also blessed to ensure good harvests, and religious or magic rituals were carried out. Despite this, average yields were probably significantly below current levels.

Seed was sown by broadcasting. Not all seed sown was one variety alone, such as wheat or oats. Some was mixed – *dredge* or *drage* was barley mixed with oats, *maslin* was rye and wheat. The grain depended heavily on the region.

Workers would walk up the land casting the seed in one direction, casting it in the other direction on the way back. The land was then immediately harrowed to cover the seeds. When the cereal was ready for harvest, it was cut with a sickle, then left in small piles to partly dry. It was then tied in sheaves and set up in shocks to allow it to ripen fully and dry. It was threshed two to three weeks later (around August). Remaining produce was gleaned after harvesting. Communities frequently restricted gleaning to the poor, to help ensure they had enough to live on.

Two-wheeled carts might be used for transporting the harvested goods; wealthy households might use carts with four wheels. Other farm equipment included a great variety of tools and implements for a great range of tasks, ranging from daily household activities such as cleaning and cooking to farm tasks such as building sheds, ploughing, planting and harvesting as well as animal husbandry. Equipment ranged from nets and traps, through knives, buckets and brooms, to mattocks, ladders and wheelbarrows.

Over our period, agriculture by and large became more crop-intensive. Farming of arable lands and crops was intensified from about the eleventh century, which may have reduced the amount of meat in the diet as grain increasingly became the focus of farming. Cereal production was thus a focus of the vast majority of peasants, even in mixed-farming areas.

The Paris region was well known for its grapes, especially the vineyards of the abbey of Saint-Germain-des-Prés, and the vineyard of the abbey of Saint-Denis. England was a major destination for the wines produced at these abbeys, as there were not as many grapes grown for wine in England.

While vineyards were exclusively for growing grapes, gardens and orchards served for the cultivation of many different plants. Orchards were stocked with trees bearing fruits and nuts; the exact kind of tree depended very much on the climate and, thus, the region. The most general word for garden was *hortus* or *ortus*, and a gardener was frequently called an *ortulanus* or *gardinarius*. In England, a garden was mostly called a yard or equivalent, which was translated into *gardinum*, *ortus* and *virgultum*. The actual meaning of the word was land with grass, trees and cultivation, often enclosed by a wall, hedge, fence, wattle fence or ditch. Some gardens had kerbed stone paths. Words for places of residence, such as croft or cottage, often implied a garden.

Gardens also existed in towns, where they served similar purposes as gardens in rural areas: they were mostly used for private sustenance, though a few were used to generate income, especially around major towns. Their decorative value was also much appreciated. Some of the variety of gardens is reflected in the medieval Latin words used to name them: *pomerium* was an orchard to produce fruit for the table or for sale, *viridarium* or *virgultum* was an orchard which was grown more for pleasure, a *gardinum* was a kitchen garden, while a *herbarium* was a specialised garden, which for example produced herbs for medicine or grew flowers for use or for sale.

In addition to the mostly functional gardens, there were also what might be called pleasure gardens. There was no completely strict division between pleasure garden and functional garden, however, and pleasure gardens might also have been used for produce. Most evidence we have for pleasure gardens comes from the late twelfth century and after.

Pleasure gardens could be quite large, with a size of up to 8 acres not uncommon. A typical pleasure garden would have rich soil and a turf-based lawn planted round with sweet-smelling plants such as basil and sage. Square gardens might have plantings arranged to correspond with their four quarters. Lawns could be rolled or beaten to compress the turf and make them even and attractive. There was a level and large lawn at Westminster Palace, known from a 1259 illustration. Lawns could be used for sport as well. There would also be flowers, for example violets, lilies and roses. Seats and shade trees were provided for enjoyment, with some of the shade trees chosen for their perfume or fruit. Some gardens might also have boasted water features.

The nobility often had gardens that were designed to impress, perhaps linked to a park. There is some suggestion that the gardens of the wealthy grew in size in the thirteenth century.

Henry I bought land outside Windsor Castle in around 1110 to make a garden. He also had a stone-walled enclosure at Woodstock, which sported exotic animals. These were not his only gardens, however; he had more, for example at Kingbury and Havering. The Tower of London had two pleasure gardens: a small walled one inside the premises, and one outside, on Tower Hill. Other notables, like Hugh de Noyers at the very end of the twelfth century, also had fenced enclosures so that they could keep animals. Technically, animals kept in a garden were kept for aesthetic purposes, and those kept in a park were farmed for use. Just as with the plants, this boundary might have been quite blurred in practice.

Where there was no formal garden, plants might still be used to beautify a building. Wells Cathedral, for example, had elms planted outside its west front in 1243 while it was still unfinished.

Typical tools for tending gardens were iron-shod spades (wooden spades with an iron rim) and probably picks and narrow hoes with long blades. Pottery watering pots are known from as early as the eleventh century, though it is hard to tell how common they were. They were often shaped like narrow-necked bottles, with a flat, perforated base. A small hole at the top enabled the user to control the water flow using his or her thumb.

Other Resources and Their Exploitation

Many medieval industries relied on the exploitation of resources from plants and animals, but others needed metal, clay or stone. Their exploitation was also closely tied to land use and to ownership. For instance, mineral rights were largely the property of the king; concessions to work the mines were obtained from the ruler, in return for royalties.

Metal

Metal is a very versatile material, and metals were thus very important and widely used. They can be grouped into ferrous metals, non-ferrous metals and precious metals. Ferrous metals are iron, steel and iron or steel alloys (all ferrous metals are magnetic). Non-ferrous metals are metals with no appreciable amount of iron. Precious metals used in the Middle Ages were silver and gold; technically these are also non-ferrous metals, though they are often grouped separately due to their much higher value.

Only very few metals can be found as native deposits. These include silver, copper and gold. Other metals have to be processed from ores. Native metals as well as ores can be extracted from the ground by mining. Ore deposits closer to the surface are easier and safer to exploit than deep deposits, and surface mining was thus the preferred method of extraction during the Middle Ages.

While some larger mines existed, ores were mostly mined on a smaller scale. This was either done by farmers having mining rights and exploiting ore resources on their own lands or by specialist miners working on a small scale. The latter may also have been itinerant miners. Specific isotopic fingerprints of metals can even make it possible to link a metal item to the mine where the ore came from.

Many different non-ferrous metals and alloys were in use during the Middle Ages. The most important metals were tin, lead, copper, zinc, silver and gold. Of these, tin, lead and silver were mined in noticeable quantity in many places. For example, in the southern French region of Massif Central, mainly lead and silver were mined in the eleventh and twelfth centuries. England not only saw mining of these two metals but was, in fact, the major European producer of tin. Tin and lead prospectors were allowed to look anywhere for their metal except for gardens, orchards, churchyards and the highway. They were permitted to cut wood, dig peat, divert watercourses and make roads. They even had their own courts.

Devon and Cornwall had been major sources of tin for a very long time. A lot of it was cassiterite, readily available from alluvial deposits. It only needed washing and smelting in a peat or charcoal fire before it was useable. Tin was taxed, which means we have better records of it than for other metals. For instance, in 1198, 869 lbs of tin were produced (or at least made it to the taxation records) and Jewish tin miners were recorded.

Lead was so crucial to so many industries that it is reasonably well documented. Not only was lead important in itself, but since it was often found together with silver, it was also mined for its silver content. Lead mining in England was concentrated at Alston Moor, Yorkshire, the Peak District in Derbyshire, Flintshire, the Mendips and south Devon. The Derbyshire mines were the source of much lead used on the Continent.

Lead miners could work independently, with a percentage of the ore found going to the owner of the mineral rights, or they could be employed on a piece-work basis. In 1298, at the Beer Alston mine, miners were paid 5s for a load of ore (each load consisting of nine dishes, each around twenty-seven kilograms). If a miner was prospecting, he was paid a low daily wage.

The production of lead was not always trouble-free, despite its importance. In the 1170s, for instance, the political disruption in England caused lead production in northern areas to trickle, which caused a lot of problems down the line for builders and craftsmen, and for the miners themselves in terms of making a living.

Copper was mined from the thirteenth century in Cornwall, Cumberland and Yorkshire. However, it was far more likely to have been imported raw into England during our period. Coppersmiths worked at the mine, doing the initial smelting of the metal. Some of these smiths travelled from place to place to obtain work, as the mines were small and shallow with a rather low yield.

In contrast to non-ferrous metal, iron and steel cannot be found as native metal, and thus were extracted from ores by smelting. Iron as an ore was very common in both England and France. Smelting the ore was a lengthy process quite similar to smelting copper, but requiring higher temperatures and thus considerably more fuel. Charcoal was used to heat the specially built kilns, and the resulting material – iron with fairly high amounts of impurities and carbon – had to be worked by hammering and reheating to clean and homogenise it. Smelting and refining required considerable expertise.

The most important sources for iron in the Middle Ages in England were the Forest of Dean, the Midlands, South Yorkshire, Cumbria, Durham and Northumberland. In the twelfth century, the Forest of Dean had a near monopoly on iron for the southern counties, and used Gloucester as its distribution centre. The Forest of Dean was still important in the thirteenth century, though its status was challenged by the Weald (Sussex and Kent), which had the advantage of being closer to London. International sources of iron included Sweden and Germany.

Mining and smelting activities had strong and long-lasting effects on the forest cover and the soil quality, leading to changes in vegetation and to pollution of the soil with lead isotopes. These traces can be used by scientists today to find otherwise undocumented mining areas.

Clay, Stone and Sand

Clay, stone and sand might seem much less spectacular than metals at first glance, but they were no less important as a resource. For instance, most pots were made of clay; stone was used for representative buildings and sand was the main ingredient for making glass.

Clay was not only crucial as potter's clay; it was also essential for making daub-and-wattle walls. Tiles, including decorative floor tiles, and building bricks were also made from clay.

Raw clay could come from a variety of places and could usually be dug up rather easily. For example, around 1275, clay was excavated from the Tower of London moat and sold to local tilers. Raw clay was processed into pottery or building clay by homogenising it and mixing it with additional materials depending on the intended use.

Stone was also used in a wide variety of ways and for many purposes. Quarried and sometimes shaped stone was used as foundation and building stone or turned into sculptures. Stone slabs were used for roof tiles; slate was especially suitable for this. The use of stone depended on its type, quality and availability. Limestone and sandstone were most often used for building and sculpting purposes.

Hillsides or riverbanks were stripped of their topsoil when stone was quarried. Poor quality, friable stone came away in small pieces. This rubble was used as cheaper building material, for instance for simple functional walls, for foundations of houses or to fill up the core of thick walls (such as those of castles). Blocks of stone were cut and extracted using iron wedges.

Limestone rubble or chalk was fired into caustic lime using lime kilns. Chalk in particular was quite readily available in much of England. Caustic lime is best known today as a component of mortar, but it was also an ingredient for paint and for glue.

The price of stone depended on its availability, quality and on the demand for a specific stone type at the time. A dark limestone variant known as Purbeck marble, for example, was outstandingly popular in England from around 1170, with demand particularly strong after 1250, and some of it was even exported to Normandy. The vast bulk of surviving worked Purbeck can be found in churches, especially in tombs and funerary monuments. Purbeck marble effigies were especially commissioned from around 1230 to 1280. In thirteenth-century London, marblers set up shop to shape and sell Purbeck marble.

The French equivalent of Purbeck marble was Tournai stone, which was also imported into England. It was used chiefly for architecture, graves, monuments and ornaments.

Sand was used as a filler in clay for pottery, as material for building purposes (such as one of the ingredients of mortar) and also as the main raw material for making glass.

Finally, special earths such as ochre were used as pigments. A mixture of clay and other substances was known as fuller's earth and was used for finishing textiles.

Peat and Coal

Apart from wood and charcoal, other fuels that could be used were peat, sea coal and brown coal. Peat is formed by partially decayed vegetation, especially moss, in wetlands. It was dug where it was available and dried before use as fuel. The most spectacular instance of peat harvesting was probably in Norfolk, where around 900 million cubic feet of peat was dug, creating the Norfolk Broads.

Both sea coal and brown coal can be found in deposits close to the surface in some regions; black coal requires deeper mining and was not in use in the Middle Ages. There was very little use of both sea coal and brown coal relative to modern usage, though; the big change in fuels only occurred in the eighteenth century. All types of coal were useful for very hot fires needed for industries, especially for smelting ores, blacksmithing or glass making, but may also have been used in better situated homes and kitchens.

7

Working and Making
Craft and Artistry

Raw materials grown and harvested, collected from the wild, or obtained by mining and quarrying were turned into items for special as well as everyday use by a variety of craftspeople.

A lot of the medieval items that are regarded as art today were not crafted as art pieces, but as items with a purpose, for example holding relics or serving drinks. This holds true even for most paintings and sculptures. Altar paintings, for instance, were needed to educate and aid in worship. Pieces considered to be art today were a means of communication, teaching and remembering, intended for everyday use or brought out as part of festivities. The modern concept of 'artist' is hard to fit to this: the vast majority of medieval art and architecture was made by craftspeople whose names are unknown today. These craftspeople would, however, have developed reputations for their fine work and good quality, and would have been known to their contemporaries. The art of the Middle Ages was no less appreciated because it was also (or perhaps mostly) regarded as high-quality craftwork.

One aim of modern art history research is to try to distinguish artists, scribes or individual workshops by their characteristic traits. Evidence suggests they were mostly lay people, though monastic artists certainly existed as well.

Today, medieval art is often described with the terms Romanesque and Gothic. These are modern terms that originate from the description of architecture, and they refer not only to a style, but also indicate an era of origin. Neither of them was known or used contemporaneously. In addition, the term Gothic has gone through a variety of nuances in meaning: in the eighteenth century it referred to disorder, patchiness or an over-ornamented mess.

Romanesque architecture, which was heavily influenced by Roman, Byzantine and Islamic designs, was characterised by rounded arches and horizontal lines. Just after 1000, a variety of vaulting systems began to appear, and the size of the Romanesque buildings increased over time. Barrel vaults were typical for the early Romanesque period. The British Isles developed their own variation of the style after the French Norman Romanesque was imported to England after the invasion. This is characterised by extreme length as compared to the more vertical building style on the Continent.

As the Romanesque style developed, it included pointed arches and rib vaults. Pointed arches were known during the eleventh century, but were chiefly used from the twelfth century. Rib vaulting was known in England by 1100. Durham Cathedral, where building started in 1093, sports this type of vault. When the ribs in these vaults changed from being decorative into being constructive, the development that led to the Gothic style began.

Perhaps the only true Gothic invention was the flying buttress, since most of its other elements had already been used in Romanesque buildings. However, the typical Gothic style equalled more than the sum of its parts. Mature Gothic style is strongly connected to rib vaults, a prominent verticality and a light and airy feel due to high vaults, slender-looking columns and large windows. The iconic flying buttresses that make the outer appearance of Gothic churches so distinct developed as a structural device for this airiness. While earlier vaults were supported either by the walls directly or by buttressing that was concealed in the design of the walls, the flying buttresses took this support away from the walls. This allowed the architects to build thinner walls that included very large windows. Flying buttresses may not have appeared until about 1175 at places like Notre-Dame de Paris, and the peak in their use was from 1195 to 1230.

The hub of architectural development was France, and style changes travelled from there throughout Europe. In England, Gothic style began in the 1160s, while it came considerably later – in the beginning of the thirteenth century – to Germany and Italy. Early Gothic was not a unified style, and while the later Gothic style from the thirteenth century onward was dominated by the influence of Chartres (1194), Reims (1212) and Amiens (1221), there were adaptations and distinctive variations of the style in Europe.

The Gothic period is generally divided into several different stages. English Gothic has been given the labels Early English Gothic, Decorated Style and finally Perpendicular Style. Lincoln Cathedral (finished between 1192 and 1270) with its extremely long nave and Purbeck marble accents is a typical example of English Gothic style.

Large churches and cathedrals of both Romanesque and Gothic style would have dominated the landscapes around them. Their splendour was meant to show God's greatness, the large stained-glass Gothic windows intended to give a glimpse of heaven. However, a few people deplored these churches as being built on usury, avarice and general wrong-doing.

There is less surviving architecture from other medieval buildings, both public and private. For these buildings as well, France – northern France in particular – led in style, in innovation and in technique. Our period was one of the great periods in Western European architectural history and saw an amazing flourishing in growth in building techniques and growth in major building projects. This, however, was overwhelmingly a phenomenon of the Christian community. Very little Jewish architecture survives. And while synagogues resembled other buildings of their time, following the change from Romanesque to Gothic style, the Christian community often demanded that they be unobtrusive buildings. Not even the most prosperous Jewish community was permitted to build a Jewish equivalent of the great cathedrals.

Just as with other developments in technology, art and fashion, change in architecture was not instant. Different buildings constructed at the same time may show features typically considered earlier or later. A single building can show earlier or later architectural traits, since construction work took its time, and styles could be adapted to more modern looks while the work was still going on. Finally, regional preferences and style differences, personal preferences of the architect or the constructor, or the wish to emphasise continuity with an older building were influences on how a building would look.

Crafts

There was a vast range of crafts undertaken in the Middle Ages, using a wide array of materials as well as specialist tools. Despite this, crafts have not been classified as holistically as architecture, though some craft items also show changes typically connected to a timespan or fashion phenomenon.

Medieval people in general were in closer contact to crafts than modern people are. For example, anyone who wanted to build a house would have to be in contact with different craftspeople, such as carpenters, maybe masons, roofers, smiths for metal fixtures and fittings, plasterers, painters, possibly also glassmakers and, of course, general labourers to do menial work. Good-quality work would have been recognised more easily by a wider range of people than today and appreciated for its level of craft skill; the same is true for complex and especially time-consuming items.

While much craft work was done as a part of regular household work (such as spinning or smaller-scale woodworking), craftwork was equally likely to be undertaken professionally. Some towns had good reputations for certain crafts, such as London for silk work and embroidery and Paris for goldsmithing.

The main aim of a craft was not personal entertainment such as in hobby crafts today, but to make necessary items. Thus crafting tended to make efficient use of both energy and equipment. Nevertheless, a lot of time was invested in some craft processes, for example in making fine textiles or exquisite bookcovers.

Techniques and tools are in many cases forgotten or were transformed gradually into other techniques, so it is not always possible to reconstruct processes. This is also a reason why craft research is difficult. Very often, basic techniques seem to be very similar to those still used today in traditional crafting, but details of tools, techniques or materials have changed. In many processes used in crafts, these changes are crucial and have a huge impact on the process as a whole. Furthermore, there were different means to achieve the same end: varying tools or processes can be used to make almost or completely identical items. Tools were usually rather simple, but used with efficiency.

Finally, a large number of craft techniques were not documented in detail during the Middle Ages. Techniques only done by a small number of professionals, or mostly used by people for their own needs, may not have been documented at all.

Craftspeople produced goods for international, regional and local markets as well as for household use. Goods thus ranged widely in quality. For items that covered basic needs, such as an axe or a bucket, quality might be different, but the form tended to stay stable over a long time.

It is not always possible for modern experts to tell whether a medieval item was homemade or professionally or mass produced. Mass production is not usually associated with medieval industry, but was definitely done for a range of goods such as cheap tin or lead dress accessories or bone items like dice and beads.

The crafts that were most influential were often regulated in some way in towns, and the freedom to practice in a given town was not granted to everybody. Typically, it required an apprenticeship and the acceptance by the other masters of the craft, sometimes tied to paying a fee. Guilds functioned both as regulators of crafts and quality control as well as protection of the crafters.

The regulations of crafts also provide a good source for modern scholars to learn about medieval crafts. For instance, the provost of Paris kept records of a very large number of businesses in the thirteenth century that can give us evidence concerning crafts in population centres.

Women as well as men went into professional craftwork, but they are usually much less documented. The number of women achieving senior status was likely to be significantly smaller than that of men. The typical crafts where women dominated included silk-spinning, embroidery or small-scale brewing, while those dominated by men mainly required greater physical strength. A few crafts, such as tapestry weaving, were not particularly gendered.

Metalworking

The metalworking crafts ranged from the more artistic goldsmiths and silversmiths to blacksmiths who specialised in rural equipment, including shoes for animals and common items such as nails.

The chief non-ferrous metals in use were copper, tin, lead, zinc and the precious metals silver and gold. Metal from mines is not completely pure, so small amounts of other metals can be found in many objects, but they were not deliberate additions to alloys. Extraction of impurities was done to a degree, but evidence suggests that it was not done to current high standards.

Copper was rarely used in its pure form. Instead it served as the main base metal for alloys. Tin, lead and zinc were added to the copper in varying proportions, changing the melting point and other characteristics of the metal, such as its hardness, considerably. The zinc needed for making brassy alloys was most probably imported from China or the Islamic world; it was not worked in metal form in Western Europe.

Copper alloys were used for all kinds of items: buckles, pins, bells, accessories, reliquaries and jewellery. Alloy mixtures and ratios did vary, but brass (copper and zinc) and gunmetal (copper, zinc and tin) were at least as common as bronze (copper and tin), according to metal analysis of dress accessories found in London. Modern technical definitions of brass and bronze, though, are not very useful for talking about the actual metals of the Middle Ages. The metals themselves ranged considerably in their components, and there were no alloy composition standards.

All of the non-ferrous metals can be either cast or formed with help of a hammer. They get harder during forging and can be rendered malleable again by annealing (heating and rapidly cooling). Annealing was especially important when forming bowls or similar items from sheet metal by hammering.

Clay crucibles – made from clay specifically tempered to withstand high temperatures – were used to melt metal. These crucibles had a limited lifespan. The simplest moulds for casting could be made by pressing a model into sand. More complicated or delicate pieces were cast in reusable stone moulds from one or more pieces, or made using the lost-wax procedure. A lost-wax process was also used for bellfounding, and bells made in traditional workshops are still cast using the same techniques as in the Middle Ages. Considerable expertise was needed for both casting and for making moulds. Single cast pieces could be put together by soldering.

Very hot fires were used to melt and cast, anneal or solder objects from non-ferrous metal. Coal and charcoal are especially suitable for producing sufficient heat, though a wood fire may have been hot enough in some cases. Since relatively little mined coal was used in the Middle Ages, charcoal would have been the most common fuel. Bellows could be used to increase air flow and thus the temperature of the fire considerably. Typical tools for working non-ferrous metals included hammers, chisels, files, tongs and punches or engraving tools.

While copper and copper alloys were important materials for all kinds of goods for daily life, ranging from needles and nails to cooking vessels, silver and gold were mainly used for jewellery, precious vessels (especially liturgical vessels) and for embellishing paintings or textiles.

Silver was used far more frequently than gold, so much so that there were specialist goldsmiths called finers who specialised in refining silver. The silver of Limoges was particularly renowned for its purity. Devon silver was marketed internationally through London and was very popular.

A very cheap alternative to silver was tin or pewter (an alloy with tin as the main metal). This metal could be polished to look quite similar to silver at first glance. Pewter was used for items such as pilgrim's badges, tokens or spoons. It was also used for ecclesiastical items such as cruets and crucifixes. Pewter was generally cast; since its melting point is very low, it could even be cast in moulds of wood. Round objects cast from pewter could be finished on a lathe. Tin or pewter can also be easily worked by soldering or abrasives. Some items (including possibly some types of flagons) were made through soldering together strips of pewter that had been cut from a flat sheet.

While some pewter plates and other household items survive, they are hard to date. At least some domestic pewter was in use during the twelfth century, even though the peak of the industry was in the fourteenth and fifteenth centuries. The oldest current find is a spoon bowl from the late eleventh or early twelfth century. The earliest guilds for those working in pewter, however, appear to date from the thirteenth century, with one in Paris from 1268. Pewter was often recycled, with the recycled metal costing only two-thirds of the price of new metal. This has unfortunately led to a low survival rate for items made of pewter.

Lead was crucial to the building industry, and lead workers had their own trade, appearing quite early by occupation in the public record. For instance, Walter Plumarius was in the 1175–6 *Pipe Roll*. Other surnames related to lead work included le Plumbere and le Plummer. Lead has a low melting point and is easily malleable.

Roofing lead was cast on a bed of sand into sheets, while lead pipes were made by rolling sheets in wooden shapes and soldering the seams. Window-leading was cast in two-part iron moulds.

Iron was just as crucial to medieval society as the non-ferrous metals. Iron and steel were used for everything from buckles, hinges, wool comb tines and hooks to carpenter's saws and swords and armour. They were, however, not cheap materials. Items such as spades or shovels were wooden and only reinforced with iron along their lower edges.

Items made of iron were a key part of the economy and of society. Some items were so important that they could be provided in lieu of financial or service payments. For example, in 1253, the sheriff of Sussex provided Henry III with 30,000 horseshoes and 60,000 nails for the army. Smiths also produced the basic tools for many other trades, making them extremely important to medieval society.

In contrast to non-ferrous metals, ferrous metals are soft and malleable only when heated. Heating changes the microstructure of the material, and sudden cooling from higher heat was used to produce a much harder finished product. Steel hardened in this way is quite brittle, which can be amended by tempering the piece – this lets the smith achieve the right balance between hard but too brittle and soft but too malleable.

Iron can be welded together with help of hammer and anvil when hot enough, and fire-welding was a quite common technique. Pattern-welding, a procedure when iron and steel were welded together in layers, was mostly before our period. It was probably an attempt to replicate true Damascus steel from India, called Wootz steel today. Wootz is steel of very high quality that shows a banded pattern similar to pattern-welded steel.

Damascus steel items, both from Wootz steel and pattern-welded, were however a rare item in our period. Monosteel pieces, or items like knives with the main part made from softer iron with a steel strip welded on for the blade section, were much more common. Cast iron was not used in our period. The earliest cast iron is documented for Continental Europe from the fifteenth century onwards as it was difficult to bring ferrous metal to liquid form before then.

For working iron and steel, relatively few tools were needed: an anvil, a hammer and a pair of tongs plus a chisel are the basic equipment. Historical anvils were much smaller than the anvils in use today and had no horns. Their size and relatively small weight enabled smiths to travel from place to place, offering their services. Hearths to heat the metal could be as simple as a hole in the ground fitted with bellows. Stationary smithies, however, would have hearths of a more convenient height and bigger bellows. Forges were run with sea coal as well as charcoal, and the quality of the fuel also influenced the quality of the material that was worked using it.

Pottery, Brickmaking and Tilemaking

Another important material, both for medieval daily life and for modern archaeological research, is ceramic. Clay was readily available in most regions and was thus a cheap material. Fired pottery is a hard, brittle, yet still porous and durable material very well suited to storing or cooking food. The durability of fired clay also led to its use as a building material, such as roof tiles or floor tiles. Ceramic products were therefore at least as ubiquitous as metal and textiles. However, ceramic crafts were generally not as high in status as most other crafts. During our period no guilds, therefore, developed for potters.

Making pots did not require a large workshop, though there were some larger commercial ventures which made pots for more distant markets. Those were usually high-quality pieces; most other pottery that travelled did so as a container for other goods. The many smaller-scale potters sold their wares in local or regional markets.

In spite of the easy availability and rather low status, pottery was not a throwaway item. We have surviving examples of pots repaired, for instance by plugging a hole with lead. If the pot was a complete write-off, its shards could still be used for other purposes. They could, for example, be shaped into spindle whorls or counters for board games.

Most potters were rural and paid rents like other tenants. Pottery was only one aspect of their working lives. For example, a potter in Longbridge Deverill in Wiltshire in the thirteenth century had a flexible arrangement for dues owed, indicating that he did not rely on pottery for his whole living, but made pots according to demand. Evidence suggests that clay was sourced locally, and that most potters travelled no more than a day to obtain it. In addition to the clay itself, which could be of varying quality depending on the region, workers in any kind of ceramic needed a ready supply of tempering materials (for example sand), water and fuel.

Clay has to be prepared before pots or tiles or anything else can be made. Tempering (mixing other materials into the clay) is done to prevent cracks and fissures during the drying and firing process. A variety of tempering materials is known for medieval pottery, such as sand or very fine stone grit, crushed seashells or organic materials (like chaff). The amount and type of tempering material depended on their availability, the type and quality of the clay basis and the products to be made. High-quality pots, for instance, were usually made with fine clay.

The clay was also left to rest for a period to ensure homogenous moisture. The weathering process during this time improved the malleability of the material.

Pots and other ceramic vessels could be hand-built or wheel-thrown, or formed with a combination of both techniques. Wheels could be turned by hand (these slower wheels were also used to finish hand-built pieces) or by foot. The modern wheel with a heavy fly-wheel base was probably not known during the Middle Ages.

Tiles were usually formed with help of a mould. The tiling industry only rose to prominence after the late twelfth century, but then became very important; for instance, many roofs in London had ceramic tile, supplied by tilers on or near the outskirts of the city such as Smithfield.

Wood was the typical fuel for firing pottery. The firing temperature used for medieval pottery was usually high enough to form a hard ceramic piece, but not high enough to lead to sintering. Thus the pieces stay porous.

Firing larger amounts of pottery was done in specially built kilns. Single items or smaller batches, however, could also be fired in a pit dug into the ground or even in a normal hearth fire. Proper kilns allowed better control of the firing and the atmosphere: pieces burned in a bonfire or pit more often turned out black or partly black due to lack of oxygen in the process. Enough oxygen resulted in cream, yellow or reddish tones. Controlled firing with enough oxygen thus was crucial for pots decorated with slip or glaze. Glazes contained lead to lower their melting point so they would melt in the kiln. Glazed pottery was, however, not common before about the late twelfth century. From then on, glazing became used more widely, with green glaze being especially common.

Surfaces could be decorated with grooves, scratches, shallow cuts or impression patterns, polishing or roughing of the surface and applied bands or other semi-plastic elements.

Many decorations also had an influence on the properties of the item: roughed surfaces led to more evaporation and therefore better cooling of the contents; applied bands enhanced stability; and glazes sealed the porous surface and made the pottery waterproof.

The different forms and decoration of ceramics changed from region to region and over time and can thus be used by archaeologists to date other items, making old broken pottery an important part of modern research. For example, the twelfth century saw a period of major stylistic change that also affected simpler household pottery. Patterns and styles of very simple functional pottery were, on the other hand, quite consistent over time.

Woodworking

Wooden items are rare finds in archaeology, since wood decays in the ground; furthermore old, worn-out or broken wooden items could be burned as fuel. We do know that wood was used to make all kinds of things for daily life – from a boat to a cup or a ladder. It also provided the basis for artworks such as sculptures and paintings.

Wood is a renewable resource and a material that is insulating, tough, yet easy to work when fresh. The exact properties of a piece of wood depend on the tree species, the surroundings of the tree during its growth including the climate and the part of the tree that the wood was taken from.

Woodworking techniques thus varied. Axes as well as wedges and hammers could be used for the rough formation of the desired shapes, for example for splitting logs into pieces. Adzes and axes were very important tools for woodworking. Smaller pieces could be worked using a knife or a more specialised toolset including chisels. Pieces with rotational symmetry – such as dowels, cups and vessels – could be turned on a pole lathe using specially formed irons. Saws were not a standard tool; they were probably not introduced before the twelfth century.

The sort of wood to be used was selected according to the intended use, though probably influenced by availability and affordability as well. Oak, for example, was the preferred structural timber, though elm, ash and aspen were used for building as well. Elm wood was known to be very durable in wet conditions, while ash was used where supple and flexible wood was needed.

The most valued wood for making furniture appears to have been oak, but other woods were also used, including walnut, poplar and pine. Woods were even imported in some cases, such as the Norwegian soft woods used for the king's tables at Winchester in 1253.

In addition to these timber crafts, some tree kinds such as willow and hazel also provided supple shoots for light fences and hurdles, basketry and wickerwork. Other containers could be made from thin strips of wood, woven together and formed into basket-like shapes, or staves that were bound together with willow or metal rings into buckets, cups, bowls and barrels.

Bone, Antler, Horn and Ivory Crafts

Bone (and the similar materials antler and ivory) and horn are not much used anymore, their niche for everyday items having been taken by various plastic materials. They were, however, an important material in the Middle Ages. Antlers were shed yearly by deer, and bone as well as horn could be harvested from dead animals, both wild and domesticated. They were cheap, rather hard and durable, but still easy to work with and suited to a wide range of tasks. Bone and antler are known, for example, from pins and combs, board-game pieces and dice.

Antler seems to have been preferred as a raw material, though bone was also available and has more standardised forms. Bone was also probably easier to source.

Ivory, the tusk of elephants or walruses, was a very valuable raw material. While ivory was important, it was not commonly used. Most surviving twelfth-century pieces of ivory from England and France are religious items such as liturgical combs – used for ritual grooming in preparation of Mass – or small cases for relics. In England until the end of the twelfth century, mostly walrus ivory was used. Elephant ivory became important from this time onward in England. It had, however, been used in France before that time.

Finally, horn (usually of cattle, sheep or goat) could be used for a variety of items as well. Horns are not shed yearly like antlers and can thus only be obtained by killing the animal. Horn is more or less translucent and becomes soft when heated. This enabled horn-crafters to flatten sheets of horn that could be used as a glass substitute as well as worked into other items such as combs. Horn unfortunately decays very easily in the soil, and thus the full range of items made from horn in the Middle Ages is probably not known. Most evidence for horn-working comes from the discarded horn cores.

Parchment, Fur and Leatherworking

Animal hides can be processed into parchment, leather or fur, with these processes resulting in very different end products. For all three, the animal is skinned and the flesh side of the skin scraped to remove fat and non-skin tissue. For making leather or parchment, the skin is then put into a bath containing ashes or lime. This prepares the skin for the following processes, including loosening the hairs. For tanning furs, the ashes are only spread on the flesh side and only left on for a short time so that the hair would stay on.

Parchment is made by stretching the de-haired, prepared skin in a frame, scraping and drying it. Before the rise of paper in popularity in the fourteenth and fifteenth century, parchment was the most important material for writing. For one Bible, the skins of about 170 calves or about 500 sheep was needed; especially large and pompous manuscripts used even more skins.

Objects made of leather ranged from shoes to gloves, belts and knife sheathes through to saddles and small containers. This meant that almost every place had some kind of leatherwork, while some areas even relied heavily on manufacture and trade of specialist leather goods.

Leatherworking was the most important trade in York in the thirteenth century, and Northampton was a centre for boots and shoes by the middle of the thirteenth century: Henry III ordered 150 pairs of shoes to give out as alms in Northampton in 1266.

For producing leather in the Middle Ages, three different methods could be used. All three methods keep the collagen fibres in the skin from deteriorating. The first method yielded the most resistant leather by chemically changing the skin. It was made by soaking and working the skin over a long time in a bath containing tannins, typically derived from oak barks. These leathers have a brownish or reddish colour.

Finer leathers could be tanned minerally, using alum. This resulted in a soft leather with a light colour. Finally, fat could be used to turn the skin into leather, yielding a very fine and soft but not very resistant end product. Leather production was a water-intensive industry and also resulted in significant amounts of waste liquid. This is especially true for vegetable tanning, and those workshops were usually situated downstream and in the outer areas of a settlement.

Animal skin was also turned into furs, including skins of squirrels or cats. Furs could only be tanned using alum or fat tanning methods. In contrast to tannin-cured leather, these leathers are still attractive to vermin and keep less well in the ground, which may be a reason why medieval fur is very rarely preserved.

Leather goods were ubiquitous in the Middle Ages. Three major techniques were used to make objects out of leather. The most common technique was sewing. Holes for seams were made using awls. The thread for stitching was usually flax or hemp yarn treated with pitch and beeswax, attached to a pig's bristle that served as a flexible needle. Objects could also be made by gluing the edges together with hot animal glue. This was often used for box coverings, for instance. Finally, objects could be made by moulding the leather. This technique was especially favoured for armour, drinking vessels, bottles (a very common way of carrying and serving drink) and buckets.

With these techniques, leather could be formed into almost every shape desired. Its surface could be decorated by embossing, incising, carving and punching. Colour decoration was done by gilding, dyeing, embroidery or painting the surface.

Textile Crafts

Another crucial group of crafts were the textile crafts, since textile items were needed everywhere for an immense variety of functions, from ropes and sails on ships, bags and bale covers for transport of goods, to household textiles and, of course, clothing. The textiles were often not purely functional, but also denoted status and wealth of their owner.

A multitude of materials in different qualities were available for the medieval textile-maker. Best known for use in the medieval period are linen, wool and silk, but other fibres were also in use: hemp and nettle fibres or hair from animals other than sheep. Cotton was imported, though it is not completely clear when imports started and whether the fibre was used as a stuffing only, or spun and woven.

Preparation of the fibres depended on the material and its quality, and processes could vary considerably. Before spinning, though, each material needed to be prepared by getting rid of residual debris and aligning the fibres at least roughly into one direction. While it is technically possible to spin from a jumble of fibres, the resulting thread will not be of a good quality – which most threads surviving in archaeological textile finds are. The typical procedure for preparing wool was to wash it (either while on the sheep or after shearing), then loosen the fibres, then comb it with a set of long-tined wool combs to prepare one long band of aligned fibres.

The main spinning tool throughout the Middle Ages was the hand-spindle, always used together with a distaff to hold the fibres. The distaff could be held in the hand or tucked into the belt or under the arm; some images also show long distaffs standing on the floor. The first forms of the spinning wheel are documented from about the end of the thirteenth century. These were simple spindle wheels, however, and far different from the pedal-driven spinning wheels known today.

Today, textile work and especially spinning are often seen as predominantly or exclusively female work. Textile production in the medieval era was, in any case, not exclusively a female task. Since the spindle was the symbol of the active, busy woman, this may have lead to women being depicted with a spindle whether they were actually spinners or not.

After spinning, the yarn (whether dyed or undyed) can be made into cloth by weaving.

Woven cloth was manufactured on looms. Two types of looms are likely for our period, according to current research: the vertical warp-weighted loom or two-beam loom (with a second beam instead of the individual loom weights), and the horizontal treadle loom. Both the two-beam loom and the horizontal loom are hard to trace archaeologically, as they lack the telltale loomweights. The horizontal loom is supposed to be in use from at least the eleventh century; however, for complex patterned weaves earlier than this, coming from the Mediterranean or the Far East, the use of a horizontal loom can also be assumed. As the treadle loom became more and more common, the vertical looms were probably less frequent, though their use cannot be excluded completely.

The weaves that can be produced on all three types of looms range from the simple tabby weave to very complex weaves. All woven fabrics have at least two thread systems running perpendicular to each other, the warp and the weft. For a tabby weave, each thread in one system passes alternatingly over and under one thread of the other system.

This results in a fabric with no textural pattern and provides maximum stability and stiffness possible with the threads used. A tabby weave done with fine, soft threads and a loose weave can, however, still be very soft to the touch and drape nicely.

Twill weaves, characterised by their diagonal lines, require a slightly more developed loom. In twill weave, the threads of one system go either over two threads and under one thread of the other system, or over two, under two. The next wefts shift in sequence, resulting in diagonal lines in the fabric. Twill weave can be used to weave cloth with two differently coloured sides. Twill is the most frequent weave known from textile finds of the Middle Ages. Twill weaves, in comparison to tabby weaves, have a reduced number of thread crossings, making it more supple and resulting in a fabric that is quite elastic on the bias.

Other weaves, such as satin weaves, have even fewer binding points, resulting in even more drape of the fabric and a more pronounced difference between the warp-dominated and the weft-dominated side.

Finally, complex weaves have survived in some cases. These complex weaves have more than one weft or more than one warp (or both), enabling the weaver to create very complex patterns both in texture and with several colours. These complex weaves were very demanding to make and are thus typically used with higher value materials such as silk. The two most frequent surviving complex weaves are called samite and lampas; samite (sometimes wrongly translated as velvet) was in use mainly from the fifth to the fourteenth century. Lampas starts to supersede samite from about the eleventh century onward, reaching its heyday from about the fourteenth century. Both were heavy, smooth-surfaced fabrics that could show elaborate patterns; for the most costly fabrics, some of the pattern wefts could also be made from gold thread.

Fabric widths depended on the loom widths and were generally narrower for the very costly silks than for wool or linen. For the latter, fabric widths of more than 1 metre, roughly corresponding to the most common widths today, seem to have been quite frequent.

In addition to weaving, other textile techniques were employed to make narrow wares, such as bands, or fitted textile items such as caps, gloves or stockings. Tablet-weaving and rigid heddle weaving, used to make functional or decorative bands, are still (or again) known today. Medieval tablet-weaving was much finer and used different patterning methods, though, than most modern bands in that technique. Nalebinding is a technique related to needle lace and was used for making stockings and gloves, best known from finds in ecclesiastical contexts. Knitting is a technique that is rather hard to trace, but seems to slowly emerge from the thirteenth century, not earlier. Felting is similarly hard to trace, but was definitely used for making hats.

Stoneworking

Worked stone from the Middle Ages is mostly associated with buildings having public and semi-public functions, such as churches, cathedrals, castles, mansions and rich burghers' houses, and with rich stone sculpture found, for example, as church decoration or as epitaphs.

These decorations are probably the best known example of medieval stonework. They could range from fanciful column capitals to realistic freestanding figures.

Romanesque sculpture is especially known for semicircular carved panels called *tympana*, which often decorated the main portals (doors) of the church. Gothic sculpture, on the other hand, is known for more realistic human figures with flowing draperies and detailed faces. Tomb sculptures or effigies were sometimes used to show an image of a person as they might have appeared in life. Stone sculptures, beautiful reliefs and portals as well as valuable marble and Purbeck Stone decorations were important decorative work. Worked stone was also used for other purposes, such as building stone bridges. It found uses completely separate from the building crafts as well, for example for making millstones – both large ones and those used as hand querns – or stone troughs.

After the stone was quarried and roughly dressed at the quarry site, the mason or masons worked it with tools suitable to the material and the intended end result. Stones with sculptural elements would be worked with different toolsets than stones just made into blocks for building. Known stoneworking tools include axes, hammers, punches, chisels, stone saws, borers and ravels. For rough dressing, tools also included wedges, mauls, crowbars and picks.

Gem-cutting was an entirely different form of stoneworking. Medieval gem-cutters polished and carved both semi-precious stones, such as rock crystals, which mainly came from Germany, Switzerland and France, and amethysts from Germany or Russia, and precious stones, such as rubies, turquoises and sapphires, which were imported from the East, and emeralds from Egypt. Jet was found near coal measures at Whitby. Diamonds were only rarely used in our period, becoming more common only in the fourteenth and fifteenth centuries. Both precious and semi-precious stones were traded widely.

The typical form of a medieval gemstone was the cabochon, acquired by rubbing and polishing the stones. The more reflective and brilliant form of cut planes did not evolve before the fourteenth century. Stones with differently coloured layers could also be carved into *cameos* and *intaglios* by removing parts of the upper layer to form a two-coloured design. Just as stones from old buildings were re-used for making new buildings, old gemstones were used again for jewellery. This included the Classical cameos and intaglios surviving from the Roman period that were still highly prized in medieval times. Cameos and intaglios, whether old or new, were especially well-suited for use in seals and rings.

Other uses of cut and polished stones besides jewellery were elaborate book covers, precious containers, such as those holding relics, or smaller settings that could be sewn to clothing as ornaments. Cabochons of coloured glass set in the same way could be used to simulate precious and semi-precious stones.

Glassworking

Glass was less ubiquitous than the other materials discussed here: it was not a mass product affordable to everyone, such as ceramic pots or wooden vessels were.

Glassworking crafts are mainly the production of the raw glass and the crafts that turn the raw glass into vessels or sheets. Glass was produced by melting quartz sand into a homogenous, translucent mass with the help of fluxing agents to lower the temperatures needed for melting. The Romans used natron, an imported naturally occurring sodium, as a fluxing agent. This made it possible to produce highly translucent, good-quality glass. However, the trade in natron slowed and came to a stop due to political troubles in the eighth and ninth centuries. This led to the development of glasses using potassium instead of natron, with the potassium derived from plant ashes (called forest glass). Beech was a popular source of the plant ash in England.

The new chemistry in glass making also required an adaptation of the craft procedures, and early items made from the potassium glasses were often non-homogenous and of low quality. Good glass-making sands were not available everywhere, and colourless forest glasses were rare. Forest glass was typically tinged green due to the metal contents of sand and the plant ash used; however, a variety of other colours could also occur naturally, as evidenced by much of the glass used in the York Minster windows.

Glass colour could be influenced purposely by adding different metals, such as iron, copper or zinc. Glass with a relatively high lead content is also known and seems to have been the preferred glass for use in enamelling.

Raw glass was formed by heating it up until soft, then manipulating it. Vessels were formed with help of a glassblower's pipe. Glass blowing was also one step in making flat glass: a large cylinder would be blown, then cut open and flattened out to make a sheet of glass.

Modern glass is made with sophisticated temperature controls that reduce the number of pieces shattering due to fast or localised temperature changes. Such controls were not available in the Middle Ages, and thus making large pieces of glass was much more demanding and consequently much more expensive than small pieces. Accordingly, windows were put together from many small glass pieces, held together by lead strips.

A special form of glass windows were stained-glass windows, one of the crowning artistic glories during our period. For stained-glass windows, a pattern or motif was drawn by an artist and glass pieces in various colours were cut, placed and leaded accordingly. Details and fine shading could be added by using a special kind of paint, made from ground glass with iron oxide or copper, which was fixed on the glass by heat curing. Sometimes pictures were painted with this mixture on clear glass, resulting in a black-and-white picture that is today known as *grisaille*.

Churches and cathedrals were not the only buildings sporting stained glass: some synagogues also did, though none of these windows have survived. Glass windows, both simple and stained, were also used for secular buildings. Since glass was becoming more affordable with time, the rather small and rarely seen glass windows became larger and more frequent during our period.

Just as in other crafts, it is very rare to know the artists or the craftspeople who made a specific piece. One instance of a signed piece is in Rouen Cathedral, where a window dating from around 1220–30 was signed by Clement of Chartres.

Decorating Crafts, Artistry and Design Crafts

The use of colours and colourful materials was as important in the Middle Ages as it is today. Contrary to modern prejudice, life was not all in brown and grey hues. Colour and decorative motifs were widespread and could be found on all kinds of things and in all forms, such as brightly dyed textiles, painted walls and doors, enamelled metal and, of course, statues and manuscript illuminations.

The materials used for decoration were just as varied. Charcoal, ink and lead or silver pens could be used for line drawings. For coloured work, a wide range of pigments could be ground up and mixed with carrier and binding materials for different kinds of paint. The cheapest pigments generally were earth pigments such as ochre. A typical use was mixing them into fresco paint and decorating the outside of buildings, for example with geometrical motifs. Similar paints were used for murals, a common art form during our period. Most surviving ones are found inside churches and represent religious subjects, but mural decorations were also used in private houses and depicted secular themes. On the other end of the spectrum were rare, very high-quality pigments derived from grinding up gemstones such as lapis-lazuli. These were used for small and high-quality paintings, for example illuminations in valuable manuscripts.

Between these two extremes were many other pigments. There were colours extracted from plants, reclaimed from dyed textiles and various metal oxides. The final outcome of the colours depended on the type, quality and amount of the pigments, the mixture and, of course, the surface they were applied to. Different media resulted in different choices of pigment or colour, so that even if the artist intended to show the same scene, it was not always possible to match colours across media.

The preparation of the pigments, colours and the surfaces to be painted was usually done in artists' workshops. This preparation would have ranged from selecting a piece of parchment to applying multi-layered gesso to wood or priming a textile for painting. Gold and silver could be beaten into leaf metal and applied to parchment, leather and gesso. With appropriate preparation of the gesso, these metal leaf coverings could even be polished to a high sheen.

In some rare cases, pre-drawings and sketches have survived that clearly helped the artist or crafter plan the work. A special case of pre-drawing was when designs were made by artists for other crafts, such as embroidery or tapestry-weaving. Motifs for embroidery could be inked directly onto the cloth, while full-size sketches were drawn onto some other material and placed behind the loom to serve as template for the tapestry. Sketchbooks or sketch pages holding numerous examples of people and things have also survived, though rarely. These may have been practices or studies, but might also have served as patterns.

The motifs of decorative art varied widely and ranged from geometric designs and ornaments inspired by plants, to more or less realistic depictions of plants, animals and humans, to grotesqueries and half-human, half-animal beings. The actual designs used depended on the time, region, circumstances, the intended function of the decoration and the artist as well as on the one commissioning the design.

Jewish artistry had a considerable amount of overlap of style and theme with Christian artwork. Although Judaism prohibited representations of humans in theory, Rashi notes wall frescoes illustrating scenes such as David and Goliath. In England, Jewish signet rings have been found that bear human likenesses.

Writing and Related Crafts

Not all medieval crafts would be considered crafts today. The primary example for this is the craft of writing, whether it was copying text from one manuscript to a new one or writing something entirely new.

Scribing was regarded as a craft, and professional scribes were found both in monasteries and in secular surroundings. Medieval books from before the fifteenth century were all manuscripts, which means that they were all handwritten.

Manuscripts were generally a quite expensive commodity; consequently, few people had books or libraries, and books were valuable enough to serve as a security deposit.

The standard format for manuscripts was the codex, the form we associate with a book today. Some manuscripts were also in the form of a roll. For this, parchment was sewn together to create one long piece that was rolled up. Torahs, genealogical histories and the *Pipe Rolls* are typical examples for this format.

The scribing of manuscripts, especially religious manuscripts, was very often done in monasteries. It is not clear whether every scribe knew how to read well or how to read at all – copying letters onto new parchment was a task that did not technically require knowing how to read. By the twelfth century, professional non-monastic scribes would have written most of the texts in centres of learning such as Paris. This led to the increased importance of such centres of learning in the production of books.

The writing tasks were not necessarily all done by a single person. Most texts did not include illumination or much decoration beyond very simple reading aids such as differently coloured initials. Illuminated manuscripts are, however, the best-known manuscripts today since they are much more spectacular than the more common undecorated ones.

For the elaborate manuscripts featuring illuminations, the usual process entailed a number of specialists working together. Planning the manuscript layout and deciding on the number, size and placement of illuminations and elaborate initial letters was the first step. The parchment was cut to size, and pricked holes were used to keep the writing aligned throughout pages. Scribes or writers then took care of the text, using inks and quills. Typical writing quills were strong feathers from the wings of birds such as geese, with the feather vanes removed and the tip hardened and cut. Rubricators or miniators took care of the headings and initials as well as the illustrations, using a larger number of colours and sometimes gold leaf as well. Finally, another specialist would take the finished pages and bind them into a codex format. The more elaborate and expensive the book itself would be, the more money would also be spent on the covers for binding it, which could range from simple leather covering the wooden boards to heavy covers with exquisite ornamentation made from metal, carved ivory or gemstones. Sometimes, money seems to have run out during manuscript production, and spaces for pictures are left empty or show only sketched outlines.

Making manuscripts was thus more a collection of crafts than a single specific craft. It is also a very good example of how the single crafts, or craft branches, interacted. None of them was isolated or working only by and for itself, and interaction ranged from sourcing tools and materials from other crafts to working together on specific items or projects.

The crafts listed in this chapter are also not a complete description. Innumerable more crafting techniques existed that are not covered with the simplified and very general descriptions given here – from very basic techniques such as making straw or rush baskets (for instance to serve as beehives), to more elaborate ones such as plaiting straw for hats. There has also been no mention of the many very specialised crafts working with more than one kind of material and on more than a basic first process of the material, for example wheelwrights, cartwrights, fullers and saddle makers.

8

People at Play
Leisure Activities

Life in medieval times was not all work, of course, and free time led to leisure activities. The choice of activities a person might make depended on factors such as the region, social circles, wealth and status, other people involved and the time of year. In addition to reading, listening to texts being read or storytelling as important pastimes in our period, there were many other leisure activities. They included everything from gambling, sports, bear baiting and board games to going to the fair or the baths and drinking with friends.

Leisure activities thus took place in many different surroundings, but generally, public spaces including cemeteries were often used as open spaces for games and general enjoyment. Gerald of Wales reports a complaint made by a priest from Worcester that he could not sleep because of the local community dancing in the graveyard at night. Bloodshed was, however, forbidden in a cemetery. Jocelin of Brakelond wrote about gatherings at a burial ground in Bury St Edmunds during the Christmas period, where the abbot's servants and the townsfolk had wrestling matches. Unfortunately, it escalated into real fighting with bloodshed, and so the participants were stripped, whipped and forbidden to meet in the cemetery again.

Sports and Tournaments

Just as with many other things, the pastimes and leisure activities of the upper parts of society – nobles and the wealthy – are better documented than the leisure activities of the majority of people. The favourite sports of the nobles included chess, hunting and tournaments. Chess was introduced into Europe from the Islamic world around the tenth century. European chessmen from as early as the eleventh century have been found. They were generally made of bone or antler and are seldom works of art. However, two eleventh-century wills bequeathed valuable chess pieces to St Gilles Monastery (one set made of quartz and the other proudly proclaimed *ipsos meos schacos*, or 'my very own chess-pieces'), so precious sets were known at the time. Chess may not have been introduced into England until the thirteenth century; if it was played before that, it would have been as a curiosity. In the thirteenth century, it pushed the popular game *hnefatafl* (of Scandinavian origin) from its central position as a popular game, even though it was still played after the rise of chess. *Hnefatafl* was a strategic two-player game: one player tries to bring a special piece, the king, to one of the corners of the board, while the opponent tries to capture the king piece. Passion could run high with board games: in London, around the middle of the thirteenth century, a man killed a woman over a game of chess.

Hunting was a prestigious sport and required not only animals and appropriate weapons – for example bows and arrows, spears, dogs, ferrets and birds of prey – but also the right to hunt in a given area. Hunting smaller animals with birds of prey was a sport for both men and women. Hunting birds were an important status symbol as well and accorded different ranks and values, the gyrfalcon being one of the most prestigious birds and the sparrowhawk the least. The prey may have been driven into enclosures or was even farmed to guarantee availability. This applied to both smaller animals like rabbits and larger animals such as deer or boar. The more dangerous hunt for wild boar was a male activity.

Hunting was not always restricted to nobles, though: London citizens also had an interest in hawk and hound, and were entitled to hunt in Middlesex and Hertfordshire, among other places.

Tournaments, like many sports, were leisure activities both for the active participants and the spectators. Medieval tournaments were, however, also part of military training for maintaining fitness and skills. They are explained in this chapter, therefore, but they have close links to the military. For instance, sometimes the tedium of sieges was allayed through both parties engaging in mock combat. In 1141, during the siege of Winchester (Queen Matilda besieging Empress Matilda), the combatants held daily jousts against each other.

The medieval legendary view of the origins of tournaments was that they were founded by Godfrey de Preuilly (d. 1066), a French knight. In fact, however, there were tournament-style mock battles earlier than this. These mock battles shifted to tournaments alongside the new forms of fighting with couched lances, and the chief prizes were the booty gained from the vanquished. Weapons were supposed to be blunted, and thus less able to hurt or kill.

From about 1150 to the end of the thirteenth or beginning of the fourteenth century, most tournaments were massed meetings, with between thirty and 200 fighters on each side, like the melée section of a battle. They covered large amounts of countryside, and were quite dangerous. Juliet R. V. Barker suggests that this style of tournament represented the perfect chance outside war itself to practise closely massed charges using the heavy lance. Despite the emphasis on the lance, other melée weapons such as swords and maces were also seen in these mock battles.

During the thirteenth century, a different form of a tournament developed: the Round Tables, which became very popular by the end of the century, during the reign of Edward I. The knights who participated might take on the roles of Arthurian heroes. The Round Tables included interludes of role play by the tournament hosts. These events included singing, dancing and revelry, as well as fighting.

Near the end of the thirteenth century, the normal form of tournaments changed to jousts in restricted spaces, where knights fought one on one. Previously this had been part of the preliminary entertainment of some tournaments, rather than the chief focus. It was also more audience-friendly, and audiences on stands and specialist judges became typical for them.

At their best, tournaments were the place where the romance of the poetic world overlapped with military reality. Participants demonstrated skills in weaponry, horses and teamwork, and had enough personal discomfort and even danger to make it exciting; furthermore, it could all be done for an audience.

Tournaments were not only a practice ground, but also offered opportunities: a knight could use them to build a career. Some individual knights travelled looking for tournaments, especially between around 1150 and 1250. They might travel alone, with squires or even with a close friend. One of the best-known knights to seek fame through this means was William Marshall (c. 1146–1219), who followed the tourney route in France and, with a friend, captured 103 knights and their ransom in ten months.

This was not without risk, however: there was a good chance that a knight might die or suffer serious wounds or financial losses in the attempt. Thus tournaments were quite often restricted or even banned in England. For instance, they were banned under Henry I, which led to many nobles travelling to the Continent to attend tournaments or attending illegal tournaments in England. Henry II himself attended tournaments on the Continent, such as the one at Beaucaire in 1174. Some were held during Stephen's reign and Richard I licensed tournaments in England from 1194; the culture of tournaments was probably at its peak during his reign. Edward I permitted them, but passed the *Statuta Armorum* to control them in 1292.

Tournaments were so much a place for the ruling classes to congregate that they were used to cement rulership. Some nobles travelled to tournaments to recruit fighters for their next war, such as Baldwin of Hainault in 1183. They could also foment trouble. Unlicensed tournaments, in fact, were quite possibly rallying points for those in opposition to the Crown. The *Magna Carta* barons used tournaments as an excuse to meet and plot, for instance, and so did the rebellious under Henry III.

The tournament was very much a male sport, including the spectators. Attendance by women did not become standard until the early thirteenth century in France, and the first attested instance of women in the audiences in England was not until 1279.

For non-nobles, other sports than tournaments served the double function of providing a competitive event and being social gatherings. On Sundays in Lent, young men who could obtain suitable horses engaged in contests in the fields outside London. These contests included running in circles and a variety of mock battles. Older boys might have a lance and a shield, while younger boys tended to use forked spears (without points). When the king or great lords were in town, these young men would be joined by their households. People probably gambled on the results, as they did for cockfighting, bear-baiting and other sports. Other games were played in the fields outside Smithgate (the east gate of London) as well as racing, since it was a favourite haunt of clerks and young scholars.

Sports and entertainment for summer feast days included archery, running, jumping, wrestling (in pairs or in teams), slinging stones, hurling javelins and fighting with swords and bucklers.

Ball games were another common form of entertainment of this kind, and they seem to have been especially popular at certain times of the year. Children might kick a pig's bladder around in autumn, when the pigs were killed for winter, for instance. School attendees in London are known to have played ball in the fields after dinner. There was also a game a bit like football, where two teams (probably of variable size) tried to get a ball across a set boundary. It was not, however, a placid game, with some matches becoming quite violent. We have evidence from the fourteenth century of games using balls thrown at sticks (a little like baseball). These probably originated during our period, but we have no more evidence of them than that. A game called *boules* was also popular, especially in France. The rules are somewhat similar to the modern French game of boules.

Water sports included swimming, boating, fishing and mock naval warfare. In twelfth-century London, for instance, a kind of naval warfare game was played every Easter. A shield was fixed in the middle of a stream, and boys tried to break the shield with a lance while standing in a boat. If they fell over, they lost, even if they broke the shield. Swimming was a recreation enjoyed by both men and women, although it was not without danger. In 1244, for example, a London woman drowned while swimming alone.

Sports-related injuries in general were not uncommon. In ball games, for instance, the knife hanging from a belt was a danger when people cannoned into each other (and one man died of such an accident). In another accident, in Eston, England, a woman called Alice died from a stray archery arrow in 1249.

Games and Gambling

Other pastimes were less physically oriented. One important leisure activity was gambling. Gambling could be tied in with many different activities and entertainments, such as betting on the outcome of other sports or games. Dicing appears to have been a passion during our period. Many dice have survived (even some loaded dice), as have records of court cases and gambling debts. Dice games were popular even among the clergy. Cards (and therefore card games) were not popular until the late Middle Ages.

Board games were also popular. Chess has already been mentioned, but many different games existed, from very simple ones like three-in-a-row to games with complex rules, and from those relying on pure luck to win to those with elaborate strategies. As with all other games, the rules are not always known and may have differed from place to place and changed over time. The boards for board games varied depending on what the game was. Both boards and gaming pieces could be made of many different materials, and ranged from simple scratched lines to elaborate masterpieces made from precious materials. Luxury boards (possibly from our period, possibly later) have been found with a chessboard on one side, *merels* on the other, and opening out to show a backgammon board. Playing pieces could be made from materials such as antler, bone, ivory, glass, clay or metal. In addition, it is always possible that items such as pebbles, pottery shards, coins or wood scraps were used as simple playing pieces or tokens.

Some of the boardgames played during our period can be reconstructed with help of texts, pictures and archaeological finds, though their rules are not always clear. The earliest evidence we have of three-in-a-row in England is from around 1100. These games were possibly introduced by crusaders. Some versions have links with modern games. Nine holes, for instance, was possibly the ancestor of noughts and crosses. It was played either on a noughts and crosses hatching or on a grid of four squares. Each player had three pieces; the aim was to line up the three pieces, with moving pieces allowed (and considered a turn). Evidence suggests that this game was popular with clerics and scholars.

Normans brought with them to England a game called *merellus* in

Latin. It was known in English and Old French as *merelles*, *merels* or even *morals*. It was played on a board that comprised two squares (one inside the other) linked by four lines connecting the four sides of the squares to each other, and sometimes diagonal lines linking the corners as well. Pieces were placed on the corners and where adjoining lines touch, with the aim of lining up pieces in rows. This game was equivalent in importance to chess and tables.

Tables may have been a direct ancestor of modern backgammon. A board and table-men dating from around 1066 have been found at Gloucester. The board looks rather like a modern backgammon board, used with carved disks. The disks are normally cut from antlers or animal jawbones.

There was an eleventh-century board game called *rithnomachy* (*rithnomachia* or *pugna numerorum* in Latin). The best descriptions of it are unfortunately later than our period, and the rules that date from our period are hard to determine. It was played on a checkered grid, eight squares deep and sixteen squares wide. Each player had twenty-four pieces. It was a distinctive game for England and France, although it was also played in Germany and Italy.

The name *alquerque* was not used for only one game, but for several variations, probably played on the same or similar boards. A 1283 Spanish manuscript that describes games talks about two simple games that were rather like *merels* (*de tres* and *de nueve*) and one more complicated one (*de doze*), which had a strong strategic component that brought it closer to chess. This *de doze* game may have developed into checkers and draughts after our period, with the major change to effect this transformation being that moves were made from within squares, rather than from the points of them. Thus, the game in our period was probably played using the corners and edges of the grid, not the squares.

Other forms of entertainment connected to gambling involved the use of animals, for example for horse races, but also for fights between animals. Horse racing was popular, but usually run fairly informally. During Henry II's reign, every Saturday at Smithfield (outside the London walls) teenage boys raced sale stock to show it off. In bear-baiting, dogs were set on a bear that might have been harried in addition to this to make it more aggressive. Bets were taken on how many dogs would survive and for how long, and also on how long the bear would survive. Bull baiting operated similarly. There were no wild bears in England during our period; they were imported for the sport. School attendees in London in the twelfth century are reported as bringing fighting cocks to school and having a holiday declared so that everyone could watch them fight.

In winter, leisure activities were restricted by the weather. Activities on feast days might include watching animal fights (boars, bulls and bears). Winter sports, such as ice games, were also known. These ice games included skating on animal shinbone skates with the aid of poles shod with iron.

Music and Dance

Enjoying music and dance was also a part of medieval entertainment. We know that people danced at certain religious feasts, almost certainly at weddings and possibly at funerals. There were also some clerical dances, either to religious tunes or maybe even in church during service. This suggests that dance was enjoyed by many people during our period.

Since dances were not described or documented in any detail, little is known or can be reconstructed about medieval dancing. The only sources available are artworks that show dancing people and surviving music, plus a wide range of mentions of dancing in literature. Most of these sources come from the thirteenth century or later.

This makes it impossible to reconstruct crucial information such as the sequencing of steps, how long dances lasted and even approximately how fast they were. The name of one dance form, *estampie*, suggests that at least some dances had a foot rhythm accompanying the musicians. They might also have had percussion backing up the rhythm; since the few surviving notations of music only show the melody line, this is impossible to know for sure. It is likely that there was significant overlap between popular and courtly dance, but there is insufficient evidence to prove this.

During our period, the dance for which we have the most details is the *carol*, a dance usually in a circle formation. It was probably the most common dance. Other types of dances for which we have some records include the *estampie*, the *ductia*, the *nota* and *rounds*. These dances seem to have ranged from very simple to very complicated and elaborate, and from gentle and subdued to wild and vigorous. Common setup forms seem to have been single or multiple lines or circles.

Despite modern popular belief about the ancient nature of morris dancing, we have no evidence for morris dancing in this period, and most of what we know of as folk dance from both England and France is considerably later. The vast majority of dances done currently from medieval tunes for our period are invented, not reconstructed, due to lack of sources. Many dances performed at places like medieval fairs are from after our period (some, indeed, are Renaissance). These include the *basse* dance, *saltarello*, *rotta*, *troto*, *galliard* and *pavan*.

Due to the nature of our sources, the information on dancing we have is strongly biased towards the Christian aristocracy, that is, towards the fashionable dancing of the era. Courtly dances as well as single specific dance figures probably had names, and reflected current fads. In 1285, for instance, Jacques Bretel mentioned a dance called the *chapelet*. Dance figures might also have names: these were mocked in the pastoral *Le Jeu de Robin and Marion* (Adam de la Halle, 1285).

Generally, as far as we know, dancing can be split into three categories: popular, courtly and clerical dances. Popular dancing included circle dances, dancing to singing and dancing that included miming.

Clerics sometimes objected to popular dancing. This was not only when singing and dancing in the churchyard bothered the local priest, but also when servants or young husbands slipped away from their duties to dance. Clerics were particularly wrathful at people missing church services to dance. In 1208, the Bishop of Paris said that it was wrong to dance the *carol* in religious processions, and in 1209 a Church council at Avignon made an edict declaring that dance was obscene and therefore not appropriate for vigils of saints' days. These are indications that popular dancing was widespread and a rather frequent pastime.

The main festivals where dancing took place at court were Christmas and Pentecost. There are some hints to dancing being more widespread, though. We know that children were taught dancing tunes (carols) as part of their music education, from a comment by Batholomew Anglicus. But what sorts of dances were preferred by which group, and how frequently people danced together is still a mystery. There are reports of dancing being mainly an activity for spring and summer, and that dances occurred in the country as well as in the city, in streets and roads as well as in churchyards.

Almost nothing is known about how the Jewish population danced in the Middle Ages. We know that they danced at weddings and the bridal feasts that followed, during festivals and on Sabbath. There is a tradition of Jewish instrumental dance music that reflects these dances. It is likely that Jewish dance and dance music had a significant degree of overlap with that of the non-Jewish communities. However, we do not know whether Jews joined Christians in dancing or stood aside. It is likely that in some places and at some times, Jews might not have danced in public, simply because of the dangers of being Jewish.

The earliest dance music we have is from the thirteenth century. The dances themselves are not recorded; in the best case, they are described in a more or less vague way. Some scholars suggest a link between lyric poetry and dance, since quite a few types of poetry share names with dance forms: *rondeaus* and round dances, ballads and the verb *balader* (to dance), *virelai* and the verb *virer* (to twist) and carol and the dance known as a *carol* (a circle or line dance). Music for all of these forms has survived. Johannes de Grocheio (who described music in the Paris area around 1300), for instance, mentions a circle dance done by clerics as a *rotundellus* or round dance accompanied by singing.

No polyphonic arrangements appear to have survived from our

period for dance music. This means either that they were monophonic or that they were not written down. The latter is much more likely.

Music, whether for dancing or not, was often improvised and seldom relied on written music. Pilgrims, crusaders and other social and religious groups probably also had their own songs. There was the music played by travelling musicians and scholars, and the music of the religious year, both Christian and Jewish.

Most of this music has not survived. We have the texts of some songs through literature and records of the words of some of the street cries. The more private songs, though, have scarcely been recorded; for example, we have no lullaby melodies from our period. We have a very little Jewish sacred music, and quite a lot of Christian sacred music. We also have some of the music that accompanied the work of minstrels and their like, especially when linked to major courts.

Most musical scribes were associated with churches, which means we have more church music written down than secular. Very few minstrels could read or write at all – for them, music and words were passed on in a personal context or were improvised. Medieval music can thus only be reconstructed in a severely limited way, and we cannot know how a medieval musician would have interpreted, or how a listener would have received, a given piece of music. It was certainly a different thing to modern music. For example, our modern idea of an octave above being an equivalent note to the octave below did not apply. Up to around 1200, the fourth, fifth and octave were considered harmonious, with thirds, sixths, seconds and sevenths being dissonant. Gradually, from around 1200, the third and the sixth were also considered harmonious.

Music can be seen either as a liberal art (the Church-sanctioned theoretical approach) or as a practical craft. Medieval composers came from a number of backgrounds, with very different training. They could work from within the Church where the composition of music would have been secondary to their other duties. Secular composers might be dedicated musicians, either with a patron at a court or as a wandering musician. They might be a teacher of the seven liberal arts or a clerk. Full-time professional composers would have been very rare, if indeed they existed at all. Musical performers mostly had low social status (especially if they depended on the music to make a living and were unsuccessful in attracting a good patron). This is why most of the named composers have strong links with the Church and various courts: these are the places where prestige lay.

Different types of music influenced each other, sometimes obviously, sometimes less so. The troubadour songs from southern France were major influences on lyric songs in England, for instance. It is also very likely that the synagogue song and the Church song interchanged elements: where people heard something and liked what they heard, they copied it. However, documentation is so rare that it is usually very difficult to know which way the influence ran, and how often music was borrowed. In fact, the earliest surviving popular music collections only date from the second half of the thirteenth century.

Christian musical notation started earlier than that, around the tenth century. Throughout the Middle Ages it was, however, still very different from modern notation and provides much less information. Jewish musical notation (cantillation) was formalised around the same time.

Music would have been made by many different people in all kinds of places and circumstances, on a wide variety of instruments and in many ways. Most knowledge we have about musicians, however, is about professionals. The best-documented professional musicians frequented courts and were steeped in their culture. In some cases, they even had noble backgrounds. They would sing mainly songs that reinforced the courtly view of the courts themselves. Others made a more parlous living and would only have sung the courtly songs where the popular view accepted them.

For some of these musicians, we know the regional names. For example, *goliards* were poets, musicians and buffoons who travelled across Continental Europe in the eleventh and twelfth centuries and mainly sung in Latin and vernacular, while *jongleurs* were general entertainers who performed dance and acrobatics in addition to music sung in Old French and possibly Middle English. They toured France and England throughout our period. *Ménestrels*, on the other hand, worked for patrons mainly in northern France. Epic legends and stories of antiquity appear to have been far more important to a troubadour's repertoire than the lyric poetry they are famous for today. A poem by Giraut de Cabreira mocks a troubadour called Cabra for his lack of knowledge, listing everything he should know and does not. It is an impressive list, covering a vast amount of literature.

We know that not all professional musicians were Christian, although it is probable that most were. Through a complaint made by Jacob Anatoli around 1230 concerning the practice of Jewish musicians singing love songs and romances, we know not only that Jewish musicians existed, but that they had similar taste to their Christian counterparts! Jewish singers wrote in the vernacular, even when they were writing on biblical or rabbinical subjects. However, we have no information on individual musicians or their lifestyles.

Most of our knowledge of secular music comes through literary sources, thus the words of songs were far more likely to be recorded than the melodies. Although the styles we know mostly come from courts, the fact that many musicians moved from place to place also made it highly likely that the love songs and satires, and in particular the long epic legends, were also the music of the people.

Singers were trained to use their memory, rather than to rely on written texts. In fact, written music was only available to very few people. Christian religious singers would begin learning with the psalms, hymns and canticles. Songs and instrumental music were not limited to religion, entertainment or music for dancing, though – street cries to announce wares or food might be classified as a form of music, and private prayers as well as literature read out loud could take the form of a song or chant. Music formed an important part of religious services both for Christians and Jews as well.

Church music included chants for Mass and for office, a daily cycle of services involving psalms and prayers, as well as music for specific occasions, like requiem Masses for the dead. The music for all of this varied from simple recitation right through to fancy solos. The presentation ranged from simple melodies to dramatic re-enactments. The complete collection of church music for all parts of the year is called an *antiphonary*. Around the beginning of our period, there were new feasts and new music added to the Church's religious year, leading to major developments including the increased use of polyphony to ornament solo chants. Chants could be used in liturgy, but they could also be used for dramas and as music for processions, which were an important part of the cultural aspect of religion.

Jewish religious music was also a type of chant, probably very similar to that which can be heard in synagogues today. Some medieval melodies have survived for particular prayers, but, since the rest was recorded using the cantillation system, we do not have precise records for the bulk of it. The singing habits of important rabbis and cantors were carried on by their successors, which means that strong learned (but not written) traditions developed in different areas over time.

Cantillation did not just help with singing synagogue music; it was also a grammatical aid for the text itself. In the eleventh and twelfth centuries, some cantillation signs represented the shape of the hand signalling used to lead the singers. Rabbis generally felt that music had to be edifying: the beauty of the melody was not itself sufficient. No instrumental playing was therefore allowed during services, no women's voices and no copying of Christian or Muslim religious music.

Musical instruments for all kinds of music were many and varied. The main instruments played by non-professionals appear to have been Jew's harps, bone pipes and flutes – all of which have survived. Wooden and other perishable instruments were also likely used, but have not survived.

Instruments were not standardised in form or type, and a single name could cover a very wide variety of instruments. The examples given here thus do not reflect the full range of possible instruments. Additionally, a single instrument could have a number of names and an even larger number of tunings. Tunings were also not standardised during our period; instruments in a group would be tuned to match each other, not to a set tone as is common today.

Instruments can be classed roughly into three categories: strings, wind instruments and percussion instruments, with keyboard instruments making a tentative fourth. They were not only played solo, but, as today, in combination with other instruments for a better and more varied sound. The combination of pipe and tabor was common in the thirteenth century, and possibly also earlier than that, and was even played by a single musician. The pipe, with its two finger-holes and one thumb-hole, was a one-hand instrument that had a range of two octaves; the second hand could be used for playing the tabor, a small drum, as percussion.

Stringed instruments could either be plucked or played with a bow. The vast majority of strings on musical instruments seem to have been made of gut, with some being metallic and a very few possibly being made of horsehair or silk.

Bowed string instruments can be grouped under the generic name of fiddle. Some of them were played with each string sounding separately, like most modern strings, but some were played as a drone accompanying other instruments. Bows were strung with horsehair and could be either arched or straight. The fiddle was the standard instrument for the courtier from Provence, while *veilles* were regarded by some contemporary learned commentators by 1300 as the queen of stringed instruments. Other stringed instruments include the rebec, lute and harp.

Lutes were not known in England prior to the late thirteenth century, and were possibly introduced during the time of Eleanor of Castile. They were known in the south of Europe before this time and may have been played in Provence. A lute had a vaulted back (as opposed to the flat back of a guitar). Guitars appear in art of the thirteenth century, but before that are somewhat unusual. Both lute and guitar really came into their own, musically, after our period.

Wind instruments were extraordinarily varied. Wind instruments can either have a means to modify the sounds played by physical changes, most commonly finger-holes, or the different notes are played by modulating the breath and lip pressure. The instruments themselves can be made from many materials, ranging from a simple branch of willow or an animal horn to precious wood, ivory or metal.

Instruments with finger-holes were the pipe, the flute and their many variants. Pipes had either no finger-holes at all or a small number of them, often only three or four. It is possible the recorder (a pipe with eight or nine holes) was played during our period, but earliest finds date from the fourteenth century. The flute was usually held transversely, unlike pipe variants, and is edge-blown. It spread very slowly from Germany and does not appear to have been played in England at all.

Reed instruments use the vibration of a cut reed in the airstream to make sound, and the best-known type of these instruments is the bagpipe and its variants, such as the bladder pipe. Other reed instruments include the *shawm* (the predecessor of the oboe) and hornpipes.

Finally, some wind instruments had a mouthpiece like the one associated with brass instruments today. This mouthpiece transforms lip vibration into sound. Horns and trumpet-like instruments could be very loud and were thus also used for signalling, including for military purposes. They were referred to as a *cors* or *oliphant* in medieval literature. The most famous of these horns was the one Roland refused to sound to summon Charlemagne's army at Roncesvalles, leading to all his men being massacred.

An instrument that seems odd to modern eyes is the *cornett* (also called *zink*). This instrument combined a brass-instrument-style mouthpiece and finger-holes. Even though it had its heyday at the end of the Middle Ages and after, it was in use already in our period.

Though the typical use for percussion instruments is to provide or mark a rhythm, they can produce a variety of sounds. Percussion instruments can be as simple as two sticks struck together and are easy to improvise – stomping on the floor or hitting tables, chairs or boards can provide a rhythm as well.

Drum forms usually consist of a frame or bowl with a drum skin pulled taut across the opening, and played either with hands or with drumsticks. The tabor was the most popular drum and might have been tunable. While it could be played with two sticks, it was generally played with one. The crusades introduced the *nakers* or *nacaires*, drums of North Africa, to Europe. They were small kettle drums which were generally played in pairs, each member of the pair tuned differently. They were not introduced to England until about 1300, and became very popular only later than our period.

One form of percussion instrument often associated with the Middle Ages in the popular mind is bells. Chimebells (*cymbala*) could be arranged on a rod or frame and hit with a hammer. There was also a wide variety of larger bells, the most notable being the church bells so important for religious use and marking time. Frame drums may also have been fitted with additional bells or jangles, such as the *timbrel* or tambourine. Entertainers possibly used small bells attached to the body or to clothing as a percussion instrument.

There were several instruments that were played with help of a keyboard. The most famous example of this is the organ. Organs are an array of pipes that are supplied with wind by bellows, and the keyboard is used to select which pipes will sound. More important churches generally had an organ. Positive organs were smaller and more mobile, but still required someone to work the bellows. A small and portable form, the portative organ, did not appear until around 1300. A related instrument is the *organistrum*, which was played during the twelfth century, mostly in churches without sufficient money for an organ. It was a stringed instrument with a keyboard related to the hurdy-gurdy. It required two performers, one turning a crank to produce sound and a second person to play the keyboard by pulling the knob-like keys upwards. A later, smaller version of the *organistrum* was called a symphony or *sinfonia*; it was played by a single person and may have had keys to pull upwards or the newer keys that could be pressed.

Feasting

Feasts can also be regarded as a special leisure activity or a form of entertainment. They were not purely that, however. Just like the menageries kept by kings, with exotic animals that might include lions, leopards, elephants, camels or polar bears, feasts also showed social status.

Feasts took place on special occasions and invariably had more ritual than everyday meals. Some of this was visual, some of it was ceremonial and some of it was gustatory. People would dress in better clothes than normal, and the head of the table would look down at the rest of the hall, where those who were not the family or special guests sat. The best dishes would be used, and the meal would be extended by entremets, entertainment or visually interesting dishes. Unfortunately, there is little evidence of actual menus before the fourteenth century. Some of these dishes might be subtleties, where pastries were made as castles, for example. Others might be practical jokes, such as pie shells filled with live birds, or with mincemeat with marzipan worms. There would also be music, mummery, chivalric sports, tale-telling and dance. The entertainment could be provided by professionals, or by the diners themselves.

Ceremonial aspects included formalising everything, including such basic functions as carrying in food, the washing of the hands both before and after the meal, handing out food from the high table to favourite individuals below, serving more courses than usual and saying a formal grace after the meal. Dishes would be bigger and better than usual, with strong distinctions between the high table and the rest of the diners, in terms of rare and unusual ingredients, and between nobles present and any commoners present. Commoners were fed the most everyday food. We know this structure best through records of royal feasts, where the king and his table would be served both additional courses and extraordinary dishes such as peacock and porpoise, with

Top left: 1. Record of grants of land in Suffolk by Roger Bigod, Earl of Norfolk, to the sons of William de Risinges. Bigod received in return a riding horse, a windmill with land and an annual fee. The document is written in chancery script. Note the remnants of the seal: it shows a figure on a horse on one side and a lion on the other. Dated *c.* 1201–05.

Top right: 2. Childhood in the Middle Ages was a distinct stage of life. While children had some responsibilities, they also had time to play. Modern interpretation, Middelaldercentret, Denmark.

Bottom: 3. The Harrowing of Hell (an episode from the Gospel of Nicodemus). This scene shows the hellmouth itself and a conquered devil. Psalter, first quarter of the thirteenth century, central England.

4. The Vices and Virtues. Diagram of the seven vices represented as devils: Superbia (Pride), Invidia (Envy), Ira (Wrath), Accidia (Sloth), Avaricia (Covetousness), Gula (Gluttony) and Luxuria (Self-indulgence). Each one is subdivided and countered by doves representing the seven gifts of the Holy Spirit, a knight on horseback (the 'Just Man'), who carries the shield of faith and is armed with virtues, and an angel. The armour of the knight and the trappings of the horse are labelled with the names of virtues. England, after around 1236 to the third quarter of the thirteenth century.

Left: 5. A papal bull of Clement IV, dated 1266. Unsigned and untranslated; marked with a lead bulla (papal seal) on a silk band.

Right: 6. Genesis, the opening words of the first book of the Torah, with an illuminated initial showing dragons. Miscellany of biblical and other texts, northern France, 1277–86.

Left: 7. Excavation of the *mikvah* in Milk Street, London, 2001. This *mikvah* consists of a semicircular chamber, with a set of steps leading down into the water. The *mikvah* was built around the middle of the thirteenth century and situated in the basement of a house. Excavation by Museum of London Archaeological Service.

Right: 8. Education for fighters included learning how to use bow and arrow and started at a young age. Modern reproductions of a medieval longbow and arrows in a living history scene.

9. A hunting scene. Dogs were an important part of hunting parties. Note that the hunter is armoured: hunting was not a safe sport! Image from a bestiary from south-east England, second quarter of the thirteenth century.

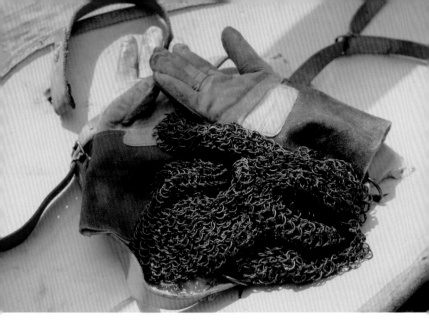

10 & 11. Details of armour and shield: riveted ring mail, padded protective garment and the inside of a shield. Modern interpretation of medieval sources.

12. Hedgehogs. Northumberland Bestiary, England, *c.* 1250–60. Tinted pen-and-ink drawings on parchment.

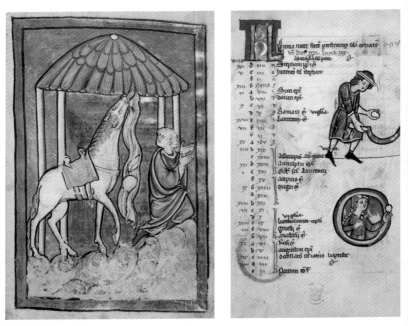

Left: 13. Saints sometimes had a special relationship with animals. St Cuthbert's horse, for instance, is said to have found him food. Note the saddle, which is quite different from modern riding saddles. Bede's prose *Life of Cuthbert*, northern England, last quarter of the twelfth century.

Right: 14. August calendar page from the Psalter of Lambert le Bègue, 1255–65, France. Note the illuminated initial, a picture of a man doing harvest work, and the zodiac symbol of Virgo. Illuminated calendar pages such as this are one of our sources of knowledge about agricultural tools and procedures.

Left: 15. Building a wattle-and-daub wall. The wattle parts are set in timber frames that form the main structure of the building and are coated with a clay mixture. Modern interpretation, Middelaldercentret, Denmark.

Right: 16. Lincoln Cathedral is an example of the Gothic style in England, with the iconic flying buttresses and massive windows.

17. Barfreston church, twelfth century. This Romanesque church, partly built from flint and partly from imported Caen stone, shows strong French influences. It is famous for its carvings as well as for the wheel window.

18. Axes, cudgels, knife and materials used for woodworking, and a half-finished trough. Modern interpretation of medieval tool finds and probable working techniques, woodworking by R. Metzner.

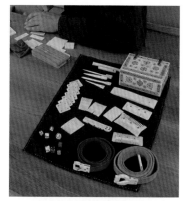

Above left: 19. A parchment maker at work. Modern reconstruction of a medieval stretching frame for parchment.

Above right: 20. Various bone items such as a casket and different forms of combs. Work by M. Opitz, modern interpretation of archaeological finds.

Right: 21. Harness pendant for a horse from cast copper alloy with original enamel décor and attachment loop on the bottom, set at 90° to the plate. A hole has been drilled through the plate opposite to the attachment loop. This pendant type dates to the twelfth or early thirteenth century.

Above left: 22. Making a stave cup: fitting the bottom of the cup and the staves together. Modern interpretation.

Above right: 23. Chessboard and chess figures, modern interpretation of a higher-status chess set based on illustrations and archaeological finds. The colourful decoration of the board reflects the general enjoyment of colours in the Middle Ages. Chessboard M. Megner, chesspieces C. Niato.

Left: 24. Man playing a stringed instrument. Detail from a manuscript about music. Southern France, last quarter of the eleventh or first quarter of the twelfth century.

Middle: 25. Page from the Gradual of Crowland Abbey, showing notation for music to be sung on Christmas Day. Northern England, first half of the thirteenth century (after 1220).

Right: 26. Juggler. Detail from a manuscript about music; the juggler represents one of the musical modes. Southern France, last quarter of the eleventh or first quarter of the twelfth century.

Left: 27. Early modern wooden stairs of the type frequently used in medieval buildings: narrow triangular steps mounted on two supporting beams at a very steep angle. Town gate of Schlüsselfeld, Germany.

Right: 28. Glass oil lamp – one of various methods for lighting a room. Glass being a luxury item, this lamp also signified status. Modern interpretation of medieval sources.

Above: 29. Wallholder spike for illumination. Modern reproduction of an archaeological find by C. Niato.

Right: 30. Modern interpretation of a medieval lantern, based on illustrations and archaeological finds. Brass body with horn panels that let the light through. Execution B. Megner.

Above: 31. Part of the Great Conduit of London, built in the thirteenth century. The conduit brought water from the spring at Tyburn into the city. It shows both the importance of clean water for the city and how sophisticated medieval technology was. Excavation by Museum of London Archaeology Service.

Left: 32. These scenes of the Wedding at Cana and the Expulsion of the Moneychangers show a table set for a feast and the rare depiction of a clearly recognisable trestle table. Psalter, first quarter of the thirteenth century, central England.

Below left: 33. Changes in the shapes of knives are a good example of subtle differences developing over time: the knife on top shows shapes and characteristics from knife finds of the early thirteenth century, while the knife below shows the characteristics of knives dating to the fourteenth century. Modern interpretation of archaeological sources by N. Hofbauer.

Below right: 34. Wax tablet with soot-blackened wax and stylus (stylus after a London find). In the time before cheap paper, writing education would be done on a medium that allowed it to be erased, such as a wax tablet. These could also be used for taking notes or even for less formal contracts. Modern interpretation of archaeological finds by N. Hofbauer.

Opposite below: 37. Guide to palmistry. Manuscript pages showing the Hands of Prognostication. England, second half of the thirteenth century.

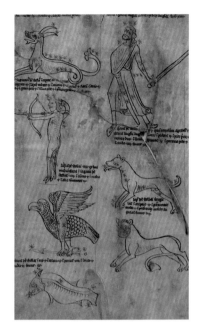

Left: 35. Parchment leaf, from England *c.* 1300. The original manuscript was a Latin translation of the *Physics* of Aristotle (book 5 of the *Physics*, the middle of chapter 6 to chapter 7). The page is frame-ruled and the script is Gothic. The red and blue are running headings and paragraph marks. The colours help orient the reader so that they can keep their place easily.

Right: 36. Recognising the zodiac at night: basic astronomy. Part of texts on the *quadrivium*, early twelfth century (the manuscript has some later additions). Pen and coloured ink on parchment.

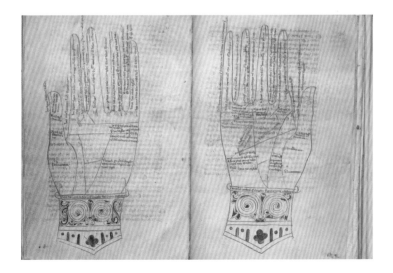

Left: 38. A scene from the Prose *Lancelot*, devoted to the adventures of that hero. In this scene, a lady is bathing in a wooden tub and Lancelot approaches to rescue her. Northern France, last quarter of the thirteenth century.

Right: 39. Detail of a unicorn being held by a woman and pursued by three men, one of whom spears it with a lance, and another with a sword. Note the cloven hooves of the unicorn. Bestiary, south England, second quarter of the thirteenth century.

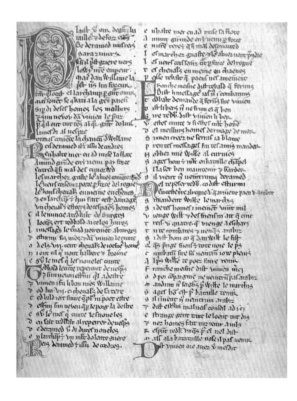

Top right: 41. Fabrics made from wool, dyed with natural dyes according to reconstructed historical procedures and recipes. Colour comparison chart is shown on the far right of the picture. Dyeing work by S. Ringenberg.

Right: 42. Knife and decorated leather scabbard after finds of the early thirteenth century. Modern interpretation of archaeological knife finds, modern replica of a London scabbard find by N. Hofbauer.

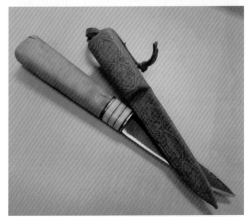

Below right: 43. Shoemaking equipment and a finished shoe on the last, ready to be taken off and turned to the right side. Note the boar bristles and the awls as main tools. Modern interpretation of tool finds and archaeological shoe finds, shoemaking work by S. von der Heide.

Bottom right: 44. Copper alloy brooch, dated *c.* 1200 – *c.* 1300, front with decoration of collets with remains of a white paste inside and beaded domes.

Opposite below: 40. Manuscript page of the *Song of William,* an Old French epic written in England concerning the exploits of William of Orange (Charlemagne's cousin). The coloured initials structure the text and a large puzzle initial opens it. Second or third quarter of the thirteenth century.

45. The English Park is probably the oldest cattle breed in Britain today. They were held in parks to be hunted, hence the name.

46. A Tamworth pig, considered to be Britain's oldest pure pig breed and similar in appearance to the Old English Forest Pig. Of all the native breeds, the Tamworth experienced the least influence from imports of Asian pigs during the eighteenth and nineteenth centuries.

47. Medieval water wheel from the mill at Fountains Abbey, Yorkshire. This wheel is normally submerged in water and is a fine example of medieval everyday technology.

Left: 48. Smaller water vessels like this would have served a lot of the transport needs for people and goods. Modern interpretation of medieval sources, Middelaldercentret, Denmark.

Right: 49. Sailing ships were dependent on favourable weather and winds and generally stayed close to the shore even on long travels. Modern interpretation of a smaller ship that would have been in use in our period, Middelaldercentret, Denmark.

50. Travellers on foot more frequently encountered narrow paths than wider roads. Modern interpretation.

51. Lead pilgrim's ampulla, *c*. 1180–1299. The ampulla is decorated to look like a scallop shell and has a small 'W' on the back, which might indicate it came from the shrine at Walsingham Priory, Norfolk.

52. An explanatory drawing of a method of finger counting. Finger and thumb positions are used to mark ones, tens, hundreds and thousands and can be used for numbers up to 9,999. A miscellany of works on *computus* and astrology, northern or central France, end of the eleventh or beginning of the twelfth century.

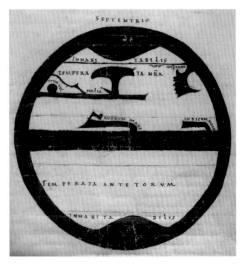

53. Surviving maps are mainly diagrams for instructional purposes. This one shows the oceans, the inhabited area and the inhabitable zones. Illustration for Macrobius' *Commentary*, II.9.1-7 on the ocean. Eleventh century, Germany, written in Latin.

the lords and ladies having two courses and dishes such as lamb and the commoners having to be satisfied with roast beef, which was not considered an aristocratic food.

At a big manor or estate, the feast might be held outdoors, to accommodate more people, since generosity with food was considered a sign of good lordship. The meat could be roasted outside, the trestles were set up outside, but most of the food would be prepared in the kitchens and carried out. One important occasion for tenants that entailed a special meal at the manor was when they appeared to fulfil their reaping obligation.

Entertainment was as much a part of feasts as the food was. It could be expensive. For example, in 1286 over £53 was divided between 125 minstrels for playing on Christmas Day for Edward I. While many of these minstrels were indeed musicians, some were acrobats (such as Matilda Makejoy, who appears in English Royal Household Accounts from the end of the thirteenth century), mummers, fools and jugglers among others.

The generic term for an entertainer was *joglar* or *jongleur*. This included singers, instrumentalists, jesters, jugglers, clowns, acrobats, those skilled in court conversation and even bird imitators. They varied from the socially tolerable to the near outcast. The Church particularly mistrusted those who entertained using obscene gestures and dances, nudity, magic and masks. John of Salisbury argued that actors and other entertainers should not be given sacrament; they were on the very edge of acceptable society. Those who were more tolerated told stories of saints or sang epic legends.

One important element of entertainment was tomfoolery. There were several different types of fool during our period. Some might take on the role of fool just for a feast or a holiday, for instance, while others might be fools professionally. Some people were fools for life. Today, most people think of the fool as a person opting to act foolish; many historical fools, however, were actually mentally disabled people. These were individuals with intellectual defects who were given a home and a job as fool at a court because they were regarded as simple. These people were known as naturals. There are many other modern fictions about medieval fools. Motley was not worn until after our period. Another common belief is that they had nonsensical names. While some had the suffix *Stultus* (fool) or *Fatuus* (stupid) attached to their given name, the majority of their names appear to follow regular naming patterns, that is to say, they were not distinctive.

Fool was the English term, while *sot* was the word used in Old French. In Latin, fools were called *joculatores*. Other terms were used to describe fools: one used around 1300 was *cachinor*, accompanied by a picture of a near-naked man frolicking. He was wearing a two-eared hood, a single shoe, a sword and was carrying a bauble. Many fools were likewise deprived of some or all clothing, carrying a bauble and wearing an eared hood. It was not universal, but it was as close to a uniform as existed during our period.

The word jester was not commonly used until the Renaissance; however, some professional fools were, in practice, court jesters. They were identified with a single patron, and taken care of by that patron. These court jesters appear in literature as well as in administrative records: in the thirteenth-century romance about William the Conqueror's father, *Robert le Diable*, a character disguises himself as a court jester.

Fools were such a standard part of personal entertainment for the very wealthy that the Council of Paris (1212) had to step in and forbid bishops and monasteries from keeping them.

9

Where to Live?
Homes, Castles, Villages and Towns

Medieval households were as varied as the people who lived in them, and accordingly required varied structures. These could range from very simple, temporary huts to stone castles and manors. Lifestyles and built structures intertwined and were additionally influenced by climate, regionally available materials, and, of course, the wealth of the owner.

Much of our knowledge about secular buildings is gained from surviving buildings such as manors, castles and halls. Smaller, less important structures, such as private houses belonging to merchants, burghers or peasants, survive less often. While archaeological excavations can show the footprint and sometimes even the floor size and wall construction of a building, other elements can generally only be conjectured.

Accordingly, there is quite a lot of speculation and theories regarding medieval houses, lifestyle, house decoration and the medieval view of house and home. Michael Thompson, for instance, suggests that larger medieval houses should be seen as comparable to an army barrack, where the hall dominates and the other areas have specific complementary functions. Each household was different, depending on its size and the occupations of the householders, but more documentation is available for larger households than for small. Knowledge on matters such as finances, upkeep, workspaces, housing or staff depends on written data, most of which is not readily available for our period. Archaeological research can improve our knowledge of the layout of large buildings and thus increase our understanding of workspaces and living spaces, but information is still patchy. There is also more documentation available for households from the fourteenth and fifteenth centuries than for earlier ones, so most descriptions of household organisation and operation are based on late medieval sources. The larger the household, the more complex its structure and management, with very large households having distinct areas and staff for most major functions, from cookery through to military matters. The high levels of comfort and convenience that we are used to, however, such as central heating, large windows and running water, were definitely only available in very few, exceptional medieval buildings.

Building Work

Very little is known about the common varieties of medieval building and their organisation. Most of our knowledge comes from larger, more elaborate or expensive buildings, where building professionals were hired. For the other end of the spectrum – simple, smaller houses and structures such as barns or sheds – next to nothing is known; they may have been built with or without the help of professionals. There is certainly evidence for both very substantial, sturdy buildings as well as for flimsy and rather unstable ones, with no hint as to the identity of the builders for the vast majority of them.

When professionals were involved, the builders were mostly hired by the day, with the fortunate ones being employed for forty weeks of the year. The very fortunate ones worked on big projects such as castles or managed to attach themselves to monasteries or castles all year round to see to repairs and modifications. Builders operated often in a very hierarchical manner, depending both on their skill and on the materials they worked with. On top of the hierarchy were the free masons and carvers, elite craftsmen who formed the finest stone. Below them were, for example, the layers, settlers and wallers who worked with the finished stone pieces. Below these were the workers who did the rough and unskilled work.

Primary building materials for all structures in our period, from shed to mansion, were most frequently wood and stone of different quality – both locally available stone (including chalk or flint) and imported stone – or wattle and daub. Wattle and daub, as well as other types of wall using clay as the main substance, were used together with a timber frame that gave stability to the building. Stone walls could be made as dry-stone walls, set with mortar or, for prestigious buildings, from exactly masoned stones that also needed no mortar. Very thick walls could be achieved easily and cheaply by building two walls and filling the space between them with earth or rubble and mortar. Timber walls, banked up with earth, were also in use. Earth walls were not necessarily only found on humbler properties; they were, however, frequently in need of rebuilding. Brickwork is mostly known from the fourteenth or fifteenth century, and little is known about brick use before this time: it appears to have been used only occasionally. The type of materials used defined not only the status and outer appearance of a building, but also imposed certain limitations on size and proportions. Most buildings, for instance, had their width limited by what was possible to span with the wooden beams used in the roof construction.

In many regions, wood was generally cheap and easy to obtain and thus used for less expensive buildings as well as for temporary structures, for example a shelter for an itinerant miner. Houses made with at least a significant amount of wood, such as half-timbered houses, were very common.

Stone was much more durable, but also meant additional building expenses and a greater need for experienced crafters such as masons. Even though stone from old buildings could be re-used to reduce costs (a common practice – York Minster, for instance, features re-used Roman stonework), stone houses were usually only built by the wealthy. They were, accordingly, more likely to have other expensive fixtures such as larger windows, a cellar, drains, lead pipes for water and sophisticated heating. Dressed stone was the most expensive building material, and thus was mainly used for windows, doorways and other key construction areas.

Stone buildings, or at least stone cellars, were also the preferred choice of wealthier merchants for storing and even selling their wares, since these buildings were much less in danger of being destroyed by fire, and thus offered protection to the goods stored within. Stone cellars with vaulted ceilings were an especially expensive part of a building and could easily cost more than the rest of the building. They were, however, best suited for the safe storage of expensive goods: chances were high that even if the upper parts of the building burned down and collapsed, the cellar and its contents would still survive. The history of Rouen shows that this was indeed a concern: the city burned six times between 1200 and 1225.

Mortar, with its main ingredients of quicklime and sand, was used to keep stones or bricks together. Plaster was also used in buildings, more extensively in the later parts of our period, after the thirteenth century.

Roofs always rested on a wooden structure, whether the walls were stone or wood. The actual roofing material could vary greatly, from straw or reed thatch (or similar plants suitable for thatching, such as rushes or even heather) to ceramic tiles or slates. Straw and reed were widespread as thatching material, and shoots of hazel or other supple woods were used to fasten them. While these materials, just like wood shingles, were flammable, they only caught fire when a chain of conditions like very dry weather, the right amount of wind and hot embers landing on the roof chanced to come together. Thatched roofs had a limited lifespan, but materials were easily available and cheap. Thatching was thus usually not used for important or prestigious buildings.

Slates and shingles were an alternative to thatched roofs. Shingles were cut from wood and were more common in regions where suitable wood was in good supply; oak shingles, for instance, were common in Winchester from the twelfth to the thirteenth century. Slates were split from suitable stones, such as limestone in the region around Leicester. Slates were considered as a more luxurious decking, used for example for the twelfth-century royal buildings at Winchester, and transported across considerable distances from the quarry to building sites in both England and France.

From the twelfth century, ceramic roof tiles were also in use. Sizes of these tiles varied, as well as their price. Roof tiles were produced unglazed as well as glazed. Ceramic tiles were used mainly in England and Normandy, and production for the English market was mainly in south-east England and the London area.

House Types

While the range of available materials for houses and other buildings was limited, many different kinds of structures were erected, and only very few of them survive. Researching houses or house types (as well as types of other buildings) is remarkably difficult in most cases. The few surviving houses are for the most part special buildings, such as manors or houses of very rich people. Thus, they offer little information about general building activities, and archaeological sources usually only yield limited information. It is easier, therefore, to find out about the dimensions of the ground floor and where the fireplace was located than what rooms there were or how furniture was arranged.

Generally, though, we can assume that medieval buildings were functional constructs designed as living and working spaces. Various building materials were chosen according to what was available, well suited and affordable. In contrast to most modern building, there was little standardisation of materials and few to no pre-manufactured parts such as windows. This led to a higher variation in buildings than is typical today. The houses would be adapted to the environment, to personal as well as to social needs and thus would vary hugely, not only from small and simple huts to grand manors and well-defended castles, but also from hut to hut and manor to manor.

An example of social influences on buildings is the rise of stone as a material in England: the Norman preference for stone stimulated stone building in England in the early part of our period. It became the building material of choice for representative or luxury buildings. Other examples of social and also religious influence can be found in the detailing of a building, such as little hollows dug out of the doorway at the right-hand side. The doorway of a Jewish house had either this hollow or a religious scroll in a wooden case (*mezuzah*) attached to it.

Houses might have just one floor and be open into the roof, have a second floor used as a storage area or to live in with working areas downstairs, or have more than one floor to live on. For access to upper stories either from within the building or from the outside, the options were ladders or stairs. A frequently used type of stair was a narrow flight, built from wood, with either massive block stairs or boards set into slits. Stairs were a way to access spaces and usually built narrow, taking up little space – representative, large staircases only came into use long after our period. Buildings with several storeys were probably more frequent in towns and cities, where space was limited, and less often found in rural areas. Limited space encouraged the building of houses with a smaller ground floor, but with several floors.

Floor plans varied according to wealth, the activities and work undertaken in the house and in its surroundings, building materials (for different materials supported different sized rooms) and locality. While some rooms were intended for a special use, such as workshops or kitchens, most of them could serve multiple uses, with screens or wooden partitions being used to divide larger spaces where necessary. In any case, house use would have been according to the individual needs and preferences of the family living inside. The arrangement of the rooms depended on issues such as family needs and business needs, but also on the space available.

Matthew Paris, a Benedictine monk, described a prosperous London house of the thirteenth century. It had its own chapel, several bedrooms, an orchard, stables, a kitchen courtyard, a garden and a well. In fact, quite a few English town houses were arranged around courtyards.

The terms hall and solar are often used in connection with medieval buildings. Generally, the hall was a relatively large central room used for various purposes, located on the ground floor in some regions and on the level above in others. The solar was usually smaller and located above the ground floor. Furthermore, the solar was a personal room and the hall was considered as a public space, though these concepts were different from the modern standards of private and public. Both hall and solar are hard to define, however, and the knowledge we have about their use comes mostly from documentation of specific circumstances or special events. Their day-to-day use remains rather unclear, as neither documents nor archaeological evidence yield sufficient information about it.

Halls could be very large and sometimes called a great hall. Typically, they had a high ceiling and a paved open hearth, which was usually about two thirds along the hall; this changed relatively little over time.

Wooden doors were the typical means of closing off the entrance to buildings as well as rooms inside buildings. Very few wooden doors survive and those that have often come from more important secular or ecclesiastical buildings. Metal hinge straps or other iron reinforcements could be plain or be decoratively shaped, ornamenting the door while strengthening it. Bars and locks, also made from wood or iron, could be used for additional protection. Locks used on doors could be fixed to the door, but padlocks (with the lock body most often shaped like a barrel) were also known. Locks offered some protection, but could, of course, be picked or forced. A description of a break-in into a Norwich house tells us that the robbers first broke through the oak door and its iron bar, then entered the courtyard. From there they proceeded into the hall, then the chamber.

Gardens in towns were, to the best of our knowledge, seldom in the courtyard but rather at the back of the house. While some people had vegetable gardens, we know of a Jewish physician, also in Norwich, who had a private herb garden. Gardens provided space to grow some produce, get rid of waste materials in middens or pits and to keep poultry and animals: they were an important part of living in towns and very common.

As with many other areas of research, rural housing is even harder to grasp than town housing, since rural buildings survive even less often. How solid peasant housing was and what the standard of living within these houses was is a matter of debate. However, it is reasonable to assume that since peasants lived in varying degrees of wealth and prosperity, their houses would accordingly range from small, very simple cots that had at most two rooms to farms consisting of several sturdily built houses, barns, stables and sheds, and that the quality of building would likewise vary.

A relatively typical rural building in England and northern France was the longhouse, built of timber and wattle and daub or unfired clay blocks. Longhouses were up to 30 metres long, but only about 5 metres wide, with the average size being 4 to 5 metres by 8 to 15 metres (or about the floor space of a one-bedroom apartment). On one side of the house was the dwelling area, the centre of which was the main room with its central hearth. On the far side, with a connecting door, was a byre, storeroom or an inner room. Judging from documentary evidence such as tax records, the longhouse was probably the most common dwelling for moderately prosperous peasants.

In the south-west or north of England, where mixed farming was standard, most houses had byres for the animals, while in places like the Midlands, where arable farming or industry was the norm, the same space was used for storage or as a workshop.

An early thirteenth-century French poem describing what rural people needed suggested a house, a place to keep hay and a place to keep grain (implying three separate places: perhaps a house and two barns or storage buildings). The poem also mentioned a place to hang the ham by the fire, somewhere to keep the water for the house, a tub to bathe in, a bench, a table, a bed, other furniture and a kneading-trough. It is one of the few hints we have about houses and their equipment in rural areas.

Fortifications, Castles and Manors

Castles and castle life are somewhat better documented. In modern minds, the castle is the epitome of a fortified stronghold in the medieval period. However, while castles did play an important role, they were not the only fortified buildings. Wherever more protection was needed due to reasons such as unrest close to borders, fortifications were more common than in quieter regions. A relatively cheap and easy way to fortify a building or a group of buildings was a moat in combination with an earthen embankment. Most moated sites in England were developed in the twelfth and thirteenth centuries. They enclosed gardens, orchards, chapels, churches, various places of residence and even farm buildings.

Even more spectacular regarding their sheer size were fortifications around towns. Some towns had a wall around their area and an additional castle inside, but towns without a castle could also be enclosed. Walls were built and maintained around wealthier towns in danger of being affected during war, such as York, Colchester, Winchester, London and Exeter. Some towns in dangerous areas, however, did not have walls, as they lacked the funds for construction and upkeep. The expenses for keeping fortifications in fighting condition could be considerable: for instance, £6,600 was spent on Dover from 1180 to 1191.

Castles were built only partly for military reasons. They also served local functions, including administrative and residential functions and served as a display of authority and power. Castles and manors were key for regional administration, including courts, and even served as jails. Lydford Castle was, in fact, built originally as a court and jail in the 1190s. Castles played significant roles as places to live and cores of settlements, economic units and status symbols; they were embedded in the surrounding landscape – both geographic and social or political – and had a deep impact upon it. In other words, castles were not simply fortifications: they were more complex than that, served many functions and developed their own communities.

The type of staff employed echoed the uses to which a castle was put, including its military purposes. Additionally, the number of people in residence or working in a given castle could fluctuate greatly, depending on whether the household of the castle's owner was in residence or not, and whether there was peace or war in the region. Lambert d'Ardres described the Ardres castle in the twelfth century as employing an extensive system of retainers and employees as well as their relatives. Those paying labour service were housed for up to three months at Ardres to give that service.

Ownership of castles, manors and their land was mostly determined by household. In many circumstances, the head of the household represented all those who lived and worked there and was usually the one counted when numbers were taken or taxes were collected. This makes it very difficult to determine the actual number of people who lived in most castles and manors until the later Middle Ages, when household accounts give us more information about their arrangements. Even this information is, however, very limited.

When the owner of the castle was abroad, it was usually commanded by a castellan. He was overall supervisor of the various roles the castle had (especially during times of conflict), including management of supplies, care of arms and materiel for war, barracks, training ground, smithy and ordinary residence. He also had a very direct influence on the countryside for many kilometres around, as the reach of the castle (economically, socially and politically) could be as far as 40–50 kilometres from the building itself. The castellan was responsible for keeping the castle running and in good order when its owner was not in residence.

Large households could have a steward (seneschal), who was head of the servants and took care of the non-military administration of the household. Especially in very large households or those of high nobility, this was considered a very prestigious position. The steward's counterpart for the military side of the household was the constable. A marshal was head of the staff responsible for care of the horses, both military and non-military. This part of the staff was often kept quite separate from the rest of the household.

There was no universal design or location for a castle. Most were agglomerations based on the specific history of that castle. The site, the history of the site, the building materials, the money and labour available, the date when the castle was built and the fashion of that period and the actual needs of the person who owned the castle all played a role.

Castles usually took the location into account in some way, such as being situated to make the best use of hills, cliffs or rivers for their defence. Not all castles were on sites that made very good sense in military terms. Those places might often have had the remains of an older fortification or building, or even enclosures or sacred places, and the newer castles sometimes integrated or re-used them. For instance, the French castle Grand Caux used a place that had been sacred in pagan times, while Rochester re-used older fortifications.

The functions of castles had more in common with each other. They granted protection to those inside and usually also had some control over the surrounding region or important features such as rivers, river crossings or roads. Sometimes, this was reason enough for nobles to erect castles illegally. These adulterine castles were, if possible, taken down by sheriffs with a team of people to help them.

The defences castles used were varied. They ranged from ditches or moats to sturdy curtain walls around the castle complex. These walls could be combined and stacked inside each other, resulting in several enclosed spaces. In addition to the large and well-defended main entrance into the castle, they often had smaller and therefore less obvious additional gates known as the postern gates. Those could turn out to be both a weakness, if foes found a way inside through them, or a strength if they allowed the castle occupants a successful sortie. A keep or donjon – the main building of the castle, and the one dominating the inner ward – stood at the heart of the castle. Parts of the inner courtyard might be connected by covered passageways for additional protection. Some castles had barbicans to defend the main entrance, featuring a gateway and usually a ditch.

The layout of castles also changed over time. Tenth-century castles were, by and large, wooden towers with moats, and were basically fortified farms. Wooden castles, whether from this time or from later centuries, usually did not survive. In the eleventh century, stone started replacing wood, and fortified donjons were built. From the twelfth century, the donjon moved to a more purely defensive role, with a second building in the castle enclosures serving as main residence. In fact, from the end of the twelfth century, a second enclosure was quite frequently built for lesser dependents and for refuge at times of war. Castles prior to around 1200 might have had smaller towers and most would not have had large halls. A roughly normal interior space for a hall would be about 6 by 5 metres. The hall was generally within the bailey section of a motte and bailey castle. Mural towers were towers that were built into the curtain wall, and curtain walls with these extra fortifications were usually built some time after the beginning of the thirteenth century.

Castle defences could also include a series of sections with walls that could be closed off, high towers to observe distant happenings and as a firing-point for artillery and sally-ports. Preparation for the case of a siege included a secure supply of water and store rooms suitable for large enough amounts of food. Many castles took their water from cisterns or from the ground through deep wells, often situated in the keep or inner courtyard. This could result in quite sophisticated water management. Dover, for instance, used lead pipes to move water through the building from its almost 74-metre-deep well.

Typical parts of a castle in addition to the defensive structures included room for people to live and work in, buildings to house animals, kitchens, storage spaces and a chapel or similar place for religious service. Residential areas could be solars or other rooms in the main building, but also separate residential buildings, either freestanding or as a lean-to structure attached to walls and other buildings. Most of these structures have left little trace, so our knowledge of them is very patchy.

Statistics of castle building are sadly unreliable, but overall numbers increased during our period. The numbers for England are probably around 250 baronial castles and forty-nine royal in 1154, and 179 baronial and ninety-three royal in 1214.

Building a castle, even a small one, was a large and costly project requiring a substantial work force. For example, 950 labourers worked on Harlech in the summer of 1286 and 2,000 worked on Beaumaris in 1295. These people were paid 1¼*d* or 1½*d* a day.

Another building type with similar importance and similar functions to the castle was the manor. The distinction between a manor and a castle is not always easy to make, and daily life would not have been very different. Where manors belonged to great households, not even the people were very different, as much of the household would have travelled from estate to estate.

Legally, the medieval way of distinguishing a castle from a manor was by its crenellations. In reality, the differences between the two were not great. Castles served the same functions as manors in everyday life, and it was usually only in times of war that the differences in military capacity became obvious. Thus manors were lived in by those who had administrative, legal and military responsibility for the region, just as castles were. They served as bases for rent collection for the district and the administration of other services, for collection of dues and for most legal matters. Their residents shared these tasks with the village, which provided constables, for instance. The residents of castles or manors might be quite senior barons, or quite junior knights, and their level of wealth and influence was often apparent in the nature of the building and the size and complexity of the household. At the upper end of wealth and influence, manors might have pleasure gardens and deer parks, for instance, while at the poor end, they were little more than glorified halls.

Halls were very important to the functioning of the manor: they were used for meals and for courts; the noble dead were laid out in them and gatherings were held. Some scholars suggest that people slept there at night, although evidence to sustain this is seldom cited. The dimensions of halls varied hugely. Town halls were considerably smaller than castle halls, for instance. The largest hall in Europe of its time was Westminster Palace (built from the eleventh century), which was 77 metres by 74 metres, divided into twelve bays. It originally had a wall gallery and possibly had aisle arcades (like a church) or an arcade down the centre.

Household Organisation and Use

While the exterior and especially the above-ground parts of a building are often problematic to reconstruct, even less evidence exists regarding the interior of houses and the use of the rooms. The size and shape of individual houses influenced size, shape and organisation of the rooms inside. For larger buildings or building complexes such as castles, special purpose rooms like chapels, kitchens or special storage rooms like the buttery (for ale) and the pantry (for bread) are documented. It is not known how typical rooms with a specific use were in private houses – probably the smaller the house, the more multi-purpose its rooms.

All houses would have contained a main room with a means of heating. In the simplest instance, this was just an open hearth in the middle of the room, also used for cooking and to provide light. In that case, the central elements of home life – food and sleep – were thus all taken care of in one single room.

The Middle Ages only knew two sources of heat and light: the sun and fire. During the day, windows allowed natural light in, though not in the same way as modern windows. Medieval windows were typically rather small and could either be left completely open or covered with translucent material. Glass windows were expensive and therefore rare. The use of window glass is known from royal houses and palaces by the end of the twelfth century. What was used as cheaper alternatives is much less known – oiled parchment, oiled cloth, sheets of horn or translucent slates of stone are all possible materials. Whether with or without any translucent cover, windows were also equipped with wooden shutters to close them completely.

The second source of light, fire, was an omnipresent thing – not only as lighting, but also for heating, for cooking and as part of many craft processes. An open hearth or comparable fireplace was part of every house.

Fuels for lighting and fire were different depending on the person's wealth, the region and what the fire was needed for. Locally available fuel was usually the most affordable, and wood or brushwood were common choices. In some regions, people gathered dead wood from the forests; this was a right that was fought for, if necessary, especially by rural dwellers. In regions with peat or coal, they were dug for fuel. Peat was the standard fuel in East Anglia due to its availability, and the Norfolk Broads had enormous peat extraction areas. Coal was mostly not used as a domestic fuel, but in crafts and industries, where high temperatures were needed. The wood available also varied regionally, and there are huge differences between various kinds of wood regarding the speed and heat with which they burn. Fuels could be stored indoors, for example in a shed, or in a protected space outside.

Contrary to popular modern belief, lighting a fire was not a hard or time-consuming thing to do. The typical technique was to strike a spark onto tinder using an iron striker or fire steel and a piece of flint. The material used as tinder carries the ember, and different substances such as punkwood (rotten wood), tinder fungus or cattail seeds all work as tinder materials. The ember is placed into a nest of substances that catch flame easily, such as straw, fine brushwood, wood shavings or birch bark, and the small fire fed on successively larger pieces of wood or other fuel. Alternatively, it would have been possible to start a fire using a fire drill. Rashi also described glass devices, which were filled with water and exposed to the sun, for setting fire to chaff.

The omnipresence of fire and thus hot ashes and embers meant an ever-present residual danger of uncontrolled fire spreading and devastating houses or entire settlements. However, since fire was a part of daily life, it was usually familiar enough to be controlled well and easily, and everyone was aware of its dangers, much like people today are aware of the dangers of modern traffic. Precautions were also taken to prevent fire-related disasters, such as the curfew, a bell that was rung in towns to remind people to cover their open fires for the night. This bell had its name from the *couvre-feu*, a pottery cover with air vents that could be used at night to cover the fire and protect the surroundings. It also helped to slow down the consumption of fuel and preserve the fire overnight.

Fireplaces used for heating the rooms and for cooking were a key element determining the house's floor plan. Earthen fireplaces or earthen, mason work and brickwork hearths are often found in archaeological digs. Simple, undecorated tiles were, for example, used to build the central hearth. This was done even before the general rise of tiles and brick as building materials. In addition to the fixed fireplace, portable heating was also available, for example in the form of braziers.

The smoke from fires rises upwards, and in simple houses it dissipated through the roof, which may or may not have had openings at the gables. The smoke could be used to preserve foodstuffs, and it also helped to keep the upper parts of the house and the roof pest-free.

Smoke was also a nuisance. While it is possible to build a fire low in smoke by choosing good-quality, dry fuels and having enough ventilation for the fire, there will always be some smoke coming from it. Chimneys to channel the smoke and lead it outside faster appeared from the eleventh century. They enabled the wealthy to reduce the amount of smoke, and the accompanying smell and soot, inside the house. Since the smoke also carried away a considerable amount of heat, chimneys were for the well-to-do only, as a chimney meant that more fuel was needed for heating the house. Wealthier town houses had fireplaces with flues and chimneys by the twelfth century. Baked clay chimney pots were used from the thirteenth century in east and south-east England, although not elsewhere. They are normally associated with ground-floor halls or manor houses with timber roofs.

No matter how the house or room was heated, additional insulation could help the inhabitants to keep warm. This insulation could take the form of curtains, wall hangings, cushions and back-rugs, as well as wooden shutters for windows or more elaborate room fixtures such as wood panelling. There is very little known about these, however. The few surviving examples we have are often very elaborate and colourful, showing clearly that soft furnishings were also very important for their decorative effect. Even less is known about floor coverings such as straw, rushes, herbs or mats and other textiles.

While the main fire in a room or house would also have provided some light, a wide variety of additional or alternative lighting means were known and in use. These ranged from cheap and simple – usually with more of a smell, more smoke and less light – to more efficient expensive versions. Most of the time, it is impossible to tell where lights would have been put. However, exceptions to this are small niches built into stone walls that are supposed to have held lights.

Basic lighting means were simple spills of resin-rich wood or rushlights made by dipping a rush into oil, fat or wax. Oil lamps, either standing or hanging, could also be used for lighting. The hanging lamps were shaped like a cone and were hung from chains; if made from glass, they would also illuminate what was below them. Standing lamps could be made from pottery or stone, though stone lamps are mostly known from ecclesiastical sites. Candles were made from tallow or from beeswax, with the latter being the most expensive material.

Candlesticks, both cup and pricket versions (with a spike to keep the candle in place), are known from our period. Cupped holders were used from the late eleventh century, but not really common until the late thirteenth century; prickets were generally preferred during the earlier part of our period. The candleholders were made of various materials and either stood on a flat surface or had a spiked end that was stuck into walls or boards.

For use as outdoor lighting, a relatively wind-resistant torch was one option. Another possibility was a lantern that protected a small flame (such as a candle flame) from being blown out. Some lanterns are known from archaeological digs: they are metal cylinders with a door, with decorative punching to let some light through. Thin, translucent sheets of horn or oiled parchment were also suitable for use in a lantern.

Both types would not have given off a lot of light. Lanterns with large glass panels, as they are common today, are not documented for our period.

Apart from heating and light, two more basic needs had to be taken care of in daily household life: water supply and waste removal. Clean water was necessary for consumption by humans and animals, hygiene and for manufacturing and crafts.

Water was generally obtained either from a stream or a well. Wells were dug down until groundwater was reached and lined with wood or stone to keep them clean and open. Rainwater or water piped in from a spring could be stored in a cistern. Generally, the larger a town and the denser its population, the more water was needed, and it sometimes became a challenge to supply. In London, this was solved by piping in water from outside the city and storing it in cisterns, known as the Conduits, where citizens could supply themselves. Buckets, carried in hand or with a beam across the shoulders, were a common means to transport water.

Inside the house, water could be stored in buckets, troughs or barrels. Running water was available in some houses and can be seen as a very prestigious thing. Monasteries sometimes had running water, for instance Fountains Abbey in Yorkshire. At least some castle keeps also had that commodity, such as Dover Castle in the late twelfth century.

A description by Rashi suggests that hot water supplies were available in some households. He described a samovar-like structure with a large pot of water on one side and a smaller, attached container for hot coals on the other side.

Dirty water could be taken care of by throwing it out into the street or discarding it into a garden plot belonging to the house. For other refuse, such as human and animal excrement, kitchen rubbish and other broken or discarded bits, several different possibilities existed. As usual, those depended on regional customs as well as on individual circumstances, including the wealth of the household. The exact way of dealing with dirty water and refuse within a house was sometimes quite different from modern expectations – for example, before the installation of a conduit in 1260, the smell of the outgoing water from the king's kitchens at Westminster was discernible in the hall, leading to complaints.

As most houses had at least a small garden plot and domestic animals were very common, a midden or dung-heap on the plot was an easy and common way to take care of human and animal excrement as well as domestic waste, organic floor coverings and animal bedding. In stables or stable-partitions of longhouses, a drain or sump could be used for easier cleaning. Once the dung-heap had rotted down, the material could be spread on the garden beds to serve as fertiliser. An alternative, especially necessary in towns where garden space was limited, was to have the collected material taken away and deposited somewhere else.

Pits, either lined or unlined, were also used to collect rubbish. Unlined pits with privy waste or domestic waste were documented in rising numbers from the tenth to the thirteenth century, when they were increasingly replaced by pits lined with stone or brick. Sometimes, they were lined with wickerwork; evidence for this comes, for instance, from tenth- to twelfth-century London. While not all pits used for dumping rubbish were indeed dug for that purpose, there were plenty of lined and unlined pits dug especially for wastes. They were used for collecting and temporarily storing the rubbish, which was taken out periodically for storage or use elsewhere.

Rubbish was also dumped into deep holes such as old quarry pits – for instance for stone, chalk, sand, clay or bog iron – disused wells or cellars, or other pits and holes. Medieval records also tell us about unauthorised middens that were created in other spaces and encroached on market squares or roads and could even block lanes. Vacant plots or abandoned buildings, whether secular or religious, were also places for opportunistic dumping. In many towns and possibly also in some villages, common muck hills were also available as rubbish disposal places. It was also used to level up hollows or for other filling purposes, such as the infilling of waterfront revetments. In towns with extensive iron-working, such as Gloucester or London, slag might be used as a road material.

As towns became more densely populated, the number of regulations regarding rubbish increased. Many larger towns had passed regulations by the early fourteenth century and, in many cases, also organised a system of rubbish collection and street cleaning.

For the collection and disposal of human waste, similarly different solutions were available. Great houses as well as monasteries often had latrines that emptied into cesspits. We also have some evidence of indoor toilets (in cellars) in Oxford. Small lean-to privies attached to the main building are known from at least the later twelfth century, and attached outhouses or indoor privies became more common in the thirteenth century. Where larger houses had accommodation on the upper floors, privies served by latrine chutes developed.

The toilets were usually fitted with seats not dissimilar to modern solutions: Rashi described a privy stool which looked like a folding chair but with an opening in the leather seat. From York, archaeologists have uncovered twelfth-century wooden toilet seats. The latrine would have been underneath them, possibly with a wicker screen or a similar sight shield in front for privacy.

Many larger towns also had communal latrines. When possible, these were conveniently situated close to water, such as directly on waterfronts or on bridges, next to rivers or streams or set up to empty into a moat or deep ditch. Documentation of these, however, is scarce

– they mostly get mentioned when they needed maintenance, or when a crime happened in them. Winchester, for instance, had public latrines over a stream, which have appeared in legal cases.

Finally, sewage and slops could be taken care of by throwing them out into the street, or by dumping them into a river or stream.

With heating, lighting and waste removal taken care of, daily life in any house was based on the use of various domestic items necessary for running both household and workshops. The number and types of items that could be found in a household were as different and varied as the houses and households themselves. Typical furnishings of a house might include sitting and sleeping places for the inhabitants; a table for working and eating; at least one place to make fire for lighting, warmth and preparing food; and something to store clothes, food and other items. There is, however, only very limited information about the look, the function and the placement of medieval furniture, so what we know does not form a coherent picture.

There is very little surviving furniture from the Middle Ages, and most pieces come from religious surroundings. Soft furnishings, such as rugs, wall-hangings, cushions, back rugs for benches and curtains, survived even more rarely.

Some information about medieval furniture can be gained from illustrations. Written inventories also give an indication of what was used. Judging from these sources, most households did not have a plethora of furniture. Frequently mentioned are beds, chests, benches, stools and cushions, as well as maybe a trough of some kind. However, inventories only list the furniture that was valuable enough or seen as important, and such lists were only made for a small number of households. There is no way to discern how typical a given household inventory was.

Research about medieval furniture is made even more difficult by the items originating from the Arts and Crafts Movement and their successors in the nineteenth and early twentieth century. Modern technological and art historical analyses show that most of the pieces in museums, castles and private collections thought to be from the Middle Ages or the Renaissance are, in fact, objects constructed in the nineteenth century, using modern methods of construction and resulting in more modern forms. This holds especially true for the furniture that seems to be best preserved or most richly decorated. Those modern re-interpretations have significantly shaped our idea about how furniture looked in the Middle Ages.

Illustrations showing furniture are thus quite an important source, since they may also depict types that have not survived, as well as possible placement in a room. These illustrations, however, cannot always be taken at face value.

For a secular household, there is definitive evidence for tables, chests, beds and some form of seating furniture. Decoration of these items could be achieved by different means, such as painting or carving. The motifs for decoration were often close to architectural forms, such as rounded arches. This furniture was probably complemented by pegs, rods, boards and similar possibilities for hanging or standing things.

Tables were a key piece of furniture and used for eating as well as to provide work surfaces. They could be fixed tables or trestles. Generally, fixed tables are more stable, while trestle tables were much more flexible and could be put up or placed out of the way according to circumstances. They were especially handy for use in multi-purpose halls, where they were placed in order to meet the needs of the day. Some tables also show evidence for particular uses, such as game boards marked directly onto the table top, or grids used for counting and accounting purposes.

Table linen is documented as well, though we do not know how frequently it was used outside formal meals. Tables set with a table cloth are shown on illustrations of feasts or similar special occasions. Typically, these cloths were white and may have been decorated either through a decorative weave or other means such as embroidery.

Seating arrangements and the type of seat depended on the wealth and status of a given household or person. Just like all other furniture, the seats themselves could be decorated by carving or other means, such as using differently coloured wood or paint.

The simplest and most common form of seat was the stool or plain bench without a backrest. Stools could be shaped in many different ways, and could rest on either three or four legs, with or without cross-bars between the legs. Three-legged constructions will stand securely with less precisely worked legs and regardless of uneven floors.

Chairs – seats with a back, with or without arms – were a more prestigious type of seat. The right to a chair or the most important chair at a given occasion depended on precedence rather than on absolute rank. The junior people at a gathering were given lower status seats such as benches. Other ways of indicating rank through seating included adding a footrest, cushions and raising the seat by putting it on a dais or step.

There are two additional special types of seating: fixed seats and especially mobile seats. Fixed seats were part of a building, such as the window seats or benches fitted into walls that are sometimes found in castles or churches. Just like the more mobile seating, they could be outfitted with cushions, back rugs or similar textiles to provide more comfort and more insulation.

On the other extreme were seats designed for itinerant households: folding chairs or folding stools. Though it would have been possible to make folding chairs from wood, no evidence for these cheaper versions has survived – folding chairs or stools that are known today are made from metal and leather. Those were especially prestigious and served as a mobile throne for monarchy as well as seats for travelling bishops and other high clergy. These chairs could even be used to emphasise a connection to other, preceding rulers. For example, Abbot Suger of Saint-Denis (d. 1151) had an earlier folding seat altered for his use, declaring it to have a connection to the Frankish kings. The importance of the folding seat can also be seen by its appearance on the French royal seal. Some folding chairs and folding stools survive, and they are typically quite elaborate and very well-made. Furniture designed for a travelling lifestyle was not limited to seating, of course – other pieces were also made with travel in mind, like chests or beds.

Chests were ubiquitous and used for storing all kinds of things, including clothes, linen and wool fabrics, grain or flour and plates and other household items. They provided additional seating, and they could be taken along as luggage when travelling. While dugout chests made from a hollowed-out tree trunk survive in some churches, the typical medieval chest was constructed from split boards. The four boards forming the ends of the front and back, or the two boards forming their sides, extended below the bottom of the chest, serving as feet to keep it off the ground. This protected both the chest itself as well as its contents from moisture. The lids of these chests were either flat or gabled, roof-shaped lids; there is no solid evidence for rounded lids of chests. The lid was often attached using no metal at all: the back part of the lid and the upper edge of the chest's back were shaped to interlock, fixed together with a wooden or metal dowel that served as hinge. While some scholars interpret the gabled-lid chests as used purely for storage of grain or fodder, this is by no means sure.

Chests used for storing garments or household goods, as opposed to grain-storage chests, were usually outfitted with a small, inset box for keeping smaller items, and they could even feature secret compartments. For securing the contents, chests could be fitted with one or even several locks. Some chests or other containers for storing valuable personal possessions were not kept in the household, but deposited elsewhere, for example in a church or cathedral, for safekeeping.

Surviving medieval chests often look quite long to the modern eye, and they were all rather large – often about 2 metres or more in length. The wooden boards used for their construction had considerable thicknesses as well. Those chests were, accordingly, very heavy, which protected against theft of the whole chest. Elaborate metal reinforcements could additionally strengthen them. Examples of these reinforced chests again mostly survived in churches and monasteries where they were used to store valuable garments and liturgical equipment.

Cupboards in the modern sense, as upright storage furniture closed off with one or several doors, were much less common than today and much less important than chests. Just like chests, most surviving cupboards are from religious buildings, but other evidence suggests that this was indeed where most, if not all of them, were used. They became more common in secular circumstances only very gradually.

Other means of storing items were boards for display and storage, or rods fixed to the wall or the ceiling. These have usually not survived, but are known from illustrations. Architectural structures, such as the beams in an open roof structure, could also be employed to stand or hang something.

Finally, we do not know very much about another essential type of furniture: beds. Our knowledge about beds and bedding is almost entirely from written and pictorial evidence, which skews our knowledge toward the more sumptuous. When beds are shown, their construction is usually hidden because of hanging bed covers and blankets.

Many beds in these illuminations had four posts as vertical construction elements; in artworks, these posts can be seen standing out above the bedding. How side, front and back boards were fitted, and how the mattresses were supported, is hard to tell. Mattress support may have varied from rope webbing or a sheet of leather or strong cloth to slats or boards set into the bedframe. Mattresses could be made from cloth stuffed with some filling, such as straw, rushes, furze or broom, but again we do not have much firm knowledge. Some beds had wood or metal canopies, which was probably a sign of status. A low railing or decorated boards at the head and foot were also possible. Full bedding and bed linen, according to written sources, included a mattress, underbedding, pillows, covers and sheets. These may have included blankets made completely or partly from furs; rich textiles on the bed were used to show one's wealth and importance. Whether beds were shared by several people as a rule, or not, is also hard to tell from our sources. For small children, cradles are documented both in art and in writing. Although most evidence of what cradles looked like and what they were furnished with relates only to the very highest levels of society, we know that other households used them as well. A French list of the thirteenth century, for example, makes clear reference to cradles in peasant households. Some cradles may also have had straps to keep the child securely in.

Many more small furnishings and personal items survived, mostly known from archaeological excavations. For both furniture and smaller everyday items, such as spoons and knives, there can be considerable differences in form and material between a typical medieval and a typical modern item, even though they served the same function.

In some cases, it is hard to tell whether medieval people would have regarded an item as part of the household furnishings or as personal. This can differ widely from how these things are regarded in our time. For example, though spoons were generally personal possessions, they could also be supplied at a formal dinner. Knives used for eating were usually personal items and not part of a supplied table setting. They were seen as so personal that it was only socially acceptable to share a knife between people very close to each other.

Smaller objects around the home were mostly made from pottery, wood and bone. Pottery was used for everything from bowls and pitchers to candlesticks and colanders. Smaller items found in households included pots and pans, bottles and cups. Glass objects were unusual except in the homes of the wealthy. There was a gradual increase in the use of glass during our period, with very little in use before the thirteenth century (unless earlier glass has perished). The use of glass domestically is thought by archaeologists to have possibly been a by-product of window glass. Metal was used relatively sparingly, but was essential for things such as knives or locks.

Typical items found in a home included pots in different shapes and sizes. Because pottery was low status, it was common and varied considerably in shape and size and function between regions. While surviving vessels are usually made from clay, wooden ones were probably at least as common, and metal was also used in some cases. Vessels ranged from everyday sizes (as trenchers, drinking bowls or cooking vessels, for instance), through sizes large enough to be used for cooking or storage (typically 5 to 10 litres), to enormous ones for specific purposes such as brewing. In 1244, two cases from London are documented where women fell into lead vats and were scalded to death. Wooden trenchers, bowls and troughs were items as frequently documented as buckets, pails, barrels, boxes, baskets, pegs or hooks, brushes, brooms and small tools such as hammers, spindles and distaffs. Small boxes, cases and caskets could be used for safekeeping of smaller, highly valued items (such as letters, documents or jewellery). In contrast to the large chests for storage, more shapes are known for these small storage units, including cases with a rounded lid. They could also be elaborately decorated by carving or painting, or covered with leather, which in turn could be decorated. For less valuable things, barrels, sacks, nets and baskets in different sizes and shapes could be used for storage.

The vast majority of household items have not withstood the ravages of time. Stray items turn up in archaeological digs or are mentioned, often in passing, in literary sources. These instances remind us of the many varied things found in an ordinary domestic household, even though most of them have disappeared from our sight.

Towns and Other Settlements

While there may have been isolated hamlets and single farms, most medieval households were grouped into a kind of settlement. Much of our evidence concerning medieval lives comes from the examination of these different kinds of settlements. Whether a town, a village or a single homestead, all settlements had some common needs and concerns. The inhabitants needed space to live and work in, water and food supplies, a means of trading and some way to get rid of refuse. Settlements larger than a single farmstead needed a road and path network as well. As villages and towns grew, trade and production grew with them and travel between them became easier. Opportunities also differed between life in rural areas and life in towns. Women, for instance, were able to lead quite different lives in towns than they did when they lived in isolated hamlets. The shift of the population from relative isolation into towns is one of the hallmarks of the Middle Ages.

The more people who lived in a given location, the more complex it became, and rules and regulations developed for government and administration. In addition, larger cities or towns had more influence on their surroundings and also more political influence due to their wealth, leading to more mentions of the places in written sources. Thus, much more is known about towns and cities than is about villages and farmsteads – for the latter, archaeological excavations are the main source of information.

Technically, a village was self-sufficient in food but may have had little in the way of external trade. On the other hand, towns and cities often depended on food brought in from the nearer or wider vicinity. Those foodstuffs were either sold at stalls in a marketplace, in shops or by peddlers. Both shops and peddlers could sell a very great variety of goods.

Individual houses and garden plots were the most frequent components of any settlement, but not the only one. Key structures that were needed in every settlement larger than a single farmstead or a very small village were a church and a graveyard. One or several common water sources were necessary for water supply. Marketplaces were areas for trading, but also important places for social and cultural activities. When there was enough need, common buildings or structures could be found, such as ovens for baking. Communal ovens were an asset for Jewish communities as well, since they could be used to cook Sabbath stew. They were certainly used for Passover to bake matzah (unleavened bread).

The topography of the place depended on many different influences, such as the region and history, the lay of the land, the property distribution, already existing roads or commons and whether the settlement was planned or developed slowly over time. A frequently found village type in England was one centred on a shared village green or common. Other villages developed along a road, for example, or to support a castle. In the north-west of Europe, villages were often centred on a church, which may have been the only stone building, though a wooden church was also quite common. The actual structure of a given village depended on its region and history.

Some areas were more closely built, and medieval tenements were not unknown. However, open spaces existed both in villages and towns, and typically houses had a garden plot even in more densely populated parts of the city, such as High Street in Winchester. Towards the outskirts, open spaces would have been even larger and may have included arable land and pastures either held by individual people or used as common lands. While commons were used mainly for grazing, and so always had cows, sheep and other farm animals, they were also used as a source of other materials. For instance, the furze, bracken, rushes and reeds that grew there could be harvested.

Larger and richer villages or towns sustained a larger variety and quantity of crafts as well as a higher level of specialisation. Crafts that were needed in rural life, such as smithing or pottery, were probably found more often in smaller or more rural settlements than more refined crafts such as glassmaking. More available capital also made it easier to build or to maintain communal defences such as city walls; smaller settlements thus remained mostly without defensive structures. Walled villages were very regional.

The twelfth and thirteenth centuries especially were a time of urban expansion. More people lived in towns than previously, and their numbers grew continuously. Some towns (known as *bastides*) were purpose-built, fortified and carefully planned. These towns are often found in the parts of France that were under English rule, usually in Languedoc, Aquitaine and Gascony. With this urbanisation came a change in self-definition of people as townsfolk. In fact, the earliest known appearance of the word bourgeois in this context was in 1134.

A charter granted special privileges to a town or city that might include the right to have a seasonal or permanent market, the right to have foreign trade or hold a fair, tax exemptions or political independence. Many towns, however, still owed their allegiance to a lord when their charter did not grant them the right to be self-governed. Not all towns had their own charter, but those that did were often attractive to live and work in due to privileges and relative independence. A charter would thus usually lead to some growth of the settlement. Towns were also the places where one might find a mint, an administrative point for the Church or a permanent judicial court.

Royal boroughs reported directly to the king through his officers;

seigniorial or mesne boroughs were held by lords. The governor of the town – king, lord or town council in self-governed towns – had the power to issue regulations and approve privileges. Some towns also had more than one governor. London, for instance, was governed by different lords as well as through the City of London. A single town might also have multiple governors due to many reasons; for example, a town might have grown together from several smaller settlements that were originally within different jurisdictions. While more towns became independent boroughs during the twelfth century, such as Oxford, most towns and villages were still under a lordship.

Special rights or institutions in a town also depended on who held the town or at least a part of it. Royal boroughs may have held a king's court, for example, known as the *portmoot*. Guilds developed in towns due to the need to control the practice of crafts and trading. The word guild (or *gild*) comes from the Old English word *geld* (payment, contribution). While it could also apply to people forming something like a mutual support club, it usually means a group of people pursuing financial and crafts interests together and restricting the influx and practice of new town residents in the craft.

A very town-specific thing was the freedom, a special civic status. Not all towns offered freedom for inhabitants. If they did, it could be attained through different means, for example by inheritance or through purchase. It basically meant membership of the town corporation and usually included payment of annual fees, for example 12*d* per annum in Wells in the twelfth century. Freedom might link towns – the payment of 12*d* per annum in Pontefract in 1294 also gave privileges in Grimsby, for instance. Acquiring freedom might mean acquiring the right to buy, sell, mortgage and bequeath property; access to local power; commercial privileges; or tax exemptions.

Towns were also a place of special opportunities. If a town was outside the jurisdiction of a serf's landlord, they could escape to the town and live there for a year and a day, which in most cases made them free.

The location of towns and villages had important repercussions on the life of people. Trade routes might lead to commercial prosperity. Some towns were relatively isolated, acting as regional centre and not much more. Others were key destinations for foreign merchants involved in international trade, for example La Rochelle, London, Winchester and Montpellier. Border towns, on the other hand, were at the mercy of the political situation. Hereford was sacked by Gruffydd ap Llywelyn in 1055, for instance, with canons being killed.

Some towns, especially during the eleventh century, had customs and feudal obligations. The amount and extent of the dues paid by a given town, and to whom, depended on what region it was in and the history of the particular settlement. Over time, obligations might be transformed, such as the obligation to upkeep a bridge translating into a cash payment.

The actual lifestyle in any town or village also depended on the choices people made and their access to markets, their family connections and actions, their neighbours and outside influences, customary law and the Church and on the local aristocracy. These choices and influences would have had a very large effect on how strong a community in a given settlement was, how much access to what sort of culture and crafts people had, how far the community was torn or built up by internal politics at a given moment, how far it made its own decisions and how far it depended on the lordship and the Church for important decisions.

No matter whether it was large or small, each settlement was unique, not only in place, but also in time. Each place possessed its own fluid and changing culture. Some settlements were dynamic and some were dying. Some were prosperous and some were poor. Some followed fads and some practiced old traditions. And many would have combined all of this in different people.

Town Life

Towns were places where trade happened. The big difference between towns or cities and smaller settlements was the potential to develop financial capital through trade and crafts. This financial capital ensured wider lifestyle choices and increased personal security, at least in theory. Wealthier merchants usually chose to live closer to the commercial centre, with more comfortable houses. In walled towns, they lived safely inside the walls wherever they could. Towns were also the most likely to have a range of professions and crafts represented. More people would be able to earn a living by specialist work of one variety or another. The larger the town, the more variety and specialisation was likely to occur.

The range of occupations and trades included not only crafts, but all kinds of other trades such as selling old clothes, selling wax, making pancakes, making garlands, running baths, washing hair, dealing in peacock feathers, making church vestments and making felt. In Paris in the late thirteenth century there were 321 professions recorded as tax-paying, of which women were definitely active in 108. Many did not exclude Jews. Evidence of Jewish servants, doctors, teachers, butchers, vintners, cheesemongers and fishmongers suggest that money lending was not the only option for Jews, despite popular belief.

Poverty, however, was ever-present. The poorest practitioners in these many professions and those who did not earn enough to appear on the records (for they did not pay tax) did not make enough to live on: these working poor relied on alms for sustenance.

Despite all this evidence for a generous array of crafts and trades practiced in towns, by no means all of them were town-based: the industrial revolution and the concomitant shift to towns was still a long way away.

On the edge of towns and outside the walls were often found the noisy and polluting trades such as blacksmiths, bellfounders, potters, tanners and fullers. The riverside was also frequently an industrial zone. Mills were normally found on the edge of towns or in nearby villages. Most mills during our period were watermills, although windmills began to be built in the thirteenth century. Major towns had mostly sorted out public water supplies by the thirteenth century. Public wells were common and made handy meeting places for townsfolk. Archaeological studies have also shown that most towns probably had trees and shrubs.

Towns had plenty of issues, too. For example, they were far more likely than the countryside to be flooded when there was heavy rain, especially as the towns grew in size. One of the major problems attached to flooding was possible contamination of drinking water.

Streets were usually narrow, so traffic was another issue. Iron wheels damaged roads, and animals being driven to market could be severe obstacles to anything or anyone else. Having specialised streets to sell different produce helped with the traffic problems, as did having animals for sale only entering using certain gates.

Responsibility for the upkeep of streets was often divided, which could cause maintenance problems. Frequently, the houses next to a given section of road were responsible for its paving. Not much is known about the quality or standards of work, although the maximum width of gutters in England was apparently twelve thumbs.

Where there were no houses or where the area was public (such as a market), which was more frequent in the thirteenth century than earlier, it was paid for by a tax called *pavage* (collected from visitors to the town), which was probably also used for work on major streets.

This urbanisation led to the expansion of old settlements and the founding of new towns. New towns might be a planned town (a *bastide*), in which case it had a regular layout that was likely to be symmetrical and would generally include a church, market and town wall.

Existing towns expanded where they could to meet their residential needs. It was not always possible to build outwards into fields, so innovative means were found of extending residences. Buildings might be taller, for instance, than in the surrounding countryside. Or they might be built on the riverbank, on reclaimed land. Jettied buildings are found quite frequently in English towns.

Houses in towns might be rented or owned outright. In Norwich in the late thirteenth century, houses cost between four and thirteen shillings per annum to rent. These were not luxury houses at that rental – they were more likely to be made from wood and plaster. A spectacular stone mansion at the top of the rental market would go for much more – at about £5 per annum.

Permanent shops would have probably been common in larger towns by the twelfth century, but we have little record of them. However, the records we do have are telling. For example, the so-called Norman House in Lincoln had an undercroft, a row of shops on the ground floor and a hall on the first floor. While most shops were not standardised in size, a street frontage of around 2.5 metres and a depth of maybe 6 to 7.5 metres seems common.

Major towns might have town residences for lords and senior ecclesiastics, including accommodation for those who worked for them. In London until the middle of the thirteenth century, these residences were mostly in the City itself or in Southwark (because of its proximity to markets and the port), but after this time the centre for lordly activity gradually shifted to Westminster.

Lords and townsfolk did not necessarily work together very well. Lords demanded their rights, for instance inheritance tax, and the right to interfere in other people's lives, especially when it came to marriage. In these battles, women and Jews were mostly the losers. They were more dependent on the goodwill of others to have their rights and needs observed. Sometimes, the issues between a lord and his town could result in actual violence, such as in Amiens in 1115 and Laon in 1111. Matthew of Westminster wrote around 1199 that King John hated London, and Richard of Devises said of John's brother, Richard, that he would sell London if a buyer could be found. Towns also had their own views of the politics of the day, and their own involvement. For instance, Rouen rioted in 1090 at the instigation of the sons of Henry I and of the nobility.

Jewish communities often formed their own sub-settlement inside towns, with their own organisation. The official head of the community was the *parnas*. There were many other roles, both religious and secular. The president of the synagogue, for instance, directed liturgy and was often also responsible for the synagogue building. The Beth Din (community law courts) depended on rabbis and other learned men for judging and teaching. Rabbis were not synagogue officials in their own right, but were religious teachers who maintained the community's religious and legal knowledge base.

Social standing of individuals in towns was just as important as in the manor or in the country. Two main factors seem to have controlled standing: wealth and acceptance into certain circles (such as the great families of merchants, the senior members of the most important guilds). The key players in areas dominated by trade were the big merchants, naturally.

10

Learning for Life
Education

Education was not organised by the state as it is today, and formal education was not universal in the Middle Ages. Some people were more likely to go to school than others. Boys, for example, were more likely to obtain a basic education than girls, as were children of higher social standing than those of lower. Serfs were very unlikely to have the same opportunities: wealth and position in society were definite factors in being able to access basic education.

Literacy was essential in several spheres – religion, administration, the law and, to a lesser extent, trade – but most people probably didn't use writing in their daily lives. Artisans, workers and peasants had no real need for literacy. Merchants were often literate and even more likely to be numerate, but their focus was on business communications and thus they were not regarded as literate by many medieval scholars. While literacy of the elite in society was inconsistent (ranging from the most educated people in the country to people who couldn't read at all), the typical education levels of priests and Jews were consistently higher than the average. Still, priests for distant and lonely parishes might have had little more than the reading basics. Learning more than just one language was also considered important by some classes of people, and they took great pains to ensure their children could speak, for instance, Old French. In the thirteenth century, Denise de Mountchesney commissioned Walter of Bibbesworth to write a rhyming vocabulary so that her children would have language resources. How much education women had is a matter of hot controversy, for the evidence is extremely patchy and often hard to interpret.

Formal education (beyond reading and writing) consisted of specific disciplines. Many modern disciplines such as history and languages were not formally studied, while others such as the sciences were quite different to today's subjects. Many of the disciplines that we regard as related to formal education – engineering, for instance, and the capacity to compound medicines – were taught informally (for example through apprenticeship) in the Middle Ages. It was quite possible to have advanced skills related to these disciplines without being able to read or write. There was also a big difference between the theoretical knowledge of matters as taught in a university and the practical application as used by craftworkers. The discipline where these two overlapped most frequently was probably alchemy, which had a theoretical underpinning (and was studied in higher education) and also many practical applications. Its modern equivalent subject is chemistry.

Given the paucity of records, it is difficult to know just what proportion of the population was educated. We can be certain that the number of educated people grew over time, though even with schools becoming more widespread, not every child attended them. Many families of great houses sent their children away for fostering, training or service in connection with their education. For example, a young noble would take service as a valet. The service would include household, military and administrative work, where the boy learned the skills and knowledge necessary for functioning in a noble household or at court. Cup bearing was one of the skills that all would-be knights and courtiers were expected to know and perform before they reached higher levels. A courtier, in an ideal world (and obviously with ideal levels of ability), would also be functionally literate, have musical skills and be versed in games like chess, have good social skills and manners and, of course, hunting and fighting skills. One of the reasons boys were fostered into great households was to obtain skill sets such as this.

Whether early education was received during service, given by an individual tutor, in little groups or in school-like organisations is for most cases hard to tell. The more formalised education processes in schools are much better documented than other forms of teaching and learning.

While most formal education in the Middle Ages was given by religious authorities, Nicholas Orme argues that in England the increase of secular schools from the twelfth century provided the principal source of education. In these secular schools, the master and scholars might be linked to the Church, but generally had not taken higher orders and were clerks rather than religious. Acceptance of a child into school was technically independent of social rank, though children in towns and from wealthier families would have had better chances of attending school than poor children or those from remote rural communities. Entry into these schools was through acceptance by the master and through payment of a fee. Endowed schools (free from fee) were more of a fourteenth-century development. In monastic schools, the students were either of free birth or had their lord's permission. In the twelfth century, they paid around ½d or 1d twice a year for their studies. There was some charitable provision for bright and needy students.

Over thirty schools are mentioned in English records from the twelfth century, with a significant increase in numbers in the thirteenth century. The exact number of schools is almost impossible to establish, however, as there was no central governing body nor any licensing system for these schools. Great scholars could be found at some of them. For instance, Geoffrey of Vinsauf – a famous rhetorician – taught at Northampton. Lincoln was a major centre of learning under William de Montibus. Oxford had several famous teachers, such as Gerald of Wales and Alexander Neckham, and the scholar Adelard of Bath studied at Bath.

An alternative to schools was the private tutor, available to the well-to-do. These tutors might focus on formal schooling, but were equally likely to be able to assist with other skills such as hawking. It is not possible to tell how much formal education was taught by tutors, and it probably varied widely.

Education for Christians

Early Education

Early education mostly covered learning how to read. The technique for learning to read was to start with learning the alphabet, then to move to syllables, then words, then phrases. The texts used for teaching were in Latin. Pronunciation of Latin was learned alongside the learning of syllables. Some students (probably mainly in religious institutions) also had singing incorporated into their learning from this point on.

A reasonably standard way of learning Latin syllables would be to learn the psalter by heart. Most students would have stopped at the psalms, being able to read aloud more or less fluently. They may have had little understanding of what they were reading unless they had also been taught Latin. Knowledge of that language was not always a given; some teachers needed glosses (vocabularies) in their native tongue to use the teaching texts.

Beyond this, once the students could read words, they were taught basic grammar and then the initial texts were re-read for real understanding. Popular texts for this were Cato's *Disticha* and the Bible. More advanced students also read Aelius Donatus' works and Latin Classics. Christian students thus usually learned the alphabet, psalms, some antiphons and, if the teacher had the requisite skills, how to read music.

Higher Education

Higher education was restricted mainly to Christian males. It covered quite a different range of subjects to modern higher education. It was also significantly different to early education. All higher studies were in Latin, so there were no language barriers between scholars coming from different parts of Europe.

We have quite a bit of evidence on how subjects were commonly studied for higher education. To take natural philosophy as an example, each section of a major work by Aristotle was explained. Then the teacher asked the students a question. The students would present their answers, then the master would resolve the question, citing many authorities in the process and leaving the students with an understanding of both the basic question being examined and of the intellectual field that had looked at it. This question method (known as *quaestio*) was key to medieval scholastic method and very important for higher education, especially in Christian France.

Major centres of higher education included Hereford, Oxford and Lincoln. There were no formally instituted universities in England in the twelfth century, and even after this, the only universities were in Oxford and Cambridge. English students mostly went abroad for their advanced education. The most popular destinations for students were Salerno for medicine, Bologna for law, Paris for theology and general studies and Orléans for general studies. The university at Paris had so many students from England they even had an 'English nation'. Advanced students in places that offered extra subjects and further qualifications could also specialise.

From the thirteenth century, universities were formally set up, partly due to political reasons. Not all of the established centres of education became universities, however. These institutions were primarily targeted at Christian scholars, leading to a marked difference between the formality of Jewish and Christian advanced education. In fact, most universities did not accept Jewish students. Montpellier is the only one documented as doing so.

The aim of higher education was to educate religiously, and the highest levels included topics such as religious philosophy. Before advancing to these studies, an adequate knowledge of the seven liberal arts was needed. This was technically also a requirement to be a preacher or a religious teacher. They covered the basic rounded education of a person with higher learning.

The seven liberal arts consist of the *trivium* and the *quadrivium*. The first and most important three, grammar, rhetoric and logic (the verbal arts), were the *trivium*, and the mathematical arts, arithmetic, music, geometry and astronomy, made up the *quadrivium*. Although these seven subjects may seem familiar to us, they were not as clearly defined as their modern namesakes. Each of these arts comprised a variety of topics, and there might be considerable overlap between the arts. For example, history was considered a part of rhetoric, and etymologies as well as numerical symbolism were a part of grammar. One subject might also be covered under two different arts.

The vast proportion of treatises on the subjects of the seven liberal arts were written by masters for the schools and universities. The seven were not immutable, and increasingly knowledge extended and even challenged the limits of the liberal arts structure. The twelfth and thirteenth centuries were periods of great intellectual growth and change, and the changing structure of knowledge reflected this. Nevertheless, the liberal arts remained the building blocks of Christian advanced education in the Middle Ages.

Trivium

The *trivium* consists of grammar, rhetoric and logic or dialectic. Grammar was one of the most common subjects, being taught at every cathedral church from around 1179. It was the ground on which other education rested and was the most important of the liberal arts.

Grammar was subdivided into several areas including prose, metre, rhythm and, most famously, poetry. One of the best-known writers on poetry was Geoffrey of Vinsauf. Hugh of St Victor was perhaps the most well-known eleventh-century grammarian and William of Conches his equivalent in the twelfth century.

Most modern scholars divide the use of ancient grammar (the works of Donatus and Priscian) from medieval grammarians in the twelfth century. Popular medieval texts included Evrard of Bethune's *Graecismus* and Alexander de Vila Dei's *Doctrinale*. Aelius Donatus was a fourth-century writer whose treatise comprised questions and answers on the eight parts of speech and their inflections. Not only did Donatus' system break sentences into parts of speech (noun, pronoun, verb, adverb, participle, conjunction, preposition and interjection), but it analysed their attributes (quality – common or proper; comparison – positive, comparative or superlative; and gender, number, form and case). This was the most common model for the learning of grammar.

The other main author used in teaching grammar, although less important than Donatus, was Priscian. His *Institutiones grammaticae* were referred to for language theory and as teaching texts. They were required reading in Paris and Oxford for anyone studying the liberal arts.

From the thirteenth century, Oxford was the centre of English grammar teaching, with a series of grammar schools operating alongside the university. The aim of these schools was to create school teachers and to teach would-be university students.

Rhetoric was a system of rules for and ways of doing things that governed literary writing and formal speeches such as sermons. It applied to both prose and poetry. The main aim of learning rhetoric was to help writers prepare poems, hymns, letters, sermons and other written materials, although there is discussion in some rhetorical works of its use with the spoken word as well.

Rhetoric is frequently divided into three subsections. The oldest of these is *ars dictaminis*, the art of writing letters, dating from the eleventh century. *Ars praedicandi*, the art of saying things, is really about how to write a sermon, and an immense number of manuals treating this subject have survived. Finally, *ars grammatica*, grammar, was also important for the study of rhetoric, and considered a subsection of it as well as being taught on its own as one of the liberal arts.

Rhetoric proper was generally organised around five topics: arrangement, delivery, invention, style and memory. Some scholars also looked at the context of the speech, for instance whether it was meant for judicial, political or ceremonial purposes.

Logic was also known as dialectic, and was a formal, theoretical study. It was the art of rational argument and inquiry, and was particularly important with the rise of scholasticism from the twelfth century. It was viewed as a subject more advanced than grammar and rhetoric, but its contents were not clearly defined. Various scholars explained it quite differently.

Logical study in the twelfth and thirteenth centuries was based on works of Aristotle and Boethius (with Boethius being particularly important), plus Isagoge of Porphyry and a couple of others. This was *logica vetus* (old logic). A second branch was the *logica nova*. *Logica nova* included some of Aristotle, plus Gilbert de Porree. *Logica modernorum* was a twelfth-century movement which included recent major thinkers such as Abelard, Ockham and Gerbert.

Quadrivium

The first of the four *quadrivium* subjects was arithmetic. Arithmetic was the theory of discrete quantities. The main topics were the number in itself, the ratio (relationships between numbers) and the proportion or mean (the relationship between three numbers). Numbers could be looked at in three ways in the Middle Ages: as a basis for calculation using either numbers or the Hebrew script, depending on the training; as a basis for arithmetic; and as elements of mystical or religious lore. All of these were linked, but who looked at numbers and how they looked at them in everyday life would depend very much on who the person was and what their background was. Scholars, by and large, were only interested in *computus* (calculations, a part of mathematics) if it led to philosophical ends. The basis of medieval arithmetic was Boethius' work on arithmetic.

The second *quadrivium* subject was music. There was a big difference between the scholarly study of music and the actual practice by musicians. Music was taught as a system, with a focus on harmonics and rhythm. The harmonics could include tones, intervals of sound, models and different chord types. The explanations of rhythm in music theory began with basic units of time.

This was linked closely to mathematical theory and cosmological and astronomical theories. Studying music also involved studying proportions. Major treatises used were by Boethius and Martianus Capella. According to Boethius, music was the daughter of arithmetic and an important tool for understanding the workings of the cosmos.

Geometry, the next subject of the *quadrivium*, was a more advanced use of numbers and their manipulation and theoretical understanding than arithmetic. Hugh of St Victor divided it up into three subjects: investigating heights and depths, finding the extent of a flat surface and measuring the circumference (especially of the world itself). Technically, then, medieval geometry was closely linked to modern surveying. The main schools for learning it were at Liège and Cologne.

Finally, astronomy was considered the most useful of the sciences in the Middle Ages, for both practical and religious reasons. It not only helped with navigation and prayer times, it also aided people to understand God's workings and will through improving their understanding of the universe. The most important tools were Euclidean geometry, plane and spherical trigonometry and algebra. It could be divided into three components: celestial physics, mathematical astronomy and astrology.

The basis of medieval astronomical study was a variety of texts on cosmology and the stars.

Cosmology underlay all studies of the heavens and their relationship to the Earth. It regarded the universe in a broader sense: what it was shaped like, for instance, and how it operated. In the twelfth century, Honorius of Autun pointed out that the universe was shaped like a ball and that the very centre of that ball was Jerusalem.

Basic astronomy teaching included the names of the fixed stars, the four compass directions and elements and use of the astronomical tables. A more practical part of astronomical study included the use of tools to gain astronomic information such as the time of sunrise, distances to and position of heavenly bodies, telling time and predicting other astronomical events.

Both Christian and Jewish astronomy were based on standard writers such as Al-Farghani and Averroes. Ptolemy's *Almagest* was particularly important, containing astrological techniques as well as mathematics. Claudius Ptolemy (*c.* 150 CE) integrated earlier astronomical work, calculated the earth's circumference and established the size of planets, to produce a system of astronomical size and difference. Astronomy books by Europeans (based on these books) included Johannes de Sacrobosco's (John of Holywood) very popular *De Sphaera* (*c.* 1250) and a twelfth-century book ascribed to Gerard of Cremona, *Theorica Planetarum*.

The main textbooks from the thirteenth century included two by Sacrobosco: *Computus* (time-reckoning) and *Algorismus* (arithmetic for astronomical calculations).

Astronomy postulated a spherical earth at the centre of a spherical universe. Learned people knew the earth was round, and literature suggests that most other people knew this too. Earth was circled by the planets in seven spheres, with another sphere containing the stars on the outside, rotating from east to west. Outside that, a ninth sphere was known as the crystalline heaven. Astronomers also calculated movement of fixed stars and a third movement for varying rates of star progression. This understanding of the physical universe underwent important changes during the twelfth and thirteenth centuries due largely to the improvement in understanding of Greek science.

Astrology was closely linked to astronomy, both in Judaism and Christianity. Astrology was used to cast horoscopes and to help find the best moment for events. Astrology was also used as a tool in other disciplines, for example in medicine, to find the appropriate treatment. It was how scholars could link the cosmological theory with their everyday reality.

Astronomy was used by formally trained teachers because of the understanding it gave of the natural and the occult worlds. This could be very mathematical, for instance calculations of the planets and their effect on daily life, or it could relate to the qualities of heavenly bodies, for example how parts of the body fell under different zodiac signs and what the significance of that was. The scientific approach to the cosmos was part of the curriculum of formal education. It gained in importance from the twelfth century, as more people had access to formal education. Popular astrology mostly concentrated on phases of the moon and their influence.

Philosophy

Other subjects were taught beyond the *trivium* and *quadrivium*. Philosophy was considered to be more advanced than the seven liberal arts, and development in philosophical thought was considered very important. According to the medieval worldview, philosophy incorporated all other knowledge, including science (the word *scientia* in medieval Latin simply meant knowledge). It generally consisted of three parts: natural philosophy, metaphysics and moral philosophy. The chief aim of studying philosophy was to better understand the Bible; this meant that philosophy was very much influenced by Christian religion.

Until the twelfth century, many Christian scholars followed Plato in dividing philosophy into physics, ethics and logic. In about 1120, the influential Hugh of St Victor classified philosophy into theoretical, practical, mechanical and logical. This was a subject of discussion in medieval education and scholars did not always agree on the divisions.

Christian philosophers based a lot of theory on the work of Philo of Alexandria. However, the medieval versions of Greek philosophical texts were often different from the originals. This was because of translation, attribution (such as pseudo-Cicero) and textual tradition, but also due to the borrowing of ideas and words from a source, then changing them to fit a new context.

Education for Jews

Early Education

Jewish children, boys especially, were given basic education from an early age. In many cases this education continued until the child reached religious adulthood, which was at the age of thirteen for boys. From the twelfth century, boys younger than this were not encouraged to participate in services like adults, which suggests that initial religious education continued until at least thirteen where possible.

We have evidence that at least some Jewish boys were given a special ceremony on their first day of elementary school. They were five to six years old, and, ideally, started their school education on the festival of Shavuot (Pentecost).

While some Jewish groups stated that they were not in favour of women being educated, a student of Abelard gives us evidence that this position was not universally adopted. In fact, judging from this evidence, Jewish women tended to have a higher level of education than Christian ones. He pointed out that Jews educated not only their sons, but also their daughters. Rashi, one of the great Jewish scholars and teachers, was noted for his daughters also being outstanding scholars and teachers. The actual position is probably that Jewish girls received less education than Jewish boys and that their education stopped earlier, but would still provide the Jewish women with a solid basis.

Jewish education included some of the same basics as Christian education, but not all. As literacy was valued, most English Jews appear to have been literate in Hebrew and some in Latin. Most Jews used Hebrew characters for writing, both when using the vernacular and when writing Latin.

Once the basics were learned, Jewish students moved on to study Talmud, which meant learning Aramaic as well as Hebrew. While Talmud provided the legal background necessary for the community, a learned Jew would have to add many other subjects. These might include mathematics, astronomy, medicine, rhetoric, poetry, grammar and logic. Perhaps the most famous formal grammatical treatise in the Jewish spheres was written in Provence by Rabbi David Kimhi (*c.* 1160–1235); however, many of the standard texts were Greek.

Higher Education

Jews obtained an equivalent level of education to Christian scholars through Jewish communities with a strong educational focus, for instance in Lunel in southern France, or in Paris. There appears to have been no major Jewish centre of education in England.

Particularly important for the study of Jewish law and theology from the twelfth century were the Tosafists. This was a group of scholars who played a key part in influencing how the Talmud should be learned and interpreted. A key Tosafist was Jacob ben Meir (Rabenu Tam), a grandson of Rashi. The Tosafists produced a huge collection of short texts that resemble Christian law glosses in format, but, obviously, not in content! Their chief sphere of influence was Germany, northern France and England, and the most important influence on them was Rashi. One of the distinctive features of their work was the production of *responsa* (answers to queries by the public) that were long and explanatory and, in fact, taught the religion rather than just rendering a verdict on a case.

Jewish writers also saw philosophy as a discipline for advanced thinkers only. Many Jewish thinkers used Greek philosophy to give direction, but during our period philosophy using Jewish texts (such as the Torah and Talmud) was gaining ground. Medieval rabbis don't seem to have used Philo of Alexandria's work as much as Christians did. Jewish philosophers were as influenced by Aristotelianism as Christians, and, for both of them, this caused problems of explaining the point at which reason and faith met.

There were other significant differences between the Jewish view of things and the most common Christian interpretation. For example, the Jewish cosmology stated that the cosmos was created by a name. This had wider repercussions; for instance, if one used the letters of that name it was possible to perform powerful magic, including the creation of life.

Overall, it is much harder to trace Jewish formal education than Christian. Jews may have been more or less welcome in the places for higher education that were not universities; however, more modern research is needed to be certain.

11

Crossroads of the Mind
Science, Magic, Medicine and Technology

When people in the Middle Ages looked at the world, they interpreted it using a mixture of popular culture and learned culture. The specific mix that anyone used would depend on a range of factors, such as religion, social status, level of education and literacy, how travelled they were and on their personality. The Middle Ages was a religious period, however, and this aspect of the world view underlay everything else. Much of the practicality – how people use their view of the world to interact with it – emerges in other chapters. For instance, political decisions and social choices, even decisions on what furniture is necessary, all are subject to the cultural assumptions that belong with world view.

This view of the world also affected the medieval approach to science as well as to magic, technology and medicine. Medicine and magic were at the nexus between learning and folk culture, between the theoretical understanding of the world and what people actually did to effect changes in that world.

The world view of the Middle Ages was very sophisticated and complex. Dividing it up into categories, which must be done to explain them, creates artificial breaks in ideas that were seamless. It can even suggest that everyone had the same view of science and magic, the same approach to and use of technology, made the same choices and had the same material in their lives, told the same stories and shared the same lifestyles as each other. This was, of course, not true. One of the hallmarks of the Middle Ages was the capacity for individual interpretations of this complex reality. There was no printing press or mass media to reinforce shared viewpoints, and even the sermons by priests were not uniform.

Science

The Middle Ages was a time of great intellectual flowering, especially during the twelfth century, and many advances and changes to styles of inquiries were made that laid foundations for modern thought. This is very true especially of scientific thought.

The natural science of the Middle Ages, however, is not directly comparable with our modern version. This is one of the reasons why apparently scientific texts do not meet our modern canons of scientific presentation. They were *not* scientific texts, but were regarded as literature intended to help understand the world better.

Essentially, medieval science was based on a fundamentally different description of reality to modern science, resting on and relating to a different world view. Physical reality, that is nature, was seen to have innate qualities. These qualities were the Aristotelian qualities: hot, cold, moist and dry. Objects could also be imbued with special qualities by the influence of the stars and planets. This influence was generally described as occult (meaning 'hidden'). However, it still related to the natural world – occult properties in scientific descriptions of the Middle Ages did not refer to anything mystical, but simply to what was not visible. Astrology was thus a natural tool for many medical practitioners. Another quality of objects was their metaphysical qualities, which might be known from experiment or might be derived from their appearance. For instance, a doctor might recommend a herb with dragon-shaped leaves as a remedy against worms or snakebite. This concept gave rise to a form of sympathetic magic, where people harnessed these metaphysical qualities, likenesses to attract or differences to repel, to try and effect change. This principle of sympathetic influences underlay many scientific studies and much intellectual inquiry, as well as doctors' and others' everyday work.

There are two particularly important works in our period that outline the scope and the nature of science. They are Hugh of St Victor's *Didascalicon* (twelfth century) and Robert Kilwardby's *De Ortu Scientiarum* ('On the Origin of the Sciences', middle of the thirteenth century). Hugh of St Victor discussed the difference between theory and practice, while Kilwardby (1215–79) divided science into divine (biblical) science and human science. Human science was, according to his definition, philosophy and magic; he recommended, though, avoiding magic.

Philosophy itself was similarly divided into two subfields, divine philosophy (speculative knowledge) and human philosophy. Divine philosophy included natural science, mathematics and their subfields geometry, astronomy, perspective, music, arithmetic as well as metaphysics. Human philosophy was further divided into operative and verbal. Operative philosophy was ethics including monastics, economics and politics as well as mechanical (farming, cooking, medicine, tailoring, arms-making, building and commerce). The verbal included grammar, logic and rhetoric. This understanding of science is global, therefore, and comprises an understanding of how the world operates. Although there were some experimental scientists (one of the most famous being Roger Bacon, 1214–92/94), most people who studied science were involved in theory and undertook thought experiments rather than physical experiments.

Scientific development, in fact, was largely divided between the craft development (engineering and technological progress) and intellectual development, with little contact between the two. The well-known scientific thinkers were not working for industrial purposes, but for religious. World understanding and interpretation was very important, and there were many writers who used scientific approaches in their work. The vast majority of people involved in scientific inquiry during our period were not questioning the basis of their understanding of the world so much as interpreting it, and, through disciplines such as alchemy, finding ways of manipulating the world itself. Alchemy especially had a big influence on development in crafts. Though some alchemists were looking for keys to transmutation and to the philosopher's stone, even more were occupied in a more practical branch, interested in the qualities of glass and ceramics, in painting pigments and in metallurgy for everyday use. These pursuits might not be as glamorous as the modern view of alchemists, but they were much more useful to goldsmiths and others, and hence much more lucrative. Work in these practical areas brought with it major strides in chemical knowledge and application. Both branches of alchemic work involved the making of elixirs. Elixirs were substances that could cause chemical reactions, rather like modern catalysts. A second unifying factor was the alchemists' interest in changing the material world.

Southern French scholars were particularly important for the interface they could provide between the Arab and Christian worlds. Scholars who could read Arabic translated these texts into Hebrew, Spanish and Latin. Among other key texts, they made Ptolemy's *Almagest* available for Western audiences, which had a huge impact on the development of science.

Among the writings used for astronomy, the *Almagest* was important, but the classic book on the nature of things, used in many universities, was by Bartholomew Anglicus, an English scholar writing around 1230–50. His book was called *De Proprietatibus Rerum* ('On the Properties of Things'). Other key authors included Euclid, Aristotle, Averroes (who was a crucial author for Europeans), Alhazen, Galen, Hippocras and Avicenna. They utilised mathematics (Euclidean geometry, plan and spherical trigonometry and algebra using both the decimal and sexagesimals systems) as a tool. A good example of a thinker laying foundations for modern science is Adelard of Bath (*c.* 1070 – *c.* 1160). He believed that to call something a miracle should be a last resort, and before doing that, other explanations should be sought. He explained many natural phenomena in his *Quaestiones naturales*. This kind of striving to explain phenomena and mysteries, however, was not universal: there were many scholars who preferred their mysteries to remain unexplained. Other important twelfth-century scholars included Bernard Silvester (who wrote *Cosmographia* around the middle of the century) and William of Conches (who interpreted the outside world critically and objectively and lived *c.* 1090 – after 1154). The best-known Jewish scientist was probably Jacob ben Abba Mari Anatoli (*c.* 1194–1256), who lived in Provence. He was the only known Jewish experimental alchemist from the period. This may be either because too little has survived concerning Jewish alchemy or because Jewish alchemists may have been unusual. He and Michael Scott (1175 – *c.* 1232) were at least acquaintances and possibly friends.

Magic

The medieval views of magic are just as different from modern concepts as the medieval view of science. Magic was not something separate from religion or science, and would not have been defined during our period in quite the way it is defined today. It consisted of a wide range of practices, all with the intent of changing the world. Probably the most frequent uses of magic were for influencing health and love; however, it could be used for everything from predicting the weather and ensuring a safe journey, to killing enemies or at least rendering them impotent. It was mentioned in literature or records when it brought a sense of wonder (when curing the ill using a relic and when reporting a miracle) or evil (the dread doings of someone who dealt with demons), but it was far more widespread and far more everyday than this suggests.

Magic might be achieved by prayer (supplication) or by spells (manipulation). The difference between the two was that the manipulative magic relied on the order of the universe rather than on the power of the deity. The manipulative magic tied in with such concepts as the medieval cosmos, the four elements and the four humours. The two could also work together: the distinction between prayer and spell is by no means an absolute one, nor is it always easy to make.

Magic was inextricably linked with how people saw their world. Richard Kieckhefer suggests that magic was a crossroads where different pathways in medieval culture met: religion and science, popular culture and intellectual culture, literature and everyday life.

While the practice of magic varied amazingly, magic was well known throughout our period. Evidence of Anglo-Saxon magic, for instance, survives in manuals of medicine, which shows that it was linked to both the folk cultures of Europe and to Classical learned ideas of the world. Anglo-Saxon clergy were firmly against soothsayers, charms and love potions, confirming the use of magic for these purposes. The most famous manual for magic in our period is known as the *Picatrix* and is a thirteenth-century Latin translation of an Arabic text. However, treatises on subjects other than magic, such as lapidaries, herbals or bestiaries, may contain information on how to practice magic.

There was no definable group of magicians or witches in our period, nor even one simple set of universal practices. People ranging from priests to housewives, both Christian and Jew, practiced some sort of magic as part of their daily lives. We have evidence of thirteenth-century magic used for recovering lost items, foreseeing the future and conjuring spirits. Erotic magic was important: many people, from many walks of life, would have thought of using magic to enhance their love life or their sex life. A woman might keep a consecrated Host in her mouth and kiss her husband to retain his love. A man might use vervain or place a wad of wool soaked in bat's blood under her pillow while she slept to make a woman sexually pliable. Some magic was novelty, such as palm-reading (chiromancy; the earliest treatise we have on this was attached to a psalter around 1160). Some magic was part of daily life, such as miracle cures or even reading the shoulder blade of a sheep: the Flemings who settled in Haverford West in the middle of the twelfth century were particularly noted for their skill in this art. Only some magic was practiced by specialists. The archetype of the good magician in popular tradition was Solomon. In Jewish folktales, his ring was of particular significance, being able to control demon-kind and enable the wearer to understand birds.

Types of magic included religious magic, which was based on the belief in miracles. Religious miracles meant that the natural order was changed by God, often at the request of an intervening saint, or Mary. Other forms of religious magic were the Kabbalah, religious charms, prayers, curses and exorcism. It might also include remnants of pre-Christian practice, especially in the eleventh century, such as well-worshipping. Relics of saints were the religious equivalent of amulets in terms of power and operation. The major difference is that amulets were not venerated (although Jews may have regarded them as semi-sacred) – the religious context of relics added an extra component. It was one of the safest forms of magic in Church terms.

Other kinds of magic were prophecy and divination – telling the future or interpreting natural phenomena. The central prophet in medieval popular tradition was Merlin, and Geoffrey of Montmouth's *Prophecies of Merlin* were best-selling and much copied. Crystal gazing and gazing into shiny objects were used for divination, at least from the twelfth century. John of Salisbury reports in his (somewhat unreliable) *Policraticus* of having encountered it as a child. Basically, a reflective surface was used after preliminary incantations. John of Salisbury explains that his teacher used his fingernails anointed with chrism, or a polished basin. Alisson, a fortune teller (*divinatrix*) in the middle of the thirteenth century near Toulouse, told the Inquisition that she cast molten lead for readings to make money.

Another kind of magic was the use of numbers and names of God. This is a very typical part of learned Jewish magic, copied by some Christian clerics. The use of arithmetic and letter magic in Europe has been linked by modern scholars to the spread of Islam; however, it may also derive from the practice of Kabbalah, first developed in France. Kabbalah was a complex narrative, intended to lead to a higher understanding. Letter magic included making magic squares (the most famous using the words *rotas/opera/tenet/arepo/sator*) or writing words on an object such as an amulet or a charm.

Amulets were well accepted among both the Jewish and Christian communities. Popular amulets included items decorated with religious pictures, blessings or adjurations or magic phrases or words which apparently made no sense. The items carried as amulets could range from precious objects to simple bits of parchment with writing on them.

Healing magic was used on its own or together with medicine. Healing magic used the occult properties of material objects or the objects plus charms to promote (or even negate) physical well-being. Health and medical treatises, and even information about plant properties, usually contained elements that we would call magic, such as saying certain words while preparing something or using the occult properties to achieve a certain goal. These worked together with both scientific understanding and practical healing.

Magic also intertwined with science in astrology, alchemy and all other sciences where one manipulated the occult virtues of the natural order to achieve certain outcomes. Astrologers and alchemists would not have considered themselves magicians. However, some scholars of the day might have considered them to be dabblers in magic. Some scholars during our period also held the opinion that magic recipes worked mainly through the power of suggestion.

The magic of the intellectual elite was heavily influenced by the writings of the Classical world and by religious writings, especially the Bible and the writings of the early Church. Popular magic might have been influenced by the views of the intellectual elite mediated by people such as priests and the literate, but it also had a large dollop of popular tradition. This would have led to differences in practice. Regional history and religious history would have influenced how magic was considered in a given place, such as whether there were strong pagan influences, and what level of magic was acceptable in daily life.

While the obvious qualities of material objects (such as how the balance of the four qualities of hot/cold/moist/dry sat in them) and the occult qualities of things (how they resonated in the wider universe) were used by learned magicians, some objects were particularly strong in and of themselves and could bring about magical effects. The most famous of these is the mandrake, which was so potent it had to be pulled out of the ground by a dog.

Even the use of powerful items such as this, however, did not always save learned magicians from being regarded as fraudulent. Varieties of manipulating magic were liable to be seen as fraud because of their link with magic tricks, used to entertain the gentry at feasts. Roger Bacon had some trouble in this respect, for instance.

The vast majority of magic practices were considered part of daily life or religious belief and were not regarded as sorcerous. Sorcery was magic done with the intention to do harm; typical examples of sorcerous magic were witchcraft, demonology and necromancy. They intended to change the natural order of things through (non-religious) spells and appeals to demons, or employing the dead. Contrary to modern popular belief, very few people were burned for witchcraft during our period. Necromancy borrowed its theory from a wide range of places, and could include such components as conjuring spirits and animal sacrifices. Of all magic, it was the most heavily condemned; interestingly, most of those accused of necromancy were clerics. Sorcery was not sanctioned by the Church, and practitioners would be excommunicated; they had to work their magic secretly and circumspectly. The Church generally had no problems most of the time when people healed the sick or foretold the weather using non-sorcerous means such as reading omens. So some types of magic were tacitly condoned by the Church, and some were not. The practitioners of the types of magic least tolerated by the Church were occasionally made to wear distinctive clothing.

The Christian view thus defined religious magic resulting in miracles as God's gift, but other forms of magic as perversion. This view was not universal, though. Non-miracle magic was described generally as demonic up to the twelfth century. The technical names given to it were derived from the work of Isidore of Seville (*c.* 560–636). Isidore's claims that actual magic involved demons (the offspring of men and bad angels) was very important to learned notions in the early part of our period.

Jewish views of magic also had this divide between good and bad. Magic due to the power of the Torah was fine, because it came from

God. Sorcery was not, as it called on something other than God to do work in God's realm.

In Jewish magic, the most important component was always incantation. In fact, this was often the only component. The positive verbal magic comprised mainly prayers and blessings. Jews used verses of the Bible for very specific purposes, including protection overnight, against other magic, for love, for success, against highwaymen and to help animals grow. Prayers were directed to God, Mary or saints, asking for intervention. Blessings were also religious, but were directed at the person needing it; for instance, in case of an illness, 'May you get well' would have been used. More negative were adjurations or exorcisms, which targeted whatever was wrong, such as the sickness itself or the being responsible for it. Curses were simply inverted blessings: they had the same structure but the opposite intent. 'As the Egyptians died in the Red Sea, may so-and-so come to such-and-such a fate' was a typical format.

All these variants of magic were not discrete areas: they all linked in together through the medieval understanding of the working of the world.

Health Care

Medieval health care had several layers, including hygiene, medical diagnosis, medication and other treatments, special diets to help with health problems or promote good health and possibly magic or spiritual practices. As in many other areas of medieval daily life, some of the beliefs and approaches seem very foreign to a modern person, while others have remained much the same. An example of this is the recommendation of a monk and physician from the late eleventh century on how to stay in good health: Constantinus Africanus recommended exercise, regular bathing, a good diet, sufficient sleep and an active sexual life.

Hygiene and Cosmetics

In contrast to modern popular belief, hygiene was considered important for health and cultural reasons in the Middle Ages. Washing and personal cleanliness were considered to be very much signs of civilisation. Baths were more common than modern stereotypes suggest. One of the big negatives of the *villain* in medieval poetry was that he went for as long as six months without washing. This was not said with any positive feeling. Generally, cleanliness was important because of the tight link between material and non-material: cleanliness and moral purity were seen as closely allied.

References for bathing recommendations survive, for instance, where they deal with bathing young children. According to these, babies were ideally bathed one to three times a day. The water should be clean, lukewarm in summer and hot in winter, and the bath taken before nursing. It was recommended that until age seven, children should be given daily baths, but from age seven to puberty two or three a week would suffice, ideally first thing in the morning. We also have records of special bathing arrangements for (noble) women for the weeks after birth.

Bathing arrangements for the very rich could be quite sophisticated: water from a cistern was pumped directly into the king's and queen's chambers at Westminster under Henry III and Edward I. This water was largely used for bathing. For the less wealthy, there are many fewer sources about bathing and hygiene. However, we can assume that very few households would have had a bathhouse with tubs for one or more people, or a room set aside only for bathing. More houses may have had a full-size bathtub for one person, or a smaller tub that could be put up when required. For the poor, this may also have been unavailable. An alternative was visiting a public bathhouse, where taking care of hygiene needs and social functions could mix. Public baths may have had steam rooms for sweating as well as tubs.

Bathtubs were mostly wooden, built from staves and bound with hoops similarly to barrels. Soap could be used for washing hair and body. Soap might be made at home, but could also be bought by the load or cake. The soaps of Marseilles and Savona (Italy) and Castille were particularly admired. It is likely that a harder soap for washing clothes was made at major soap-making centres such as Bristol.

The water for bathing could be scented with herbs and rosewater, and scented water might also be used for rinsing. Scents may also have been used as part of personal grooming procedures. While the early history of perfume in France and England is little known, Phillip II of France had granted a *Perfumer's Charter* by 1190, and we have some indication of the plants and some of the other substances that could be used in perfume manufacture.

Musk and floral perfumes were traded mainly from the Islamic world, along with spices and dyes, and appear in the records of the Pepperer's Guild (which start from 1179). A common technique of extracting essential oils was to use fat or beeswax with flowers, leaves or roots, or to heat the plant in water. Perfumes were thought to ward off disease as well as to be a nice fragrance. Rosewater, sandalwood, lavender and nutmeg were popular scents. Pure fragrances often had a musk base. *Eau de Chypre* was the name of a perfume that became popular in Europe after Richard I conquered Cyprus.

Good outer appearance was not only improved by cleanliness and fragrances, though. It could be helped along with grooming and the use of cosmetics. Ear scoops were used to clean the wax from ears, and hair could be plucked with tweezers. The implements for this often came in sets together with a toothpick-like implement. Copper and its alloys were the most common substances used to make these accessories, especially in the thirteenth century.

Another important piece for grooming was the comb. They could be made of wood, horn, antler or ivory, though horn and wood combs rarely survive. Antler or bone combs may have been the most popular until the late twelfth century, but it could also be that the wooden combs from this period have disappeared over time, since wood is very perishable.

Two types of combs appear to have been in use: a double-sided comb, with finer teeth on one side and coarser on the other; and a comb with teeth only on one side, all the same size. Combs could be made from one piece or from several pieces of bone or antler, riveted together (composite combs). Some are decorated in the flat section above the teeth or between the teeth with words or abstract designs.

Composite combs from antlers were made in the early part of our period, but gradually disappeared until they were rarely seen by 1300. They were replaced by combs made of bone, wood (especially boxwood), horn and (the luxury combs) of ivory. People increasingly preferred a one-piece comb to the composite one.

Sources on cosmetics are, unfortunately, very rare. Mentions in literature do hint at the use of cosmetics to enhance physical beauty, but what substances were used and in what extent throughout the population is hard to evaluate. Clear, light skin, bright eyes and red lips were generally desired, and cosmetics to enhance these desired characteristics were used. Recipes for hair dye also exist, suggesting that some people might colour their hair. A lye-based soap, made from wood-ash and water, was used to clean hair. A common white powder used by women to maintain their fairness was called *blaunchet* in Anglo-Norman, and was made of wheaten flour. While modern popular sources suggest that lead was used to whiten the face, only a couple of sources back this up (Bartholomew Anglicus is the most quoted). Both rouge and exfoliating pastes were used to add blush to cheeks. Antimony was used to colour the eyebrows and lashes black. Borage, red powder, saffron, resin and silver were also known to be used in cosmetics. Applying make-up had its drawbacks, though. A face with heavy make-up was likely to be mistaken for the face of a prostitute!

Less obvious was the use of other cosmetics. Lined faces were not as admired as unlined, which suggests that creams, moisturisers and other lotions were used. We have evidence for women doing so. These cosmetics would have been made with bases of lard, olive oil or almond milk. They could have been scented with essences of flowers and herbs, such as violet or lavender. At least some cosmetics (but probably many) were home-made, with the most important tools being mortar and pestle. Spice peddlers and traders were important sources of some of the ingredients and even of finished products.

Mirrors were a necessary item for applying cosmetics by oneself, and they were closely linked to women in medieval literature and art. They were rather small and expensive, with the best glass often imported from places like Germany, from very specific prestigious manufacturers. Surviving examples have a hinged metal case, made of a copper alloy or a lead and tin alloy. The glass was cemented in place. The more expensive cases were probably made of ivory. All surviving mirror cases are decorated. Larger mirrors may have been used, but no complete example has yet been found, and no mirror or mirror case has been found earlier than the thirteenth century. This does not mean that they did not exist; the mirrors themselves are surprisingly perishable.

Medicine

Medieval medicine was based on a sophisticated understanding of the human body and its relationship to the outside world. This understanding was, again, not the same as the one used in modern medicine, but was clearly based on the medieval world view.

Medicine had to deal with the aches and pains of everyday life, illnesses like smallpox and cancer, emotionally based disorders and mental illnesses and with catastrophes such as the fever and famine that overtook England in 1087.

Several illnesses that pose no or little threat today were considerably more dangerous in the Middle Ages. Diseases like smallpox had not been eradicated, and colds and bacterial infections were more likely to be fatal, since antibiotics were unknown. Arthritis was well known too, and bone analysis has shown that many religious had knee problems from too much kneeling. Rickets were a particular problem for children in areas of low sunlight, among which it might be possible to count the crowded parts of major towns. Scurvy was not limited merely to sailors, but could be a seasonal problem in winter.

Parasites were also rather frequent and posed a threat by taxing the body. While parasites can be hard to trace, they have been found through archaeological investigation. Common parasites included whipworm (*Trichius* sp.) and maw-worm (*Ascaris* sp.).

Amoebic dysentery and smallpox were present and were virulent. Breast cancer was not only recognised as one of the most common cancers, but early treatment was recommended. Tuberculosis was also a common and dangerous illness. There has been a dispute among medical historians as to whether syphilis was known in our period or not; as yet, there seems to be no final conclusion. Finally, a common and much-feared sickness of medieval times was leprosy.

Leprosy was hard to diagnose. If leprosy was confirmed, the leper suffered a change in social status and was isolated. Lepers were not accepted in ordinary hospitals or in monasteries. *Leprosaria* were often found outside the city walls or at least at a distance from other buildings; they served not only as a home and care facility for the sick, but also meant segregation of these people, to protect the healthy from contagion. A common size for leper hospitals was about twelve residents. Around 130 of them were founded in England in 1150–1250. Many of these institutions were given enough land so that the lepers were not fully dependent on charity, but could grow their own food.

Lepers wore special clothes, including gloves. In many cases, a *claquette* was a prescribed accessory to warn the healthy that a leper was approaching. Lepers were not allowed out after curfew, nor were they allowed to go past the boundaries of their institution. If they did not abide by the often strict rules of their leper hospital – intended to keep the danger of contagion minimal – they were forced to leave and to wander the roads, begging.

While leprosy was one of the ailments seen as incurable or curable only by magic and miracles, cures and remedies were available for most other illnesses. Medieval medicine can be divided into two categories: scholarly medicine, learned through the university; and medicine learned informally through an apprenticeship or through family tradition. This, however, does not mean that the two were fundamentally different: there was significant overlap.

Sources for scholarly medicine are more readily available, as more of this formal branch was written down. We have most information about the Latin-trained physicians who used manuscripts and who, late in our period, went to university. The formal branch is thus by far the best documented and studied, especially from the thirteenth century onward, when university medical studies began. Thus it forms the basis for our modern understanding of medieval medicine. It was, however, the medicine of the wealthy and important.

Many of the principles of scholarly medicine were from Ancient Greece, mediated and changed over time. New work and new translations following the lines of this earlier tradition were undertaken from the eleventh century right through our period. From the late twelfth century, Galen was considered pre-eminent among the ancient authors. Nancy G. Siraisi points out that the original medicine from which the medieval principle derived contained some very astute observations on disease and its progress. While the Greek basis was important, early in our period only a small percentage of it was available, mostly to do with treatment of patients. Knowledge of the anatomical and physiological theory that underlay these treatments rose dramatically through our period, as translations of more texts were made.

In scholarly medicine, there were three important categories that had to be taken into account by medical practitioners: the natural, the non-natural and the contra-natural. The natural included such things as the elements, the humours, the parts of the body and the *spiritus* (which was manufactured in the heart and was distributed through the body by the arteries).

Most illnesses were attributed to an excess in any of the four humours, and cures were intended to rebalance them. All of this was based upon the analysis by Aristotle of the four fundamental qualities: hot, cold, wet and dry. Every aspect of the body partook of these qualities, and the ideal balance of the humours was different from person to person, as it was also influenced by their temperament.

Gender, ethnic background, geographical location and even age were also important factors in determining the balance of the natural elements. For instance, women were considered melancholic by nature and expected to die earlier than men, since death is a cold and dry state, and these are also the qualities of melancholia. (Albertus Magnus pointed out that women actually lived longer than men, but that this was only accidental, due to intercourse being more exhausting for men and menstruation being an effective cleanser of impurities from women's bodies. He also claimed that men working harder was a factor.)

The non-natural category of scholarly medicine consisted of six elements which were crucial for diagnosis and therapy. These were food and drink, air, sleep and being awake, evacuation and repletion, passions or emotions and motion and rest. With proper attention to these, the medical experts thought that the body would be less likely to turn to illness. The contra-natural category basically referred to pathological conditions.

For diagnosis, different methods were usual. Inspection of urine was a key diagnostic tool, as were blood and faeces and checking the pulse. People often brought their urine in flasks for diagnosis. The other preliminary diagnostic tools were examinations used to check for symptoms such as pain or fever.

Direct physical examination of women by male medical practitioners seems to have been unusual, although it was common for women to be treated by men. There were, however, female medical practitioners, especially earlier in our period. And it was recognised that women had very specific complaints: anaemia was accepted as more likely to strike women than men, and the recommended cure was increased meat and legumes in the diet.

A special diet was the first line of treatment for many conditions.

This was, if necessary, followed by drugs and then by surgery as the last recourse. The most common evidence for treatment in skeletons is trepanation, but also amputation and dentistry. Trepanation – making a hole in the skull – was used to treat a number of complaints, such as headache, epilepsy, migraine or head injuries. Other remedies included warm, fragrant baths and cupping or bloodletting. Baths were often recommended by doctors especially for gynaecological complaints, kidney stones and to relieve chronic pain and discomfort.

For cupping, a small heated vessel was applied to the skin. When the air inside the vessel cooled down, the resulting negative pressure lead to more circulation in the skin and muscle tissue under the cup. The skin may have been scratched before applying the cup. Cupping was used for different ailments, for example on the neck for eye trouble, bad breath and facial blemishes, or on the lower back and buttocks for internal problems, especially those of the liver and the kidney. Cupping the upper arms was considered useful for arthritis and gout, while work on the thighs assisted the bladder and reproductive organs. Blood was not drawn when the aim of the cupping was to eliminate fumes and venom as in cases of flatulence or a blocked nose.

Bloodletting was often done as a regular part of a person's medical routine, to enable them to release bad humours. In some cases, blood was let every two weeks, in others, every six weeks. When bloodletting occurred, it was usually followed by three days' rest and a nourishing diet, which included large amounts of red meat.

Some people earned a living as specialists in bloodletting. The major veins of the arm were the standard places to do a bleeding except in special circumstances (such as treatment for melancholy requiring the use of a vein in the forehead). It was normally done surgically, by opening a vein through cutting, although leeches were known and also used. The very old and young, the very weak and the pregnant were not normally bled.

Other aspects of the scholarly medical tradition came from popular practises and still others from the observations of individual medical practitioners, passed down through the apprenticeship system. Magic was a legitimate path of medical treatment, using both charms and the innate occult properties of objects. Astrology, likewise, could be an important part of the practice of some doctors: the signs of the zodiac were linked to parts of the body and this was also used medically. For example, Taurus related to the neck and the throat, while Pisces related to the feet and Gemini to the shoulders, arm and hands. Scorpio matched the genitals, Aries the head and Leo the chest.

For some afflictions, medical aids were employed. This included eyeglasses for those who could not see well enough; 1280 is the earliest dated evidence for the use of glasses for reading in Western Europe. Other aids for the disabled include crutches and prostheses. Simple forms of prostheses, such as peg legs and bent-knee pegs can often be found in medieval artwork showing the very poor and beggars.

Finally, there was a certain amount of care and thought to be taken for what ought to be done in the name of medicine and what ought to be left to God. The Church especially had a strong belief in the efficacy of prayers and faith healing. Some religious used them in addition to other treatments, but some even employed them instead of traditional medicine. In fact, the Church put spiritual health above physical well-being: it was seen as more urgent to fetch a confessor than a doctor in emergency cases. The vast majority of pilgrimages were also for medical reasons. Sometimes they were undertaken after recourse to treatment, sometimes instead of treatment.

Just like the spectrum of cures and approaches to medicine, the range of medical practitioners was very wide. Besides university-educated physicians and wandering doctors, they could include the lady of the manor, midwives, nurses (who provided home care for a few), country healers, herbalists, apothecaries, barbers, surgeons, priests and monks and rabbis. Although they did not usually have access to the formal university training, Jewish doctors were well-reputed. Some of the practitioners were approached by patients looking for relief, others actively solicited custom by door-knocking. And many knew the role that belief in cures played in healing.

The most prestigious practitioners (physicians and surgeons) often had university training, at least in the thirteenth century. The highest formal medical qualification was an MD, which required a minimum of ten years study, first of the seven liberal arts and then of subjects for a specialist medical degree. The bachelor of medicine took several years of study, but followed only initial training in the liberal arts. These formally trained physicians based their medical practice on theology and philosophy. Their cures, most importantly, were designed not to conflict with Church teachings. For instance, a popularly diagnosed illness was lovesickness, to which a standard cure was sex. University-trained physicians often either sought other cures (such as wine) or advised the patient to put up with the illness. Formal degrees were only obtained by very few, and those few had the chance of riches at the other end. There was a saying comparing medicine with law: 'Galen gives wealth and Justinian office'.

Formal medical accreditation appears quite late in our period, whether through the universities, through guilds or through ecclesiastical authorities. The hierarchy of medical practitioners, as demonstrated by university degrees, was slow to develop. Licensing of both secular and regular doctors began in the twelfth century.

Universities that taught medicine were Paris (founded *c.* 1200), Oxford (founded *c.* 1200), Montpellier (founded *c.* 1220), Cambridge (founded *c.* 1225), Toulouse (founded *c.* 1229) and Angers (founded *c.* 1250). English practitioners were most often trained in Paris or Montpellier, where both Christian and Jewish medical teachers could be found. Another major source of medical knowledge and learning for the English, from around 1100 onward, was Salerno (Italy). Salerno did not actually boast a university until the thirteenth century. Students at Salerno were basically taught Greek medical ideas through a Latin framework. From around 1120, education included anatomical dissections using animals (human dissection was not known until the fourteenth century unless undertaken as part of a biopsy for legal purposes). Most teaching was done through commentaries of the major authors and on the *Viaticum* (literally, the 'Guide for Travellers'). A widely copied book was the *Antidotarium*, which gave cures for various illnesses.

Books and treatises as well as other written aids were an important part of scholarly medicine. Several kinds of books survived that were used by doctors on the job, in the training of doctors or as reference books on medical subjects by physicians and apothecaries. But it should be noted that not all medical practitioners had access to any kind of literature, and those at the lower end of the spectrum were not necessarily literate.

Some doctors may have carried small (often folding or pleated) charts with them as ready references when they were working. These references had key information on them, such as the parts of the body and how they operated in schematic form. Some manuscripts also gave sketches of the body, and some even illustrated delicate operations such as on eyes and haemorrhoids.

Herbals were frequently used as reference books, both for information about the plants and their characteristics, and for instructions on how to make remedies. Medicinal herbals were often arranged following the human body, from the head down, for easy reference. This followed the model of the *De Medicina* ('On Medicine') by pseudo-Pliny, which was comprised mainly of artfully re-arranged extracts from works by Pliny. Other books had remedies to solve specific disorders – these could be pharmaceutical, religious or magic in nature, and were often all included together in a book. Books used on a regular basis, as opposed to books for show, often had fewer and more sparse illustrations, due to the cost of illustrations in manuscripts.

While Galen was the standard model, some Anglo-Saxon medical manuals survive from the eleventh century, demonstrating that Anglo-Saxon medicine was practiced right up to the twelfth century and possibly beyond in some circumstances. Some of the typical elements of Anglo-Saxon medicine include the worm or *wyrm* as a cause of disease (tapeworm, ringworm, maggot and other parasites), the definition of elfshot as a cause for sudden illness, knowledge of venoms, and, perhaps most importantly, the use of the doctrine of names (attribution of nine diseases and nine healing herbs) for diagnosis and treatment.

From the twelfth century, medical writings were frequently translated from Arabic to Hebrew to Latin and so became increasingly available. These new translations incorporated a higher level of mathematics and a different approach to pharmacology, surgery and everyday practice. They also sparked off new thought and developments in the Latin Middle Ages, resulting in a very different understanding of medicine in the thirteenth-century university-trained physicians to their equivalent in the eleventh century.

Several gynaecological manuals in Latin, Hebrew and even Anglo-Norman also survive. These are especially associated with Trotula, the famous (and possibly legendary) female doctor from Salerno. Roger Frugard's book on surgery (*Chirurgia*) was used as a basis for surgical teaching in the university, covering a range of injuries and maladies that included facial wounds suffered in fights. Since it was translated into the vernacular, we know that it had a wider audience than many textbooks.

The non-scholarly stream of medicine usually consisted of apprentice-trained physicians and doctors. These included most Jewish doctors, since only Montpellier University admitted non-Christians. Practitioners of the non-scholarly medicine often inherited their parent's business, but it could also be taken on by non-relatives. Those who ran infirmaries and the lady of the manor were often the people of first recourse for simple illnesses, along with apothecaries and locals with knowledge of folk and herbal remedies. While there were many attempts to prevent Jewish medical practitioners from treating Christians, these did not stick.

Medical practitioners, whether they were apprentice trained or university trained, were often known by the Latin description of *medicus* or *medica*. Some doctors in England were described as 'leeches' and surgeons as *surgicus* or *surgica*. Not every practitioner was necessarily available for all medical processes, though. For example, the Fourth Lateran Council (1215) forbade clergy in the major orders from practising cautery or surgery.

Surviving information about medical practitioners suggests that only 1–2 per cent of them were women during our period. This is quite possibly an underestimate, as records of male medical practitioners are more likely to have survived and documentation only takes into account the top end of the medical marketplace. Healers who learned through apprenticeship are largely absent from documentation, as are midwives and the informal sources of medical advice that most people would have used before they called in a professional. Few women doctors were rich or big taxpayers, and therefore would not have made much of an impact on records. Most records we have about women doctors are when they appear in court, which is hardly a typical situation. Women would have appeared in all groups of practitioners except perhaps the thirteenth-century university-trained doctor. They could be Jewish or Christian. They could be and were apothecaries, midwives and other practitioners. The areas where women were likely to be the typical practitioner were in midwifery or in taking care of a specific client group. Midwives did not draw on the same theoretical material that the university-trained male doctors had access to.

We have only very limited evidence on where practitioners worked. Apothecaries and peddlers of cures are an exception: we know that peddlers or traders of remedies would have wandered from place to place. Apothecaries, on the other hand, would have had a shop to sell drugs. (They also sold spices and rare goods.) Apothecaries could be very well esteemed in the community. For instance, in 1273 John the Spicer was the mayor of York.

Medical institutions apart from the *leprosaria* already mentioned did exist, but were usually not purely for curing the sick. Hospitals were intended for the sick as well as for the poor and for travellers. One of the largest hospitals in England until 1300 was St Leonards, in York. It had 225 ill or poor people on its books in 1287. A more typical hospital, in terms of size, was probably St Saviours, at Bury, which had twelve poor men and women on its books. Hospitals were often situated at town gates and directed by the Church. Hospitals for the poor grew in number from the twelfth century, with the largest number of new foundations from the very end of the twelfth and right through the thirteenth century. While *leprosaria* and hospitals were available for either Christian or Jewish sufferers, monastic infirmaries were solely for Christians.

The full extent of medieval medical understanding concerning scholarly medicine or the more informal understanding and practice in different communities is not yet fully known by modern scholars. Much of the evidence for medical practice relates to only a small sector of society. More work needs to be done in this area, but there are very few surviving sources.

Technology, Inventions and Innovations

While there were many significant inventions during the Middle Ages, the modern systems that allow us to celebrate the work of individual inventors (the patenting system, for instance, and public acknowledgement) were absent. This means that we know about inventions through their wider use and through their documentation in works such as Theophilus' *De Diversis Artibus* (around the middle of the twelfth century) on mechanics and making things, and from passing comments in documentary sources, but we do not have many details concerning when they were first developed and by whom. For instance, Rashi mentions the *atbi*, a small notched stick of wood. Documents could be slotted into the notches. This demonstrates that something similar to paperclips was known in the Middle Ages, but gives us little indication of how widely or when they were first used. Another very good example of the difficulties of tracing the origins of inventions is the history of nitric acid, where the first clear European recipe appeared in a Latin treatise around 1300, but which could have been known before this time inside and outside Europe. Any timeline of medieval inventions and technology is therefore only approximate and indicates first traceable use from our perspective (using surviving documents, archaeological inquiry or pictorial evidence) rather than the actual date of first invention. Even the countries of first invention are likely to be based upon extrapolation from limited evidence, and the religion or nationality of a given inventor is as hard to determine as the year of actual first use.

Some of the key inventions of this period were by-products of scientific thought applied to the needs of crafts. The preparation of sulphuric acid, for example, was described in a Byzantine manuscript from the end of the thirteenth century. Others were developed in agriculture, such as an improved plough, the three-field system or the artesian well.

Each field had its own specialist equipment, and looking at that field enables us to gain a fair idea of overall invention and technological development within it. In astronomy, for instance, the most common tools were the astrolabe and the quadrant. The most important variety of astrolabe was the *planispheric*. It incorporated an observing bar (*alidade*) that rotated to measure the altitude of the sun and other bodies. The quadrant was a quarter-circle of brass, used to measure altitudes and to calculate the time. In the thirteenth century, the functions of both instruments were combined in a new quadrant, possibly invented by Jacob ben Mahir (also known as Profatius the Jew, *c.* 1236 – *c.* 1304).

By the end of the thirteenth century, daylight tables and probably also the *torquetum*, an instrument for measuring and converting measurements, came into use. Many instruments were not developed for use just in one field. Astronomical instruments were not used solely for astronomy or star chart calculations; they were also used for navigation.

By the late thirteenth century, clocks were available as a method of timekeeping. The water clock measured longer spans of time quite reliably and was thus also very useful for astrology and astronomy, as well as getting people to church at the right time. It could even save lives: a big fire at Bury St Edmunds in 1198 was extinguished using water from the water clock. Eyeglasses were known by the late thirteenth century and wheelbarrows were used in various industries. The mineral acids (nitric acid, sulphuric acid and hydrochloric acid) discovered in the Middle Ages, as follow-ons from distillation, led to rapid changes in chemical technology, making assaying precious metals easier and more precise.

This patchwork of knowledge reflects our access to information rather than any lack of technological advances in the Middle Ages. It was, in fact, a time of significant invention. Architectural advances, agricultural developments and use of new technologies in various crafts were all hallmarks of the Middle Ages. Itemising technological advances and ascribing exact dates and places to them may be difficult, but the effects of these advances on daily life for many people were immediate. The discovery of a working formula for gunpowder, for example, was to completely change warfare in Europe by the close of the Middle Ages, while the agricultural advances during our period sustained far denser populations than lived in Western Europe until the eighteenth century.

12

Written and Spoken Words
Languages and Their Literature

Much of the medieval culture and social landscape we know today has been reconstructed from texts that directly or indirectly describe social activities, entertainment, or leisure pastimes. Literary texts were themselves part of culture and also part of social activities, since the medieval society had a tradition of reciting texts or reading them aloud. This semi-oral culture meant that even a person with no direct access to books or texts for reading could have had access to literature, both secular and religious. The culture of preaching also ties into this semi-oral culture and spread ideas from religious and polemical texts to the public.

Linguistically, England was dynamic. It was a polyglottal society, with different languages used to communicate in different spheres or in different social groups. For instance, the language of farming was Middle English and the language of the court or of international trade was Old French. For some groups, Old French was also the everyday language, while it was a second language or a specialist language for others. Large groups of the English population were likely to speak dialects of both French and English as native languages and to use them for different purposes. The language that was used depended on the geographic area, but also on the speakers or their background and social circumstances and, in texts, even on the nature of written work. For instance, French was often used for law issues in late thirteenth-century England.

Given the language use, it was possible to be a native speaker of more than one language. The religious and administrative function of Latin was so important that the most proficient in them would also have had native-level use.

The vast majority of educated people would have learned second languages when learning to read, or by using a language in a specific context. We have a wide range of thirteenth-century texts which are

Hebrew but glossed in French: in order to understand the Hebrew, Jewish scholars used Old French to explain it. French seems to have been frequently used to teach Latin as well, which means that higher-level literacy in England implied a reasonable level of French/English bilingualism as well as knowledge of Latin.

Choosing a particular language for a particular purpose, therefore, also helped clarify who belonged to which profession or social group. Proficiency in Latin would have been expected from a scholar, but would have been very surprising in a farmer or peasant.

Written texts, too, tend to differ in relation to the language they were in, or – put the other way around – different types of texts were usually written in different languages, and there are differences tied to the language even in corresponding genres. For example, Latin epics were literary endeavours that tried to follow Classical models that often used hexameters, and thus were very different from the Old French epics, which had irregular stanzas of ten or twelve syllables to a line.

Large numbers of medieval texts were translated into one language from another and even back again. Medieval translators, however, were not necessarily working in a way similar to modern translation. They might be undertaking *remaniement* – taking a known subject and writing it with their own words – instead of creating a more or less literal translation. For most texts, rewriting was considered a virtue and not a betrayal of the original. Meaning had to be retained, but otherwise improving on the original was an admirable trait in a translator.

Changes in texts were not limited to translations, however. They also applied to the copying of manuscripts, albeit to a lesser degree. Individually writing or copying each volume lead to a uniqueness of each manuscript beyond the choice of script and the individual hand of the scribe. Texts usually differ at least slightly, whether by scribal error or on purpose. This means that there are often several variations of the same story or the same manuscript, and it is usually not possible to determine a correct or original version.

The vast majority of texts from the Middle Ages, including literary works, are anonymous. For every named author, there are many about whom we know nothing but what we can glean from the text itself. Literary culture moved away from monastic centres from the eleventh century, with most literature produced outside monasteries by the end of the twelfth century. Material was produced in schools, universities and cathedrals, but also in commercial centres, especially in places with important courts and commercial development, such as London and Troyes. Monastic culture was still very important, but a secular culture was growing.

Latin

The impact of the Latin language on philosophy and other theoretical disciplines was enormous. When people talked about these subjects in Old French or in other vernacular languages, they used Latin terms, for Latin was the main language used for working in these areas.

Medieval Latin (often called Church Latin) became distinct from Classical Latin from about the ninth century; about the same time as Romance languages such as Old French emerged.

While in the eleventh century the balance of Latin literature was on the side of the religious, after the mid-twelfth century there were more secular writers. We owe most of our knowledge on subjects such as medicine and cosmology to Latin writings. Most Latin literature is therefore discussed indirectly under other subjects in this volume.

It being the primary scholarly language, Latin texts were read across national borders. Widely read texts in Latin were, for instance, the Bible (the most read book in the Middle Ages), early Christian poets (including Ambrose and Prudentius) and theological, philosophical, scientific and medical texts. Law books were also spread quite widely. While many Classical authors were read, Horace was probably the best known of them.

Some themes were more popular than others and appeared across a wide variety of texts. Visions of heaven and hell (and especially of hell) were particularly popular, for instance. Current events also resulted in new writing fads; after the death of Thomas Becket in 1170, he became a popular subject, and quite a few authors instantly turned their hands to prose lives of Thomas. These included John of Salisbury, Herbert Bosham and Benedict of Peterborough, who was a personal friend of Becket.

England's cultural strength appears to have been history, with two important twelfth-century writers being Henry of Huntingdon and Geoffrey of Monmouth, both of whom focussed on the history of England. Most history texts were written in Latin prose, though this very important topic of medieval literature was also covered in other Latin genres.

Other types of literature included collections of curious trifles and tales by Walter Map and Gerald of Wales, lyric poetry on both secular and religious themes, animal fables, commentaries on almost everything, religious texts of innumerable variety, instruction books, moral literature, encyclopaedias and lists, satire and comic writing. There was a plethora of saints' lives and a variety of histories. Writers eulogised Mary, wrote debates or political discussion and described the world around them (both institutional and physical). There were works on prophecy (the most famous being about Merlin, by Geoffrey of

Monmouth) and works on all areas relating to medieval learning, which included grammar, rhetoric, philosophy and law. Some tastes were regional: Caesar's commentaries were particularly popular in northern France, for instance. The range of Latin literature was enormous, and the quality ranged from the brilliant to the sublimely bad.

Satiric poetry probably peaked during the thirteenth century, although some of the classics were penned before that (such as the *Gospel of the Silver Mark*, *c.* 1150, a northern French work). Hymns were a particularly important form of Latin poetry during our period, especially in monasteries. This was largely due to St Benedict, who added hymn singing to the daily monastic religious service.

Latin poetry was as varied as vernacular poetry and was abundant in quantity and very varying in quality. The vast majority of these poems are anonymous, and some even have fictional names (for instance Golias the Archipoeta) attached to them.

Old French

Old French was a Romance language, like Italian and Spanish, that is to say the language developed from Latin roots. It has been called *Langue d'Oïl*, reflecting the way 'yes' was pronounced in the north of France, as well as Old French. It was not only spoken in France and England and used as a common language in international trade, but it was also one of the most important literary languages of Western Europe. Old French dialects were native not only to northern France, but also to England and part of Belgium.

The dialect that mostly influenced modern French is from the Ile-de-France, and is today often seen as the standard dialect. The dialect spoken in England was Anglo-Norman and was closely related to western French dialects such as Poitevin.

Some dialects were more fashionable than others, and some speech usages were regarded as inferior. The accent of the Ile-de-France was most prestigious socially, although the bulk of literature was written in other dialects, especially Champenois, Anglo-Norman and the western French dialects.

The first apparent mention of Old French we have is from 813 (the Council of Tours) and the first written text we have is the *Strasbourg Oaths*, from 842. Between this period and the late thirteenth century, the language is called Old French. By the late thirteenth century, French had changed sufficiently that linguists generally define it as Middle French. The change was, however, gradual.

Surviving Old French literature is wide and varied. The vast bulk of surviving Old French literature from before 1150 was written in Anglo-Norman – that is by English writers who were native French speakers.

This is a by-product of the polyglottal society mentioned earlier. While most writing in Old French was on themes relating to France even when the work was produced for an English audience, there are several works with significantly English themes. There is a historical romance in Old French about William I of England written in 1165, for instance, and one about his father in 1195.The most popular genre was the epic legend, followed by chronicles of various types.

From the thirteenth century, there are over 440 surviving texts, covering a far wider range of genres and also the full range of dialects from northern France. Old French epic legends and histories were still popular, but Arthurian and other romances were equally important.

The types of text ranged from the religious (instruction and explanation, sermons and retellings of the Bible), through the historical (chronicles and epic legends), romantic (such as Arthurian romances or the *Roman de la Rose*), short poems of all sorts and even some bawdy literature (for example the *Roman de Renart*). Epic legends are known from the eleventh century and were popular throughout our period. Arthurian literature was chiefly popular form the twelfth century, with key authors being Béroul and Thomas (for versions of the Tristan story), Marie de France and Chrétien de Troyes. In the thirteenth century, poetry was still the main vehicle for literature in Old French, but significant prose works became more common. Examples for this are the chronicles by both Guillaume de Tyr and Villehardouin. In the thirteenth century, manuals such as legal texts previously only written in Latin also began to appear in Old French. Short (lyric) poetry was at its height in the twelfth and thirteenth centuries.

Most of the remaining French literature falls roughly into one of three categories. These categories correspond with those described in the epic *Chanson des Saisnes* ('Song of the Saxons'), where tales are divided into three matters, those of France, those of Britain and those of Rome the Great. These in turn roughly correspond with the three modern categories epic legends (*chanson de geste*), Arthurian romances and romances of the ancient past.

The term *chanson de geste* is Old French for songs about action, exploit or history. They were the archetype of the medieval epic legend, written in a poetic form and generally very long. The most famous (though not the most typical) is the *Chanson de Roland*, whose earliest manuscript dates from the second quarter of the twelfth century.

Arthurian literature is not one genre but several. It is one of the major literary phenomena of the Middle Ages, and it created many ideas that linger in the present. Old French literature concerned with Britain is mostly Arthurian romances, although Arthurian material can be found in other genres and in other languages. The author mostly associated with Arthurian romances today is Chrétien de Troyes. Chrétien, who wrote in Champagne in the twelfth century, was one of the great writers in the French language. He was the writer forming the genre, and many of the ideas adopted by later Arthurian romances were borrowed from Chrétien's innovative work.

Marie de France was the pre-eminent writer of short Arthurian fiction. Her Arthurian court is a place of fairytale. Marie was the classic writer in Old French of Breton lays, relatively short works which relied heavily on folkloric and Arthurian themes and on Breton tradition. One of her most famous works is *Chevrefeuil*, a delicate lay about Tristan.

The third group, romances of the ancient past, is less discussed by scholars today. They all have a historical basis (like the epic legend), are primarily in verse and all deal with major heroic episodes of the past, such as the deeds done in Ancient Troy or by Julius Caesar.

Old French historical writing reflected Latin historical writing to a large degree. The most important Old French chronicles are the histories of the kings of France, of the kings of Britain and of the dukes of Normandy. There is a genre of verse chronicles that deal with the history of England, such as the verse tales of Gaimar and Wace which often focus on Arthur to the exclusion of much else, but the main Old French chronicles were written following the crusades, such as Villehardouin's chronicle of the Fourth Crusade, *The Conquest of Constantinople*. Historical writings also included universal chronicles (which started as early as possible, often with Adam, and ended in the present day) and other genres.

In addition to these longer texts, a great deal of short poetry, largely on the themes of love and crusading, were written in Old French in both England and northern France.

Old English and Middle English

English changed so much from the eleventh to the fourteenth century that it is generally described as two different languages by scholars. Middle English is primarily derived from Old English (also known as Anglo-Saxon), which was chiefly a composite of the languages spoken by the migrants into England from the fifth century. These migrants mostly came from northern and central Europe. Old English changed significantly with the arrival of Old French speakers into England in 1066, when it adopted large quantities of French vocabulary.

Old English was mostly a spoken language, and extremely few documents in Old English are known today. While little Old English appears to have been used from the late eleventh century, one particularly important text is the *Anglo-Saxon Chronicle*, which is a key literary source of English history. Verse texts in Old English that we know of were on heroic subjects (*Beowulf*), historic subjects (the Battle of Maldon), or religious subjects (Biblical subjects, lives of saints and mystical poems such as the *Dream of the Rood*). There were also short poems and riddles, charms and other unclassifiable texts. Prose works apart from the *Anglo-Saxon Chronicle* include translations from the period of Alfred the Great and homilies (commentaries on scripture readings). Most surviving Old English texts can be found as copies of older text in later (mostly twelfth century) manuscripts.

Most modern discussion of Old English during our period is based on the dialect of West-Saxon, an important dialect both politically and for literature. West-Saxon is probably also the dialect that developed into Middle English. Despite its importance, it was not the only Old English dialect and was neither the dialect of King Alfred (r. 871–99) nor of *Beowulf*.

Middle English is considered to run from about 1100 to 1500, even if it was quite different at the end of this period to at the beginning. Pronunciation in particular shifted during that time. Middle English first appears to have been used for formal written documents around the middle of the thirteenth century, although it was still an unusual choice of language for such documents, with both Latin and Old French remaining the more usual choices.

Middle English dialects can roughly be divided between two (or three) main groups: the dialects of the north and east of England as opposed to those of the south and west. London was in the overlap area, and was the conduit by which northern vocabulary reached the south. During our period, the divisions between these dialects were still very clear: the language of the north, especially from around the York area, was hard to understand for southerners.

Middle English was written down far more than Old English. We have romances, dialogues and debates, religious texts (including sermons and paraphrases of the Bible), saint's lives, historical writings, short poems and homilies. Much of it was based on Latin or Old French originals. For example, romances written in Middle English telling tales of knights and love were mostly modified versions of Old French romances, with only a few (such as *Havelok*) having English origins. Some are set in the court of King Arthur, some in the time of Charlemagne. The earliest romances in English date from the thirteenth century.

A few short lyric poems have also survived from the thirteenth century, some of which were obviously intended to be set to music. Of these, the best known is undoubtedly *Sumer is I-Cumen in*, written around 1230–40. The oldest surviving English play also dates from the thirteenth century.

Other texts appeared as the uses and perceptions of English changed and as writing became more widespread. Important examples of this include Layamon's *Brut*, a verse adaptation of Geoffrey of Monmouth's history of the British. Despite these early texts, the heyday of Middle English in literature was really from the fourteenth century.

Hebrew

Hebrew is often not included in listings of medieval languages of England. It was, however, an important language for Jews; it served as the equivalent of Latin for Christians and should thus not be omitted. It was also known to some Christians: Roger Bacon (1215–94), for instance, wrote a Hebrew grammar. Other Christian Hebraists in England included Herbert of Bosham and Ralph Niger.

Hebrew was mainly a literary and religious language, but could also be used as a lingua franca between Jews who spoke different vernacular languages. The literary language of northern French Jews was known as medieval Ashkenazi Hebrew. English Jews to a large degree also used this language.

A minimal education in Hebrew was required of any man in the Jewish community, and many Jewish women probably also acquired at least a basic knowledge. As with Latin, the lingua franca for Christian scholars, there were differences due to the background of the speaker. For instance, people who came from the Arab world would have slightly different Hebrew.

Hebrew literature was very varied. It ranged from liturgical texts, through books used for other festivities and texts that taught Judaism and Jewish law, to secular texts such as poems. The most common books used by Jews were prayer books or religious texts. The Five Books of Moses and many other key religious texts were often glossed as well.

Talmudic literature was very important as a genre. It comprised rabbinical commentary on the Bible. These commentaries were mainly explanatory, clarifying the text of the Talmud for instance, or were critical, examining specific issues.

One of the most important forms of religious poetry was called *piyyut* (plural *piyyutim*). These poems embellished the normal liturgy. Some of the most famous writers of this kind of poetry worked in England, or were well known there, and some of the poetry they wrote is still used in the Jewish liturgy today.

Since an unknown number of Jewish texts were destroyed by non-Jews, it is hard to know how many were produced or the full range of their contents. Law books, such as the Talmud, and commentaries and glosses on the Bible are the most famous Jewish literature from France during our period; there is, unfortunately, not enough evidence available for England.

Other Languages

In addition to these main dialects and languages, others were also spoken in various regions. Romany, though, did not arrive in England until the fifteenth century. Some Flemish was spoken or understood near the Welsh border (in Pembrokeshire) from the reign of Henry I until the late twelfth century, due to some Flemings having settled in that region. Welsh was used in England around the Welsh border and even appears in English documents. There was possibly a related Britannic language that survived in the north-west of England until the twelfth century, but there is insufficient evidence to prove or disprove this. Manx Gaelic was spoken on the Isle of Man, even though the region was held by the English. It is not known how far the Scottish Gaelic of the south of Scotland reached into England, but one well-known native speaker, Malcolm Canmore (1058–93), lived in England for fifteen years.

Danish might have been spoken in remote parts of England to the early twelfth century: there is a little evidence of Danish being used in the Carlisle region to around 1100. There was also a Scandinavian imprint on English due to its links with Old Norse lands, which were stronger in the north than elsewhere. Additionally, there were some Scandinavian settlements on some islands and even in mainland north-west England right to the tenth century. This means that Scandinavian languages might have been understood in that region for a while. This would have been reinforced by the rule of Cnut and Harthcnut (r. 1040–2).

Cornish was used mainly west of Bodmin by 1100, having declined considerably, and around 1200 in the east of Cornwall only. Old Cornish was used roughly from the tenth to the twelfth century, with glossaries being the only surviving texts. Middle Cornish describes the language from the thirteenth to the sixteenth century. No Cornish literature from our period has survived.

Drama and Performances

A special form of literature was dramas and, connected to them, dramatic performances. Our understanding of medieval performance, especially in England, has changed significantly over the last thirty-five years. Close studies of surviving material (ranging from dramatic performances to mentions in various administrative records) has broken English drama into regions and looks at it region by region. This study has led to a detailed understanding of how plays in Middle English or Latin operated as part of society in each of these regions. Religious play cycles were the exception in medieval English life, not the norm as earlier scholars thought. The subjects of both these cycles and other plays, however, fit in with the wider subjects of literature, and are heavily inclined to the religious (although not lacking in comic relief). On the other hand, none of the folk and mumming plays we have trace back to anything near our period, and most of them are from the eighteenth or nineteenth centuries.

Folklore: Tales and Traditions

The vast bulk of folklore, tales and traditions belonged to a very strong oral tradition. Some of these tales can be extrapolated from literature, as they were to some extent embedded in texts and art. Examples are the collections of writers such as Walter Map, or records of what the Church preached against. However, most tales and traditions were things not considered interesting enough to be written down, glamorous enough to be turned into written stories, or outrageous enough to be condemned, and are thus lost to us.

Walter Map and Gerald of Wales both compiled popular tales in their writings, as did Orderic Vitalis. These are important sources of folklore, as are sermons and resource books for sermons due to material such as the condemnation of folk belief. There were also writings by Jews that incorporated this material. For instance, Berakhiah the Punctator wrote *Mishle Shualim* ('Fox Fables') in northern France or England around the late twelfth and early thirteenth century. These tales take their narratives from many sources, including Christian and pagan folklore, and add Jewish moral teachings. The need to place folktales in a moral context is quite typical of the Middle Ages.

Folktales were a place where Christian and Jewish cultures could crossover unobtrusively in many cases. These stories could be tailored to meet the needs of the religion, while fitting into the overall culture of the time: Marie de France wrote *Bisclavret* for a courtly audience, about a werewolf knight, while later popular Jewish tradition had its own unknightly version of the tale.

Stories about heroes, or those in their circles, were very popular. This is especially true for the heroes dubbed the Nine Worthies in the fourteenth century. These were three pagan heroes (Alexander, Julius Caesar and Hector), three Jewish heroes (David, Joshua and Judas Maccabeus) and three Christian heroes (Arthur, Charlemagne and Godefroi de Bouillon). Tales concerning these heroes account for a significant part of the folk stories we can still grasp today.

Other heroes included many that were linked to the legends of these nine, for example William of Orange and Roland (linked in with Charlemagne and the epic legends), and Gawain, Lancelot and Perceval (linked in the English histories and the Arthurian romances).

Several of the popular heroes were sleeping heroes: they were considered not to have died, but to lie somewhere sleeping or, alternatively, to live and rule somewhere else. Sleeping heroes were expected to return when their country needed them. The best known of these today is probably Arthur. The earliest account of Arthur sleeping appears to be by Gervase of Tilbury in around 1211. This belief was held firmly: there was a riot in Bodmin in 1173 when canons of Laon, touring their relics to raise money, claimed that Arthur was dead. Another example of a sleeping hero was Ogier the Dane, a combative leader in epic legends, who was seen at the time as the sleeping saviour of Denmark. Yet another of these heroes is mentioned in Walter Map's *De nugis curialium*. He tells of King Herla, who finds that three centuries have passed when he leaves his castle.

There were also outlaw heroes who, unsurprisingly, did not link in neatly with the more noble heroes. Famous outlaws included Hereward (eleventh century, English), Fulk Fitwarin (thirteenth century, Norman, and the original robber baron) and Eustace the Monk (thirteenth century, French; a rare case of a pirate monk). There is no English literature about Robin Hood from our period, though the legend may have existed in the thirteenth century.

Popular beliefs can also be extrapolated from stories as well as from other sources. Examples for folk beliefs were ghosts as well as extraordinary creatures.

These extraordinary beings were fabulous animals such as dragons, griffins, unicorns and similar creatures. They were not only important in folklore, but comprised a category in the medieval system of classification of beasts. In the popular imagination, they fitted very nicely alongside heroes.

Dragons were generally considered to be oversized snakes, with wings, a tail, feet and sharp talons. They might also breathe fire and have impenetrable scales. They were associated very strongly with evil in the Christian mindset, helped by the popular tales of heroes such as St George and St Michael slaying serpents. Many saints were praised for killing dragons or serpents, which were actually demons in disguise. One of the most popular in Provence was St Martha, while in north-west France St Michael was popular. St George was not the only dragon slayer of our period, and he may have entered the popular tales late, from the thirteenth century.

Griffins were popular decorative beasts. They appear on caskets, on the Bayeux Tapestry, on saint's reliquaries and in manuscript margins. Bestiaries list the griffin's traits as greed and hate for humans. But they could be gentle guardians, too. Richard de Revers, earl of Exeter, had a griffin on his coat of arms in 1167.

Descriptions of unicorns in the Middle Ages were heavily dependent on a third-century compilation of animal descriptions called the *Physiologus*. Unicorns were considered small but very fierce and swift;

they are pictured more like goats in size and shape, down to the cloven hooves, and not as much like horses as modern unicorns. Bestiaries added to this the idea of the only way of catching a unicorn being to use a virgin, who is often depicted naked. The horn of the unicorn was considered a sovereign protection against poison, and, powdered, as a preventative for plague and leprosy. Unicorn horns – the horns of the narwhale were considered and sold as this – were a cure for the rich, being terribly expensive.

There may only be a few sources for tales of werewolves during our period, although the subject has not been extensively investigated. Gerald of Wales, in his book about Ireland, tells about a wolf that talked. Walter Map also has a werewolf tale. Marie de France wrote *Bisclavret*, a tale about a noble werewolf who was mistreated. And for the learned in medieval society, Ovid's *Metamorphoses* were a key source of information about a wide range of amazing beings.

Wild men – hairy, wild, human-like beings that lived in forests – were given numerous names, ranging from the Old English *wudewasa* and the Middle English *wodewose* or *woodehouse* to the Latin *fauni*, *silvestres* or *pilosi* (hairy). Wild men appear in literature as madmen; when heroes lose their wits, they could wander in the woods as wild men. These heroes have generally undergone a temporary fit of insanity or, like Perceval, have been brought up without the amenities of civilization. In enchanted forests such as Broceliande, wild men could be found guarding enchanted springs or other sites.

The female equivalent of the wild man was the wild woman. She was generally described as a *lamia*, and was associated with woods. Another description was a *strix*, or witch. These descriptions are hardly immutable, however, as German speakers also had a *lamia*, which was associated with the sea rather than the land. Thirteenth-century mentions of this creature occur in the works of Gervase of Tilbury and of William of Auvergne (Bishop of Paris).

Fairies were more the stuff of romantic adventures for the learned and courtly than the stuff of everyday life. Most of our references to them come from Old French romances and from lays, although they also appear in writers' prose work such as William of Newburgh and Walter Map. We do not really know, in fact, how most of the fairies in the romance tradition carried over into ordinary belief, apart from their use as important ancestors to certain families. As L. Harf-Lancner pointed out in the classic study on the subject, fairies really belong to the twelfth century and later. Fairies were hard for many people to classify in the Middle Ages, which makes it even more difficult now. Romance writers were clear on their view of fairies: they were beings of great beauty and power, with at least a hint of magic. All the beings were obviously supernatural, but the exceptional beauty of the goddess, the forest-living of the nymph and the capacity to influence human destiny of the fate were obviously characteristics that the writer was trying to match with Classical norms. This may be one of the reasons they were not always trusted. William of Auvergne is an example of a writer who distrusted all fairies. He argued that they were demonic in nature. Certainly they did not fit comfortably in Christian reality.

Female fairies fall roughly into four groups. The first is the fairy lover, who often disappears after having children and when someone disobeys a limit she had earlier set down. A classic example of this is Melusine (who appeared first in Geoffrey of Auxerre's twelfth-century writing – he did not like her!), who turned into a *guivre* (a serpentine magic being) and flew away after her husband looked in on her on the one day he promised not to. When she had gone, she moved into the second group of fairies: ancestral. The combination of human and fairy produced the illustrious Lusignan dynasty. The third group is the fairy who takes care of people. An example for this is Lancelot being taken care of by the Lady of the Lake. Finally come fairies who guard places and objects.

The classic fairy is, of course, Morgan. She was known as Morgane or Morgue and the words 'the wise' or 'the fairy' were often attached to her name. Unlike most fairies, who were preferred more in one country than another, she appears to have been known in both England and France, and more widely than just in the court circles where the Arthurian romances were most favoured.

Christian scholars equated elves with demons, but they were more like fairies in that they were supernatural rather than malevolent. English folk considered them to make mischief: being elf-shot meant having a disease brought on by them. 'Elves' is perhaps a generic term for many types of supernatural creatures. The English elves developed from the Anglo-Saxon tradition and were not seen. They were very different from French or Scandinavian beings called elves. Despite this, elves were primarily creatures of the German-speaking lands and of Scandinavia, which are the routes by which they reached England.

There was also a strong belief in giants during our period. Honorius of Autun wrote about them in the twelfth century, for instance. The existence of giants was corroborated by the Old Testament, the foundation legends of England (known as the *Brut* chronicle), heroic stories, Graeco-Roman myths, which were becoming increasingly popular among the learned, and texts of well-known authors such as Flavius Josephus and Augustine. It was probably a medieval Jewish belief that gave rise to the Christian view that giants escaped from the flood of Noah's day due to their immense size. Their heads remained above the floodwaters and so they escaped God's wrath. The most famous of these giants was Og or Aapalit ('the one who escaped').

Giants were generally not nice to know. In the prose romance about Tristan, one appears as an incestuous cannibal; very few were thought of favourably. These included St Christopher, depicted as a giant man, and giant heroes of epic legends who were either Christian or converted to Christianity. Some giants were humorous in their blundering innocence, although the humour tended towards blood and gore.

The golem was literally a body without a soul, a man-made man. Its creation and use were linked to the *Sefer Yetzira*, an important Jewish mystical text; however, the idea of it originated in Talmudic literature. The golem was more of a scientific and/or religious experiment than a magic one: the Jewish Pietists of the twelfth and thirteenth centuries believed that they could change reality using mystical practices. The golem story as we know it first emerged in tales told about the Pietists, and in particular about the rabbis Samuel and Judah. Most modern golem legends relate to later scholars, especially a sixteenth-century Prague rabbi, but the theory of golem-making was around during our period.

13

Clothes Make the Man
Clothing and Fashion

Throughout human history, outer appearance has been used to show one's status and wealth; the medieval era is no exception to this. Textiles, especially in the form of clothing, were an immensely important part of daily and social life. Clothes did not only cover the body. Through their more or less fashionable cut, the quality of their material, their colours and how accessories were used with them, they showed the social status of the wearer and advertised the wearer's taste and wealth. In terms of status symbols, clothes were both the most important and most accessible way of showing one's importance. They could also tell something about the social circles that someone belonged to, both through the free will of the wearer, or through imposed rules. Prostitutes, lepers, clerics and Jews were groups who could be especially affected by this. For example, Jews generally wore the same clothing as the rest of the population, but in some places, at some times, Jews were supposed to wear an identifying badge. It was often possible to bribe your way out of wearing this badge, however, through buying an exemption. The badge was most consistently enforced in 1218 in England. It was a piece of white cloth or parchment in the shape of the stone on which the Ten Commandments were carved. By 1275, the badge was yellow, not white. Because of the unofficial exemptions, individual towns instituted their own Jewish badges.

A multitude of source material has information about textiles and clothing, but no single source or type of source is perfectly reliable or detailed enough to provide a complete picture of medieval garments. Archaeological finds of textiles and therefore of clothes are a very rare thing. Most textile finds are only tiny scraps of fabric, for instance left over from re-working a piece, and turned a dull brown colour by the soil. In addition, the surviving textiles discovered archaeologically are mostly made from animal fibre such as wool or, for costly pieces, silk. Vegetable fibres such as hemp or linen usually degrade in the soil, so the surviving cloth does not necessarily give an accurate picture of the range of fabrics used for clothing. Images and texts also tell us about clothes, but whether they show an image of actual lifestyles or whether artistic licence was used freely is not always discernible. Lists of garments included in wills or inventories give a rough overview of the amount of textiles available in a given household, but do not provide detailed descriptions of these pieces. Legislative texts provide some information about quality control and standards in textile production and trade, but do not show what happened in everyday life, how far the legislation was observed, or what choices individuals made for their home-produced cloth.

Just like food and drink, textiles and clothing are a part of daily life that has a very deep influence on us. For the Middle Ages, as for most of our history until recently, it will never be possible to reconstruct accurately and entirely the look and feel of garments worn and fabrics used. Even the best-preserved surviving textiles may have changed significantly due to their age, and they are usually much too fragile to allow handling that would give an impression as to their feel and drape, or how they would have worn. For such an impression, it would be necessary to do a fully accurate reproduction of the fabric, starting from the fibres: and this is where problems begin. Such a full reproduction first requires a very well-preserved item that has to be analysed from a number of angles. For instance, one of the necessary analyses is an accurate survey of the fibres used in the textile, which typically means some loss of material. With this information, fibres for the reconstruction can be sought, but as both plants and animals have been changed significantly by breeding since the Middle Ages, it may not even be possible to find a sheep that delivers wool closely similar to the sort used in a specific textile. For the reconstruction of historical garments, we are thus always faced with at least some conjecture, even with all the information that has been gathered about historical textiles, their production and their use.

With the available sources it is, however, possible to say that textiles were very important and very valuable, and that there was a definite development and a sense of fashion not only in the late Middle Ages, as is often stated, but long before. From our sources we can glean an understanding of style over a long period, but not of regional differences or short-lived fads or personal styles. Texts give us tantalising glimpses on these more localised developments. For instance, Guibert of Nogent commented in around 1100 that women's sleeves widened and that bodices were tighter, but we can't interpret how widespread these fashions were, how fast they spread or how long they lasted.

Fabrics

The look and feel of garments is largely defined by the fabrics they are made from. For our period, the rare textile finds show a multitude of different fabrics, ranging from fine and soft (such as fabrics for veils), over fine but dense and therefore less supple (for instance for garments), to coarse, rough weaves (used, among other things, as packaging materials). Most of the surviving fabrics are made from wool, so there is a definite bias in the archaeological record.

While the variety of historical fabrics is very great, they are still distinctly different in feel and drape from the modern fabrics available today. Medieval woollen fabrics were made from tightly spun threads, which make the textile hard-wearing but stiffer and more firm than modern woollen cloth of similar thickness. Silk textiles were prized for their sheen; fabrics from spun silk similar to modern coarse silk fabrics are unknown archaeologically, and the preserved silks are not the soft-flowing fabrics we know, but have a more firm handle, similar to a densely woven fine linen cloth.

In contrast to woven cloth, leather is only very rarely mentioned as a garment material in texts, and archaeological finds of leather garments are almost non-existent, though we have ample evidence for leather shoes. Since leather as material for clothing has about as many disadvantages as advantages – it is resilient and windproof, but also heavy, relatively stiff and less breathable than fabric – it was probably only used very rarely and in special circumstances. Leather armour or armour parts, as well as leather protection in the form of aprons, gloves or similar items are, on the other hand, rather probable.

Woven fabrics were the mainstay of garment production, but details, reinforcements and embellishments could be achieved by narrow woven or tablet-woven bands, braids or decorative stitching and embroidery. Smaller items, such as stockings and gloves, may also have been produced by nalebinding, and hats may have been sewn or felted. Knitting is mostly traceable after our period, and the exact date of its origin is unknown; there may or may not have been knitters in England in the late thirteenth century.

While leather garments seem to be an absolute exception, fur linings or fur trimmings were in use and could add much warmth to a garment. If expensive fur was used, the lining and trimming also added to the representative value of the clothing. Fur linings or trimmings are often shown in illuminations, but survive only very rarely in archaeological finds.

Clothing

Medieval garments were probably thought of differently to the way we approach clothing today, with work, leisure and special occasions having their own distinct sets of clothing. Instead, a good and new set of clothes could first be used for special occasions. Once a piece of clothing started showing traces of wear, it would be used as normal daywear, and even more worn pieces were used for activities where garments would get dirty or maybe damaged easily, such as hard and dirty fieldwork. Worn clothing was also handed down to those lower in status as an act of charity, or sold.

Apart from used clothing, there was probably little ready-to-wear clothing available for purchase. Instead, it was common to bring cloth to a craftsperson and have the garment of choice made up from it. All new pieces, therefore, were more or less made to measure. The time necessary for tailoring a garment would have depended on a number of things: the complexity of the cut, the fabric, whether a lining was added, whether it included fastenings (such as eyelets or buttons) and, of course, the individual's working speed (and maybe morale). Smaller pieces such as hoods or hose probably took half a day to a day to make, while larger garments such as tunics would have needed several days to complete.

It is not possible to say how many clothes were made by professional or semi-professional tailors and how many were tailored and sewn as a part of household work. Surviving garments range from having rather simple shapes that would be easy to cut and sew, even for a novice, to very elaborate, tight-fitting pieces that would have needed more expertise for cutting, fitting and sewing. Whether a simple garment was made by a tailor or a precisely fitted, complex garment in a private household probably depended a lot on the circumstances and personal abilities or preferences of the individuals.

Generally, medieval clothes were able to withstand a lot more wear and tear than is typical for modern clothes. The high twist yarns in medieval textiles greatly increased the durability of the cloth. It was thus not uncommon for a good garment to be handed down to the next generation: wills include them as named items.

To protect clothes against dirt or damage, aprons could be worn. The simplest form of an apron is a piece of cloth tucked into the belt or knotted around the waist. Most depictions of aprons, including this very simple form, are from after our period, however. Damaged clothing could be patched or, once parts of the garment gave out, re-worked into other pieces of clothing. A good example for this is the bog body of the Bockstensman in Sweden, where the upper part of a tunic with the neck-opening was re-used as a foot rag.

Describing medieval clothing is made more complicated by terminology problems: we cannot determine the exact meaning of the medieval terms. Not even undergarments, outer garments and outerwear are exactly the same as our modern conception of these categories. To avoid possible confusion, therefore, we will not use these terms here. Instead, we have grouped garments into layers, starting at the skin with the first layer of clothing.

Similar to modern underwear, first-layer clothes were usually not shown in public, but covered with other garments. Key pieces of the first layer were shirts and underpants. Most literature that mentions these pieces describe them as being made of linen or, less frequently, of silk.

There is very little archaeological evidence for this first layer, and it is seldom shown on images. Men usually wore *braies* (very wide underpants) and a shirt. For women, a longer shirt or shift is a typical garment. There is still a lot of discussion among scholars whether women did or didn't wear underpants. Pictorial evidence and texts usually hint at them not wearing more than a shift, but a reference to a *coiffe au cul* in the thirteenth-century fabliau *Boivin de Provins* suggests that this may not be the case. We also lack evidence for how menstruation was dealt with, a problem also connected to the question of female underwear.

Generally, first-layer garments had a very simple cut. For example, a shift might have a straight body part with sleeves either completely straight or slightly narrowing towards the wrist, but with no armscye (the rounded hole cut for the sleeve) and rounded sleevehead. To avoid rips below the arm, a small square gusset was inserted. For a longer shirt or shift, the sides were either slitted or gores were set in with side seams to allow ease of movement.

The second layer makes up the clothes that were seen in public. Wool was the most common material for these, although the better-off also wore silk. Both fibres can be made into quite insulating fabrics that helped the wearer to keep warm in winter and cool in summer. A woollen dress can be surprisingly comfortable even in very hot weather, especially with a linen layer underneath.

Typical second-layer clothes for women were dresses of at least floor length. The dresses were worn with a belt that could be used to tuck the dress up, making it shorter so it could keep off the ground. For most of our period, the dresses probably followed a simple construction principle consisting of a rectangular front and back panel plus triangular or trapezoid side gores. This construction also helped the wearer appear slim. Armscyes and rounded sleeveheads were known and used, and the sleeves could be rather tight, especially around the lower arm. The construction with armscye and rounded sleevehead also worked to achieve an overall tighter fit around the upper body, showing off the woman's curves.

Men wore hose and tunics on top of their first layer. The hose were cut on the bias, with feet or a stirrup strap attached to the bottom, and fixed to the belt holding up the *braies*. They were tight-fitting to show off the male legs: good legs were the medieval equivalent to the modern six-pack. A tunic covered the upper body. Tunic lengths varied over time and possibly over region. For the simple tunics of the less wealthy and the working classes, however, a typical length was between mid-thigh and knee length. Slitted tunics were worn by riding men to allow them to straddle a horse. The slits in surviving tunics are invariably cut into an additional triangular central gore, not into the front and back panels themselves. The additional gore helps the slitted tunic to cover the wearer and avoid showing his underwear.

A third layer could be added to this clothing, either for protection against cold or bad weather or as a show of rank or ostentation. The half-circle cloak worn by nobles and courtiers, for example, was mostly a garment for show. In some circumstances, these third-layer clothes became necessary aspects of proper appearance of higher-status people, making a distinction between the second and third layers difficult. On the other hand, this gives us a better knowledge of the third layer for those of high status.

Especially in the earlier part of our period, third-layer clothing for non-nobles can be even harder to trace than the second layer, as there are only few illustrations showing them in the daily life of peasants or craftspeople. Some forms of hoods, with or without a *liripipe* (tail), seem to have been worn from at least the twelfth century onwards, and pictures showing the labours of the months also show forms of capes or wide tunic-like garments. Furthermore, it would also have been possible to layer several dresses or tunics over each other for more warmth instead of using special, distinct garments for the third layer.

From about the thirteenth century, a sideless tunic (today also called a *pellote* or sideless *surcot*) was possibly worn. The earliest evidence of this garment comes from the royal tombs of St Burgos in Spain, where several of these tunics with very wide arm-openings and traces of fur lining were found. It is hard to say, however, how fast such a fashion or garment style would have travelled through Europe and into Britain: there may have been *surcots* worn in England before the fourteenth century when depictions of them became rather common.

The worth of garments – both their actual monetary worth as well as their worth as a status object – was only partly defined by their cut. The material and type of weave, their colour and decorative elements such as embroideries, applications, trimmings or linings were also important.

Coloured fabrics could be achieved by dyeing either the yarns or the finished fabric. The dyestuffs available were derived mostly from plants. The dye plants that led to the most vibrant and durable colours are madder (*Rubia tinctoria*) for red, woad (*Isatis tinctoria*) for blue and weld (*Reseda luteola*) for yellow. The most prestigious colour was true purple, gained from a mollusc and very expensive. Countless other plants can be used for dyeing, however, and each plant can be used for a whole range of colours depending on a variety of influences such as water hardness, the pot used or the mordant chosen to pre-treat the fibres. For instance, weld can be used to dye a spectrum ranging from a very bright yellow through olive-green hues to a medium brown. Generally, bright and vivid hues were considered best and most precious, while broken or subdued colours were less desirable.

Natural dyes, when applied with care and knowledge of the dyeing process, are both wash-fast and light-fast, though some dyes (especially the yellow colours) have a tendency to fade when exposed to sunlight.

Patterned textiles were also used. It is quite likely that patterned cloth was used for clothes as well as for decorative textiles such as curtains, cushions or other furnishings. For very complex patterns, a special kind of loom was necessary as well as considerable expertise in weaving. Most of the surviving patterned textiles are woven in coloured silks using a complex weave. This process resulted in very heavy fabrics that have no modern equivalents.

A method of decorating clothes that is often associated with the Middle Ages is the use of *dagges*, that is, decoratively cut edges of garments. While the earliest examples of *dagges* already appear from the middle of the thirteenth century, the heyday of this clothing element only came in the middle of the fourteenth century and later, so after our period.

Ecclesiastical clothing – the garments worn by priests – was largely separate from secular fashion. It developed along different lines and at a different speed, and its forms did not change or change much over long periods of time. The chasuble, the outer garment worn during Mass, was a bell-shaped garment during our period, made from a half-circle of cloth sewn together at the front. The sides were usually gathered up during Mass so that the priest could use his hands. Bishops wore a special headdress, called the mitre. Gloves with religious symbols on the back of the hand, an insignia ring and stockings were other typical parts of their dress, as were burial garments for bishops. Ecclesiastical garments were often heavily decorated, costly pieces.

Monks and nuns also dressed differently. They wore habits as prescribed by the rules of their order, which also restricted how many items of clothing each person might possess, their colours and their materials.

Accessories

In addition to the garments, personal attire was completed by shoes, headwear and various types of dress accessories. Just like the main items of clothing, these things could show wealth and status through what they were made of and how well they were made.

Low-quality mass-produced items were available in the Middle Ages.

Production methods may not have resulted in the quantities we are used to, but cheap items were replicated and used. The low end of the market wasn't the whole market, but it is worth knowing that not everything made in the Middle Ages was lovingly crafted by hand to a high degree of beauty. The quality of items was mixed; the style of use was mixed too.

People wore these accessories and handled them according to their personal means and according to their skills and personality. Sometimes possessions were lovingly and skilfully repaired. Sometimes they were patched up poorly. Sometimes they were thrown out at the least sign of wear and tear. Sometimes they were kept in good condition from beginning to end. The Museum of London archaeologists have observed that people were more likely to try to repair better quality (that is to say, more expensive) items than the very cheapest. Some things never change!

Some accessories were made from materials that were traded internationally, as was, for example, Mediterranean coral, though most may have been made from material obtained in England. Some were made from substances that could have been available locally or traded internationally, such as beads that were made in London from jet and from amber and were available from either route. Mounts made of sheet copper and cast buckles and loops for straps were made in England, but may also have come from greater distances.

Most of these pieces were not purely decorative: brooches were employed as fasteners and purses and pouches were the medieval equivalent of pockets. Belts or girdles held the garment closer to the body in the waist area, could be helpful to tuck up the lower part of a dress or tunic to shorten it temporarily and served as an attachment point for other items such as a small pouch or a knife. Knives may also have been counted as a personal accessory, since they could be worn on a belt and were a very personal item.

Dress accessories such as belt fittings and brooches were made from copper alloys as well as iron, pewter, lead, tin, bone and, more rarely, precious metals. Tin, silver and gold could also be employed to coat other metals. Tin coating protected iron items against rust, as well as making them appear shinier. Gold and silver coatings were rarer and provided a cheaper alternative to items made completely out of precious metal. Which materials were more commonly used depended, again, on the time and possibly also on the region.

Belts

Belts were usually quite narrow compared to most modern types. Very wide belts were more typical of the fifteenth century than earlier. The width of the buckle bar and the width of the buckle plate are major sources for our knowledge on the width of the belt strap. While some outstandingly valuable or artistic belt buckles and strap-ends have survived in treasuries, the majority of surviving belt buckles come from archaeological excavations. They cover a large range of shapes and sizes, and the simpler forms may indicate different uses of similar materials and shapes, such as horse harnesses.

The frame was the main element of the buckle and was usually made from copper alloy before the middle of the thirteenth century. Most double frames are from after our period, though there is a London example dated to the mid-thirteenth century.

One way of attaching buckles to the belt was by folding the leather or textile strap around the frame and sewing it together. In many cases, however, the belt was fitted together with an additional buckle plate, which was a metal plate folded around the buckle frame with a hole or a slit for the pin. The plate covered the front and back of the strap and was riveted in place. An alternative was two separate pieces soldered together with the buckle frame itself.

Buckle plates, as well as their counterpart on the other end of the belt (the strap-end) offered flat surfaces suitable for decoration that could either be engraved or three-dimensional.

The belt strap itself could be as simple as a narrow strip of leather or as elaborate and costly as, for instance, a brocaded tablet-woven band such as the belt called Eric of Pomerania's Belt. Leather belt straps could be dyed or painted and decorated with stamped, engraved, punched-out or incised patterns or embroidery. The free end of the belt strap was sometimes knotted around the belt and buckle, as many illustrations as well as a few archaeological finds show.

Shoes

Shoes were an essential part of dress. A typical shoe type for much of our period is an ankle-high shoe closed with a drawstring, though other, lower-cut shoes were also in use. Shoes were made from leather, with thicker and stronger cow leather used for the sole and finer, more supple leather – such as sheep or goat leather, or calf leather – for the uppers. Fashionable shoes might be decorated with embroidery or made partly from cloth. Since leather is preserved more often in the soil than cloth, shoe finds are relatively frequent and allow better tracing of changing styles and fashions than garment finds.

Shoes were sewn inside-out around a last (a wooden form) and turned around after sewing. These types of shoe fit closely around the foot, more comparable to a glove than to a modern shoe in fit. Over time, they would mould to the wearer's foot, showing individual patterns of wear as well as evidence of deformities if the person was suffering from an injury or from a foot condition such as bunions.

While the soles made from thick leather – several millimetres in thickness – could protect the foot from cold or sharp and pointy objects on the ground, they still allowed the wearer to feel the texture of the ground through the sole of the shoe. The soles were usually waisted at least slightly in the region between the ball and the heel of the foot, giving the shoes a distinctive shape. There were also left and right shoes.

Shoes that needed lacing were mostly tied with a drawstring or several drawstrings around the ankle, though side-lacings were also used in some cases. Another possibility for shoe closure was the use of straps and buckles or toggles. Archaeological find catalogues from larger excavations, such as those published from London or York, can give a good overview of the different forms of shoe used in a given place or period.

Finally, there is the possibility that, instead of full shoes, some people wore leather soles that were attached directly to the cloth hose. Whether this was already done in our period or not is, however, hard to trace.

Worn-out or damaged shoes were either repaired or discarded. It is hard to evaluate what percentage of shoes were repaired, although undoubtedly some were. For those shoe finds that do show repairs, they were frequently made to the sole, and often a repaired shoe would have been patched up more than once, up to five or six times. Some shoes were also taken apart, probably for re-use of the uppers with a new sole to make a refurbished smaller shoe.

It is also not entirely clear how long a shoe would have lasted, and records about this are hard to find. In some cases, shoes were part of the wages for a person. This hints at some people using at least one pair of shoes per year, although it might not mean that the pair was completely used up and beyond repair after that time.

It will probably never be possible to estimate how many people went barefoot, and under what conditions. Several scholars researching shoes and shoe finds have, however, illustrated that at least in the northern climates, even the poor wore shoes. Probably only the very poor who could not even afford remade shoes and young children went without shoes. Children's shoes are found in archaeological excavations, but not always in numbers that fit to the estimated numbers of children who wore shoes.

Pattens – wooden under-shoes used to raise the foot above the ground and protect the shoes from cold, wet, dirty or rough grounds – are known from about the early thirteenth century from archaeological evidence. They seem to have been relatively uncommon around that time, though. Most documentation for *pattens*, both archaeological and from artwork, is dated to the fourteenth century and later.

Headwear and Hairstyles

Both headdresses and hairstyles were important parts of personal appearance, similar to clothing, and just as connected with status and social distinctions. For instance, headdresses were a must for married women outside the home. The style and form of headdresses, however, varied depending on time, status and region. The simplest and most timeless solution was to wear a long, rectangular piece of cloth that was arranged over the head by help of sewn-in folds, needles, wrapping techniques or knots. From the twelfth century onwards, a headdress called the wimple gained acceptance for married women, demonstrating their social status and marking their identity.

Other elements of headdress included the *barbette* and the *fillet*. The *barbette* was a band that covered both ears, running from the top or upper back of the head to the chin and back around to its starting place; the *fillet* was a cloth circlet or perhaps a flat cap that sat on the head, covering the hairline on the forehead. The *fillet* could be accessorised by putting a circlet around it. Together, they could also be worn with a hairnet. Archaeological finds of these hairnets are usually made of fine or very fine silk and sometimes splendidly decorated with embroidery. Their size was adjusted with the help of a band sewn to the lower edge of the meshes in front of the net and pulled through the meshes in the back part of the net. Medieval hairnets were large, generally covering the complete head and with a bottom circumference much wider than a normal head circumference.

Caps may also have been worn by women during our period, though they are usually associated with men. While the cap-like headwear called *coif* is only named as a male garment, other pieces that could be caps are listed among women's headwear, and illustrations do not necessarily show clearly whether an item was a piece of cloth wrapped and bound around the head, a hairnet or a cap.

Another piece of headwear, the circlet, is best known from pictures showing unmarried women, and is frequently depicted as worn with free-flowing hair.

The specific head cover chosen depended on the time and probably also the region as well as social circumstances. Hairstyles are a more difficult topic, since we have less useable depictions of how women wore their hair; we have better pictorial evidence of male hairstyles. They did, however, also differ from region to region. For instance, it is said that King Harold's scouts, who were used to long-haired and bearded men, reported that the Norman army consisted almost entirely of priests, since the Normans were shaven and short-haired. In some circumstances, different hairstyles were used to mark ethnicity, such as in medieval Ireland. In any case, the possibilities of hair are limited, and a long or short hairstyle can be interpreted differently depending on the time, region and social circumstances. For many early medieval societies, there was an equation of (male) long hair with high birth, and this association continued into our period.

In the late eleventh and early twelfth centuries, a craze for long hair swept through the male upper classes in England and northern France, and it was fairly well documented since it was regarded as scandalous by more conservative factions.

For both men and women, a shorn head was associated with subjection, servitude and humiliation. Cutting of hair could be a sign of a penitent, though some also grew their hair to represent their state. Lay knights might also cut their hair before a battle, signifying their submission to God. For women, long, flowing hair was both the sign of maidenhood and virginity and of sexual availability, generating an interesting and possibly titillating tension for the medieval viewer. The cutting of women's hair was part of the ritual of consecration into religious life as well as a possible punishment for convicted prostitutes. Another example of fashion in hair, this time traceable through archaeological finds, is the use of hair pieces to augment the natural hair.

Mourning was another circumstance where treatment of hair was particularly important, and many medieval texts give examples of tearing or shaving hair from head and face as an expression of distress. Mourning women – wives and widows – might also let their hair down, stepping outside the normal social code, though whether this was also practised in England is not completely clear.

Closely cropped hair was, according to the Bible (First Cor. 11: 7) only obligatory for the clergy. Beardlessness and, since the fifth century, a tonsure also marked members of the clergy. The Council of Liège in 1287 exhorted members of the clergy to renew their tonsures seven times a year, and the Council of Aachen in 816 had demanded twenty-five haircuts per year. However, records and rules as well as decrees prescribing punishment show that clergymen may have frequently disregarded these rules and worn their hair long and fashionably styled, neglecting the tonsure.

Ordinary members of the clergy were forbidden to wear a hat in church. Outside church, customs and regulations seem to have varied between wearing no hats or wearing specially stipulated hats. The first prohibitions regarding priestly headgear made their appearance in the eleventh century, but in the thirteenth century, wearing a hat in public became obligatory. Synods frequently objected to priests and clergymen wearing worldly hats, however: they were not supposed to wear fashionable and precious headwear.

Only girls and unmarried women were not expected to cover their heads. In practice, though, even they would not always have gone bare-headed. Generally, women were expected to cover their hair in church. Religious sources are very clear on this. It is pointed out, for instance, in the *Rationale divinorum officiorum* by Wilhelm Durandus (d. 1296), a widely disseminated handbook on liturgical questions. Whether this extended to unmarried women or whether unmarried women were allowed to go into church bare-headed, though, remains unknown.

Young, unmarried women were often depicted in art wearing their hair uncovered, which represented their unmarried state. It is, however, not very practical to wear long hair down and uncovered during field work or household work. It is more probable that they also put their hair up and out of the way, and that a kerchief or similar hair covering would have been worn by them as well to protect the hair from dirt and from getting caught during work.

Since married women covered their heads as a rule, and unmarried women were represented with hair worn down, we have only very limited insights into women's hairstyles.

Both the pictures of unmarried women, shown with their hair loose and flowing, and the few text passages that mention female hair length point to long hair being the absolute rule. Hip-length or longer hair is described both through images and through the rare mentions or hints in texts. Hair of this length is impractical if worn down, but on the other hand, is easy to put up and out of the way. This can either be done with loose or with braided hair – the braid adding more protection against tangles. A knot or bun could be fixed and held using a stick or pins (for example U-shaped hairpins, similar to modern hairpins) with or without additional bands to wrap around the hair or bun. Decorative pins from the Middle Ages also survive: they may have been used as hairpins or for pinning veils and other headgear.

The best sources for medieval hairstyles both for men and women are illustrations or other artwork. A few collections of hairstyles throughout the ages are available in modern book form. Due to printing and copyright issues, the illustrations in these books are often only re-drawings. Frequently, these books are also vague about their sources; they should thus not be regarded as completely reliable.

Unfortunately, hairstyles have not been the focus of much study, so it is possible that the depictions of hairstyles are strongly influenced by symbolism that may not be obvious to the modern viewer. A good example of this is indicating unmarried women through showing their hair loose, as described earlier.

Male headwear is similarly hard to describe in detail. For men, a headdress might symbolise their social status, serving as a marker of age, office, rank or dignity. At least from the fourteenth century, every man wore a hat or cap, and we know that hats were made from leather or cloth, felt or fur. The strong connection of hats with the concept of personal freedom only emerged in the sixteenth and seventeenth centuries, though. During the medieval period, especially before the late Middle Ages, references to attitudes towards the hat are seldom to be found. Hats were, however, not exclusively male: masculinity was shown through hair and beard more than through a headdress, and women are documented to have worn styles of hat associated more with men in some cases.

Bare-headedness also had different implications for men to women. While women kept their headwear on, the men's hats and caps could be taken off and put on as part of the social code. Raising a hat or cap could signal deference or recognition of a social superior, for instance. Male uncovered heads could also indicate humiliation, self-abasement, public penance or even asceticism.

Dress Accessories and Jewellery

As well as the more socially obligatory head coverings, it was also possible to dress up one's clothes with jewellery and other accessories. The range in quality was considerable. For those less well off, mass-produced items made from lead, tin or copper alloy set with glass stones could imitate silver and gold accessories set with gemstones.

In Christian England, paternosters made from beads were also an important accessory. They were a predecessor of the rosary we know today, and used as a help when praying. Paternosters were a common use of larger beads made from a variety of materials. Paternoster beads were worn attached to the girdle or a brooch, or sometimes worn hanging from the wrist, arm or neck.

Paternoster-making flourished in both London and Paris, and guilds were established that divided the makers by the type of materials they used: coral and shell, amber and jet or bone and horn. Paternosters made of costlier materials, such as pearls and precious stones, only appeared near the end of our period.

Necklaces and bracelets were unusual during our period; there is little evidence that they were worn at all. Some chains have been found, but are hard to date. They may have been used for religious rituals or for chain collars. Since bracelets and necklaces were unusual, most pendants hung elsewhere. For example, pendants were occasionally worn inside the clothing as prophylactic charms or talismans. There are some paintings that show earrings, but not many, and naturally, pendants worn inside the clothing would not appear in a painting. Most pendants were probably directly attached to clothing.

Rings, though, were worn as jewellery, and we have a large number of surviving pieces. Most rings were decorative, but some were amulets, which were considered to have magic properties. Rings were made in various shapes: stirrup-shaped rings were popular from the end of the twelfth century, often decorated with a sapphire, ruby or garnet. However, they vary considerably in size and weight. As today, rings could be plain metal, or could be set with stones (or fake stones made of coloured glass). They could also have cameos. Precious rings could be made of silver or gold, though gilt silver was more probable than pure gold. Some rings were engraved using a fine chisel, with a name, heraldic device and even with inscriptions. Most inscriptions (although not all) were on the outside of the hoop. By the twelfth century, love rings (*fede* rings) were known: they were often two intertwined hands on a bezel.

In the eleventh century, rings made of lead appear to have been quite common. Quite a few were made in London, although others were imports from places such as Paris. Lead-alloy rings grew in popularity from the beginning of the thirteenth century, and were made using different techniques. Some rings were mass-produced, and quite a few reflected the same decoration as pilgrim's badges and were worn as religious souvenirs. Enamelled rings were not known prior to the fourteenth century, although enamel was used on objects such as shrines and crucifixes in the twelfth and thirteenth centuries.

Pins could be ornamented with heads of glass, pearls, coral or decorative metal heads. Uses for pins were diverse, including pure decoration, fastening of dress parts or fastening of a headdress to the hair of the wearer.

Buttons, made of cloth or from other materials such as glass or metal, probably came into use as everyday dress items in the early thirteenth century.

Brooches were used to fasten garments, for example a slit in the collar area. They were often round but could also have lozenge shapes or multi-cornered forms, or even take the shape of (stylised) animals, people or other figurative designs. Religious elements were often a part of the design. These may have served for private devotion in addition to their decorative effect. Moreover, older objects, such as those from Roman times, were sometimes re-used, possibly because they were believed to have significance or to construct links with the past.

Another type of dress accessory were badges. Religious or pilgrim badges made of lead or pewter were very popular during our period. The English ones tended to have more openwork and to be made to hang, while ones from the Continent often had small rings at the corners so that they could be sewn in place.

These badges were sold at religious shrines and served as souvenirs or mementoes of a pilgrimage that retained something of the blessedness of the shrine. Even miracles were occasionally attributed to pilgrim badges. For example, a priest of Chartres was said to be cured of a serious illness when his mother laid a badge on his chest while praying to the Virgin. Cockleshells were originally sold as badges at the shrine of St James of Compostela, and these were later made of lead. In England, the shrine of St Thomas Becket was especially popular, providing badges featuring a pewter ampulla containing drops of water mixed with blood from the martyr's wounds. Gerald of Wales wore one of these badges around his neck when he was visiting the Bishop of Winchester.

Pilgrim badges could have been decorated with any number of religious or symbolic images, but there are few surviving examples from our period, so it is difficult to describe them with any certainty. Badges of allegiance might have been worn during our period, but there isn't a lot of evidence for this. Many small pieces worked in metal have been melted down to recoup the materials in later times.

While dress accessories such as simple rings, brooches, pendants and dress pins often show similar forms and choices of material, their spectrum is still so large that describing the shapes and styles here is not possible. Archaeological find catalogues as well as museum catalogues can give an overview of their designs. Small finds are also listed in catalogues for metal detector users.

Purses and pouches were the medieval equivalent of the pocket and used to contain small items, including coins. Archaeological finds of purses made from cloth are very rare, but there are some of them, as well as finds of leather purses. Leather purses could be decorated with the same methods as leather belts, and cloth pouches might feature embroidery.

During our period, the shape of these purses was quite simple; more elaborate purses with metal frames and flaps only occur after the fourteenth century. Judging from archaeological finds as well as from illustrations, the purses were typically rectangular and had a drawstring as closure at their upper end. They were attached to the belt with a strap or narrow band, hanging down freely from it, and seem surprisingly small to the modern eye. In the fourteenth century, purses with wider leather straps for attachment or purses slotted directly onto the belt become common; how far into the late thirteenth century their use started is hard to tell.

Everybody Needs to Eat
Food and Drink

Food is one of the most-discussed aspects of the Middle Ages. This is not surprising, as food and drink are cornerstones of daily life, and something that everybody can relate to. It is also easy to imagine that food in the past would have been different from modern food, just as dishes and preferences change from region to region.

Regarding medieval food and cuisine, however, there are many modern popular errors that abound. Some notions of foodstuffs, the culinary arts and eating must be shattered at the outset. Firstly, table manners were important in the Middle Ages. Secondly, people did not eat spoiled food without suffering the consequences, which makes it highly unlikely that expensive spices were used solely to disguise the flavour of rotten meat. Thirdly, some staple foodstuffs of our time were not yet known. This includes tea, coffee, potatoes, tomatoes, pineapples, chocolate and related products. French beans and green peas were also not known, though white peas were known and eaten. Any peppers or chillies came from America, as did corn and turkey, and were thus unknown too. Note that references to corn during this period were to corn as a generic name for grain and not to maize. Asparagus, melons and pumpkin probably became popular after our time. Bananas were known since the crusades, but they were not popular.

Knowledge about recipes improves dramatically for the fourteenth and fifteenth centuries, so most popular studies focus on these centuries rather than on the earlier Middle Ages. Less than a handful of thirteenth-century recipe collections have survived. They were for the literate classes, and we have little evidence for how these volumes were actually used. They might have been used for household management, enjoyment or to take recipes from one household to another. They only relate to the upper classes, and give no indication of what food was eaten every day.

Copies of Anthimus' tract on eating wisely were made in the eleventh and twelfth centuries. These also would have been the product of the literate upper class and the religious. It indicates that there were people who took their food seriously, just as the recipes that appear in medical manuals and other books do, but they still do not give us any indication of how often these recipes were prepared or in what situation they were enjoyed.

Recipes from manuscripts have been used to try to reconstruct how medieval food may have tasted. However, since every single person has his or her own cooking style, even a perfectly described simple modern dish can taste different depending on the cook. This phenomenon is made even more influential in reconstruction of historical recipes, due to the nature of medieval cookery books: they do not list full instructions for making each dish like modern recipe books do. Many things are just assumed to be known or maybe the cook's decision and thus are left unexplained or unmentioned. This is true for both contents and cooking techniques needed, and leads to a lot of necessary interpretation even for simple recipes.

Finally, there were differences in who ate what, and when, and we have much more information about specific dishes the wealthy ate, such as feast dishes, than about specific dishes anyone else ate.

For all of the period, the availability of food underlies all questions about what was eaten and when. The main factors of availability were regionality and seasonality. Although preservation techniques were known and used, availability of foods outside their season was still limited. A reason eggs and dairy were blessed around Eastertide, for instance, was probably their renewed availability. Salted boar was most often a winter dish, and fresh peaches were only eaten when they ripened in summer. Verjuice (sour grape juice, used to make sauces) was best in January and February. Trout was normally eaten between March and September, and hare was generally a summer dish. Despite attempts to eat well and to store foodstuffs, dietary deficiencies were more likely to happen in winter, when the diet included a far higher proportion of dried and preserved foods.

Regionality was another important factor. While some ingredients could be traded, these were more widely available in places where more trade happened, and bulk foodstuffs were seldom traded. Typical examples of traded items were sugar, pepper and other spices, such as cinnamon. Overall, the regions were dependent on what grew there, and strong regional cuisines developed.

The most common cooked dishes would have been soups and stews, pottage or *pot au feu*. Consequently, the most common cooking techniques used were the ones that made these dishes and to bake bread. For seasoning, both local herbs and imported spices could be used, with the latter being an option for the more wealthy.

A standard peasant pottage would probably have had a base of grain. Peas or legumes were important parts of the diet as well, supplying protein in addition to carbohydrates, and also suitable as a base. Vegetables such as onions or leeks were also common additions. The grain base for the pottage would have been the most readily available grain, varying from region to region. Other vegetables were probably important to peasant food (such as mushrooms, berries, fruits and wild greens), but we have little evidence. Only the poorest would not have had some sort of fish or meat in the diet.

We know that peasants in both France and England often ate bread, together with another dish, for a main meal. This other dish was called, in generic terms, a *compagnium*, that is, something that accompanied the bread. The best-known *compagnium* was pottage, but the food that accompanied the bread could be fairly diverse. Sometimes we even have an indication of the food consumed by workers. For instance, Norfolk harvest workers, in the thirteenth century, were given an approximate daily allowance of around 3 kilograms of wheat and barley bread (with more barley than wheat), 70 grams of oats for pottage, for about 1.6 litres of ale, 100 grams of meat (pork and fowl), about 440 grams of fish (mostly herring), eggs and cheese and about 1.6 litres of milk. This may have also fed their families.

Meals did not all have to be home-cooked: hot dishes were sold in major centres for instant consumption. In Winchester in 1148, for example, there were nine commercial cooks. In big cities like London or Paris, in particular, there was a roaring trade in ready-to-eat food due to the density of the population, the number of transients and the surprising number of people who lacked cooking equipment or could not afford fuel. Those who might eat ready-to-eat meals included travellers, boatmen and deck workers, those with limited kitchen facilities or those with no cooks or cooking skills. Fast food was already very important to the working poor.

In London in the late thirteenth century, you could buy pastries (spiced or unspiced, made with meat or fish), cooked meats, cooked game or poultry, cheesecakes, flans and wafers. Some cook shops offered to fill a pastry with meat the client brought with them, and to bake it for them. One of the earliest London cook shops we have information about is from the 1170s. Other pre-prepared foodstuffs were also available in towns: Norwich in 1287–8 has records of a mustard seller and of pork sausages for sale.

Staple Foods

Grain was the major source of carbohydrates in medieval England. One of the mainstays of the diet, bread, was made from ground soft-grain wheat, barley or oats. When these were not available (due to a bad harvest or poverty), beans or alternate flours – for instance from acorns or hazelnuts, seeds of weeds and even bark – were probably used. Hard-grain wheat (the predecessor of most modern commercial wheat) was hard to grow in England.

While wheat was obviously an important grain, rye was used for bread, although it was susceptible to a fungus called ergot. Ingesting ergot can cause internal bleeding, fatigue, giddiness, huge hunger, a feeling of creepiness and, in high quantities, gangrene and death; ergotism was well known under the name of St Anthony's fire.

In the north and midlands of England, oat, rye or a rye/wheat mix (called *maslin* or monk corn) were popular for the less wealthy in the late eleventh century, with beans used instead of any of these in bad years. All of these grains make a reasonably heavy loaf. The south of England used more wheat, which meant that the higher quality, lighter loaf was available to a larger part of the population.

Bread was prepared and baked using a number of techniques that probably varied again from region to region. Large loaves needed proper ovens, constructed from bricks or clay. They could be large or small and were private or public (communal) ovens. Small loaves could be baked on a hearth. One possible method was to place the small loaf on the hot hearthstone, cover it with a pot and bury the pot under hot embers; this method was, for instance, used in Devonshire and Cornwall. Flat pieces of dough could be cooked on a griddle over the open fire, resulting in griddle bread. The most common type of griddle bread was probably oatmeal bread, because it was low in gluten and so was not suited to loaf form. Biscuit was bread or pastry cooked twice to make it hard (*bis* 'two times', *cuit* 'cooked'), like a cracker.

Bread was so important that it was occasionally regulated – one of the very few items to receive such treatment. A 1202 rule fixed the price of bread and the profit allowed to the baker, while in 1266 the Assize of Bread went one step further and controlled weights and prices of bakers' bread. It classified loaves in three grades based on the flour used: white loaf was very finely bolted; wheaten loaf was half as heavy again, with the flour less fine; and penny loaf used unbolted meal (whole meal). Farthing loaves and halfpenny loaves also existed, all carefully calculated by weight. Feast day bread in northern France and in England may have had spice seeds added, or milk, cream, eggs, honey and preserved fruits.

Trenchers (slabs of bread from which diners ate) were used at the dining table, though we also have some evidence that plates were used: peasants are depicted as eating their bread with the meal, not as a trencher.

Bread could be part of payments by tenants to a landlord, by masters to servants or part of donations to a monastery. This did not mean that the bread was necessarily baked at home; it could be commissioned from a commercial baking establishment.

Another staple of the daily diet was dairy. Cows were not the only source of milk, with goats' and ewes' milk also used. Towards the end of our period, cows' milk was, however, more popular. The type of milk used would have depended very much on agricultural practice (which animals were farmed in a given region), but also on the owner's wealth and the space available. Many households in English towns and villages (though not in the larger cities) had a cow which normally fed on hay or hedgerow grass. While this feed would not be sufficient for modern breeds, it was enough for the smaller, tougher animals of the eleventh to the thirteenth century. Specialised dairy farms existed, but might have contained a mix of dairy animals.

If not turned into cheese, milk was used plain, to make butter and in dishes such as frumenty, sweet curds and junkets. Most milk that was drunk was at least partly skimmed, with the cream used in cooking or to make butter. Other dairy drinks were buttermilk, whey and watered milk.

To make cheese, the milk has to be curdled. Rennet and lactic acid were probably the main agents in the Middle Ages, though safflower seeds or, for a weak curd, boiled nettle or teasle flower could be used. For a very soft cheese, vinegar would be sufficient. Most cheeses did not travel well, although there is some evidence that cheeses made in Suffolk and Essex ended on the London market. Hard cheese was made with skim milk and matured for a long time. Soft cheese was made with whole or partly skimmed milk, and did mature, but not as long. New or green cheese was actually curd cheese and had to be eaten quickly. Some cheese-makers also flavoured their cheeses with herbs; these were normally new cheeses.

Cheese was not classified by place of origin, but by texture. However, the style of cheese varied considerably from place to place. Cheeses were made in places like Cheddar and Cheshire, but since they were made from sheep's and goats' milk as much as cows' milk, they were different in taste and texture to the current cheeses of those names. The Yorkshire Dales produced a ewes'-milk cheese, and Brie was known for its soft cheeses.

A green cheese made in Normandy (with the style brought to England with the Normans) was called junket because of the *jonquet*, the rush basket that was used to drain it. It was made of pure cream curdled with rennet. Eventually, this cheese was mixed with sugar and rosewater to make a sweet dish, although we do not know the date when this first occurred.

Another frequently used ingredient was eggs. Since many families kept birds – geese, ducks, hens and doves were typical managed species

– eggs were a widely available food. They could be boiled, fried, baked or used as an ingredient in other dishes.

Meat was also standard fare. Animals were probably killed by the household on farms and estates, but in larger centres, there were specialist abattoirs and butchers. All Jewish communities technically had need of a *shokhet* (ritual slaughterer, plural *shokh'tim*) to ensure that the animal was treated humanely and that all the rules of *kashrut* were met when killing animals. Jewish slaughterers were specially trained to be able to meet ritual requirements and ensure that animals died without pain. They could be male or female (women were not banned from it as a profession until the fifteenth century), with male *shokh'tim* being more common. It is unlikely, however, that very tiny Jewish communities and even all moderate-sized ones would have a dedicated *shokhet*. Most of them were not full-time professionals during our period.

While beef and pork were the most popular varieties, a large number of different meats from different animals was consumed, like rabbit, sheep, all kinds of different birds and, of course, game. Meat might be roasted and eaten with a side sauce, in a pottage or stew or in meat pies. Of course, meat could also be grilled or fried, eaten raw, smoked or turned into sausages. A favourite dish for the less rich was *collops* (fried rashers of bacon, often done with eggs). The English also ate the brawn (head cheese) and foreparts of the boar or pig. In the thirteenth century, these foreparts were used for feasts, served with roast game birds and select spices to aid digestion.

Pigs were not only important for bacon and pork: lard was the major cooking fat in England and northern France. It was used either rendered or unrendered (straight) for frying, deep-frying, in pastries and other dishes. Though pork was a crucial meat for the Christian population, its availability nevertheless diminished during our period as the woods the pigs normally foraged in were cut down.

Birds (especially wild birds) were easier to obtain on a regular basis than cuts of meat for much of the population. Fowl was usually eaten fresh. Most birds were roasted on spits (and perhaps stuffed before roasting), then eaten with sauce. Pans would be placed under the bird to catch the drippings, which might then be used to flavour other food. Where the bird was tame and the household sufficiently wealthy, it could be fed with special foods (such as milk, grain or garlic) prior to killing to improve the quality of the meat and to add to the flavour. In London and other major centres, it was possible to buy precooked birds. In London especially, the prices of these were normally controlled. Specialist bird-catchers often supplied city needs.

Fish was an important food, but it could not be transported far without preservation. Therefore, most fish eaten was generally locally sourced, or preserved. Christopher Dyer suggests that freshwater fish was a food of the wealthy (perhaps the top 2 per cent of the population), because ponds appear to mostly be located near castles and monasteries. How important fish was as a part of the diet is reflected in the fact that fishmongers in London attained guild status in the twelfth century.

While fish could be preserved and transported, and limited transport of fresh fish was possible, this added to the price. Most people, therefore, ate fish and seafood that came from their locality, apart from species like herrings and oysters, which could be transported in barrels and were cheap. Eels and shellfish were staples for the poor. Seals and porpoises were eaten in soups on fast days.

Fruit was eaten fresh in season and, again, preserved to eat out of season. Some fruits were imported into England, because they were either not available locally, or better or more prestigious varieties were available through trade. Oranges, for example, were an imported fruit that people prized. They were bitter oranges, possibly similar to modern Seville oranges. Modern sweet oranges were not known in the Middle Ages. Lemons and pomegranates were also key imports. Although these fruits were first shipped to England from Spain late in our period, they were well known in the south of France before then. The whole fruits were shipped, as well as pots with citrus peel in sugar syrup or whole fruit in sugar syrup (known as *succade*). The juice of these fruits was used in sauces and in pottages, and the peels were saved for cooking as well. Some people made a home-made variant of *succade*, using the peel they saved from their imported whole fruit. Other important trade fruits were currants, raisins, prunes, figs and dates. The dried fruits sold particularly well around Christmas, where they made an affordable Christmas treat for poorer people in towns.

Vegetables in the Middle Ages are a vexing question. We know they were grown and eaten, but we have little evidence for how they were prepared and eaten. Sometimes, vegetables and instructions on their preparation appear in meat dishes. Otherwise, it is often not clear whether a plant that was grown in a garden would be used as a vegetable or a spice, or both. For example, John of Garland's garden in Paris (early in the thirteenth century) included such vegetables as cabbage, chard, leeks, garlic, onions, scallions and a vast array of herbs including sage, parsley, dittany, hyssop, fennel and violet. He also had herbs, which, like violet and fennel and parsley, could be eaten as vegetables. Vegetables may have been prepared in a multitude of different ways, just like today, and with regional or local differences. In England and possibly north-western France, raw salads were a low prestige item; we thus have very little evidence about their preparation.

Increasingly, we are finding out more about what vegetables were eaten through the work of archaeologists cross-checked against written sources. For instance, private gardens in Winchester grew vegetables, including leeks, parsley, beans, peas, vetches, sage and hyssop. Over time, our picture of what vegetables were eaten in the Middle Ages and how they were eaten will change. At this stage, all we can do is note that we do not have anything like a complete picture.

Beverages

Just like with food, we know more about prestigious beverages than about non-prestigious ones. For example, it can be supposed that clean water was important for drinking. Clean water was prized, and London was famous for its sources of good water, but very few sources mention water being drunk.

The most prestigious drinks in England were wine, mead, beer and ale, with milk-based drinks having less social grace. England and Brittany, most of Normandy, Flanders and the Vermandois in France did not produce large quantities of grapes. The wine from the small quantity of grapes grown in England may have been very light in both body and alcohol content due to low sugar content of the grapes grown in the English climate. Apparently Gloucestershire and maybe Ely in the early twelfth century bucked this trend by producing wine that was much sweeter and higher quality. Generally, only the better-off would have had ready access to wine in England.

England obtained most of its wine through import, and most of that from its French possessions. Bordeaux was the source of some, but the vast bulk of it came from Gascony. Some of the imported wine was raisin wine (made from dried raisins) and was therefore sweet and probably with a higher alcohol content. Local wines were, as far as we know, all table wines. Kosher wine was imported into England from France and Germany.

The wealthy in England and north-western France would have drunk local produce where necessary, but drinking imported wine would have been an important way of showing that they could afford those luxuries. The wealthy purchased their wine in bulk from the importer, while the poorer bought theirs a pint at a time in the taverns.

Wine became more important in England in the thirteenth century than it had been earlier. It was not always drunk full-strength, but also watered, for instance for children. Most wine was meant for immediate drinking; it was not cellared for more than a year. Wine flavoured with herbs and spices (for instance wormwood, myrtle and cubebs) was used medicinally by some people, or to promote digestion.

There were no standards set regarding alcohol content or method of manufacture, so style and alcohol varied far more than is the case today. Barrels were made of whatever suitable material was readily available, so in southern England barrels were mainly made of oak, and in the Rhine area, they were made of silver fir. Wine barrels often sat on feet to keep them above ground.

In some regions, grapes were not produced at all, thus the alcoholic beverages available to most people in these regions would have been beer, ale and cider. Cider was drunk mainly in the most important apple-producing regions. It was made with a short fermentation and not always made solely of apples. Blackberries were added to it in the west of England, for example, and cherries in Kent. And it was not always called cider. In Normandy, if an Englishman ordered a beer, he would probably be given an apple-based drink. When it was made with pears, it was called *poree* (like our modern perry); with blackberries, *moree*; and there was also a variety made with quinces. A fermented drink based on honey, mead, was also drunk in England.

Beer could be made from oats, wheat, rye or barley. Hopped beer was around in England from the late thirteenth century, but was not widely available. Ale (another grain-based beverage) was considered a labourer's drink. Hops were probably used in making it, along with many other herbs (combined to form a *gruit*, the secret of which gave the alewife's special drink its flavour) but how far hops were used as a preservative is not known. They may simply have been used with other herbs, such as alecost and pennyroyal, to improve the taste of the ale. Hops may not have been used at all in many ales, if their flavour was not to the brewer's taste.

In England, large households, and even some smaller ones, generally brewed their own ale. Taverns sold it, and so did village alehouses. Alewives might sell their product on the streets of towns. Ale was so important to England that in 1267 the Assize of Ale fixed ale prices, based on the price of grain. Even in an average village, the number of alewives ranged from eight to twenty.

Processing, Preserving and Storing Food

Many of the foodstuffs used have to be processed in some way. The most obvious, and probably the process with most logistics involved, is grinding grain into flour to use in baking. After harvesting and drying, grains need threshing and winnowing to remove them from the ears and to remove chaff. In some cases, for example in Anglo-Saxon households, a kiln made of clay was used to dry the harvest before threshing. Threshing itself was done with flails, and was hard and very dusty work. Winnowing to remove chaff and husks was one of the early winter tasks.

For the grinding of flour, hand mills were very popular during our period. They mostly comprised two stones, the upper one being moveable and with a handle attached. The best hand mills worked fast and with relatively little effort, and could even regulate the grind. Much private grinding of grain in independent households seems to have been done by women using these methods, but if a community was large enough, a mill was often built. Some mills belonged to feudal estates, and in that case people attached to the estate were obliged to take their grain there for milling. Bringing grain to a mill was hugely labour-saving, but it also meant a possibility of being cheated by the miller.

Mills were largely controlled by lords, with milling itself being a male-dominated industry. Even as early as the late eleventh century, there were around 6,000 water mills in England. Early geared windmills were in use in England by the 1180s. They were generally secondary to water-powered mills, although they spread quickly from the 1230s. Tidal mills are first recorded in England and France in the twelfth century. They were built using shallow waterways in low-lying areas, close enough to the sea to take advantage of the tide. The millers worked when the tide dictated, and tidal mills were many fewer in number than other mills. By the end of the thirteenth century, there were mills all over the place. They hindered road and river traffic, and tidal mills could inconvenience shipping traffic, as one did at the major port of Dover.

The flour could be ground to different levels of fineness. Once it was ground, it was sieved to remove leftover larger particles. For further refinement, flour could then be bolted through cloth to get rid of bran. Bolting cloth was fabric used as a sieve, especially to produce fine-grade flour. This cloth was mainly linen. The flour produced with this method would not be as fine as modern white flour, but it would still be quite fine, and would have lost all the bran. Chemical bleaching of flour only arose from 1900: flour before that time became whiter naturally during storage. Flour doesn't keep as well as the unground grain, though, so regular small grindings would have been preferable to long storage.

Preserving food to supply the household during winter was crucial, and several preserving and storing techniques were thus employed. While there are special preserving techniques for some kinds of food, such as clarifying it to make butter keep longer, the main ways of preserving food were salting, smoking, drying, candying and jelling.

Salt was a crucial ingredient for medieval cooking and housekeeping. It was produced in England, with important areas being Lincolnshire and Northumberland. One of the chief salt-producing towns in England was Droitwich in Worcestershire, where most saltpans were owned by the king or the earl. From the thirteenth century, a coarse dark salt was imported into England from France, which, combined with a purer salt, was particularly useful for preserving meat. It was called bay salt after the Bay of Bourgneuf, which was its major source, although it was produced in several places along the French Atlantic coast.

Just like fruit and vegetables, meat was a largely seasonal produce. Without preservation, it could only be eaten for very short periods of the year indeed (mainly when autumn stock was slaughtered because winter feed would not otherwise last the distance). Meat was preserved for a few days only using a light salting process by pickling in brine and vinegar. Most preserving was for the long term, however. For this, meat could be salted heavily, using a percentage of saltpetre as well as ordinary salt, kept in brine for several days and then dried in a smoky part of the house (by the fire or in the rafters – this was known as hanged beef), or it could be pickled. Cooking salt beef required prior treatment. Cooks had to simmer it for a long time in water with hay or bran added to draw the salt out. It was then generally made into pottage.

Herring was mostly kept salted, without being gutted, and was probably the most easily obtainable fish, being eaten throughout the year. Hook and line were used to catch white fish all year round, but these fish were more expensive and were often salted and sold inland or saved for fast days or Lent. Salmon preserved in brine was imported from Scotland or Ireland, and mostly ended up in the major markets such as London. One method of salting fish was layering them in a barrel with salt, which created a brine from the moisture in the fish; these were called green fish. Fish could also be dried to preserve them.

Smoking is a technique still employed as well, usually to preserve meat or meat preparations such as sausages. The pieces would be suspended over the fireplace or in the chimney so that the smoke from the fire preserved them, keeping the meat from spoiling and drying it out. In many households, smoked food would be suspended using hooks and rods. Evidence demonstrating this is much more common from the south of France than from the north or from England.

To store meat, loops of rope or metal were affixed to the ceiling, with poles to carry the sausages. The poles could be lifted down, but the hooks were permanent. Extra pot hooks were also attached where they would do most good. They could be a variety of shapes and sizes, some with links, some a single piece of metal.

Drying can be used as a preserving technique for meat as well, but was more commonly used to preserve legumes, grain and certain sorts of fish. Dried foodstuffs are lightweight and keep well in a dry environment.

Candying was mainly accomplished using honey, and was a useful technique for vegetables as well as fruit. The high sugar content of the candied food keeps it from spoiling. Acids such as vinegar or lactic acid could also be used to preserve food, especially vegetables. In some cases, the lactic acid is produced during a fermentation process in lightly salted brine, such as for cabbage.

Finally, there were other techniques for preservation that have been mostly forgotten in our time, such as burying butter in bogs to preserve it, or burying eggs in bowls of salt to keep them fresh for longer.

Places to store food were as important as using preserving techniques. Town residences may have required less storage because of the possibility of purchasing ingredients easily and frequently, but even then, they needed storage space. Liquid or moist items required jars or pitchers; other items that had to be stored dry could be hung, which also kept them out of reach of vermin. Earthenware was commonly used for storage vessels. The best way of keeping stores cold was to place them in cellars, although in simpler households, the cellar might be just a pit in the ground.

Items stored included meat, fish, butter, cheeses, oil, honey, herbs, legumes and grains. Grain could be stored by the ear, or threshed. Storing as flour was less normal as flour had a much higher tendency to turn rancid, or to develop a bad case of weevils, mites or rats. In many cases, storage times would have been less – often much less – than we are used to in modern foods.

One way of protecting against food spoiling, vermin and also against food poisoning was by keeping the kitchen clean. We have quite a bit of evidence about the importance of wiping down working benches after use, and scrubbing plates and the insides of pots with warm water. It was a never-ending task in larger households, with a low-ranking member of the household dedicated to drawing water, heating it and cleaning wherever possible.

Food Restrictions

Food and religion were integrated for both Christians and Jews, although in different ways. The time of the year according to religious law and custom led to quite a few food restrictions. There were also cultural restrictions that had nothing to do with religions, and some foods that we take for granted were just not available from the eleventh to the thirteenth century.

Meat and meat products were prohibited on fast days for Christians. Fast days were roughly one day in three. During fasts, animal fat was replaced by vegetable fat and meat was replaced by fish. In some interpretations, dairy products were not to be eaten on fast days, but according to others they were, so actual fasting practice varied.

Generally, fast days resulted in different food being eaten, and not necessarily less food or food of a lower quality. This holds especially true for the rich or powerful: for food on St Edward's Day 1257 (13 October), Henry III bought 250 bream, 15,000 eels and 300 pike. This does not suggest a quiet dinner with his nearest and dearest, although it does follow the letter of the law, since there was no meat purchased. Despite this, in England some people would have regarded fast days almost as penitential, mostly because of the English preference for meat dishes.

The Christian fast days were spread unevenly over the year, and affected food choices significantly. They also tied in with the seasons. For example, the fasting period before Easter with severe food restrictions fell at a time of year when food supplies were running out and fresh crops were still not available. There was a certain flexibility in the handling of these fast days, though: a record in the household accounts of Richard Swinfield (or Swinefield), the Bishop of Hereford, from 1289–90, tells us about a Christian October fast day being moved from Wednesday to Thursday because there was no fish available on the Wednesday. Christian monastic communities had their own additional restrictions. Jacques de Vitry tells of one monastery where monks were only allowed to eat game (meat that had been hunted). Again there were loopholes sought and found: when someone smuggled in some hounds and the hounds chased the pigs, the pigs were then killed as game.

Dietary laws for Judaism were very different to those for Christianity. They were part of the laws of cleanliness, or *kashrut*. The rules of *kashrut* include clean and humane killing of an animal, draining of blood through salting and soaking, removing certain parts of the animal and so on. Jews were forbidden to consume land animals that were ruminants with fully cloven hooves (such as pigs) or sea animals that did not have both fins and scales (such as oysters).

All food restrictions for Jews were based upon rules first described in the Jewish religious texts and on rabbinical guidance on how these rules should be applied. Special restrictions to prevent eating leavened food (food with yeasts, such as breads) were followed during the eight days of Passover. A special meal was held every Friday night, to celebrate the holiness of Sabbath; this meal was so important that in times of austerity, it was customary to eat even less during the week to have enough food on Friday night. Food with symbolism attached was important, with one rabbi expressing a preference for meat pies for Sabbath because the layers represented the two portions of manna that were delivered to Jews for Sabbath during the time of Exodus.

All Jewish communities theoretically followed *kashrut*. How far individuals followed it depended very much on the individual, and we have few records to check this. In many areas of England and France, the observance of fasts on Fridays and Saturdays by Christians was a potential cause of conflict with the Jewish community, which ate fish as a part of its Sabbath celebration. In some areas, Jews were instructed to wait until all Christians had done their shopping, and to only buy leftovers.

The households of Jews who kept kosher would have been ruled by the need to keep meat and dairy products apart. How strictly this was done remains unclear. In practice, a French rabbi suggested that if someone had cooked meat-based pies and dairy-based pies in the same oven it should be regretted, but the food could still be eaten. We have no indication of what proportion of the Jewish population kept *kashrut* in England, though.

Jewish fast days were far rarer than Christian fast days, but much more severe, as all food and drink was prohibited. Jewish fast days were immutable and not handled as flexibly as Christian fast days might be.

Both Christians and Jews proved rather inventive in order to find exceptions to the food restrictions. The explanations for these exceptions are often very interesting instances of legal fiction, such as interpreting geese as fish because they were supposed to hatch from the barnacles stuck to ships.

Finally, some foods were not eaten due to cultural reasons not connected with Christianity or Judaism. Dogs, cats and vermin were generally not consumed, except in case of dire need. In England, horses were generally also not used as meat.

Cookery

Cooking skills are an important factor regarding food, and cookery books can serve as a memory aid or an instructor for dishes. Very few medieval cooks, however, would have used cookery books.

We do have some evidence about the range of cooking techniques from these books, as well as from other sources. Even in the eleventh century, the range of techniques open to most cooks included baking, broiling, roasting, frying and boiling and procedures such as salting vegetables and serving them up with fresh butter, using clarified butter and dressing vegetables (for instance, with oil and vinegar) are recorded.

Cooking times were always a matter of skill and estimation rather than strictly timed. How far something had to cook might be done by sight and feel, but other means of estimating time might also be used, like cooking a sauce for as long as it took to sing a certain song, or pray a certain prayer, or even walk half a mile.

In a small household, cooking would generally have been done in the main room. This is not the case with lord's residences, though some finishing touches might be put to dishes in the hall. As far as we know, most cooking was done by women, but senior cooks in big establishments were likely to be male. Professional cooks from noble households did not have an easy life. They worked long hours at a difficult job, and had to deal with all the vicissitudes of life in a large household. Moreover, they usually had to deal with working in more than one well-known kitchen. Great lords moved from estate to estate, and the cook and many of the other staff went with him or her. This may have been very awkward for provisioning, but cooks were expected to feed the whole household regardless. A lot of the kitchen year would have been structured around this movement, and the need for staff to be released from other duties to pack cooking utensils, spices and food.

In the majority of cases, cooks would have ensured that they carried as much equipment as possible with them on each move, because the kitchens themselves would vary. Unlike poor households, they would have had purpose-built kitchens, with ovens and hearths and preparation space. A very modern kitchen in the thirteenth century might be away from the main residence and have recessed fireplaces for cooking, but a less elaborate kitchen could be an open space where benches had to be added and all cooking done on open hearths. Having the equipment for more complex tasks, for instance to cover the fire to make a fine sauce, or roast a series of stuffed capons, could make a major difference in the cook producing quality food on every estate.

There was a range of possible kitchen equipment that a well-equipped cook might use. It included tools for cooking over heat (pots and pans of diverse kinds), temporary storage or carrying equipment (baskets and boxes), specialist cooking equipment (graters, oven shovels and pot hooks), roasting equipment (spits, supports and skewers), serving dishes (plates and platters) and much more. The vast majority of forks in use were for cooking, for example long forks necessary to handle food in cauldrons. Skewers could also be used for the same task. Other items cooks needed included a good knife or set of knives and the means to sharpen it or them (a whetstone), mortar and pestle and bolting cloth.

Cooks needed flat surfaces (a good table or working bench) to chop or pound ingredients, enough light to work by (including artificial light for early starts and late finishes), at least one fireplace and buckets for water and slops.

A good and clean water supply was as essential to the medieval cook as to the modern cook. Vegetables had to be washed and cleaned, and dried foods set to soak. Clean water was used in dairies, as well, and was very important since unclean water could lead to fast spoiling of the dairy products. Dug wells generally provided the most easily accessible forms of potable water, and pure springs and fountains were highly valued. Pollution was a problem in some urban areas and a great deal of effort was spent trying to minimise it.

Often, water was brought in from a well or a fountain, and London and its nearby villages were especially famous for the number of fresh wells and springs they boasted.

For frying, heat-resistant fats were needed. Oil was a typical import to England in the eleventh century, especially from northern France. The best oil came from the nearby Mediterranean countries and included olive oil, walnut oil and oil of fenugreek. The oils were used to fry and to marinate, but they were also used medicinally. Olive oil was a prestigious oil, considered a luxury item in London in the twelfth century. Suet and lard were also important. Suet was particularly favoured for pie pastry, and lard for more delicate pastries. Butter was also available, although for use with higher temperatures for frying, clarifying the butter was necessary. Binding agents and thickeners were used extensively in cookery. The most common appear to have been wheat flour, breadcrumbs, ground-up toast, wheat starch, egg yolks, ground liver, ground almonds and ground rice. The choice of thickener would have depended very much on the nature of the dish. It is unlikely, for instance, that ground liver would be used in a light milk-based sweet dish.

The most common sweetening agent was honey; sugar was available, but much more expensive. Sugar arrived into England and France with the spice ships or the controlled overland trade from Venice and Genoa. Most of it would have come from the Mediterranean region. Sugar was more prized for its medicinal qualities, although those taking it for medicinal reasons saw no reason why it should not be coloured and used to coat digestive spices or flowers.

While sugar could be bought as part of pre-made foodstuffs, such as sugar-coated violets, it was also sold in lumps or other shapes, and either in the form of treacle or as purified white sugar. The most popular way of buying sugar was in a loaf. A sugar loaf was made of super-refined, very hard, pure white, brittle sugar, was generally conical and could weigh as much as 15 kilograms. Sugar was scraped off the loaf as needed.

Scholars argue about the level of spicing used with food. All seem to agree that spices were used as seasoning (as they are today) or medicinally and not to disguise rotting meat. It is likely that the amount of spice depended on taste buds, spice quality, finances and the cooking style in which the cook was trained. Constance Hieatt suggests that the English record demonstrates cautious use of spices.

Not all spices were available to all people, and there were many readily available seasonings about whose use we do not know. In a society that obviously liked savoury food and developed sophisticated kitchen gardening, it seems highly unlikely that local produce was not used in cooking. Local herbs, such as mustard and savoury, were effective in giving food colour and flavour.

There was a huge range of spices theoretically available, but the most popular were ginger, pepper, nutmeg and saffron. Also common were cassia, cardamom, cloves, mace, zedoary, galingale, spikenard and cubebs. From the thirteenth century, grains of paradise and cinnamon must be added to this list. Most of these spices were shipped from southern China, modern south-east Asia or India. They came to England and France via Venice and Genoa, and from there, they were sold at the great fairs of the Champagne region and southern Flanders. It was a slow process, and the spices were probably over a year old before they reached their final local markets and traders. Spice prices fluctuated according to availability. The cheapest were generally cassia (and later cinnamon), ginger and pepper, with cloves and mace being more expensive. Saffron was very popular as both a spice and colourant, although it was also very dear. Saffron-yellow dishes were often introduced through familiarity with Middle Eastern food, so they are connected to crusaders. During our period, saffron was mainly produced in Spain, although later on there was limited production in Essex and Cambridgeshire. Many people would have been forced to resort to safflower as a substitute.

In England, London was at the centre of the trade in sugar and spice, with produce available all year. The London market was so important (and pepper was such a key seasoning) that the Guild of Pepperers was established there. Its activities were first recorded in 1180. Regional fairs also sold spices, and communities distant from the major trade routes could buy spices from chapmen. The smaller the trader, the smaller the range of spices available, with the choice from a wandering peddler being limited to the most popular spices, such as pepper and ginger.

There were several popular named spice mixtures that were widely used, although the actual flavour and contents of the mix would have varied from household to household. In cities like London or Paris, they could be bought ready-made, or households could mix their own. Blanch powder was pale in colour, hence the name. It usually included items like sugar and white ginger. Powder fort comprised the hot, strong spices such as pepper and ginger, while powder douce was milder. Powder merchant was the lazy person's answer to spice mixing, because it was a mix purchased already ground from the merchant (no recipes for this seem to have survived). All spices were powdered using a mortar and pestle.

The look of the food was as important as the taste, especially in well-to-do households. The higher Anglo-Norman nobility seem to have had a particularly strong interest in food that was appealing to the eye, using reds, whites, yellows, greens and blues. Blood was used with suet or lard to make black puddings, or by itself to darken pottages. Pale fats alone made a white pudding. Marrow was used to enrich and darken soups, pottages and pies. Alkanet could be used for a reddish colour, saffron or egg yolk for yellow and saunders (a variety of sandalwood) for a reddish-brown. Orchil lichen (*tornesoc* in Old French) was even more useful, giving a blue colour in alkaline food and a red one in acid. Indigo could be used for blues as well. Parsley was used for green. Even burnt toast was added to make dishes darker and more appetising. Some of these colourings also had significant effects on the flavour of the dish. The most important colours seem to be yellow and green, with a happy, bright green being called *vergay*. For the seriously wealthy, ingredients such as ground lapis lazuli for a blue colour and finely beaten gold or silver leaves could also be used to impress diners.

15

Making Money
Medieval Economy

No picture of a society is complete without considering the economy and how individuals made a living. For our period, economy and commerce were quite different from modern economy, though in some areas, things seem strikingly familiar.

Any economy, regardless of time and place, is a complex system. It is influenced by and in turn influences the constant changes in trade, agriculture, society, politics and culture. Since numbers are a key factor in economic studies and data from the Middle Ages is difficult to obtain and can give inconsistent results, historical economics works with a lot of rough estimates and extrapolations based on interpretation of source material. This means that all theories and numbers for economics must be taken with a considerable amount of salt.

Economies are closely linked to demographic changes: the size and nature of population. The ever-changing balance between population, both actively producing and consuming resources, land use and trade structures is at the heart of understanding the economics of medieval societies. Unfortunately, it is very hard to deduce the size of the population in medieval times from available sources. Literary sources (for instance those that describe warfare) might exaggerate numbers of people to make the fight seem bigger and hence more important. Population centres might have shifted and been forgotten, so they were left out of the count when assembling information from sources. Whole population groups might be left out of a public count that only includes householders with sufficient property. In other words, our sources are limited and biased. Even backed up by strong work in the fields of archaeology and history, numerical data from written sources are not sufficient to tell us how many people there were. The biggest gaps are for women and Jews: judging from the mentions of women in official documents alone, only around 5 per cent of the population would have been female.

What can be said is that population in Europe grew to a peak in the late thirteenth or early fourteenth century before a catastrophic decline. David Herlihy suggests that it took until 1850 for Western Europe to reach the population density of the time around 1300 after the great decline in the late Middle Ages. Current population estimates range so widely as to be almost unusable. The estimates for England in the late eleventh century range from 1.1 million to 2.25 million, and equivalent estimates for around 1300 are 3.75 million to 8 million. Peasants comprised the largest single population group, making them the economic mainstay. However, we have many fewer written records for peasants than for any other major demographic group.

Medieval Economy

The whole of an economy can be subdivided into four sectors: agriculture, industry, commerce and the banking and finance sector. In the Middle Ages, agriculture was always the dominant sector, providing food as well as many raw materials. Industry – in our period meaning mostly crafts – was important as well, as evidenced by the high standards of crafts in medieval times. Two very important industries were metallurgy and textiles. Commerce – local, regional and long-distance trade – as well as banking and finance are closely connected to each other: they spread wealth and goods. Social and political institutions had a large influence on economics including those involved in landholding, the Church, chartered towns and so on. Change in each of these means influences on and changes in the others.

From the later eleventh century, but especially during the twelfth to the early fourteenth century, Europe experienced remarkable economic and population growth. This can be seen in the number of new settlements, both agricultural settlements and towns. In economic history, this is usually called the Commercial Revolution. Long-distance international trade and towns are described as engines of growth that fuelled population growth and thus resulted in urbanisation as well as in more settlements. Major innovations in a number of areas also fuelled this lengthy period of economic growth. The main sources of wealth, however, were still primary resources such as agriculture, wool and fisheries. Trade and the expansion of craft industries diversified the economies of both countries as time passed, but they remained heavily reliant on natural resources. Despite the rise of medieval industries during our period and despite the rapidly growing use of machinery, such as that employed in mills, France and England remained agrarian countries. Some researchers suggest that only around 14 per cent of the population lived in towns of 2,000 or more around 1300. The largest towns were London and Paris, of course. The Jewish population was spread over our region, with the lowest concentration being in rural England, north of Newcastle-on-Tyne and west of Exeter.

Medieval economies were not modern and should not be thought of as modern. They were based on a series of concepts like rights to feudal dues that were fundamentally different to the modern view on taxation. Financiers, both small and large and from many different backgrounds, provided a silent backbone to the system, as did stable rulership. Small financiers, including local monastic houses and even wealthy widows, comprised an important component in handling investments. At all levels, from local to national, the need to sort out public and private finances underlay daily life.

Good financial management was as complex and complicated in the Middle Ages as it is today, since it depended on a huge variety of factors and circumstances. For instance, the king and his court needed to manage their limited resources very carefully. This, however, conflicted badly with the notion of largesse to show off their wealth and status, something especially important for nobles. Many kings and nobles found themselves overcommitted simply because of the (real or perceived) need for representative spending of large amounts at their station in life in spite of limited income.

It was also a common part of the culture of the time to be persuasive with cash in hand. Representatives of London gave Henry I 100 marks of silver so that they could elect their own sheriff, for instance. When a witness was needed on the purchase of land, schoolboys might be bribed with 3*d* worth of cherries or a small sum of money. It was ubiquitous and simply a part of life.

The English economy was a wealthy one in the eleventh century. Overall there was positive economic growth, marked by periods of stagnation. The reigns of Stephen and John in England were particularly notable for the loss of economic momentum. There were intermittent political problems, social problems and religious problems that all had an impact on the economy, and the tensions between the English magnates and royal power were always there. The sort of financial reform undertaken by some kings would have had to be ongoing and consistent to achieve lasting stability, not relying on the interest of a particular ruler in administration, but on more fundamental professionalism in the way the administration was undertaken.

Income, Finances and Daily Life

Medieval finances were complicated, with a multitude of currencies and a coexistence of barter systems, hard cash and bills of exchange. Trading goods and services with other people is one of the core concepts of human community. Whatever the method of these exchanges, they make it possible to develop a society with a variety of specialised crafts and occupations. This in turn allows for a higher quality of goods and services overall.

The most informal kind of exchange is direct barter. The two parties exchange something of equal value directly with each other. This works best if each of the parties has something of the appropriate value that the other party wants or needs. In a small and relatively close-knit community, bartering is an easy method of trade. Trade partners know each other, and things can be bartered against future services or goods given in return. In these circumstances, money plays a very subdued part and might not be necessary at all.

When there is no counter-offer for the desired goods or service possible, or the other party is not available for a long-term bartering procedure, a stand-in of fixed value is needed; a form of currency. Medieval money generally consisted of silver coins. A pound of silver was split into 240 pennies. Pennies, like other denominations, had a fixed weight (1.3 to 1.6 grams) and a set standard of alloy for minting. English pennies were considered to be of consistent and high quality.

The penny was the main coin in use. It was part of an international system of coinage that had been in place since the ancient Romans. Since the same abbreviations were also used internationally, for example *d* for pence, pfennig, denier or denarius, all money systems looked alike on paper. This similarity derives from the Roman roots of the coinage, with the solidus (pl. solidi) twelve times the base unit denarius.

Some apparent descriptions of coins referred to them mainly for accounting purposes, such as the solidus or the mite. The mite was used for accounting in England, calculated at twenty-four to the penny (with the term coming from the mijt, the smallest coin in the Low Countries) but as far as can be determined, mite coins were not actually issued. Some coins did not exist because they were too large, such as the mark. Having coins that only existed on paper was very necessary to calculate small or large amounts. The larger sums they described were frequently paid in gold leaf, gold ingots, gold dust, or even objects valued at a certain amount.

Some coins associated with the Middle Ages were not struck until the thirteenth century or later. These include the écu, the franc, the groat (or groot) and the noble. Gold coins were also a rather late development. In Europe, gold coinage was only really available from 1252, when Florence started circulating the gold florin. The main gold coins apart from the Florentine fiorino d'or (gold florin), which was worth 240 Florentine denarii, were the Genoese genovino, which was worth ninety-six Genoese denarii, and occasional African coins. None of these coins were common outside Italy.

Minting coins was considered a seigniorial prerogative. The general approach to minting differed widely between England and the rest of Europe: the English system was centralised and closely controlled by the Crown. This led to a comparatively stable money system with little devaluation of coins over time. In contrast to this, France and other Continental kingdoms minted coins in a regional system, resulting in much less stability.

The value of a coin depended largely upon its weight and the fineness of the silver, with a small premium over bullion value related to the cost of manufacture in most cases. National uniformity in the weight standard was achieved in the late eleventh century, but from the fourteenth century onwards, the weight standards began an unstoppable long-term decline.

The bullion used for minting was usually not supplied by the state or mined in English territory; foreign coins and bullion imported as payment for exports were much more significant sources of metal for the coinage in England.

In the minting process, the metal planchet was placed between two dies that were engraved with the pattern for the front and back of the coin, and the top die was then struck with a hammer. Minting with picture and legend ensured that the coins were clearly assignable to a region and the issuing moneyer. It also had a second function: it made stealing precious metal by clipping or filing a coin much harder. This even influenced coin designs. For example, Henry III changed the basic design of English coins in 1247 from a short-armed cross to a long-armed cross. The moneyer issuing the coins was responsible for the weight and standard of the coins. Producing underweight coins or lowering the fineness of the coins meant more profit for the mint, which was a significant lure for greedy moneyers.

The mints generated profit by levying charges for the minting of bullion which exceeded the costs of production. Only in the late twelfth century do records of mint revenues received by the king's exchequer begin; for example, during the issue of short cross coinage 1180–1247, a mintage of 6*d* per pound of silver was charged for the moneyers' costs and a further 6*d* for the king's profit or *seigniorage*. The English Crown monitored the quality of coinage and would levy fines against the private owners of a mint when the product was not up to scratch. This could happen, for instance, if the wrong dies were used or the metal content was wrong. Apparently, in practice, this quality control was interpreted relatively liberally, and many moneyers debased coinage just a little to keep the unused silver that resulted.

If this cheating got out of hand, though, it could have dire consequences. According to the *Anglo-Saxon Chronicle*, Henry I was so outraged by the quality of the coins being issued that he rounded up a group of moneyers and chopped off their testicles and their right hands for punishment at

Christmas 1124. This was followed by a radical reduction in the number of mints. Henry II reformed English coinage twice, in 1158 and 1180. Following the first reform, he reduced the number of mints drastically from nearly fifty to only nine, eliminated the ecclesiastical mints (this was revoked under later rulers) and relocated the remaining mints. The old periodic recoinages were abandoned after 1158, and the deterioration of coinage in the long intervals between recoinages became a constant problem for the rest of the Middle Ages. Public concern about the state of the coinage had a crucial role in the introduction of new coinages in 1180, 1247 and 1279. Various chroniclers testified to the belief that the currency reform in 1180 was necessary because the money had been corrupted by forgers. Henry II replaced all of the moneyers and introduced centralised mint buildings instead of the individual workshops. He also instituted the royal exchangers who were responsible for exchanging old to new coins instead of the moneyers themselves.

Through use, coins could be significantly eroded and became impossible to be used normally anymore. To remedy this, a new coin with a different face and legend could be issued, replacing previous coins. This obliged people to exchange their old coins for new.

Use of coinage grew in the Middle Ages, and it also grew more sophisticated. In the early part of our period, there were more currencies and more moneyers than at the end of it. The total number of moneyers in England fell progressively during the eleventh and twelfth centuries. By the fourteenth century, control of coinage had become more centralised. Additionally, Peter Spufford suggests that in the middle of the thirteenth century there were approximately 100 million pennies in circulation in England, and that this had grown by a multiple of five or more since the twelfth century.

Knowing the content of precious metal – silver in most cases – was necessary for checking the value of money. Goldsmiths with assaying skills therefore had a significant role in the management of the royal mints. Assaying to check silver or gold content of a coin could be done using several methods. One method used was the touchstone test, where the colour of a rubbing made by the coin was compared with a standard trace from metal of a known quality. The accuracy of this depended on the skill of the assayer, but was only likely to be reliable to 2–3 per cent in many cases. Other methods of assaying were cutting the piece in half, checking its resonance or the relation between its weight and size. Weighing coins was done with scales; their accuracy depended both on the quality of the scales and the accurateness of the weights as well as on the skill and care of their user. For greatest accuracy, an assay by fire could be done, where the coin was melted down and its component metals checked. This of course resulted in the coin being destroyed, so it was only used when absolutely necessary.

Moneymaking and moneychanging were two different professions. For trade, it was necessary to use the coin of the region, which led to people exchanging their home coin for the local currency. Exchanging coins would of course mean profit for the moneychanger. Both moneyers and moneychangers were often of high status in the community.

Coin or currency values were also used to record or describe the income of a given person. Actual income figures for medieval people are easiest to obtain for those at least very well-off. In the late thirteenth century, the wealthiest earls might have £6,000–£8,000 per annum, with the lesser aristocracy having to be content with £2,000–£5,000. A rich bishopric would garner the holder more than £2,000 a year, while an average baronial income was merely several hundred pounds. Poor barons lived on tens of pounds rather than hundreds or thousands. They were still comfortably off compared with labourers, who earned around 1.5d per day.

The richest woman in thirteenth-century England was probably Isabella de Fortibus (1237–93). She was also one of the wealthiest barons, holding several titles and a lot of land. She adored litigation, so we have lots of records of her: she even sued her mother. Upkeep of her employees ranged from 1.5d to 5d a day. Also very wealthy were people like William de Valence, half-brother to Henry III. He had the lordship of Wexford and a share in that of Pembroke, a castle at Hereford and a lot of land, mostly in southern England. By the start of Edward I's reign, his income was around £2,500 per annum.

The Bishopric of Ely gave its incumbent £920 in 1171–2, which had risen to £2,550 by the end of the thirteenth century. The Bishopric of Worcester, however, gave its incumbent only £330 in 1185, rising to £1,192 by the end of the thirteenth century. So not all notables had equal incomes, although some, such as earls, were guaranteed a high one.

Income or wages were not necessarily paid all in coin, but could also be given in kind. Incomes could vary greatly, and it is very hard to determine today what a given amount of money would have bought. Buying food and drink, however, was probably the most important spending that people did, with it costing well over 50 per cent of their income. Economically, the food trade was also of immense importance: 25–40 per cent of people in towns worked in food-related trades, like retailing in shops, door-to-door sales, selling drinks and pies or in the international spice trade.

Pricing of goods was dependent on a multitude of things, just like today. It was different according to time and place, the buyers and sellers, the amount of skilled or unskilled labour going into something, the craftsperson or workshop producing it, how far an item had to travel, what condition the goods for sale were in and whether they were considered luxury goods (and thus marked up).

Prices were thus not steady, but fluctuating. Price changes could be due to a large number of causes – good or bad harvests, climate and weather differences, individual merchants or groups and their policies, to name just a few. Inflation would also be a factor in price changes. Only a few items indispensable for daily life, for example bread, were subject to price regulation through legislation.

For payment of small sums in daily life, the smallest whole coin (the penny or its equivalent), was still too large a sum of money. There were several solutions to this. One was the use of a barter system for small everyday goods, reducing the need for coins in general. The second possibility was to create smaller coins, where normal coins were cut in halves or quarters, creating halfpennies and farthings.

Statistics from coin finds suggest a very high percentage of cut coins as compared to complete ones: as many as 44–62 per cent of the individual pieces found in hoards were halfpence. The amounts of farthings vary from 15 to 26 per cent, but the small size of farthings may contribute to their underrepresentation in archaeological finds, as they are more difficult to find. Clipping of coins was, of course, much easier with the cut fractions, leading to more fraud being possible with these small coins. In the recoinage of Edward I in 1279–81, round halfpenny and farthing coins were issued, and generally coins were not cut after this time.

Another option was buying on credit. If you needed a single loaf of bread from the baker, you were not going to pay with a silver penny. Instead, you had the baker mark what you owed, and once you had racked up a bill, you came to settle it with coin. The idea to pay everything at once in perfectly matching amounts of money is a more recent one.

There were several methods of keeping tally of the amounts owed. The sums could be written down, or a tally stick could be used. That was a wooden stick marked with notches according to the amount owed and then split in half along the middle. Since the split surface was uneven, only the two original pieces would fit back together, and since the notches had to be on both parts of the stick, it was tamper-proof. The two parts could be held together again to add more notches if the debt went up, and burned after the accounts were settled.

Tally sticks are tangible evidence for the culture of loans and credits in medieval economy. Whether due to dire straits or due to large investments (such as to build a castle or cathedral, or to go to war), people might need loans for short-term financing needs. Loans for major investments depended on the project. The reality of Jewish financiers was quite different from the stereotype of the Jewish moneylender, already alive in the Middle Ages. Lenders of large amounts were usually from internationally important, widespread and very affluent families, which included some Jewish families. For instance, Westminster Abbey, in the late eleventh century, had business dealings with London Jews. Also very important were the Italian moneylenders (known as Lombards) and the Knights Templar. Cahors in south-western France produced many moneylenders as well, and the Cahorsins were well known in England when anti-Semitism prevented Jews from working in this profession. The standard rate for a short Cahorsin loan was 50 per cent per annum. The large-scale moneylenders often also guaranteed safe storage of valuables left with them.

Small-scale loans could be made within a community, for example from neighbours, family members or friends, or maybe from a local monastery. Monasteries were particularly important in providing rural credit. Credit like that needed by a shepherd or small trader was usually provided at fairs, recorded through notched tallies and promissory notes. Credit was also given for a sale between peasants, with a deposit provided, usually before witnesses. Royal promissory notes to traders had a record of not being honoured, however, especially in England.

The availability of loans and credits should, however, not be thought of as credit as we know it. There is a large difference, since the Church had a general prohibition for Christians to charge interest on money lent or exchanged. The charging of interest was seen as as usury. The existence of a religious law does not mean that it was not broken, and there is documentation of Christians lending money. While this might have been done as a kindness in some cases, there is also evidence of several ways to circumvent the usury restrictions. For loans in general, interest may have been very high, with rates up to 60 per cent and above. Items may have been given as security in some cases. Most financial records that survive tell us how much was owed, or how much was paid as a total figure. We seldom know exactly how much was paid over the amount owed and in what form, or how much of the sum written down for the accounting purposes represented real money.

Trade and Commerce

Trade played a crucial part not only in the growth of the European economies from the eleventh to the thirteenth century, but also in the increasing spread of ideas through the Western world. The number of merchants – some of them from peasant backgrounds, some from craft backgrounds – increased dramatically from the twelfth century. Women who traded in England could be recognised as a *fame sole*, that is as a woman trading alone, often unmarried or widowed.

Most of the buying and selling in our period was small-scale local trading. This was not all, however: regional and even international trade were well known in the Middle Ages. And somewhere between the local trade and the international trade of our period, we find the itinerant merchants, who spent most of their lives travelling. These ranged from small peddlers to important international merchants who travelled routes like the Silk Road. Some moved within countries, some moved between countries, some used ships, some used packhorses and some always travelled on foot. Since the most obvious way to move from being a peasant to being a merchant was by starting as an itinerant peddler, it is not surprising that itinerant merchants of many types underpin the economy.

Itinerant merchants brought material from the cities or town fairs to the smaller towns and even to smaller places. It is almost impossible to know the full extent of this trade network, or even much about which product was sold where. More portable products were likely to be preferred, such as ribbons, belts, writing tablets, veils, luxury cloth (such as silk and fine linen) and combs, but this sort of trade did not have the same level of documentation as the large fairs. In the eleventh century, the vast majority of these merchants would have sold a wide range of goods, but by the end of the thirteenth century, specialist merchants were becoming more common, and merchants' social and political activity also grew. Merchants were gradually becoming a part of the ruling class in some regions.

Local trade not undertaken by itinerant merchants included shops selling goods, produce or wares and local peddlers for goods like bread and ale who sold door to door. It also included markets.

Local markets were held regularly and frequently. They might be held in or near churchyards, in market streets, or in other central locations. The size and permanency of the marketplace indicated how much trade it had. Local producers brought goods directly to these markets and fairs.

Markets, especially the larger ones, needed infrastructure such as buildings, toll-houses, access to the town well or conduits, public quays and weighing beams. Market spaces for prosperous specialist markets could be covered to protect against weather; we know of such covered markets, for instance, for the late thirteenth century in both London and Paris. To meet infrastructure costs and to make money, the owner of the land charged rent for tables and stalls and fees for the right to break ground to set up booths. There were also tolls for a range of other things, including the right to use the official weights and measures. These rates were normally low, so as not to discourage trade.

Regional marketing networks centred around larger towns, with village markets and rural trading flowing around and into them. Where larger towns had markets, this place was typically preferred for trading, resulting in fewer village markets in the region, while smaller, more local markets were frequent in more rural areas. What is important to note is the sheer number of markets of different sizes, and the fact that they were scattered widely through the year and across the land.

Fairs were different from markets in that they would normally be annual and last for three days to a week. Fairs were another standard part of medieval commerce, acting with and on top of the regular commerce of shops and markets. Like markets, there were general and specialist fairs. Some mainly brought material from the countryside and traded it to people who wanted to take it to larger centres and had material from those larger centres for trade in return. Others had a more regional focus, and the big fairs, of course, were supremely international.

St Giles Fair in Winchester in the early thirteenth century, for instance, specialised in silk cloth, gold and silver thread, pearls, boots and spurs. St Giles was also well known for its wonderful horses and as a place to buy ferrets and falcons. If you wanted to buy horses, the best international fairs were those in Brie and the Champagne region. Most horses were bought more locally, however. William Fitzstephen in 1155 wrote about buying horses at the weekly fair near London, and the horses available there ranged from palfreys and warhorses through to farm horses. On the day of Saint Denis (9 October) was a specialist wine fair in the Paris region, where very new wine was sold at a premium price.

Customers of local markets mainly came from about a 9.5- to 11-kilometre radius, which means they could travel there and return home in the same day. In contrast, a typical regional fair might draw people in from about a 32-kilometre radius, prepared to stay a night or two if necessary. International trade fairs had an even larger radius of influence.

Trade fairs were crucial to the trading network, just as the big cities such as London and Paris were. Anyone could trade at the fairs, which made them very different to the regular shops in towns, where guilds controlled sales at least in the later part of our period. Each fair, however, had its own regulations to ensure that everything went well. Regular traders were usually grouped, and goods were often inspected prior to sale. The standards of the assizes (if they existed) were enforced by *alnagers*, a kind of fair steward, who took oaths of office for each fair.

Owners of fairs usually also employed guards or a constabulary to maintain order within the fairgrounds. In some cases, they even tried to make travel to and from the fair safer for both customers and suppliers: the Bishop of Winchester provided sixteen men a day on one dangerous section of the road to ensure the safe travel of fairgoers, including the London merchants. There was also a fair court to handle contracts, maintain the law, prevent brawls and minimise vandalism. Many large fairs instituted curfews between sunrise and sunset. Garbage and obstructions were not allowed in streets and lanes, and prostitutes and lepers were forbidden the site of the fair.

Health, like safety, was an issue for fairs as well. The main concerns seem to have been fire, livestock and illnesses. Cook shops were supervised, for instance, to avoid illness, but also to avoid fire, which was especially necessary considering the amounts of wood and cloth used for booths on the fair site. Some fairs were so serious about their fire prevention measures that the fair sites had water requirements and there were strict limits on uncontained fires at night. Others were less stringent, often with interesting results.

These preparations would cost the owner of the fair money that had to be recouped: selling or buying at a fair was not free, and different fees were charged, such as rent for sales places. An example where we know quite a bit about proceedings is St Giles Fair, Winchester. A market space there cost 3*d* a day. A market toll for goods to be sold was taken at the gates of the fair. It cost 1*d* to bring a cartload of hay or straw to sell and 3*d* for a cartload of wheat or a cask of wine or cider. For every thirteen geese brought to sell, one was taken in payment. While livestock incurred tolls, it was left outside the fair proper for sanitary reasons, together with the smiths and any other trader that might pose concerns to safety. Ditches separated these outer areas from the main fair site.

In the large fairs, the goods were normally arranged first by type and then by place of origin. All London goldsmiths would, for example, have been grouped together.

Successful trade fairs did wonders for the economy of a region. Regional authorities thus often took great lengths to encourage the establishment of a fair or to ensure its continued success. In 1242, the authorities for the big international fairs in Champagne made sure that its merchants were not robbed in northern Italy by refusing Piacenza merchants access to the fairs until robbed merchants received compensation. The fairs of Champagne, however, were unusual. In most cases authorities were more concerned about local safety.

The goods for fairs, including live animals, came from quite long distances. For trade with animals, herds of up to 800 animals were driven for up to 3,000 kilometres to reach their point of sale at a fair; for example, oxen from Hungary were brought to sale in France. Domingo de la Figuera, a famous horse trader in the late thirteenth century, traded in Toulouse and Bordeaux and less frequently in Gascony and Narbonne. Generally he traded twenty to thirty horses a time.

Merchants travelling in groups, bringing international goods, appear to have journeyed to the very earliest fairs. International merchants usually travelled themselves until the second half of the thirteenth century. After this, they often had agents and partners in other places or men that travelled for them, like Richard Lamaress, a Norman, who did the travelling for Ralph Pogal, a London merchant, in 1213. Merchants could seek safe conducts for trading purposes that would protect their men and goods. While this was no guarantee for safety, it certainly helped. Sometimes merchants appointed permanent agents abroad, but more used servants or set up short-term arrangements for local agents.

To make international trade safer and easier, merchants often formed groups from one or more cities. Some of these groupings were known as fellowships or *hanses*. By combining their activity, they had increased negotiating capacity and even the possibility of setting up monopolies. The Hanse de Londres was made up of Flemish merchants, buying wool from England and selling cloth there. The Hanse of Easterlings was German towns trading in London, and the Picardy woad merchants joined to make the Hanse of Corby, Amyas and Nelle. English merchants did not organise along these lines until later, establishing fellowships from the very late thirteenth century only.

Some merchants sent all their goods in one consignment; others sent several consignments through different shippers. John de Gard of Beverely sent wool and leather in July 1275, using three different ships. Separate assignments may also have been the preferred mode of trade for women traders such as Agnes of Ludlow, who was a wool exporter from London in the late thirteenth century.

Bookkeeping and accounting, just like today, were an important part of trade and commerce, but not many records survive for the Middle Ages. Double entry bookkeeping was used in some Italian city states in the latter part of our period, but probably not in England.

The vast majority of documented commercial transactions during the high and late Middle Ages were cash or bullion transactions. For merchants who were continually travelling and selling their wares in different regions, the continuous need to change money again and again must have added noticeably to their expenses. For large sums, bullion could also be used to pay the sum calculated in coin. Silver ingots were frequently used for this; they were produced as bars of standard weight and fineness in mining regions. Just like coin weights, their weight – one mark – also varied depending on where they were produced. The most important markets for bullion and currencies of coin were the Champagne fairs.

Carrying wealth in the form of bullion and cash, however, was a dangerous venture, and the wish for more safety led to the beginnings of a banking system and money transfers. Bills of exchange, which were documents entitling the bearer to withdraw money somewhere else, were used in trading from the twelfth century, but not really standardised until the thirteenth century. Surviving evidence suggests that one of the most important uses of these bills was for transactions between Genoa and the fairs in Champagne, again related to international trade. They had developed into a useful tool by the end of the thirteenth century, but were still used mainly by merchants; they depended on an understanding of what could be done and what their limits were. One of these limits was *usuance*, the date when bills of exchange became payable, guaranteeing the issuing party a minimum of time in which to hold the client's money. How money of account was transferred between cities is not yet properly understood, but enough evidence survives to show that it was done. In 1203, for instance, Gerald of Wales arranged for money to reach him at Troyes.

The trade fairs in Champagne were one of the first places, if not the first place, where bills of exchange became important, due to Champagne's role as the chief money and bullion market in Europe. Unlike today, bills of exchange were not regulated, so there was a certain risk to using them. When Genoa, one of the major sources of those bills, owed too much to the Church, the value of Genoan coin plummeted, making the bills of exchange much less valuable. To cut their losses, traders and travellers then used bullion where possible, until the Genoan coin rose in value again.

Trade Routes and Trade Connections

When the Western European economy started to develop rapidly in the late tenth and eleventh century, it had strong commercial contacts with three other regions: the East (the Byzantine Empire), the Middle East and North Africa/the Iberian peninsula. The Mediterranean basin was the logical centre of commercial activity and cultural exchange. In the later twelfth to early fourteenth century, the Champagne fairs in France were a key hub for trade between Italy, then dominating the Mediterranean, and north-west Europe. In the thirteenth century, Asian countries also traded with Western Europe.

Travelling merchants were dependent on roads and waterways. The most convenient of these roads became important trade routes: the backbone of international trade. The goods moved on those routes ranged from basics such as wool and cloth and wine to luxury goods, including herbs and spices, dyestuffs and medicinals. The different goods meant an array of different logistical problems in storing and transporting them.

Trade routes were heavily influenced by geography. Navigable rivers and comparatively flat, dry land routes were essential for a successful trade route, as well as port cities to connect oversea cities with each other.

There were three main trade routes connecting Western Europe to the rest of the world. The first route brought material to Constantinople via the sea, then round Italy to Marseilles and from there overland. The second came from North Africa (Mahdia) to Palermo, then by sea to Marseilles or Venice, then overland via Champagne. The third route was from Constantinople via the Slavic lands (carrying slaves, wax, honey and tallow for this leg) then to the Baltic area (where fish and amber were picked up) then by sea to the North Sea and from there to England and northern France.

The Mediterranean region was key to international trade and linked to France and England through the southern French towns, especially the principal towns of Marseilles, Arles, Saint-Gilles, Montpellier, Agde and Narbonne. So important was the region to trade that the rules of trade and navigation for the Mediterranean coast were codified from 1258 to 1266 by Catalan consulates.

Crucial to trade in England were the Cinque Ports: Hastings, New Romney, Hythe, Sandwich and Dover. Rye, Winchelsea and Pevensey also established important trading privileges later in our period.

Bulky and heavy items for trade went by water, on the whole. The main exception to this is where rivers were not navigable, due for example to low bridges, weirs and fish traps. Small boats or barges with shallow draughts could navigate even shallow rivers. They could carry about as much as an ox cart.

Transporting heavy goods by land, on roads with no firm surface, could be a considerable challenge in adverse weather conditions. Horses were preferred for the land transport of perishable foodstuff because of their speed. It was, however, expensive to feed horses, and highly bred horses were more prone to disease, so it was not as cheap as trading using water travel.

Trade Goods

Apart from the many local and regional wares for trade, a vast range of goods were traded internationally. These included wax from Byzantium, Eastern Europe and Spain; elephant ivory, ambergris and cotton, which came from places like Byzantium and Sicily; oils such as laurel, linseed and olive; paper, lead, frankincense and furs, with the best coming from Eastern Europe; and hemp, silken thread, dress accessories, mirrors, slaves (not a common trade), flint, asphalt and warhorses, for which Lombardy and Hungary were favoured sources in the thirteenth century. England imported wine, saffron, beaver skins, honey and resin through Bordeaux and the Bayonne, and also iron from Bilbao. It also imported almonds, figs, raisins and currants in large quantities. Mercery, cheaper linens and haberdashery came from the Rhineland and Flanders, and Devon silver was marketed in London to the rest of the world. Alum was imported from the eastern

Mediterranean in the thirteenth century, especially from the Greek Islands and Phocaea (near Izmir).

Wool was one of England's most important exports; so important, in fact, that there was even a saying, 'Like bringing wool to England.' Most English wool was exported as raw material. There were probably very few large producers, with the many small and medium sized wool farmers aggregating their product to sell. The average yield was one sack per sheep shorn, and English export near the end of the thirteenth century ranged between 24,000 and 31,000 sacks. Wool was seldom exported by farmers: it was middlemen who accumulated, graded and sold wool. This mainly happened at towns and markets. Wool was sold according to quality. England produced some cloth, and for export cloth Gascony was a major destination, with wine being imported by return ship.

Spices were luxury trade goods, but also essential ones due to their use in cooking, in incense (in church) and in medicine. As salt was a crucial preservative in the Middle Ages, the salt trade was also very important. It was so valuable that salters' rents were often paid in salt.

Wine was probably the most important trade between England and France during the twelfth and thirteenth centuries. By the end of the thirteenth century, most English ports traded in wine, with the biggest ports for this purpose being London, Boston, Sandwich, Southampton and Bristol. Large ports handled most of the wine for the inland trade, with smaller ports dealing mainly with local needs. This was an important trade for the government as well, with over 100 ships a year paying the royal *prise* (tax) in the late thirteenth century. For example in 1300, about 13,500 tons of wine was taxed. This made wine expensive to trade, and above all it was quite perishable. In addition, wine could be tampered with, meaning it needed expert knowledge to trade in it. Bordeaux wine was unusual on the English market until around 1200, when it supplanted the wines of La Rochelle. This change was due to politics and shows just how closely political changes and trade interrelated.

16

Getting There and Back
Travel and Transport

As the previous chapter has shown, not all people in the Middle Ages lived sedately in the same house all their lives. For some people, travel was an essential part of their lifestyle. Travel and the transport of goods and wares linked distant places and supported communication and economies. But travel was a part of life for more than just merchants and peddlers. Even though medieval roads and travel choices may seem uninviting and restrictive to the modern mind, travelling was part of ordinary life for several parts of society and, for many others, something to be undertaken as a special endeavour.

While the vast majority of people seldom journeyed beyond their local markets, some people travelled a great deal even by modern standards. Some parts of the communities were very mobile, being either permanently on the move, or travelling from one quite specific place to another on a regular basis. Labourers travelled to get work, especially masons, who moved to where big construction was happening, and miners, who travelled to new and unexploited ore deposits. Peddlers linked isolated communities. Noble households moved on a regular basis, carrying their lives with them in baggage carts. Pilgrims might make short pilgrimages, or travel as far as Jerusalem. Minstrels, messengers, merchants or their staff, outlaws, preachers, pilgrims, other religious travellers, wandering shepherds, itinerant justices, sheriffs, the higher nobility, revenue collectors, bishops and the households and retinues of any of the wealthier of these groups were people often on the move. Preachers often travelled, especially in the thirteenth century, and senior members of the Church and lay authorities moved to take up new positions. Knights, mercenaries and their support teams moved in times of conflict. Entertainers, just like merchants, might also travel as part of their profession. Not all of those on the move were voluntary travellers. However, one group associated with itinerancy today did not even exist: there were no Romany in England until the very end of the Middle Ages, well after our period.

Much travel was trade related or produce related, and it could involve moving goods such as lead, wool or salt, but also livestock, especially cattle and sheep. Anyone with something to trade had the potential to travel to market to sell it. If one were simply a small peasant with extra crops, then the travel and transport would be to the nearest market, which would be a local market and not one of the big trade fairs. Long-distance travel for trading purposes was mostly reserved for high-value merchandise such as silk, gems or precious furs. The Church's needs for incense and other specialist goods such as silks and precious stones led to long-distance travel and trade linking the Islamic and the Christian world. Religious reasons also led to pilgrimages for many.

Just like today, travelling involved a special set of logistics: food and drink for humans and animals must either be transported or procured during the travel and shelter against bad weather and cold could be vital. If the travel was connected to transporting goods, suitable packing materials for the goods for carrying by humans or animals or packing on vehicles for land and water were an additional need. Food had to be protected from spoiling during transport, and valuables needed protection against robbery.

Poor people – or those passing as poor – may have been able to beg for food and shelter, but normal travellers were expected to pay for goods and services. Travelling could thus be a very expensive undertaking, and many different financing models existed. Crusaders sold or rented their land to finance their voyage; travellers took jewellery or expensive clothing that could be sold during the journey. There is evidence that some travellers carried silver bars with them and exchanged them for local currency when they needed to. Gold dust was also theoretically possible to take along, but in practice appears to have been mainly used by merchants in the Mediterranean region. Taking goods to sell or messages for a delivery fee were also common ways to reduce the cost of travel. In some cases, friends, neighbours, brotherhoods or guilds may have helped fund a journey. Travel free of cost was possible for those accompanying a wealthy person on a journey. Those would take along travel companions for their safety and convenience, but also as a status symbol to show wealth.

Travelling was not only expensive, but overall a dicey business. Bad weather such as fog or heavy rain made fording rivers or travelling by water more perilous. Getting lost was easy, as landmarks necessary for orientation were not always visible. Orientation help in those cases could be provided by the sound of church bells, giving the travellers an acoustic guide.

The best times of the year for travelling were considered to be spring, summer and autumn, though the heat made summer months less suitable in southern Europe. Most rivers were also reasonably navigable during these months, due to the melt-off from winter snows and glacier ice. The Danube, Po and Rhône generally had enough water for ships. Other rivers, however, were problematic in summer and closed to shipping due to low water levels.

Travel was not lightly undertaken from late autumn: the weather was often bad and getting colder; food was not as easily and cheaply available as in summer and early autumn; fodder for animals was getting scarce; and crossing cold or even freezing rivers could result in death by hypothermia or infection.

In winter, fog and snow could ensure that getting lost was as easy as it was dangerous. Thus many settlements were isolated during the winter. Travel by sea was also mostly halted during winter months. The Mediterannean was considered non-navigable from November to March; the North Sea saw no ship voyages from November to February. However, when it was really necessary, voyages took place regardless of the season.

Nature was only one of many causes of danger to travellers: the greatest danger was often from other human beings. Local lords were quite capable of taking travellers and holding them to ransom. Jews in particular were liable to be captured and held for ransom, because of the good reputation Jewish communities had for redeeming captives (mandated in Jewish law). When Rabbi Meir of Rothenburg, one of the great luminaries of his day, refused to allow his community to pay the extraordinarily high ransom demanded, he lived for several years in captivity, finally dying there. This eventually led to limits placed on ransom demands. When several captives were being ransomed, noble captives were ransomed first among the Christians and women were ransomed first among Jews. The Jewish argument ran that women were more likely to be abused in captivity and therefore it should be kept as short as possible. Danger from brigands also clearly shows in documents such as the Statute of Winchester, which permitted no woods or dykes within 200 feet of roads, reducing the possible hideouts for criminals.

As time progressed, some developments and innovations made travel easier and safer. Such innovations were, for instance, the compass as a navigational aid and the use of the astrolabe and other instruments. Compasses were probably known and in use by the twelfth century, and may have originated from China. A technical innovation that aided land-based travel was the *whippletree*. This is a harnessing element first documented in the eleventh century. The *whippletree* balanced loads and made the animals more manoeuvrable, thus making draught work safer and easier.

Other aids used for travelling, such as maps, itineraries and route descriptions, are harder to trace. We only have very few surviving maps intended for travelling purposes – whether for study or actually for taking along – which might be due either to them being rarely used or to them rarely surviving.

The overall speed of medieval travel is difficult to gauge. It depended on many different factors such as the weather and time of year, whether travel was by land or sea, the lay of the land and the route, the size and fitness of the travelling group (including any animals) among others. Some data exists for the speed of messengers: an urgent letter from Rome to Canterbury in the late twelfth or early thirteenth century would travel for about twenty-nine days; a normal letter would be delivered in approximately seven weeks. Generally, however, it is not possible to know how long a given voyage would have taken.

Travel by Land

Most travel and transport was by land, especially for shorter routes. The speed of travel depended on a variety of circumstances; generally, a large entourage travelled more slowly than a smaller one, and travel was faster in easy terrain and during good weather. A large group might make on average from 16 to 24 kilometres a day. A well-organised smaller group of travellers might make 32 kilometres. Speed of travel and distance covered thus varied enormously. The average traveller on foot, in good conditions, could expect to cover 32–40 kilometres a day, while riders on horseback could do 48–56 kilometres a day. In mountain passes, more realistic estimates might be 4–5 kilometres a day. Bad conditions and other delays need to be factored into this. A realistic daily average for a foot traveller on a long voyage might be around 30 kilometres a day. People carting goods and possessions were much slower. An individual rider in a hurry could make 48–64 kilometres a day, and as many as 80 kilometres a day with changes of horse. Travelling by horse, though, was not necessarily faster than walking. It depended on the mount and the terrain. Bad conditions for riding could well lead to horseback travel being slower than travel on foot. Travel was more common and possibly easier on the four great roads of England (Watling Street, Ermine Street, Fosse Way and Icknield Way) than on other routes, as many roads were rights of way rather than paved paths.

While travelling on foot was slow, it was not an unusual way for people to travel. There was no need to feed and shelter animals, and a foot traveller could get through bad terrain such as mountains, swamps and dense undergrowth more easily than a rider or a cart. Walking as a means of transport was available to almost everybody and many

The Middle Ages Unlocked

sources give the impression that it was considered the normal and usual way of travelling.

Walkers might carry goods for delivery, including letters. In bad terrain, for example in mountains, porters were sometimes the only possible means of transport. Male porters could carry loads of up to 65 kilograms on their backs, though more often they carried in the region of 42 kilograms, corresponding to a quarter of a horse load. In some cases, and probably only across short distances, even heavier loads were possible. Female porters carried loads on their head, typically up to 30 kilograms.

Walkers could also transport goods using aids such as sleds, carts or stretchers when the route and goods allowed it. The earliest evidence of a wheelbarrow, also a transportation aid for walkers, is in the first half of the thirteenth century.

Riding was less common as a means of travel. It was considered more prestigious than walking, and men of higher social status typically rode. Women also rode, though sources are not completely clear on whether they sat astride (technically considered to be unrefined) or in side-saddle. Ann Hyland suggests that women rode astride except on very slow ceremonial occasions (when they had side saddles with footrests), which means that most of their horseback travel would have been done astride. In fact, the side saddle seems not to have widespread use until after our period.

Riding animals were horses, donkeys and mules; they were also used as pack animals for transport. Their qualities for riding or carrying goods did differ quite significantly. Horses, especially palfreys, were a very comfortable ride, but horses in general were more expensive and less resilient than mules or donkeys. Their carrying capacity is estimated at about 170 kilograms, that of donkeys at about 150 kilograms. Mules combined strength, speed and resilience, carrying up to 130 kilograms for about 50–60 kilometres per day.

It may have been possible to hire horses on some well-frequented routes (such as from London to Dover), although the evidence demonstrating this is later than the thirteenth century. Rich people sent out messengers who could double up with other duties, for instance escorting other people, or transporting valuables and legal documents. These messengers usually covered 48–64 kilometres a day, resting their horses about every 16 kilometres. Riding services (including delivering messages) could also be a feudal obligation. Records show that the English royal household had special messengers from the late twelfth century, who were paid by the Chancery. After 1234, the ten to fifteen royal messengers were paid regular wages from the Wardrobe and provided with clothes and shoes.

When the carrying capacity of people or pack animals was not sufficient, carts and wagons were a good method of transporting. They made loading and unloading much easier, and were less of a daily grind. They were, however, slower than riding and often slower than walking. In addition, they were only useful for routes through terrain that was not too steep, not forested and had enough sufficiently stable bridges or shallow fords for crossing rivers.

Carts and wagons were thus the transport methods most bound to roads, limiting the transport routes for very heavy goods or large amounts of goods. These roads were not what modern people would think of, however. Many medieval roads were rights of way rather than engineered products; today, they would be seen as scarcely more than a well-worn path marked by tracks left by wheels and animal or human treading. They often developed on the most suitable path between two places, such as the flattest route or the best route leading to or from a bridge or other crossing. They were not surfaced and apt to change with the landscape (for instance when a river changed its course), or when a bridge collapsed.

To make crossing through bogs or swampy areas safer and easier, wooden planking could be laid down to form a firm surface, but this was more the exception than the rule. In the fenlands, causeways were built for crossing. For instance, Ely had three causeways to link it to the mainland.

Other surfaced roads were, at best, found in towns or larger settlements and their very immediate surroundings. Roman roads remained in use in quite a few areas; in border territories, however, they were sometimes left to decay or even purposely destroyed to prevent enemies from using them for attacks. The lack of surfacing everywhere else made it easy for travellers to walk off the track and find a better way round, and also easy for roads and routes to shift.

Apart from transporting goods, carts and wagons could also be used for transporting people. The covered wagon especially meant for travelling was, however, a late medieval development. Being carted was seen as demeaning for men for a very long time: only women, the old and the sick rode in wagons. Men, especially lordly men, avoided wagons and were more likely to prefer a litter to a wagon when sickness or age prevented them from riding.

Streams and rivers posed a considerable challenge in land travel, whether on foot, riding or with a wagon. While small, shallow and slow-flowing running water could simply be crossed at a suitable place, crossing larger or deeper water made some help necessary.

The oldest form of river crossing was the ford, a crossing at the shallower part of a river where it was relatively safe and easy to wade across. Fords could occur naturally at certain places in a river's course. Fording a river could be assisted by a guideline or rope stretched across the river bed; this was especially helpful when the river was running high.

Bridges enabled travellers to cross without getting wet, an especially important advantage during the cold seasons. The simplest form of bridge could be a log or two placed across a stream. More elaborate bridges were constructed from stone or wood. Their construction was done out of military, economic or altruistic reasons: building bridges was seen as an act of charity.

Stone bridges were the most modern and expensive type of bridge, but also usually the safest and most durable. Often they were only wide enough for a horse, so that wagons still had to ford the river. However, they could also be massive and wide enough to accommodate buildings: London Bridge sported two towers and several houses as well as shops. Stone bridges were quite common by about 1180, but many stone bridges were only built in the final years of the thirteenth century. Royalty and nobility were particularly important to bridge building; however, bridges were also built on the initiative of religious houses or individuals. The stone bridge in London, for example, was started by the priest Peter Colechurch in 1176. He solicited donations for its building, which was finished in 1209.

The methods used to maintain bridges in good condition were as varied as the bridge types themselves. In some cases, bridges were rather neglected and fell into disrepair. Some bridges were maintained as pious acts, with their maintenance grants appearing in church records. In other cases, a group or society with the aim of bridge construction and maintenance might be formed, such as the Frères Pontifes that were founded in France in the twelfth century. The Frères Pontifes were very active, and probably responsible for the bridge at Avignon and several other bridges. Maintenance for London Bridge was partly paid for by house rents from those living on the bridge. Other sources of revenue that could be used to keep bridges in good repair were tolls collected for crossing them.

Bridges could also be fortified and used for controlling the crossing of a river. Monnow Bridge in Monmouth, Gwent, was constructed in the late thirteenth or early fourteenth century and is the only surviving medieval bridge gatehouse from our period in the United Kingdom. Research shows, however, that there were formerly at least twenty-eight fortified medieval bridges in England and Wales.

For travel lasting for more than one day, a place to rest and sleep was also necessary. The medieval traveller could choose between several different types of accommodation. The type available, such as commercial accommodation, religious houses or private homes, would have depended on the route. A number of rules or conventions were widespread, such as the host having the obligation to protect his guests or having the right to keep the guest's possessions should he die. Private hospitality – being given hospitality within a household – would have been a frequent solution for most solitary travellers or small groups. Many people saw it as a religious duty to shelter fellow believers.

Monasteries usually had rules regarding the hosting of pilgrims and other travellers. While they may have expected a gift in exchange for food and accommodation, staying at a monastery was on principle free for the traveller. This could be a significant burden on monasteries, especially in times of trouble. Guests at monasteries generally slept in dormitories, with men and women sleeping separately. Poor travellers were allowed to stay in monasteries just as the wealthier were, but they were given decidedly inferior facilities.

On well-travelled routes, commercialised and more organised forms of hosting travellers developed. Those could range from a single extra bed in an otherwise private home to a full-fledged inn. Beds were usually shared by more than one person, and could be shared with a complete stranger. Food may have been prepared by the host or by the travellers themselves. Unfortunately, the early history of inns is very hard to reconstruct. We do not know how many inns there were in our period, where they were located or how they operated, although information about their existence is available from as early as the twelfth century. Some inns seem to have offered entertainment as well as meals and lodging. They could also be haunts for gamblers, drinkers, prostitutes, thieves, *jongleurs* and quack doctors.

Taverns, a very English institution, also started springing up around the twelfth century. They offered mainly drinks and in some cases basic meals. Taverns were found especially in the south of England, although small shops or booths existed much earlier, indicating their trade with a long pole if they sold ale or a bush or vine if they sold wine (or a bush at the top of the pole, indicating both).

Hospices could also provide lodgings for a traveller. Some bridges had hospices built on them such as the Pont-Saint-Esprit. Kings and magnates were often happy to lodge travellers in their buildings, although they charged for the pleasure.

Larger travelling groups, such as the wealthy and influential travelling with a large retinue, might also carry tents with them to provide temporary shelter. When staying somewhere with not enough capacity to house all the guests, the tents could be used as additional lodgings to supplement the available rooms, for example in a monastery.

Travel by Water

For the transport of heavy goods such as stone or timber, water transport was often preferable to land transport. Travellers made use of rivers, large lakes and the sea as well, sometimes for practical reasons, sometimes because there was no real alternative to water travel. For inland water travel, streams and rivers were used.

Obviously it made a great difference whether the direction of travel was downstream or upstream. For example, it took a flat barge on the Rhône about two to five days to travel from Lyon to Avignon going with the flow of the water. In the other direction, upstream, the craft had to be propelled by other means. In some cases, sailing or using oars was a possibility, if this provided enough momentum to travel against the flow of the water. In shallow water, punting was an alternative as well. The most frequently used means to get a water vessel travelling upstream, however, was probably hauling it with aid of a rope or tow. The haulers, human or animal, walked upstream on the water's edge, pulling the craft along. This was naturally much slower than floating downstream: our vessel going back to Lyon from Avignon would have needed about a month for the journey. River travel also depended very much on the height of the river.

Water travel is typically associated with ships, but there were many different forms of vessels, among them flat barges and rafts that were much more common for inland water travel than ships. These as well as flat-bottomed ships could beach for loading and unloading, using gangplanks if necessary. Larger and seafaring vessels, such as ships, are also associated with wharfs, quays and harbours. Quays or similar structures were important for loading and unloading them. Since waterfronts and river courses usually change over time, finding medieval wharves and harbour structures can prove very difficult. An example for an excavated wharf is that in King's Lynn, an important trading centre in the medieval period.

Ships and ship forms evolved significantly during the Middle Ages. The ships used by the Vikings, long and relatively flat-bottomed, remained an important type right into the twelfth century. They were well suited for travel and fighting, more than for carrying lots of cargo. Ships of the cog type could transport more cargo, but were also used to transport fighters and as warships. There was no clear distinction between ships for military purposes and ships for transport, and individual ships could engage in both activities during their life. Ships were generally given a religious first name that was either male or female and the name of their port, such as *Margaret of Yarmouth* or *Dieu la Sauve of Yarmouth*.

Light boats could be portaged over land to cross between two rivers, for example; this was, however, hard work and especially so when the boat was intended to transport more than just the travellers. Rafts were a special case, since they were in some cases both vehicle and transported goods: timber was fastened together into rafts for transport downriver. The rafters could transport people or goods on their way.

Once the raft had arrived, it was unloaded and taken apart, and the rafters made their way back upstream over land.

There was considerable change in the shape and use of boats and ships during our period to accommodate changing needs such as the transport of horses and heavy goods. The cog, for example, grew in size over time, and by around 1300 it had developed into a large cargo ship of 200 tons or even more capacity. However, old designs were also still used. Perhaps the most typical cargo ship was a round-bottomed ship with lateen sails.

For travel across the sea, ships were the primary means of transport; smaller crafts like boats could not safely venture out into the ocean. Ships also kept quite close to land for safety. How far they could travel in one day depended on ocean currents, winds and the tide. In the Straits of Dover, the tides could be fatal. Trading voyages were typically short, or undertaken with short legs, with overnight stays on land.

Ship travel was so important that it featured in much poetry, from travel literature, through stories about saints to the Latin and Anglo-Norman narratives about the voyage of St Brendan. Ships were crucial to travel for trade, for pilgrimage and for everyday travel from England to Normandy and back, which includes the travel by rulers of both lands. Being surrounded by the sea, England had a very special relationship with ships and ship travel.

Pilgrimages

Making a pilgrimage was a particularly medieval reason to travel. Pilgrimages were very popular, and there were many sites that pilgrims travelled to. They could serve one or many of a range of important functions. The most obvious function was the opportunity for individuals to reach out to the numinous in hope for help with matters large or small. Pilgrimages also helped raise money for local ecclesiastical communities, enabled people to take a holiday from their work, reinforced religious belief, exposed people otherwise not travelling to new stimuli and helped define, remember and celebrate customs. Pilgrimage met people's need to learn, and the need for religious forgiveness. Even the early stages of crusading involved a sense of pilgrimage. It was a fundamental part of Christian and Jewish society.

A vast number of English and French pilgrimages were for medical reasons. Most of them would have been fairly regional, such as a journey to the nearest healing well. St Winefrede of Holywell is one example of such a site, as is the well at the shrine of Our Lady of Walsingham. Sometimes these pilgrimages were undertaken after recourse to treatment or in addition to it, sometimes instead of secular medical treatment.

However, certain important pilgrimages were major journeys and might be anticipated for many years. The big English pilgrimage (from the late twelfth century) was to Canterbury, to the shrine of Thomas Becket. Other important pilgrim destinations that resulted in long journeys were Santiago de Compostela, Rome and Jerusalem. Pilgrim sites usually offered souvenirs for pilgrims in the form of badges or *ampullas*. This could lead to flourishing trade for the makers and sellers of the souvenirs, but the flow of pilgrims also brought business to merchants, peddlers, moneychangers and inns or other accommodations. Souvenirs from important as well as from regional pilgrim sites would have been well known, and displaying them may have had an influence on the social status as well. The main souvenir for Jerusalem pilgrims was in the shape of a palm leaf, while Santiago de Compostela is associated with the still iconic scalloped shell.

Pilgrimages were also a part of religious life for Jews. Jewish pilgrims mainly visited places associated with biblical heroes and post biblical holy people. Consequently, there were no Jewish pilgrimage places in England.

Itinerant Households

Another special case of medieval travel and transport was the itinerant household. Some occupations, such as peddlers, miners, smiths and a variety of others, including entertainers, were dependent on travel for access to raw materials, customers or both. But travel as a lifestyle was not restricted to those people rather low in the social hierarchy: the king himself and his household were continuously travelling as well.

This travel was, like that of the itinerant justices, for reasons of governance. Moving from one place to another was a standard part of governance in the Middle Ages. Not only did travel permit the king and nobles to personally check on their holdings, but it enabled administration to reach out to governed areas. It also simplified household management, for the lords and royalty could use up produce from payments in kind in the region rather than having it transported to a central location, which would have been much more expensive and quite impractical with medieval means of transport. Finally, it allowed retainers to do essential upkeep and cleaning while the court was elsewhere.

The great households moved frequently, ranging from twelve to 100 times a year, depending on who they were and what places needed to be visited in a specific year. Furniture and household equipment were managed cleverly to make these moves possible. Personal goods were stored in suitable chests to keep things safe en route, supplemented by bags, baskets, wickerwork containers and protective sheets from waxed cloth or other fabrics. Marking otherwise common baggage pieces was helpful for organising the goods when loading and unloading. Household goods and supplies that needed transporting were loaded on carts pulled by draft animals, and the number of carts depended on the size of the household. Travel would thus have been rather slow and restricted to passable roads. Labour services owed could be used to ensure that the building was prepared for the arrival of the household, and that enough supplies such as food or firewood were in place.

There are limited sources on itinerant noble households, especially for the period before the fourteenth and fifteenth centuries. Estimating the size of a given household is therefore not always possible. Where the number of people fed each day can be estimated from daily food accounts for late thirteenth- and early fourteenth-century households, they seem to have ranged from about 100 up to several hundred people. However, not every member of the household would have received food – some received daily wages instead. Finally, the household may have included a number of poor who were fed as an act of charity. While these size estimates are grounded on many assumptions, evidence suggests that the households were indeed very substantial.

King John gave an excellent example of constant movement; the only month during his reign when he did not travel was when he was too busy besieging Rochester Castle in 1215. While he travelled least in June and in October, he generally moved over twelve times a month. Edward I was also restless. In January 1300, he had twenty-five days of moving, where he covered 575 kilometres. Royal travellers were entertained by sheriffs in the local castle or manor in England, rather than by the local nobility, as sheriffs represented the king.

17

How Many Leagues to Babylon?
Measuring Things

In the modern world, we are used to things being accurately measured, down to very small units such as seconds, grams and millimetres, even in daily life. Measuring things was also important in the Middle Ages: it was necessary for trade, accounting, crafts, cooking and many other aspects of life. However, the accuracy, the methods of measuring and the measures themselves were not as fixed as the modern ones. There could be great variation between one cartload and another. There were many administrative tools to help resolve problems caused by discrepancies or to prevent discrepancies in the first place, and this chapter will discuss them. It is important to note, however, that due to the many different weights and measurements and the changing standards, it is not always possible to translate a historical measurement into a modern one.

Numbers and Counting

Numbers were the basis of any counting. Computations were done using a column abacus or a technique of finger counting. Using joints and digits both, there were methods used for calculations up to 9,999. The results then were generally written down in Roman numerals.

Roman and Hindu-Arabic numerals were both used, with the balance towards Hindu-Arabic becoming more marked from the twelfth century. There were a number of changes connected to the rise of Hindu-Arabic numerals: counting boards (the board abacus) were gradually replaced by written calculations, as written calculations are much easier to do with the Hindu-Arabic numerals; and a zero was added to help with written calculations. Often, in earlier manuscripts, the zero is represented by a dot, but it evolved during our period to the circle that is used today. It was called *zephirum* by Leonardo Fibonacci (*c*. 1180 – *c*. 1250) and was not known as zero until the fifteenth century.

Writing conventions for the Hindu-Arabic system only developed in the thirteenth century; before this, the numerals could be written upright, on the side or upside down. However, both Roman and Hindu-Arabic numeral systems existed alongside each other for most of the medieval period. Latin and vernacular texts generally used Roman numerals until the second half of the thirteenth century.

Jewish calculations were often done using the Hebrew script rather than either Hindu-Arabic or Roman. The *aleph bet* was assigned numeric values; aleph was equal to one. The first nine letters (*aleph* to *tet*) were the numbers one through to nine, and ten to 100 used the letters *yod* to *tsade*. To express hundreds, the letters *kof* to *tav* were used. Hebrew letters used as numbers were often marked with a dot above, to indicate that they were numerals.

Weights and Measures

Reliable weights and measurements are key to economic transactions and thus important for a stable society. Much like medieval coinage, though, weights and measures were not always standardised centrally, but based on a local standard and also depended on the type of goods. This could cause some problems for interregional trade. In England, there was an ongoing effort to centralise the weight and measurement system, starting after the Conquest. It was, however, an ongoing battle, since assizes seem to have been violated quite frequently.

The weighing of smaller amounts was done using a counterweight of a known weight to balance the goods, for example in equal arm balances with two pans. Weighing implements were called *auncels*, later known as *bismars* or steelyards. They were probably a kind of hand-held balance; most evidence concerning them is from after our period.

Wholesale weighing of heavy goods was done by the hundredweight, with various definitions of what comprised a hundredweight. Eventually, 100 lbs became the standard for it. This weighing was done on a large version of scales with equal arm balances in London, called the king's beam. A second beam, called the king's lesser beam, was used for high-value goods like silk and spices. London was also where the master weights for standardisation were kept.

Capacity measurements were needed for measuring liquids, but could also be used for powdery or granular goods such as grain or flour. Most information concerning measurement of capacity comes from the middle of the thirteenth century and later. Since not everybody owned a weighing implement like larger scales, measures of capacity were often used interchangeably with weight measurements. Since the same capacity measure of different goods will weigh a different amount, the same weight unit, for example a bushel, would have a different real weight for grain or for flour.

While those weights were all relative, they could be quite precise. This was especially necessary for valuable goods such as gold and silver. The pound was used as a basis weight unit for these, and could be subdivided into 12 oz (although the London pound or *liber mercatoria* was 15 oz). The actual weight of different pounds, such as the Anglo-Saxon pound or the Tower or Mint pound, however, could be quite different. Since the number of coins minted from a pound is known as well as the alloy, pounds used for minting coins can usually be defined quite reliably in modern units of weight. Precision was also necessary for weighing medicinal goods; weights used for this were known as *troy* or apothecaries' weights.

The original basis for most of the length measures in use were body parts, and often the source of a length unit can still be seen by its name, as in foot, hand or ell. The best-known old measurements today are probably the yard, the ell and the foot. Feet were 12 modern inches long in London by the twelfth century, and the length was based on the sculpture in St Paul's, commonly known, at the time, as the foot of St Paul's. William of Malmesbury, a twelfth-century historian, claimed that the yard was originally measured using Henry I's arm and thence standardised. The Latin term for yard was *ulna* – not to be confused with its direct translation, the ell. The ell corresponds approximately to the length of the underarm. In England, the size of the ell was fixed by the Assize of Measures in 1196.

For greater lengths or for distance measurements, other units were used, such as the mile, the league, the rod or the furlong. Land was measured in acres, *quartentines* or *virgates*. For farmland, other measurements whose actual size depended on the land itself were also used, such as *oxgangs*, *bovates* or *hides*.

Calendars, Clocks and Time

Measuring and recording of time was also done in the Middle Ages, but again, the actual practice and the accuracy could be very different from modern standards.

The era that the period from the eleventh to the thirteenth century fell into was that of Grace, following the era of Nature (from Adam to Moses) and the era of Law (from Moses to Jesus). The year of an individual in the Middle Ages was structured by the seasons as well as by occupations and religious, legal and administrative calendars. The social calendar rested on these things too.

The calendar system used to measure the year was very similar to the one we use today. Medieval months had the same length as modern months. The standard calendar for Christian society was the Julian calendar, with 365 days to a year. Every fourth year was a leap year, with an extra day added after 24 February. The current (Gregorian) calendar began to be introduced in 1582.

However, the formal calendar with its twelve months was not the only, nor the most important calendar of the time. Both the agricultural calendar and the religious calendar had more impact on daily life for most people and thus provided the more important structure. Occasionally we see people linking all three types of years together (agricultural, calendrical and religious); for instance, there may be a visual depiction of the four seasons of the year as the four limbs of Christ, which are in turn the writers of the Gospels, with the twelve months representing the twelve apostles. Other illustrations include Janus as an aged man (winter) or with two faces (one looking at the old year, one at the new). A common calendar picture sequence lined up typical tasks of the agricultural year with the twelve months. In addition, illustrations representing the signs of the zodiac were also often placed in the appropriate month.

Medieval calendars – such as the Book of Hours that wealthy households and many less wealthy would have possessed – were generally not calendars as we are used to today, but a form of perpetual calendar filled with saints' names. The popular religious festivals and saint's days were a standard way of dating events within the year, not just within the Church. The calendar of saints varied from place to place. Thus it allowed the owners of the books to know what day it was in both secular and religious year, but only for their region.

While in many cases the year began on 1 January, it could begin at other times. For instance, in parts of France and England it began on the 25 March (the Annunciation), with 1 January not being the national start to the year until 1564. Some places even had December as the first month of the year (Reims and Amiens, for instance), with 25 December being New Year's Day. And the largest minority group in England used a different calendar entirely. Although they were obliged to use the Christian calendar when dealing with the Christian community, Jews otherwise used the Jewish calendar.

There were quite a few methods of calculating years. Many of these were based on the need to calculate Easter, since it did not follow the solar reckoning and Western Christianity had moved away from basing it on the Jewish calendar by our period.

One method is still used today, which is reckoning from the date of the birth of Christ; *ab incarnatione* (equivalent to our AD) was the most popular term for this. This method was frequently used in documents which needed long timelines, like chronicles. Years could also be counted from the coronation of a king. They were then stated as the regnal year, for example Henry 3 or Richard 4. In the twelfth century, reigns could be dated from the coronation or from the death of the king's predecessor. In Church matters, its equivalent was the pontifical year, counting from when popes came into office. For government purposes, the fiscal year (also known as the exchequer year) was used, primarily for tax and other public administration.

Other reckonings were mostly characterised by different dates for the beginning of the year. Starting on Christmas Day, following Bede's reckoning, was a very popular reckoning until the twelfth century. Years could also start from the indiction of September, or from Easter. Beginning the year from the Annunciation (Lady Day, 25 March) was especially used in England for calculating rents and feudal obligations. Depending on where people were and where they went to, and what dating system was being used, the calendar year the date fell in could thus be up to two years different.

The modern preference for marking days of a month by their number was not the most popular way in our period. In addition to using the saints' days to mark specific days, and equally important, was a numbering method derived from Rome. Each day was marked in relation to a key point in the month. The first days of a month were called the *kalends*, the fifth or seventh day the *nones*, and the middle of the month the *ides*. From the second to the sixth days in the months, the date is expressed as so and so many days before the *nones* (6 April is one day before the *nones* of April), and the eighth to the fourteenth of the month are so and so many days before the *ides*. There was also a third method, known as the Bolognese method, which was basically used by public notaries.

Sunday and Saturday in the religious calendar were called *domenica* and *sabbatum*, while Monday to Friday were called the second to sixth day of the week (II–VI *feria*). Their Latin names, when used in texts such as official documents, were *dies lune*, *dies martis*, *dies mercoris*, *dies jovis* and *dies eneris*. The modern and medieval Christian calendars share the names of the months, allowing for language differences.

Illustrations representing signs of the zodiac were often placed in the appropriate month. These could be transformed into more Christian versions if necessary, for example, in a cathedral: Aries as the lamb of God and Aquarius as baptism. Common signs were the ram for Aries, and ox or bull for Taurus, twins or Castor and Pollux for Gemini, a crab for Cancer, a lion for Leo, virgin for Virgo, a pair of scales for Libra, a scorpion for Scorpio, a centaur with bow and arrow for Sagittarius, head and horns of a goat (sometimes with a fish tail) for Capricorn, a young man or woman emptying a jug for Aquarius and two fish for Pisces.

The Jewish calendar was a lunar/solar calendar. It adjusted for a solar year, but was based on the phases of the moon. Nisan was regarded as the first month in the calendar, even though Tishrei was the beginning of the religious year and Simkhat Torah the beginning of the liturgical year. In terms of festive times of year, Tishrei was the Jewish equivalent of the late December to mid-January period, with many holidays. Adar was regarded as a happy month and Av as the saddest.

The destruction of the Second Temple in 70 CE was often used as year one of the Jewish calendar in the Middle Ages, in addition to the method still used today. For the first method, the year can be calculated by subtracting seventy from the Christian year, for the second method by adding 3,761 to the Christian year. For example, the Jewish year in 1200 was thus either 1130 or 4961.

The number of days in a Jewish year ranges from 353 to 385 days, with the most common being 355 days. For leap years, the thirty-day month of Adar is added immediately after Shevat. The Hebrew names of months have not changed since the Middle Ages, and with some exceptions the days of importance have not changed either.

Medieval calendars also showed lucky and unlucky days. Egyptian days were the unlucky ones in the calendar. According to one medieval author, there were thirty-one of them in a year. It was not wise to wed, to leave on a journey, to start an important piece of work or to have blood let on these days.

Unlucky or unhappy days in the Jewish world were Mondays, Tuesdays and Thursdays. Wednesdays were also bad news on the fourth, fourteenth, twenty-fourth or in the last four days of any month. Auspicious times to marry or move to a new home were the first half of the lunar month. In the second half, during the waning moon, it was not desirable to cut down trees, soak clothes or harvest. This was because things were considered to perish more quickly when the moon was waning.

It was not only possible and usual to mark years, months and days, but also times within a day. Modern-day people are used to having accurate timekeeping, and to being able to tell the time of day and mark or measure exact amounts of time. This was not the case in the Middle Ages, though the days were not without structure, and there were methods of approximating shorter amounts of time.

Every town and every church had its own sequences of bells to tell people when to pray. These would have been the main source for precise telling of time in the country, especially for peasants. While the day was technically divided into twelve hours (inherited from Ancient Rome), the most important times were *matins* (sunrise), *compline* (sunset) and *sext* (midday). From a lay point of view, the most useful hours for describing time were *prime*, *terce*, *sext*, *none* and *vespers*. *Nones* or *none* was shifted from an earlier point in the day to high noon in the thirteenth century. *Vespers* also moved into the afternoon at the same time and signalled the end of work or a break in work.

Apart from marking time through prayer times, the main recourse for telling time, especially in rural areas, would have been the position of the sun. Cities and wealthy communities (notably the Abbey at Bury St

Edmunds, with its famous water clock) had greater access to time pieces. From at least as early as the late thirteenth century, there were clocks. Water clocks could be the height of a man, and could have ornate cases that looked like towers with arcades and fancy ornamentation. Some of them had little bells that could be set to ring at pre-specified times to serve as alarms.

For telling or keeping track of shorter stretches of time without access to clocks, different methods were available. For instance, candles could be marked at specific intervals and burned down. Cooking instructions sometimes include passages such as 'boil for the duration of three Hail Marys', hinting at the use of songs, prayers or other recitals to keep track of time. It is not sure whether hourglasses were in use already; clear evidence for them comes from the fourteenth century and later.

Overall, while there were common markers of time such as church bells, and some sophisticated ways of measuring time, medieval timekeeping must have been much more fluid than modern timekeeping. Exact measurements of time as we are used to today were the exception, and in many cases not at all possible.

Maps and Cartography

Medieval maps reflect how people saw the world, and they generally show us a Christian reality based on a Classical past. By the end of our period, the centrality of Christianity became so pervasive that Jerusalem was placed in the centre of the world on certain important maps, such as the one known as the Hereford map. The size of extant maps ranges from the vast Hereford map to tiny drawings to illustrate Macrobius' *Commentaries*.

Medieval maps were quite different from modern maps, and their main use was not to guide a traveller in foreign places. Most surviving examples are not maps in the modern sense so much as explanatory diagrams; they illustrated and accompanied texts. If there were maps that were not textual illustrations but were used for navigation or travel, they have not survived. So most of the medieval maps still extant today were for armchair travellers or armchair intellectuals who wanted to think about the nature of Earth. They may be roughly to scale, but not necessarily so, and the level of detail in these maps may differ widely even on the same piece.

Maps can be categorised into four main types: OT maps, zonal maps, topographical maps and sea charts. As well as these were other styles of map, often combining the features of these four main types. East was generally placed at the top of a map, though not always (zonal maps, for instance, are north/south and depict the climate zones).

The most common maps or diagrams of the world are called OT or

TO maps today. They have a circular shape divided into three segments, depicting the continents of Asia, Europe and Africa. The waters form a circular boundary and a T shape between the continents. Their modern descriptive name is derived from the circular shape (O) and the T-shaped waters. The Hereford Map is the most famous and the most complex surviving example of this kind of map.

The TO map generally illustrates a text that itself is based on the notion that the earth is a globe, so this does not represent a flat earth as has sometimes been suggested. While the Church argued against the existence of the Antipodes and was inclined towards a flat earth policy for theological reasons, the text accompanying these maps clearly indicates a knowledge that the world was a sphere, a belief congruent with cosmological theory and mathematics.

Zonal maps were also an important form of maps, and a quite old one. They date to the sixth century BCE. Zonal maps illustrate the climate zones of the world and are mainly found in manuscripts of Macrobius' famous commentary on Cicero's *Dream of Scipio*. They are mostly circular, with the world divided into horizontal bands that depict the climate zones. The polar zones are at the top and bottom. The equator is in the centre. Immediately below the equator is the tropic of Capricorn and above it is the tropic of Cancer; these were the two zones considered habitable. They also illustrate a theory of planetary influences on each climatic zone, a theory disapproved by the Church. Zonal maps are inevitably written in Latin, as they accompany a Latin text. While zonal maps can include a continent in the southern hemisphere, they often do not.

Topographical maps were used for travel descriptions or to indicate land ownership. The earliest surviving example of the latter comes from Lincolnshire in around 1300, where cow pastures are depicted. A topographical map that was theoretically for travel is the one by Matthew Paris in around 1250, which was attached to his chronicle. It is basically a road map of Britain.

The earliest surviving sea charts date from around 1300, although we know that Raymond Lull had access to sea charts in the 1280s. Other sea charts may have been used but have not survived, or they might simply have been uncommon. It is unfortunately not known whether seafarers used map-like navigational aids, written or memorised directions to navigate new territory or found local aid in navigation.

In addition to these European styles of maps, Arab maps would have been available in Europe in a very limited way, due to Norman and trading links with the Middle East. The work of Idrisi in particular, a twelfth-century Moroccan geographer and cartographer, was available to some from the twelfth century. We know this because two manuscripts of his atlas survived, one each in Paris and Oxford.

Conclusion

Life in the Middle Ages was not simple, nor primitive, and neither is it easy to explain. There's no such thing as a single, perfectly typical medieval pot or axe, just as there is no such thing as a single perfectly typical medieval dress or a single, perfectly typical medieval story. Everyday life in all its ordinariness was a complex interplay of social factors, such as status, wealth and personal connections, cultural factors such as religion and government and natural factors such as climate and resources. These played together to bring a wonderful richness and diversity to the lives of people, and a set of dynamics that ensured those lives changed over time.

Certain fundamentals supported this complexity. The consistency and durability of these fundamentals were what gave society and daily life their stability. The most important of these was the Christian Church: religion underlay so much of daily life that the influence of religion (especially of Christianity) was critical to everyone's lives. People lived closer to the land and had more connection to agriculture and the seasons than we have today, which was another force for stability. Seasons are predictable, even when politics are not.

Within this framework, there were some cultural constants. To give an example, people demonstrated their wealth and status through dress and accessories as well as through conspicuous spending and gift-giving. The need to show status and to look good also helped keep many cultural forms quite stable, even as the shape and style of dress and accessories changed over time. The same applies to the rule of law. The interplay of the various legal systems played an important role in maintaining social stability and justice; however, those systems themselves changed over time.

Therefore, while there was rule of law and a profound religious belief in 1050 as in 1300, a snapshot of culture and society in 1050 would look quite different to one in 1300. The changes in political institutions are important in measuring the dynamic changes during our period, but so are wider literacy, economic sophistication and technical innovation, both in the country and in the towns.

To understand the Middle Ages, scholars use archives as well as archaeology; they examine the built world and the world of the mind to construct our knowledge. While we know a fair amount through this work, many aspects of medieval life still escape us. Some of this may be because certain aspects of life are alien to us and require a wider range of sources than we currently possess, such as the folk beliefs of peasants in different regions of England. Lack of knowledge due to lack of sources is generally a problem. Even for the elite, for whom we have by far the most sources, there is more information available for the latter part of our period than for the earlier: our 1300 snapshot is far more complete and reliable than our snapshot from 1050.

Our snapshot, just like any other snapshot, also contains the danger of seeing just one aspect or just one story. Having a snapshot should never lead us to think we have a complete picture. We know that people fell in love, quarrelled, disliked others and gave each other both friendly words and insults. We know that some people were rich and others were poor and have some idea of how some individuals managed these conditions. There were people with inquisitive minds bent on solving scientific and religious problems and there were people just interested in getting along somehow. In short, people were just as much individuals as they are today. Artefacts and clothes and items of daily life may be interpreted as even more varied than today's items of daily life, as there was no industrialised, machine-powered mass production, and every piece made showed the individual maker's touch.

Just as society and material culture were diverse, neither Church nor State was uniform. Medieval England was a celebration of regional and even local diversity rather than a monolith of simple belief.

Studying a time long gone by can be just like travelling into a foreign country and getting to know its customs and people. Some objects are very familiar, and some medieval objects have even survived to our day in a similar form. Many of our modern institutions and literatures are deeply influenced by their medieval origins and there is a strong thread of continuity between the two. This language in which *The Middle Ages Unlocked* is written changed from its ancient form to something much closer to its modern form during our period. Many of our literary icons (such as Arthur, Morgan le Fay and Merlin) came into our culture in the Middle Ages. Other concepts and constructs that we come across in researching the Middle Ages seem weird and foreign, and only become more familiar over time. The hardest part in getting to know another culture, however, are those things that seem clear or familiar, but are in fact very different – and these are where the most possibility for modern misinterpretation lies. Medieval science is not like modern science, nor is the medieval understanding of religion or art the same as modern. Crafts and art, in fact, bore quite different relationships to each other than their modern counterparts often do. Many interconnections between areas of daily life, religion and government have completely changed away from their medieval predecessors today, and awareness of the differences is the first step in understanding the English Middle Ages.

To understand the Middle Ages, we need this awareness of the difference between us and them, and we need an awareness of the similarities. Most importantly, though, we need to remember that something that may seem familiar can in fact be very different from its apparent modern equivalent. Our relationship with the Middle Ages, therefore, is as complex as the English Middle Ages itself.

No single book can fully describe this complexity and our relationship with it, nor can a single book explain all the developments and changes across 250 years. There is much more to discover and explore about every single aspect covered here. *The Middle Ages Unlocked* is just a beginning. Whether you are interested in money, military, marvels or mercenaries, it is worthwhile to look for some specialised literature about this topic and find out more about regional and temporal differences as well as about the scholarly arguments and theories around that topic.

To help you on your further journeys, the following section lists some of our sources and recommended books for more information and explains just how those modern resources work for the researcher. We wish you happy travelling and many pleasant hours spent on finding out more about this fascinating period in our history.

Reading More About the Middle Ages

Good books and articles concerning the Middle Ages number in the tens of thousands and more, and they cover a vast array of medieval subjects: everything from varieties of Latin to types of sheep. A volume could not list them all, much less a chapter. The aim of this part of the book, therefore, is not to present a complete bibliography, but to present a series of short overviews and links to further reading. The reading itself will link to other reading.

The focus of this recommended reading is on books written in English. There is an equal number of useful books written in other languages, and many of them were used for our research for this volume. Some specific works are mentioned more than once, when they are recommended specifically for more than one topic; we have, however, tried to keep double mentions as rare as possible. In many cases, we are just offering a single article or book as an example of specific work on a subtopic to show the immense variety of literature.

This guide is a room with many doors. We hope that the book you have just read unlocked these doors for you, and you can now explore the world of the Middle Ages for yourself. When you open the doors, and read these books and articles, more doors will open to you and so will the world of the Middle Ages.

1 Rich and Poor, High and Low: The People of Medieval England

The data we have about medieval people is scanty. Scholars piece things together from a range of sources, literary (romances, chronicles and saints' tales, for instance), archival (records of commercial transactions, of ownership and legal documents) and archaeological. Some subjects are better studied than others, because individual scholars have made it their life's work.

Some regions of England are, likewise, better studied than others for some disciplines. The regional study of naming patterns and names, for instance, have benefited from the work of Dave Postles, and we know far more about names in the regions he has written about than we do for other regions. His work includes

Talking Ballocs: Nicknames and English Medieval Sociolinguistics (Leicester: Centre for English Local History, University of Leicester, 2003); *The North Through Its Names: A Phenomenology of Medieval and Early-Modern Northern England* (Oxford: Oxbow, 2007); *Naming the People of England, c. 1100–1350* (Newcastle: Cambridge Scholars, 2006) and Postles, Dave and Joel Rosenthal (ed.), *Studies on the Personal Name in Later Medieval England and Wales* (Kalamazoo, Mich.: Medieval Institute Publications, Western Michigan University, 2006).

Much of the general work on society and its people is undergoing radical changes as we improve our understanding of how medieval society worked. This means that the picture of peasants given by earlier scholars such as Georges Duby and M. M. Postan is quite different to that in more recent works such as Freedman, P. H., *Images of the Medieval Peasant* (Stanford, Calif.: Stanford Univ. Press, 1999). It also means that the way we see medieval people is likely to change further, as modern scholarship approaches the matter of the Middle Ages from new directions. Archaeological work is being incorporated into history, for example, re-evaluating evidence such as that from skeletons: Roberts, C. A., *Health and Welfare in Medieval England: The Human Skeletal Remains Contextualised* (Leeds: Maney, 2009). Less tangible things such as emotions, too, are finally being studied in depth. Most importantly, some of the basic assumptions scholars have had about the Middle Ages, namely the nature of feudalism, have been questioned and the new understanding of people's relationship with the land, with the law and within the hierarchy will radically change our views of medieval lives.

Until these reinterpretations are brought together by scholars in the way that Marc Bloch and Georges Duby brought together previous interpretations, it is easier to look at specific elements rather than at the broad whole. For instance, pictorial representations of those outside society can be found in Mellinkoff, R., *Outcasts: Signs of Otherness in Northern European Art of the Late Middle Ages*, Vol. I and II (Berkeley/Los Angeles/Oxford: University of California Press, 1993). If we don't know precisely how non-feudal England looked yet, we do know how people outside the system looked to those from within, described for instance, in Higgs Strickland, D., *Saracens, Demons, and Jews. Making Monsters in Medieval Art* (Princeton and Oxford: Princeton University Press, 2003). A thorough look at violence, including violence in ritual, is given in Brown, W. C., *Violence in Medieval Europe* (Harlow: Longman, 2011).

Some subjects have been studied, but not published. In some instances (especially in the chapter on people), the examples given in *The Middle Ages Unlocked* have not reached wider scholarship yet, for they have not been published much elsewhere and, in fact, were mostly researched for this volume.

Looking at some of the specific topics discussed in the chapter on people, the classic text on forms of courtesy in the Middle Ages is old: Dupin, Henri, *La Courtoisie au Moyen Age* (Paris: Picard, 1931). Some of the formal etiquette discussed by Dupin was preserved in instructions on polite behaviour. Most of this is from after our period, but it is nevertheless useful. The standard English-language source for this is still Furnivall, F. J. and E. Rickert, *The Babees' Book: Medieval*

Manners for the Young: Done into Modern English from Dr. Furnivall's Texts by Edith Rickert (London: Chatto & Windus; New York: Duffield & Co., 1908), which contains a group of works from the later Middle Ages and more recently. It was originally published in 1868 but can be found in both reprints and on the internet. Courtesy can also be studied through manuals for letter writing, such as the one in Carlin, M. and D. Crouch, *Lost letters of Medieval Life: English Society, 1200–1250* (Philadelphia: University of Pennsylvania Press, 2015).

There are very few studies directly on how people address each other in the Middle Ages and on titles. Work on the use of titles has mainly been for formal written documents (studied in the field of diplomatics); this knowledge cannot simply be transferred over into other uses. The discussions in the earlier books, therefore, really only apply within very specific limitations. When Gillian Polack set out to address this gap in our knowledge, she used mainly the Old French epic legends, the romances and the lais. This original research was used alongside research by other scholars. Work on the formal titles royalty used, for instance in Morby, John E., 'The Sobriquets of Medieval European Princes', *Canadian Journal of History/Annales Canadiennes D'Histoire*, 13:1 (1978), is an example of this.

Not all literature was polite. There was in fact a quantity of obscene and transgressive literature in several languages, and the best current knowledge is not on politeness but on impoliteness. There are several solid studies on rudeness, again mostly derived from literary sources. Good examples are: Gravdal, K., *Vilain and Courtois: Transgressive Parody in French Literature of the Twelfth and Thirteenth Centuries* (Lincoln: University of Nebraska Press, 1989) and Trexler, R. 'Correre la terra. Collective Insults in the Late Middle Ages', in *Mélanges de l'Ecole Française de Rome Moyen Age – Temps Modernes* (1984), 845–902. A popular study is Mohr, M., *Holy Sh*t: a Brief History of Swearing* (Oxford; New York: Oxford University Press, 2013), which is a good collection of bad language but is a bit limited.

Not all subjects are this difficult. Heraldry, for instance, is particularly well documented and has been a fascination for many for a long time. Where a field is well known in this way, it is possible to give a quick guide listing a few works and giving direction as to what to read next. For instance, general information about heraldry and detail on how medieval shields looked can be found in Brault, G. J., *Early Blazon: Heraldic Terminology in the Twelfth and Thirteenth Centuries with Special Reference to Arthurian Heraldry* (Woodbridge: Boydell Press, 1997). The modern authority on heraldry in Britain is the College of Arms (www.college-of-arms.gov.uk), who can also help with enquiries. Good information about seals and their use, plus a catalogue showing seals, can be found in Adams, N., J. Cherry and J. Robinson, *Good Impressions: Image and Authority in Medieval Seals* (London: The British Museum, 2008).

2 From Cradle to Grave: Life Phases

While information concerning the stages medieval lives passed through is also patchy, a good recent overview of what is known from the archaeological record is Gilchrist, R., *Medieval Life: Archaeology and the Life Course* (Woodbridge: Boydell, 2012).

The substance of Christian lives, however, has its own peculiarity: it needs to be examined from more than one discipline in order to get a clearer picture. A good resource for this is Cochelin, I., and K. Smyth (eds.), *Medieval Life Cycles: Continuity and Change. Series: International Medieval Research 18* (Turnhout: Brepols, 2013). It uses archaeology, literature, iconography and the study of business documents.

There are no equivalent detailed studies of English Jews, so the Jews of England are often introduced through their shared culture with German and French Jews. Baumgarten, E., *Mothers and Children: Jewish Family Life in Medieval Europe* (Princeton, NJ; Oxford: Princeton University Press, 2004) is an example of such a study.

Works such as Dyer, C., *Everyday Life in Medieval England* (London: Hambledon, 1994) and Fossier, R. and J. Vale, *Peasant Life in the Medieval West* (Oxford: Blackwell, 1988) provide useful overviews of what was known at the time they wrote. As they are not updated frequently or consistently, the best way to access the most current results is by looking for studies of specific elements of lives.

There are quite a few solid studies on particular aspects of life phases and stages of life. The standard work on childhood in England just prior to our period is Crawford, S., *Childhood in Anglo-Saxon England* (Stroud: Sutton Publishing, 1999). For the remainder of the Middle Ages, see Shahar, S., *Childhood in the Middle Ages* (London: Routledge, 1992), Alexandre-Bidon, D. and D. Lett, *Children in the Middle Ages: Fifth-Fifteenth Centuries* (Notre Dame: University of Notre Dame Press, 1999) and Taglia, K., 'The Cultural Construction of Childhood: Baptism, Communion and Confirmation', in C. M. Rousseau and J. T. Rosenthal (eds.), *Women, Marriage and Family in Medieval Christendom* (Kalamazoo, MI: Western Michigan University, 1998), 255–88. Other useful sources on medieval children in general are: Orme, N., *Medieval Children* (New Haven; London: Yale University Press, 2001); Orme, N., 'Medieval Childhood: Challenge, Change, and Achievement', *Childhood in the Past*, 1 (2008), 106–19, and Orme, N., 'The Culture of Children in Medieval England', *Past and Present*, 148 (August 1995), 48–88, as well as B. Hanawalt's *Ties that Bound: Peasant Families in Medieval England* (Oxford: Oxford University Press, 1986).

Again, much less is known about Jewish children than Christian ones. A good starting point for Jewish childhood is Cooper, J., *The Child in Jewish History* (Jason Aronson, 1996) and Marcus, Ivan G. *Rituals of Childhood. Jewish Acculturation in Medieval Europe* (New Haven-London: Yale University Press, 1996). Some of this work is a reaction to the directions prior scholarship took. The work of Philippe Ariès in particular, today proven unreliable, presented a very negative and unloving view of childhood in the Middle Ages and influenced quite a few scholars.

There are some subjects which form part of the popular concept of the Middle Ages that are not actually medieval. The *droit de seigneur* may not have existed, for instance. A useful place to begin looking into this is Bullough, Vern L., 'Jus primae noctis or Droit du Seigneur', *Journal of Sex Research*, Bd. 28, S. (1991), 163–6.

Some other subjects are somewhat borderline – they have approximate but not direct medieval equivalents. While divorce did not exist as we recognise it in the Christian world in the Middle Ages, for example, there were legal paths that English Christians could follow to achieve a similar positon. They are discussed in Butler, Sara M., *Divorce in Medieval England: From One to Two Persons in Law*. Routledge Research in Medieval Studies (New York: Routledge, 2013). This subject is still controversial, partly due to the significant differences between the theological theory, the legal theory and the reality of personal lives.

Research on women's lives is also particularly interesting and provides very different views. David Herlihy was a major influence on women's studies, especially his *Women, Family and Society in Medieval Europe. Historical Essays 1978–1991* (Oxford: Berghahn books, 1995). Much new work has resulted because of it. For more on the lives of Jewish women see Baskin, J. R., *Jewish Women in Historical Perspective* (Detroit: Wayne State University Press, 1998). For work on young women in particular see Lewis, K. J., N. J. Menuge and K. M. Phillips (eds.), *Young Medieval Women* (Stroud: Sutton, 1999).

To build up an understanding of the life of an individual, it is helpful to use research from a range of sources covering a range of theoretical approaches, marrying archaeology with legal documents and with evidence from literature. Some existing studies have this interdisciplinary approach, making them especially valuable. General overviews about aspects of the life stages are Edwards, R. R. and S. Spector, *The Olde Daunce: Love, Friendship, Sex and Marriage in the Medieval World* (Albany: SUNY Press, 1991) and Razi, Z., *Life, Marriage and Death in a Medieval Parish. Halesowen 1270–1400* (Cambridge: Cambridge University Press, 1980), Sheehan, M. M., C. M. Rousseau and J. H. Rosenthal, *Women, Marriage, and Family in Medieval Christendom: Essays in Memory of Michael M. Sheehan, C.S.B.* (Kalamazoo, Mich.: Western Michigan University, 1998). Issues linked to marriage, such as property rights and canon law are can be found in Sheehan, M. M. (ed. James K. Farge) *Marriage, Family and Law in Medieval Europe: Collected Studies* (Toronto: University of Toronto Press, 1997) while a useful starting point for understanding marriage at the lower levels of society is Sheehan, M. M., 'Theory and Practice: Marriage of the Unfree and the Poor in Medieval Society', *Mediaeval Studies* 50:1 (1988), 457–87; McCarthy, C., (ed.). *Love, Sex and Marriage in the Middle Ages: A Sourcebook* (London: Routledge, 2004). Homosexual relations are far more difficult to understand in this very Christian society, and good places to start are Klosowska, A., *Queer Love in the Middle Ages* (New York: Palgrave Macmillan, 2004) and Sautman, F. C. and P. Sheingorn (eds.), *Same-Sex Love and Desire Among Women in the Middle Ages* (New York: Palgrave Macmillan, 2001).

The good news is that studies of gender in the Middle Ages are currently being transformed. A central new work is Bennett, J. M. and R. M. Karras (eds.), *The Oxford Handbook of Women and Gender in Medieval Europe* (Oxford: Oxford University Press, 2013). An example of the new approach to gender, examining it from more than one direction and extracting greater understanding of these issues in the Middle Ages using quite traditional sources, is Beattie, C. and K. A. Fenton (eds.), *Intersections of Gender, Religion and Ethnicity in the Middle Ages* (Basingstoke, Hampshire, England: Palgrave MacMillan, 2011). Parsons, J. C. and B. Wheeler (eds.), *Medieval Mothering* (New York: Garland Publishing, 1996) and Baumgarten, E., *Mothers and Children, Jewish Family Life in Medieval Europe* (Princeton: Princeton University Press, 2004). There is an increasing amount of literature on the nature of medieval masculinity. A good point to enter is Cohen, J. J. and B. Wheeler, (eds.), *Becoming Male in the Middle Ages* (New York: Garland Publishing, 1997).

The treatment of sexuality in *The Middle Ages Unlocked* relates almost solely to Christian perspectives predominant, for instance, in Brundage, J., *Law, Sex, and Christian Society in Medieval Europe* (University of Chicago Press, 1987). The best study of Jewish perspectives can be found in Biale, D., *Eros and the Jews. From Biblical Israel to Contemporary America* (Berkeley: University of California Press, 1997), which also gives a brief overview of Jewish marriage in the Middle Ages. Although far less is known of English Jewish views on marriage than of those from elsewhere, this book offers a general overview of a very complex subject.

The situation regarding rape and prostitution in the general community was far more vexed. Good introductions to some of the issues are Gravdal, K., *Ravishing Maidens. Writing Rape in Medieval French Literature and Law* (Philadelphia: University of Pennsylvania Press, 1991) and Karras, R. M., *Common Women: Prostitution and Sexuality in Medieval England* (New York: Oxford University Press, 1996).

Current knowledge concerning age in the Middle Ages is assessed in Sheehan, M. M. (ed.), *Aging and the Aged in Medieval Europe; Selected Papers from the Annual Conference for Medieval Studies, University of Toronto, 1983* (Toronto: Pontifical Institute of Mediaeval Studies, 1990). Good introductions to death are Binski, P., *Medieval Death: Ritual and Representation* (Cornell University Press, 1996) and Daniell, C., *Death and Burial in Medieval England 1066–1550* (London: Routledge, 2005).

3 Death and Taxes You Cannot Avoid: Government

This is a very well-studied area, particularly the political aspects.

The first tool anyone looking further into government needs is a reference book that gives the dates of rulers, the calendars for law courts and so forth. The standard reference book for all of this is the very compact Cheney, C. R. and M. Jones, *A Handbook of Dates: For Students of British History* (Cambridge: Cambridge University Press, 2004). With this in hand, there are a thousand more sources available on rulers and their reigns, on governance and on law.

The word 'feudalism' has been avoided in this book wherever possible, as it contains many connotations that are no longer considered reliable. A handy introduction to the vexed question of feudalism is Abels, R., 'The Historiography of a Construct: "Feudalism" and the Medieval Historian', *History Compass* 7 (2009), 1008–31.

While fiefs and feudal dues were a normal part of medieval government, the existence of a pure feudal system is unlikely. The outstanding discussion of this is Reynolds, S., *Fiefs and Vassals. The Medieval Evidence Reinterpreted* (Oxford: Clarendon, 1994). The standard works upon which our understanding of feudalism rested prior to the work of Reynolds is Bloch, M., *Feudal Society: Social Classes and Political Organization* (Chicago: University of Chicago Press, 1982) and *Feudal Society: The Growth of Ties of Dependence* (Chicago: University of Chicago Press, 1961). Bloch's work is still key to understanding the Middle Ages, but needs to be read with recent work on feudalism in mind.

Knowing these limits, the next step is general books that cover the period. A general introduction to the politics that also provides a handy introduction to the links of the kings of England with France is Clanchy, M. T., *England and its Rulers, 1066–1307* (Oxford: Blackwell, 2006), while a useful overview for the later part of our period is Brown, A. L., *The Governance of Late Medieval England 1272–1461* (London: Arnold, 1989). To understand the institutions of government and law more specifically, see also Jewell, H. M., *English Local Administration in the Middle Ages* (Newton Abbot: David and Charles, 1972).

A good introduction to the broader history of English law is Wormald, P., *The Making of English Law: King Alfred to the Twelfth Century* (Oxford: Blackwell Publishers, 1999). For an introduction to the history of the secular legal system in England, see Hudson, J., *The Formation of English Common Law: Law and Society in England from the Norman Conquest to Magna Carta* (London: Longman, 1996). These two works also provide an introduction to the history of the secular legal system.

The relationship between the king and legal system is crucial to make sense of medieval institutions. Pennington, K., *The Prince and the Law, 1200–1600: Sovereignty and Rights in the Western Legal Tradition* (Berkeley, Calif.: University of California Press, 1993) is an excellent introduction to this aspect.

Some institutions were in their infancy during our period. Parliament is one of the most important of these. Introductions to medieval parliaments and their early development include Davies, R. G., J. H. Denton and J. S. Roskell, *The English Parliament in the Middle Ages* (Manchester: Manchester University Press, 2005) and Richardson, H. G. and G. O. Sayles, *The English Parliament in the Middle Ages* (London: Hambledon, 1981). An excellent history of the development of the system is Lyon, A., *Constitutional History of the UK* (London: Cavendish, 2003).

English rule was never simply about England. The ties with France have already been mentioned, but conquest also played a role, as shown in Davies, R. R., *Domination and Conquest: The Experience of Ireland, Scotland and Wales 1100–1300* (Cambridge: Cambridge University Press, 1990).

Changes to governance in the Middle Ages had some important social and political effects. They resulted in significant social mobility linked to administration, for instance. For this, see Turner, R. V., *Men Raised from the Dust: Administrative*

Service and Upward Mobility in Angevin England (Philadelphia: University of Pennsylvania Press, 1988). A good study of how these different levels worked in practice is Coss, P. R., *Lordship, Knighthood and Locality: A Study in English Society* c. *1180* – c. *1280* (Cambridge: Cambridge University Press, 1991).

There are useful studies on several particular jobs/positions within the governing system; however, even more have only been treated in the broader approaches. For sheriffs, see Green, J. A., *English Sheriffs to 1154* (London: H.M.S.O., 1990) and Morris, W. A., *The Medieval English Sheriff to 1300* (Manchester: Manchester University Press, 1968). The standard introduction to the work of the medieval coroner is Hunnisett, R. F., *The Medieval Coroner* (New York: Cambridge University Press, 2008).

Within all of these studies, there are, inevitably, problems. One of the major issues facing studies of legal systems is that scholars have traditionally focussed their attention on how they work within male society. Specific studies are needed to redress the balance and to give a sense of women's lives within the law, how government affected women and women's opportunities to work within government. In more recent research, these topics are addressed, for example in Menuge, N. J., *Medieval Women and the Law* (Woodbridge: Boydell, 2003).

The different types of law have been studied in a great number of ways. This is partly because some medieval law is still in use today and modern styles of lawmaking in most English-speaking countries has been strongly influenced by medieval legal history. A useful history of medieval developments in the legal profession is Brundage, J., *The Medieval Origins of the Legal Profession: Canonists, Civilians, and Courts* (Chicago: University of Chicago Press, 2008).

Introduction to Specific Subjects

The topic of law is complex, and there are many paths into understanding the various medieval legal systems. What is given here is merely a sample.

Secular law: For common law, see Bonfield, L., 'The nature of Customary Law in the Manor Courts of Medieval England', *Comparative Social Studies and History*, 31 (1989), 514–34.

Canon law: Duggan, C., *Canon Law in Medieval England: the Becket Dispute and Decretal Collections* (London: Variorum Reprints, 1982) talks about particular problems of jurisdiction. An important study of how canon law affected Jews is Pakter, W., *Medieval Canon Law and the Jews* (Ebelsbach: Gremler, 1988).

Jewish law: Hecht, N. S., B. S. Jackson, S. M. Passamaneck, D. Piattelli and A. M. Rabello, *An Introduction to the History and Sources of Jewish Law* (Oxford: Oxford University Press, 1996). The classic study of Jewish law in English is Elon, M., *Jewish Law: History, Sources, Principles* (Philadelphia: The Jewish Publication Society, 2003).

4 God is Everywhere: Religion

Everything in the Middle Ages was permeated with and underpinned by religion. The focus in this book has been to give readers a basis for further exploration, because a single chapter cannot cover anything more. The reading here, therefore, is essential for anyone who wishes to really understand Medieval England.

The literature on medieval religion is vast, so the best approach to the subject is to find a careful bird's eye view that will help contexualise and interpret specific subjects, such as Arnold, J. H. (ed.), *The Oxford Handbook of Medieval Christianity* (Oxford: Oxford University Press, 2014). Follow this up with an overview of the Church such as that by Lynch, J. H., and P. C. Adamo, *The Medieval Church: A Brief History* (London and New York: Routledge, 2014).

A good introduction to the medieval Bible is van Liere, F., *An Introduction to the Medieval Bible* (Cambridge: Cambridge University Press, 2014). The reception and use of the Bible is evaluated in Boynton, S., *The Practice of the Bible in the Middle Ages: Production, Reception, and Performance* (New York: Columbia University Press, 2011) and Smalley, B., *The Study of the Bible in the Middle Ages* (Oxford: Blackwell, 1952). It is best accompanied by a general study such as Gibson, M. T., *The Bible in the Latin West* (Notre Dame: University of Notre Dame, 1993) and, even more, Graves, C. P., *The Form and Fabric of Belief: An Archaeology of the Lay Experience of Religion in the Medieval World* (Oxford: Archaeopress, 2000).

For an introduction to the liturgy see Heffernan, T. L., and E. A. Matter (eds.), *The Liturgy of the Medieval Church* (Kalamazoo: Medieval Institute, Western Michigan University Press, 2001). Another useful introduction is Dalmais, I. H., 'Principles of the liturgy', *The Church at Prayer: An Introduction to the Liturgy*, Vol. I (Collegeville, MN: Liturgical Press, 1987). A useful guide to how liturgical manuscripts operated is in Hughes, A., *Medieval Manuscripts for Mass and Office. A Guide to their Organization and Terminology* (Toronto: University of Toronto Press, 1982). Scholars have also collected key Church texts into volumes for easy reference. An example of one such book is Wieland, G. R. (ed.), *The Canterbury Hymnal* (Toronto: Centre for Medieval Studies, 1982).

Saints are important to medieval religion, but culthood is a complex subject. A good introduction is Brown, P. R. L., *The Cult of the Saints: Its Rise and Function in Latin Christianity* (Chicago: University of Chicago Press, 1981). The iconography of saints is important to understanding each saint's local influence as it is included in portraits and statues of the saints and in tokens such as pilgrim badges. A doorway into medieval iconography is Friedman, J. B. and J. M. Wegmann, *Medieval Iconography: A Research Guide* (New York: Garland Publishing, 1998).

For a basic understanding of how saints were made (although not necessarily medieval) see Woodward, K. L., *Making Saints: How the Catholic Church Determines Who Becomes a Saint, Who Doesn't, and Why* (New York: Simon and Schuster, 1990). Useful reference books for information about particular saints are Attwater, D., *The Penguin Dictionary of Saints. Penguin Reference Books*

(Harmondsworth: Penguin, 1965) and Farmer, D., *The Oxford Dictionary of Saints* (New York: Oxford University Press, 2003).

A good general introduction to monasticism is Burton, J., *Monastic and Religious Orders in Britain, 1000–1300* (New York: Cambridge University Press, 1994) or Lawrence, C. H., *Medieval Monasticism* (Harlow, UK: Longman, 2001). Knight, K., *The Catholic Encyclopedia* (Denver: New Advent, 2003) is also a useful reference for the basics on monastic rule and the history of various orders, as is Leyser, H., *Hermits and the New Monasticism: A Study of Religious Communities in Western Europe, 1000–1150* (London: Macmillan, 1984). Good general introductions to various orders are Lawrence, C. H., *The Friars: The Impact of the Mendicant Orders on Medieval Society* (New York: I. B. Tauris, 2013), Andrews, F., *The Other Friars: The Carmelite, Augustinian, Sack and Pied Friars in the Middle Ages* (Woodbridge: Boydell, 2006), Riley-Smith, J., *Templars and Hospitallers as Professed Religious in the Holy Land* (Notre Dame: University of Notre Dame Press, 2010). Also see Nicholson, H., *The Knights Templar: A New History* (Stroud: Sutton, 2001) and Lord, E., *The Knights Templar in Britain* (Harlow: Pearson Longman, 2002).

For more about religious institutions see Platt, C., *The Abbeys & Priories of Medieval England* (New York: Barnes & Noble Books, 1996) and Greene, J. P., *Medieval Monasteries* (Leicester: Leicester University Press, 1992). For more on mysticism in the Middle Ages, particularly relating to women, see Furlong, M., *Visions & Longings: Medieval Women Mystics* (Boston: Shambhala, 1996).

A very good introduction into the buildings, with further reading suggestions, is Rodwell, W., *The Archaeology of Churches* (Stroud: Amberley, 2012). Their internal decoration is unfortunately hard to trace today. Standing, G. and C. Hassall, 'Red-and-Black Painted Medieval Architecture: St Mary's Church, New Shoreham, Sussex', *Archaeological Journal* 163:1 (2006), 92–121 gives an impresson of original paint schemes. There are very few structures of Jewish religious life left; a big exception is the medieval *mikvah* found in Milk Street, London (http://archive.museumoflondon.org.uk/medieval/People/147010/).

For an introduction to the medieval papacy see Barrraclough, G., *The Medieval Papacy* (London: Thames and Hudson, 1968), and Morris, C., *The Papal Monarchy: The Western Church from 1050 to 1250* (New York: Oxford University Press, 1991). For information about specific popes see Kelly, J. N. D., *The Oxford Dictionary of Popes* (Oxford, New York: Oxford University Press, 1986). The Papacy's relationships with England were variable and often quite harried. The most interesting period from this point of view was probably during the life of Becket. An introduction to this, including translations of primary sources, can be found in Jones, T. M., *The Becket Controversy* (New York: John Wiley and Sons, 1970).

As with other areas, religion changed over our period. Excommunication, for example, was not systematically defined until the twelfth century, and evidence can be patchy. More about the practice of excommunication in our period, including on how secular punishments could be tied in with excommunication, can be found in Treharne, E., 'A Unique Old English Formula for Excommunication from Cambridge, Corpus Christi College 303', *Anglosaxon England*, 24 (1995), 185–212.

Our understanding of the role of religion in the everyday life of English Jews is just becoming known in an exciting new way. Previously, much of our knowledge was informed by the work of Cecil Roth, who is still important as an introductory author in the field, even though his work is dated. Modern research into English Judaism is starting to show a very different England to the one described by Roth. This is in contrast to our very stable knowledge of such basics of Judaism as the calendar, the liturgy and *kashrut*. The standard introductions to the Jewish liturgy are: Elbogen, I., *Jewish Liturgy: A Comprehensive History* (Philadelphia: The Jewish Publication Society, 1993) and Idelsohn, A. Z., *Jewish Liturgy and its Development* (New York: H. Holt & Co., 1932).

The exciting new work is best illustrated by the development of the Jewish calendar in Europe and how Jews used it in Carlebach, E., *Palaces of Time. Jewish Calendar and Culture in Early Modern Europe* (Cambridge Massachusetts: The Belknap Press, 2011), and sources such as www.oxfordjewishheritage.co.uk.

Anti-Semitism in medieval Europe, however, remains a difficult subject. It has been well studied, but interpretations have changed considerably over time. Langmuir, G., *Toward a Definition of Anti-Semitism* (Berkeley: California University Press, 1990) and Langmuir, G. I., *History, Religion, and Anti-Semitism* (Berkeley: University of California Press, 1990) both offer a useful approach to understanding it. A useful study of the development of the preaching orders (Dominican and Franciscan) and their connection to the increase in anti-Semitism is Cohen, J., *The Friars and the Jews: The Evolution of Medieval Anti-Judaism* (Ithaca and London: Cornell University Press, 1982). Jews were targets during the crusades; this is covered, for example, in Chazan, R., *European Jewry and the First Crusade* (Berkeley: University of California Press, 1987).

Some particularly nasty aspects of anti-Semitism were specific to England. Rees Jones, S., and S. Watson (eds.), *Christians and Jews in Angevin England. The York Massacre of 1190, Narratives and Contexts* (York: York Medieval Press, 2013) is a good example for a study about one of them. For an introduction to the very difficult subject of ritual murder, see Hsia, R. P., *The Myth of Ritual Murder* (New Haven: Yale University Press, 1988) and Langmuir, G. I., 'Thomas of Monmouth: Detector of Ritual Murder', *Speculum* 1984, 820–46. On broader issues of power and persecution, a useful place to start is Moore, R. I., *The Formation of a Persecuting Society: Power and Deviance in Western Europe* (New York: Blackwell, 1987).

5 Fighters Will Fight: Military

This is an enormous and very complex subject. Good introductions are Contamine, P., *War in the Middle Ages* (Oxford: Blackwell, 1984); Hooper, N. and M. Bennett, *The Cambridge Illustrated Atlas: Warfare: the Middle Ages 768–1487* (New York: Cambridge University Press, 1996) and Keen, M. (ed.), *Medieval Warfare: A*

History (Oxford: Oxford University Press, 1999). A useful book for quick reference is Nicolle, D., *Medieval Warfare Source Book. Warfare in Western Christendom* (London: Brockhampton Press, 1985).

Because warfare and the preparation for it and maintenance of matters military are all so vital to medieval England, the terminology associated with knights and their lives is vast. Useful overviews are: Bumke, J., *The Concept of Knighthood in the Middle Ages* (New York: AMS Press, 1982) as well as Harper, B. C. and R. Harvey (eds.), *The Ideals and Practices of Medieval Knighthood* (Woodbridge: Boydell, 1986) and Keen, M., *Nobles, Knights and Men-at-Arms in the Middle Ages* (London: Hambledon Press, 1996). It is also possible to venture into the subject through looking at the language of knighthood. Broughton, B. B., *Dictionary of Medieval Knighthood and Chivalry* (New York: Greenwood Press, 1988) is a useful reference on this subject.

Medieval military carries with it some quite particular problems for modern readers. Our idea of chivalry, for instance, does not at all match the medieval one; see Kaeuper, R. W., *Chivalry and Violence in Medieval Europe* (Oxford: Oxford University Press, 1999).

Many of the problems for modern readers can be resolved by examining the social system and its relation to the military. A good basic introduction to the English aristocracy is Crouch, D., *The Image of Aristocracy in Britain 1000–1300* (London: Routledge, 1992) along with Coss, P. R., *The Knight in Medieval England 1000–1400* (Stroud: Sutton, 1993) and Coss, P., *The Lady in Medieval England: 1000–1500* (Stroud: Sutton, 2000). How the aristocracy related to the rest of society (allowing for the dynamism of the system) can be found in Dyer, C., *Lords and Peasants in a Changing Society* (Cambridge: Cambridge University Press, 1980).

While there were many ways in which the military nature of social life was maintained, tournaments are easily the most fascinating to modern readers. For more on tournaments, see Barber, R. W. and J. R. V. Barker, *Tournaments: Jousts, Chivalry and Pageants in the Middle Ages* (Woodbridge: Boydell, 1989).

For warfare itself there is again a great deal of reading. Equipment and horses were essential, for instance. Overviews of medieval armour and its development can be found in DeVries, K., *Medieval Military Technology* (Peterborough, Ont.: Broadview Press, 1998) and Nicolle, D., *Arms and Armor of the Crusading Era 1050–1350: Western Europe and the Crusader States* (London: Greenhill Books, 1999), Edge, D. and M. Paddock, *Arms & Armour of the Medieval Knight* (London: Bison, 1988), and in Bradbury, J., *The Medieval Archer* (New York: St Martin's Press, 1985).

There are many studies of military horses, their development and their equipment. Good places to start are: Davis, R. H. C., *The Medieval Warhorse* (New York: Thames and Hudson, 1989) and Clark, J., *The Medieval Horse and Its Equipment, c. 1150 – c. 1450: Medieval Finds from Excavations in London* (London, UK: HMSO, 1995). Also useful is Hyland, A., *The Horse in the Middle Ages* (Stroud: Sutton, 1999).

6 Nature and Culture: Living with the Land

Although the land was of vital importance to Medieval English people, until recently the relationship of people with the land has been rather obscure. Part of this is because it does not show fully in written records, and partly because the land itself was (until the advent of new technology and its use by archaeologists) difficult to interpret due to the hundreds of years it has been lived on and worked since the Middle Ages. Recently there has been a burgeoning of understanding about how people in the Middle Ages lived and worked the land.

Keeping in mind that this new understanding of the subject is developing quite quickly, and that the explanations given in older overviews need to be read alongside the most recent work, the most useful introductions of how medieval people understood their natural surroundings are Chenu, M. D. et al., *Nature, Man, and Society in the Twelfth Century: Essays on New Theological Perspectives in the Latin West* (Toronto: Univ. of Toronto Press, 1997), Rackham, O., *The History of the Countryside: [the Classic History of Britain's Landscape, Flora and Fauna]* (London: Dent, 1993); White, G. J., *The Medieval English Landscape, 1000–1540* (London: Bloomsbury, 2012) and Cantor, L., *The English Medieval Landscape* (London: Croom Helm, 1982). A view of how scholars work is Campbell, B. M. S., and J. P. Power, 'Mapping the agricultural geography of medieval England', *Journal of Historical Geography*, 15, 1 (1989), 24–39.

A major study of the land and its formation and use to 1200 is Williamson, T., *Environment, Society and Landscape in Early Medieval England: Time and Topography* (Woodbridge: Boydell, 2013). Aston, M., *Interpreting the Landscape: Landscape Archaeology in Local Studies* (London: Batsford, 1985) is also a useful book. For an overview of many aspects of the countryside in the Middle Ages see Astill, G. G. and A. Grant, *The Countryside of Medieval England* (Oxford: Blackwell, 1988).

Our understanding of climate is also changing, and much research has been done in the last two decades, with many interesting results. There are two older works in French that bring together the evidence from written (primary) sources. They are Le Roy Ladurie, E., *Histoire du Climat: Depuis l'an Mil.* 1–2 (Paris: Flammarion, 1983) and Alexandre, P., *Le Climat en Europe au Moyen Age: Contribution à l'Histoire des Variations Climatiques de 1000 à 1425, d'Après les Sources Narratives de l'Europe Occidentale* (Paris: Editions de l'Ecole des Hautes Etudes en Sciences Sociales, 1987). One of the many more recent examples of studies is Pfister, C., J. Luterbacher, G. Schwarz-Zanetti and M. Wegmann, 'Winter air temperature variations in western Europe during the Early and High Middle Ages (AD 750–1300)', *The Holocene* 8 (July 1998), 535–52. A relatively recent overview about research methods and topics is given in Brázdil, R., C. Pfister, H. Wanner, H. von Storch and J. Luterbacher, 'Historical Climatology in Europe – The State Of The Art', *Climatic Change* 70:3 (2005), 363–430.

Another interesting area of recent study is how people shaped the land to meet their needs. An excellent analysis of how landowners did this, including their need for pleasure and hunting, can be found in Creighton, O. H., *Designs upon the Land: Elite Landscapes of the Middle Ages* (Woodbridge: Boydell Press, 2009), which works well alongside books about wood and managed woodlands such as Peterken, G. F., *Woodland Conservation and Management* (London: Chapman & Hall, 1993). A straightforward work on medieval gardens is Landsberg, S., *The Medieval Garden* (London: British Museum Press, 2004). Harvey, J., *Mediaeval Gardens* (London: Batsford, 1990) and MacDougall, E. B., *Medieval Gardens: 9th Dumbarton Oaks Colloquium on the History of Landscape Architecture: Papers* (Washington, D.C.: Dumbarton Oaks Research Library and Collection, 1986) are also useful.

One of the more distinctive aspects of land management in medieval England is the establishment and handling of forest. Young, C. R., *The Royal Forests of Medieval England* (Leicester: Leicester University Press, 1979) provides a solid overview, while James, N. D. G., *A History of English Forestry* (Oxford: Blackwell, 1981) is useful for a more formal understanding of forest and how it was used. Birrell, J. R., 'The Medieval English Forest', *Journal of Forest History*, 24 (1980), 78–85 is also a useful article. For activity within forests, especially hunting, see Cummins, J., *The Hound and the Hawk: the Art of Medieval Hunting* (London: Weidenfeld & Nicolson, 1988). Deer poaching is something that's generally 'known' about the Middle Ages. For a discussion of some of the issues involved in understanding it, see Birrell, J., 'Peasant Deer Poachers in the Medieval Forest,' in Britnell, R. H. and E. Miller (eds.), *Progress and Problems in Medieval England: Essays in Honour of Edward Miller* (Cambridge: Cambridge Univ. Press, 1996).

The best-known aspect of land management in this agrarian society is, of course, farming. Work on peasant farming techniques is still heavily dependent on limited sources (such as calendar pictures of farming work). As different sources are explored in innovative ways and as archaeology is integrated with historical studies, this picture is slowly changing. For an example of how specific local studies of quite precise sources can add to our knowledge, see Dodds, B., *Peasants and Production in the Medieval North-East, the Evidence from Tithes, 1270–1536* (Woodbridge: Boydell Press, 2007). An Old English tract from thirteenth-century England, often translated into Latin is a rare primary source, showing how a farm should be run by a reeve, available online at www.earlyenglishlaws.ac.uk/laws/texts/rspger/. It should be noted, however, that farming practices varied considerably and this offers only one example.

Weaving through all aspects of living on the land are the flora and fauna, from wolves to lambs, from saffron to mustard. Godwin, H., *The History of the British Flora: A Factual Basis for Phytogeography* (Cambridge: Cambridge University Press, 1984) is an introduction, and Hunt, T., *Plant Names of Medieval England* (Cambridge: Brewer, 1989) is a useful guide to plant names and what plants the literate might have known. A good study of herbs in the Middle Ages is Stannard, J. and K. E. Stannard, *Herbs and Herbalism in the Middle Ages and Renaissance* (Aldershot: Ashgate, 1999).

An overview of British mammals, including when different kinds were introduced, can be found in Yalden, D. W. and P. Barrett, *The History of British Mammals* (London: T & A D Poyser, 1999). On the extinction of species in Britain see Clutton-Brock, J., 'Extinct mammals', in Corbet, G. B. and S. Harris (eds.), *The Handbook of British Mammals* (Blackwell Scientific, 1991), 571–5.

How animals were farmed is at the heart of how 95 per cent of the English lived. A useful introduction to the aspect of husbandry on large estates is Biddick, K., *The Other Economy: Pastoral Husbandry on a Medieval Estate* (Berkeley: University of California Press, 1989). Aston, M. E., *Medieval Fish, Fisheries and Fishponds in England: Conference on Medieval Fish, Fishponds and Water Systems: Papers. Parts 1–2* (B.A.R., 1988) serves as a useful introduction to matters regarding fish, as do Currie, C. K., 'The Early History of the Carp and its Economic Significance in England', *The Agricultural History Review*, 39, 2 (1991), 97–107 and D. Sergeantson and C. M. Woolgar, 'Fish Consumption in Medieval England,' in Woolgar, C. M., D. Serjeantson and T. Waldron, *Food in Medieval England: Diet and Nutrition* (Oxford: Oxford Univ. Press, 2006).

A vexed issue is the introduction and farming of rabbits in England. Bond, J., 'Rabbits: The case for their medieval introduction into Britain', *The Local Historian*, 18, 2 (1988), 53–7 and the older introduction to the subject Sheail, J., *Rabbits and Their History* (Newton Abbot: David, 1971) are two works about this topic. For sheep, a good source to get started is Hurst, D., *Sheep in the Cotswolds. The Medieval Wool Trade* (Stroud: Tempus, 2005).

The aspect of life on the land that is in need of an introductory volume for modern readers is the production and use of metals. There are some dated introductions (discussed in the section on crafts) and there is a great deal of good material in archaeological find catalogues, especially about early medieval metalwork. Examples of these are Wiemer, K., *Early British Iron Edged Tools: A Metallurgical Survey* (Cambridge: University of Cambridge, 1993); Rubinson, S. R., *An Archaeometallurgical Study of Early Medieval Iron Technology: An Examination of the Quality and Use of Iron Alloys in Iron Artefacts from Early Medieval Britain* (Bradford: University of Bradford, 2010); Wheeler, J., 'Charcoal analysis of industrial fuelwood from medieval and early modern iron-working sites in Bilsdale and Rievaulx, North Yorkshire, UK: evidence for species selection and woodland management', *Environmental Archaeology*, 16, 1 (2011), 16–35. A good overview is also Brownsword, R., 'An Introduction to Base Metals and their Alloys 1200–1700' in Gilmour, L. (ed.), *Datasheets 1–24 (Finds Research Group)* (Oxford: Oxbow, 1999) or Goodall, A. R., 'The Medieval Bronzesmith and His Products', in Crossley, D. W., *Medieval Industry* (London: Council for British Archaeology, 1981).

Useful insights into mining and quarrying can be found in Knoop, D., *The Medieval English Quarry* (London: 1938). For insights into how the demand for metal helped shape the land and its use, see Delany, M. C., *The Historical Geography of the Wealden Iron Industry* (London: Benn Bros., 1921).

7 Working and Making: Craft and Artistry

With a subject as big as art and crafts, it helps to have a summary overview to place the various pieces in perspective. There are several broad overviews of crafts in Medieval England, but most of these are very dated. They are still useful to get a general orientation. Blair, J., and N. Ramsay (eds.), *English Medieval Industries: Craftsmen, Techniques, Products* (London [u.a.]: Hambledon Press 1991) also touches on subjects such as mass production. Other overview works are Coldstream, N., *Medieval Craftsmen: Masons and Sculptors* (Toronto: University of Toronto Press, 1991); Harvey, J., *Mediaeval Craftsmen* (New York: Drake Publishers, 1975); Crossley, D. W. (ed.), *Medieval Industry* (1981); and Salzman, L. F., *English Industries of the Middle Ages* (Oxford: Clarendon Press, 1923).

The best introduction to the work done in different crafts and how it was regarded is in French: Cassagnes-Brouquet, S., *Les Métiers au Moyen Âge* (Rennes: Ouest-France, 2008). Artists, their work and how it was seen are also explained in Sekules, V., *Medieval Art* (Oxford: Oxford University Press, 2001). Illustrations of craftspeople, mostly lay people, can be found, for instance, in Basing, P., *Trades and Crafts in Medieval Manuscripts* (London: British Library, 1990). Iron tools for many different crafts can be found in Goodall, I. H., *Ironwork in Medieval Britain: An Archaeological Study* (Cardiff: University College, 1980).

Medieval art operated in the medieval mindset and guides can be very helpful in interpreting it. Useful guides include: Murray, L. and P. Murray (eds.), *Dictionary of Christian Art*, Oxford Paperback Reference (New York: Oxford University Press, 2004) and Kessler, H. L., *Seeing Medieval Art* (Peterborough, Ontario: Broadview Press, 2004).

An example of a different publication about medieval art is Howard, H. C., 'Techniques of the Romanesque and Gothic wall paintings in the Holy Sepulchre chapel, Winchester Cathedral', in *Historical Painting Techniques, Materials, and Studio Practice: Preprints of a Symposium*, University of Leiden, the Netherlands, 26–29 June 1995 (1995). This is a detailed analysis of wall paintings in Winchester Cathedral, giving an impression of its complexity.

The context of craft in towns is also very important. See Rosser, G., 'Crafts, Guilds and the Negotiation of Work in the Medieval Town,', *Past and Present* 154 (Feb, 1997), 3–31 and, for the life of town-based artisans: Swanson, H., *Medieval Artisans: An Urban Class In Late Medieval England* (Oxford: Basil Blackwell, 1989). For an introduction to guilds and labour, see Epstein, S. A., *Wage Labor & Guilds in Medieval Europe* (Chapel Hill: University of North Carolina Press, 1991).

Most guild records have not been translated. *City Livery Companies and Related Organisations: A Guide to Their Archives in Guildhall Library* (London: Guildhall Library, 1989) is one of the exceptions, and a good starting place. Useful reading on guilds in general are Hickson, C. R., and E. A. Thompson, 'A new theory of guilds and European economic development', in *Explorations in Economic History*, 28 (1991), 127–68; Miller, E. and J. Hatcher, *Medieval England: Towns, Commerce and Crafts 1086–1348* (London: Longman, 1995); Epstein, S. R., 'Craft guilds, apprenticeship and technological change in pre-industrial Europe', *Journal of Economic History*, 58 (1998), 684–713. An overview of women in guilds is given by Kowaleski, M., and J. M. Bennett, 'Crafts, Gilds, and Women in the Middle Ages: Fifty Years after Marian K. Dale', *Signs*, 14, 2 (1989), 474–501. For a more recent, critical look at gender and guilds in research, including a research history, see Crowston, C., 'Women, Gender, and Guilds in Early Modern Europe: An Overview of Recent Research' *International Review of Social History*, 53, S16 (2008), 19–44; this text includes many more references (including references to medieval guilds) and mention of mixed-gender and women guilds.

Introduction to Specific Subjects

For the wide range of crafts in the Middle Ages, there is as wide a range of studies undertaken by specialists, covering specific aspects and elements. Examples of these are given here, listed by subject.

Jewellery: Bury, S., *Jewelry Gallery: Summary Catalogue* (London: Victoria & Albert Museum, 1983); Cherry, J., *Medieval Craftsmen: Goldsmiths* (British Museum Press, 1992).

Architecture and sculpture: For an introduction, see Calkins, R. G., *Medieval Architecture in Western Europe from A.D. 300 to 1500* (Oxford: Oxford University Press, 1998) and Stalley, R., *Early Medieval Architecture* (Oxford: Oxford University Press, 1999). Good initial guides to the timelines and styles of medieval architecture are Snyder, J. et al., *Snyder's Medieval Art* (Upper Saddle River, NJ; London: Prentice Hall, 2006) and Stokstad, M., *Medieval art* (Boulder, Colo.; Oxford: Westview, 2004), as well as Coldstream, N., *Medieval Architecture* (Oxford: Oxford University Press, 2002) and Clifton-Taylor, A. and A. S. Ireson, *English Stone Building* (London: Gollancz, 1983).

An orientation into the key terms for architecture and sculpture (focussed on France, but useful for England nonetheless) is Minne-Sève, V. and H. Kergall, *Romanesque and Gothic France: Architecture and Sculpture* (New York: Harry N. Abrams, 2000). For an overview of the history and meanings of the term 'Gothic', see Groom, N., *The Gothic: A Very Short Introduction* (Oxford: Oxford University Press, 2012) For the extension of the term to other arts, see Frisch, T. G., *Gothic Art 1140 – c. 1450: Sources and Documents* (Toronto: University of Toronto Press, 1997).

Metalwork: A very good overview of the items and tools made by smiths is Goodall, I. H., *Ironwork in Medieval Britain: An Archaeological Study* (Cardiff: University College, 1980); the thesis was published as a print monograph in 2011. Casting tools – crucibles and moulds – as well as other debris from metalworking are described in Ottaway, P. and N. Rogers, *Craft, Industry and Everyday Life: Finds from Medieval York* (York: Council for British Archaeology, 2002).

Information about refining and working non-ferrous metals is given in Bayley, J. C., *Non-Ferrous Metalworking in England: Late Iron Age to Early Medieval* (London: University of London, 1992). Egan, G. and F. Pritchard, *Dress Accessories*

c. *1150* – c. *1450* (London: HMSO, 1991), shows many non-ferrous metal finds, among them cast buttons, produced using moulds. More about gold and silver specifically can be found in Cherry, J., *Medieval Goldsmiths* (London: British Museum Press, 2011).

A useful introduction to tin is Hatcher, J., *English Tin Production and Trade Before 1550* (Oxford: Clarendon Press, 1973) and for pewter Weinstein, R., *The Archaeology of Pewter Vessels in England 1200–1700: A Study of Form and Usage* (Durham: Durham University, 2011) An overview over pewterers in London specifically can be found in Homer, R. F., 'The medieval pewterers of London, *c.* 1190–1457', *Transactions of the London and Middlesex Archaeological Society*, 36 (1985), 137–63.

More information about both pattern-welded and Wootz steel can be found in Sachse, M., *Damascus Steel: Myth, History, Technology, Applications* (Düsseldorf: Stahleisen, 1994). A very detailed survey of pattern-welding and knife-making is in Blakelock, E. S., *The Early Medieval Cutting Edge Of Technology: An Archaeometallurgical, Technological And Social Study Of The Manufacture And Use Of Anglo-Saxon And Viking Iron Knives, And Their Contribution To The Early Medieval Iron Economy* (University of Bradford).

Later knives are described in Cowgill, J., M. de Neergard and N. Griffiths, *Knives and Scabbards* (London: HMSO 1987). A very rare archaeological find of a blacksmith's tool chest including anvils is the Mästermyr find, Arwidsson, G. and G. Berg, *The Mästermyr Find. A Viking Age Tool Chest from Gotland* (Lompoc, CA: Larson Publishing Company, 1999) and wire-making is explained in Slater, R. V., *Medieval Iron Wire: Manufacture, Materials and Methods; An Archaeological and Scientific Investigation of the Manufacturing Technology and Use of Specialist Metals in the Production of Iron Wire and Wire Fish Hooks in Medieval England* (Bradford: University of Bradford, 2008).

Woodworking: Hewett C. A., *English Historic Carpentry* (London: Phillimore, 1980) is one of our recommended references. Woodworking information can also be found in many archaeological catalogues, for example in Morris, C. A., and P. V. Addyman, *Craft, Industry and Everyday Life: Wood and Woodworking in Anglo-Scandinavian And Medieval York* (London: Council for British Archaeology 2000). Also interesting is Rackham, O., *The Growing and Transport of Timber and Underwood* (Oxford: BAR, 1982).

Working with clay: There are many archaeological publications, including regional publications, about pottery. A good book for a first and general overview is MacCarthy, M. R. and C. M. Brooks, *Medieval Pottery in Britain AD 900–1600* (Leicester: Leicester University Press, 1988). See also Holdsworth, J. and Y. A. Trust, *Selected Pottery Groups AD 650–1780* (London: York Archaeological Trust, 1978) for changes in pottery types. Chronology of object types and forms can also be found in catalogues of finds from larger excavations, such as York Archaeology, for example Ottaway, P. and N. Rogers, *Craft, Industry and Everyday Life: Finds from Medieval York* (York: Council for British Archaeology, 2002).

A very detailed analysis of the clay and the production of pottery, including slips, glazes etc., can be found in Henderson, J., *The Science and Archaeology of Materials: an Investigation of Inorganic Materials* (London: Routledge, 2000). A typology of kilns used can be found in Musty, J. 'Medieval Pottery Kilns' in Evison, V., H. Hodges, and J. G. Hurst (eds.), *Medieval Pottery from Excavations: Studies Presented to Gerald Clough Dunning* (New York: St. Martin's Press 1974).

Overview books about floor tiles are, for example, Eames, E. S. and British Museum, *Medieval Tiles: a Handbook* (London: Brit. Museum, 1968) and for later tiles Stopford, J., *Medieval Floor Tiles of Northern England: Pattern and Purpose; Production Between the 13th and 16th Centuries* (Oxford: Oxbow, 2005).

Antler, Ivory, Bone, Horn: An introduction to the materials and the things worked from them can be found in MacGregor, A., *Bone, Antler, Ivory & Horn. The Technology of Skeletal Materials since the Roman Period* (London/Sydney: Croom Helm, 1985). One of the many publications about crafts with these materials is St. Clair, A. E. and E. P. E. McLachlan, *The Carver's Art: Medieval Sculpture in Ivory, Bone, and Horn* (Jane Voorhees Zimmerli Art Museum: Rutgers, The State University of New Jersey, 1989). Finds from York from these materials are published in MacGregor, A., A. J. Mainman, N.S.H. Rogers, *Craft, Industry and Everyday Life: Bone, Antler, Ivory and Horn from Anglo-Scandinavian and Medieval York* (York: Council for British Archaeology, 1999).

Parchment and leather: A general reference for parchment and leather is Reed, R., *Ancient Skins, Parchments and Leathers* (London; New York: Seminar Press, 1972), and Reed, R., *The Nature and Making of Parchment* (Leeds: Elmete Press, 1975). For leather and fur, a general introduction is Cameron, E. A., *Leather and Fur: Aspects of Early Medieval Trade and Technology* (London: Archetype, 1998); an example for the leather finds from a specific place is Mould, Q., I. Carlisle and E. Cameron, *Leather and Leatherworking in Anglo-Scandinavian and Medieval York* (York: Council for British Archaeology, 2003).

Pens, inks and writing materials: An outstanding introduction is Bischoff, B., *Latin Paleography: Antiquity and the Middle Ages* (Cambridge: Cambridge University Press, 1990). A useful reference on the style of work done by different scribes on different manuscripts is Brown, M., *A Guide to Western Historical Scripts from Antiquity to 1600* (London: British Library, 1990), while a good overview of the work of the scribe is De Hamel, C., *Scribes and Illuminators* (London: British Museum Press, 1992). It also covers related industries such as parchment-makers.

Many libraries now offer digitised manuscripts for a good look at the result of these crafts, such as the British Library, *British Library Illuminated Manuscripts Catalogue*, www.bl.uk/catalogues/illuminatedmanuscripts/.

Textiles: An introduction into historical textiles and their techniques is Geijer, A., *A History of Textile Art* (Leeds: Sotheby Parke Bernet/Pasold Research Fund, 1982); the London finds published in Crowfoot, E., F. Pritchard and K. Staniland, *Textiles and Clothing c. 1150 – c. 1450* (London: HMSO, 1992) give a nice overview on different fabrics and techniques. For the difficult topic of textile terminology, Seiler-Baldinger, A., *Textiles: A Classification of Techniques* (Washington D.C.: Smithsonian Institution, 1994) and Burnham, D. K., *Warp and Weft. A Textile*

Terminology (London/Henley: Routledge & Kegan Paul, 1981) are dictionary-style books that will prove very helpful.

Glass: A concise overview on glass-making and the development is given in Meek, A. S., *The Chemical and Isotopic Analysis of English Forest Glass* (Nottingham: University of Nottingham, 2011). See also Dungworth, D., 'The Value of Historic Window Glass', *The Historic Environment*, 2, 1 (2011), 21–48.

Spectacular examples of stained glass are shown in Hayward, J., C. Clark and M. B. Shepard, *English and French Medieval Stained Glass in the Collection of the Metropolitan Museum of Art* (New York: Harvey Miller and Metropolitan Museum of Art, 2003).

8 People at Play: Leisure Activities

There are surprisingly few sources on medieval leisure. Overviews are built up, therefore, largely by extrapolation or by using that very small pool of sources over and again. This means that the current view of leisure in the Middle Ages and our knowledge of particular pastimes is liable to significant change as more sources are discovered, through archaeology (our knowledge of gaming has changed significantly over the past twenty years due to the results of digs) and through examination of previously neglected sources. William Fitzstephen's description of London is one of these sources: Fitzstephen, W., *Fitz-Stephen's Description of the City of London, Newly Translated from the Latin Original; with a Necessary Commentary* (B. White, 1772); it is available as a digitalised book or in website form at http://users.trytel.com/~tristan/towns/florilegium/introduction/intro01.html. It has excellent detail about London at play, and it is unique.

Interesting works on the subject are also McLean, T., *The English at Play, in the Middle Ages* (Windsor Forest: Kensal Press, 1983), as is Reeves, A. C., *Pleasures and Pastimes in Medieval England* (Stroud: Alan Sutton, 1995). A useful study into the role of entertainers in medieval society is Southworth, J., *Fools and Jesters at the English Court* (Phoenix Mill: Sutton Publishing, 1996).

A general introduction to the wide variety of games and sports in the Middle Ages is Carter, J. *Medieval Games: Sports and Recreations in Feudal Society* (New York: Greenwood Press, 1992).

Some pastimes had particular importance. For example, chess played a complex role in medieval society. An interesting study of this is Eales, R., 'The Game of Chess: An Aspect of Medieval Knightly Culture,', in Harper-Bill, C. and Harvey, R. (eds.), *Papers for First & Second Strawberry Hill Confs. The Ideals and Practice of Medieval Knighthood*, (Woodbridge, Suffolk: Boydell & Brewer, 1986), 12–34. The prime example of a medieval manuscript regarding, among other things, chess, is Alfonso X and R. Orellana Calderón, *Libro de los Juegos: Acedrex, Dados e Tablas; Ordenamiento de las Tafurerías* (Madrid: Fundación José Antonio de Castro, 2007).

Regarding tournaments, another very important medieval pastime, two useful books are: Barber, R. and J. Barker, *Tournaments, Jousts, Chivalry and Pageants in* the Middle Ages (New York: Weidenfeld & Nicolson, 1989) and Barker, F. J., *The Tournament in England: 1100–1400* (Woodbridge: Boydell, 2008).

While chess and tournaments belonged to the elite, it is quite possible that music and dance belonged to all classes. We have little concrete information, however, as the evidence is fragmentary. A great deal of our knowledge of medieval instruments comes from pictures and from mentions of an instrument in text. A little written music also survives, but most of that is from the latter end of our period.

Three useful books on music are: Page, C., *Music and Instruments of the Middle Ages: Studies on Texts and Performance* (Aldershot, Great Britain: Variorum, 1997), Stevens, J. E., *Words and Music in the Middle Ages: Song, Narrative, Dance and Drama – 1050–1350* (New York: Cambridge University Press, 1986) and Yudkin, J., *Music in Medieval Europe* (Englewood Cliffs: Prentice Hall, 1989). A book more aimed at performers is McGee, T. J., *Medieval and Renaissance Music, A Performer's Guide* (Toronto: University of Toronto Press, 1985). A particularly interesting study of the work of women in music is Doss-Quinby, E., J. Tasker Grimbert, W. Pfeffer and E. Aubrey (eds.), *Songs of the Women Trouveres*, (New Haven: Yale University Press, 2001). The most useful introduction to dance during this period is McGee, T., *Medieval Instrumental Dances* (Bloomington, IN: Indiana University Press, 1989).

9 Where to Live?: Homes, Castles, Villages and Towns

Studies on medieval houses are quite different in terms of quality and content to studies of medieval households. Taking the latter first, the problem is that most of our sources are for the late Middle Ages and for those few big households that kept records. This is discussed by Woolgar, C. M., *The Great Household in Late Medieval England* (New Haven, CT: Yale University Press, 1999).

Most of our knowledge of lives within the walls comes from fourteenth century records. A good introduction for the thirteenth century is Labarge, M. W., *A Baronial Household of the Thirteenth Century* (London: Harvester Press, 1980). Mertes, K., *The English Noble Household: 1250–1600* (Oxford: Blackwell, 1988) is also useful specifically for England late in our period. An outstanding source of examples of the household devices and materials is Egan, G., *The Medieval Household. Daily Living c. 1150 – c. 1450. Medieval Finds from Excavations in London* (London: The Boydell Press/Museum of London, 2010). Another useful source (especially but not only for Jewish households) is Metzger, T. and M., *Jewish Life in the Middle Ages: Illuminated Hebrew Manuscripts of the Thirteenth to the Sixteenth Centuries* (New York: Alpine Fine Arts Collection, 1982).

Buildings are easier to find out about, as they appear in written record and have been explored in more depth archaeologically. Studies cover everything from building methods and organisation such as Knoop, D. and G. P. Jones, *The Medieval Mason: An Economic History of English Stone Building in the Later Middle Ages and Early Modern Times* (Manchester: Manchester University Press, 1967), to specific elements of buildings such as roofs like Walker, J., 'Late-Twelfth &

Early-Thirteenth-Century Aisled Buildings: A Comparison', *Vernacular Architecture*, 30, 1 (1999), 21–53 and Smith, J. T., 'English Medieval Roofs' in Drdácký, M. (ed.), *European Research on Cultural Heritage: State of the Art Studies Volume 4* (Prague: Institute of Theoretical and Applied Mechanics Academy of Sciences of the Czech Republic, 2006). Examples of ironwork employed in buildings, including padlocks, locks and keys, can be found in Goodall, I. H., *Ironwork in Medieval Britain: An Archaeological Study* (Cardiff: University College, 1980). Specific rooms, such as halls, form the subject of other studies such as Thompson, M.W., *The Medieval Hall: The Basis of Secular Domestic Life 600–1600 AD* (Aldershot: Scholar Press, 1995). Carpentry can be difficult, so general studies such as Hewett, C. A., *Church Carpentry, a Study Based on Essex Examples* (London: Phillimore, 1981), and Hewett, C. A., *English Cathedral and Monastic Carpentry* (Chichester: Phillimore,1985) use pieces preserved in churches as their basis.

Some subjects are better covered than others. A book that covers a range of surviving furniture (and we cannot be certain of how typical this furniture was) is Tracy, C., *English Medieval Furniture and Woodwork* (London: Victoria & Albert Museum, 1988). The classic (although hard to obtain) book on the subject is Eames, P., *Medieval Furniture: Furniture in England, France and the Netherlands from the Twelfth to the Fifteenth Century* (London, UK: The Furniture History Society, 1977).

For the many items of daily life found in houses, archaeological works are again a very helpful source. A good example is Egan, G. and J. Bayley, *The Medieval Household: Daily Living* c. *1150* – c. *1450* (London: HMSO, 1998).

Looking for specific types of building can help pinpoint good literature in the field. The best study of medieval houses, regardless of location, is still Grenville, J., *Medieval Housing*, (London: Leicester University Press, 2000). Wood, M., *The English Mediaeval House* (London: Bracken, 1965) is also useful, but dated. The following may also be useful references: Calkins, R. G., *Medieval Architecture in Western Europe from A.D. 300 to 1500* (Oxford: Oxford University Press, 1998); Dyer, C., 'Building in Earth in Late-Medieval England', *Vernacular Architecture*, 39 (2008), 63–70.; Pearson, S., 'Medieval Houses in English Towns: Form and Location', *Vernacular Architecture*, 40, 1 (2009), 1–22. For examples of houses and house fittings, with many details and nicely showing variations and possibilities for one large city, see Schofield, J., *Medieval London Houses* (New Haven: Yale Univ. Press, 1994).

A good general introduction to medieval fortifications is Kenyon, J. R., *Medieval Fortifications* (Leicester: Leicester University Press, 1990) and also Brice, M.H., *Forts and Fortresses: from the Hillforts of Prehistory to Modern Times – the Definitive Visual Account of the Science of Fortification* (London: Chancellor Press, 1999). There are many sources of information on medieval castles, for instance see Warner, P., *The Medieval Castle. Life in a Fortress in Peace and War* (New York: Barnes and Noble, 1971) or Platt, C., *The Castle in Medieval England and Wales* (New York: Scribner, 1982). For floorplans and diagrams see Gravett, C., *Norman Stone Castles 1: The British Isles 1066–1216* (Oxford: Osprey, 2003). A useful overview of castles and their historical contexts can be found in Pounds, N. J. G., *The Medieval*

Castle in England and Wales: A Social and Political History (Cambridge: Cambridge University Press, 1990). A look at the many facets and functions of castles can be found in Liddiard, R., *Castles in Context. Power, Symbolism and Landscape, 1066–1500* (Oxford: Windgather Press, 2012).

Settlements

The connection between landscape and community is important to understand medieval settlements. Everitt, A., *Landscape and Community in England* (London: Hambledon Press, 1985) and Chapelot, J. and R. Fossier, *The Village and House in the Middle Ages* (Berkeley: University of California Press, 1985) are helpful in this regard, while a good study of rural settlements is Aston, M et al. (eds.), *The Rural Settlements of Medieval England* (Oxford: Blackwell, 1989).

Recent work has begun to examine water supplies, for instance Hansen, R. D., 'Water-related Infrastructure in Medieval London' (2009, www.waterhistory.org). It is looking probable that water supplies and management in medieval towns were more sophisticated than previously thought, which means that older analyses may prove unreliable.

How the different aspects of a town varied can be seen through overviews and comparative analyses, such as Hilton, R. H., *English and French Towns in Feudal Society: A Comparative Study* (Cambridge: Cambridge University Press, 1992), Schofield, J. and A. Vince, *Medieval Towns* (Madison: Fairleigh Dickinson University Press, 1994) and Reynolds, S., *An Introduction to the History of English Medieval Towns* (Oxford: Clarendon Press, 1977). The standard (albeit dated) study of boroughs is Tait, J., *The Medieval English Borough. Studies on its Origins and Constitutional History* (Manchester: Manchester University Press, 1936) while the classic study of women in towns is Uitz, E., *The Legend of Good Women. The Liberation of Women in Medieval Cities* (Rhode Island and London: Wakefield, 1994).

More general works on towns and urbanisation are Swanson, H., *Medieval British towns* (Basingstoke: Macmillan, 1999), Holt, R. and G. Rosser (eds.), *The Medieval Town* (London: Longman, 1990), Schofield, J. and A. G. Vince, *Medieval Towns: The Archaeology of British Towns in Their European Setting* (London; New York: Continuum, 2003) and Palliser, D. M., *The Cambridge Urban History of Britain. Vol. 1, c. 600 – c. 1540* (Cambridge: Cambridge University Press, 2000). There are also many studies that focus on villages, for instance Hooke, D. (ed.), *Medieval Villages* (Oxford: Oxford University Press, 1985).

Different types of places had different layouts. A good introduction to town plans and topography in England is Barley, M.W. (ed.), *The Plans and Topography of Medieval Towns in England and Wales*. Council for British Archaeology, Research Report no.14 (1976). A study of the layout of towns that gives explanations of typical features is Hindle, P., *Medieval Town Plans* (Princes Risborough: Shire Publications, 2002). Layout of villages and the fields around them can be seen in the aerial photos of Beresford, M. W. and J. K. S. Saint Joseph, *Medieval England:*

An Aerial Survey (Cambridge [u.a.]: Cambridge University Press, 1979). For the handling of waterfronts and the buildings on them see, for instance, Dyson, T., *The Medieval London Waterfront* (London: Museum of London, 1989).

It is important to note that London was a special case. There is a great deal of specialist work relating to living in London, but it cannot be simply applied to life outside London due to the significantly smaller population bases in the rest of England. An example of a focused study of this kind is Hanawalt, B. A., *Growing Up in Medieval London: The Experience of Childhood in History* (New York: Oxford University Press, 1993). An excellent study of the effects of trade on London's everyday is Milne, G., *The Port of Medieval London* (The Mill: Tempus Publishing Ltd, 2003).

10 Learning for Life: Education

The shape of education in medieval society depends very much on the needs that literacy holds within it. This subject can be explored through Carruthers, M., *The Book of Memory: A Study of Memory in Medieval Culture*, 2nd ed. (Cambridge: Cambridge University Press, 2008) and Clanchy, M. T., *Literacy and Law in Medieval England* (London: Hambledon Press, 1992). For a broader analysis of the society see Stock, B., *The Implications of Literacy. Written Languages and Models of Interpretation in the 11th and 12th Centuries* (Princeton NJ: Princeton UP, 1983). Thompson, J. W., *The Literacy of the Laity in the Middle Ages* (Berkeley: University of California Press, 1939) is old, but still an excellent introduction to the field. A discussion of lay literacy can be also be found in Orme, N., 'Lay Literacy in England, 1100–1300', in Haverkamp, A. and H. Vollrath (eds.), *England and Germany in the High Middle Ages* (London: German Historical Institute, and Oxford: Oxford University Press, 1996), 35–56. Medieval education also depends on the shape of medieval theology, and an introduction to this is Evans, G. R. (ed.), *The Medieval Theologians: An Introduction to Theology in the Medieval Period* (Oxford: Blackwell, 2001).

Some elements of medieval education are particularly well-studied and an infinite amount of reading is available. The suggested reading in this section reflects this patchiness. Topics such as grammar and rhetoric and the work of major teachers fit into this category. Other areas (the education of girls, for instance) have many fewer resources and have to be explored through quite specific topics. An example of this is Alexandra Barratt's article, 'Small Latin? The Post-Conquest Learning of English Religious Women' in Echard, S. and G. R. Wieland (eds.), *Anglo-Latin and its Heritage, Publications of the Journal of Medieval Latin, 4* (Brepols, 2001).

Nicolas Orme provides excellent overviews in his *From Childhood to Chivalry: The Education of English Kings and Aristocracy, 1066–1530* (London: Methuen, 1984); *Medieval Schools* (New Haven: Yale University Press, 2006); and *Education and Society in Medieval and Renaissance England* (London and Ronceverte: Hambledon Press, 1989).

The single best source on Jewish education in the Middle Ages is Kanarfogel,

E., *Jewish Education and Society in the High Middle Ages* (Detroit: Wayne State University Press, 1992). A good introduction to the role of education in early childhood is Marcus, I. G., *Rituals of Childhood. Jewish Acculturation in Medieval Europe* (New Haven: Yale University Press, 1998).

In terms of formal study, the best approach is to understand how they fit within the structure of the liberal arts and then to look at specific subjects. Good introductory books are Abelson, P., *The Seven Liberal Arts, A Study in Medieval Culture* (New York: Columbia University, 1906) and Wagner, D.L. (ed.), *The Seven Liberal Arts in the Middle Ages* (Bloomington, IN: Indiana University Press, 1983).

Introductions to Specific Subjects

Arithmetic: Evans, G. R., 'From Abacus to Algorism: Theory and Practice in Medieval Arithmetic', *British Journal for the History of Science* 10:2=35 (London: 1977), 114–31.

Cosmology: Grant., E., *Planets, Stars, and Orbs: The Medieval Cosmos, 1200–1687* (Cambridge: Cambridge University Press, 1996).

Grammar: Lanham, C. D. (ed.), *Latin Grammar and Rhetoric: From Classical Theory to Medieval Practice* (London and New York: Continuum, 2002).

Logic: Broadie, A., *Introduction to Medieval Logic* (Oxford: Clarendon Press, 1993).

Music: Hughes, A., *Medieval Music: The Sixth Liberal Art* (Toronto: University of Toronto Press, 1980).

Philosophy: Marenbon, J. (ed.), *The Oxford Handbook of Medieval Philosophy* (New York: Oxford University Press, 2012); Sirat, C., *A History of Jewish Philosophy in the Middle Ages* (Cambridge: Cambridge University Press, 1985).

Rhetoric: Miller, J. M., M. H. Prosser and T. W. Benson (eds.), *Readings in Medieval Rhetoric* (Bloomington: Indiana University Press, 1973).

For more on the universities themselves see Cobban, A. B., *The Medieval English Universities: Oxford and Cambridge to c. 1500* (Berkeley: University of California Press, 1988).

11 Crossroads of the Mind: Science, Magic, Medicine and Technology

A straightforward way of assessing some of the differences between medieval and modern world view is through how the world was formally depicted. See, for instance: Edson, E., *Mapping Time and Space: How Medieval Mapmakers Viewed Their World* (London: British Library, 1997). For a deeper understanding of some of the key differences see Ward, B., *Miracles and the Medieval Mind: Theory, Record and Event, 1000–1215* (Philadelphia: University of Pennsylvania Press, 1982). An excellent introduction to the subject as a whole is Wigelsworth, J. R., *Science and Technology in Medieval European Life* (Westport, CT: Greenwood Press, 2006). This relationship is also explained in Grant, E, *The Foundations of*

Modern Science in the Middle Ages. Their Religious, Institutional and Educational Contexts (Cambridge: Cambridge University Press, 1996).

Many modern minds automatically try to distinguish between alchemy and chemistry, between magic and science, between astronomy and astrology. While these distinctions are not effective to understand science in the Middle Ages, they help refine keywords to facilitate an understanding. Focusing on alchemy, for instance, gives an introduction to its history in Nummedal, Tara E., 'Words and Works in the History of Alchemy', *Isis* 102: 2, (June 2011).

The reason for modern words being insufficient guides is that there are crossroads where different disciplines come together in ways that are not reflected in modern thought. The best introduction to magic and to how different ideas merge to create medieval culture and scientific thought is Kieckhefer, R., *Magic in the Middle Ages* (New York: Cambridge University Press, 1990). However, it only covers Christianity, and there is no overview on the Jewish equivalent in Western Europe. The best book available is still Trachtenberg, J., *Jewish Magic and Superstition. A Study in Folk Religion* (Philadelphia: University of Pennsylvania Press, 2004). However, this book was first published in 1939 and is very dated; it uses a different concept of the Middle Ages to more recent work and must be handled with care.

Moving away from the bird's eye view, many specific topics within this medieval crossroads of ideas are covered in Lindahl, C., et al. (eds.), *Medieval Folklore: An Encyclopedia of Myths, Legends, Tales, Beliefs, and Customs* (Santa Barbara, CA: ABC-Clio, 2000). New work in the field is shading Lindahl's overview and offers more nuance. For instance, literature produced within the church for sermons, for pastoral work and so forth are used by Rider, C., *Magic and Religion in Medieval England* (London: Reaktion Books, 2012). This book helps us understand the clerical response to magical practices and belief in England from the twelfth century but also looks at otherworldly beings and the church's response to them. Pollington, S., *Leechcraft. Early English Charms, Plantlore and Healing* (Ely: Anglo-Saxon Books, 2001) has some material on Anglo-Saxon magical practices. How common folk responded to magic is best seen in popular literature. The best study of the notion of the good magician and of the change in status of Merlin in various contexts and during different periods is Lawrence-Mathers, A., *The True History of Merlin the Magician* (New Haven and London: Yale University Press, 2012).

At the far end to magic in the medieval mind is the miracle. A common way of interpreting and experiencing miracles was through pilgrimage. see Finucane, R. C., *Miracles and Pilgrims: Popular Beliefs in Medieval England* (London and New York: Palgrave/MacMillan, 1995).

Beyond this, there are many medieval works that themselves explain the ideas of their time. The bestiary is particularly useful illustration, as it demonstrates how the natural world, the religious and the scientific meld. For a modern translation of a medieval bestiary see White, T. H., *The Book of Beasts* (Phoenix Mill: Alan Sutton, 1992). For more on the subject see Hassig, D. (ed.), *The Mark of the Beast: The Medieval Bestiary in Art, Life, and Literature* (New York: Garland, 1999).

Another approach to medieval thought is, of course, through medicine (both the theory and the everyday reality). Good introductory volumes to medieval medicine are Siraisi, N. G., *Medieval and Early Renaissance Medicine. An Introduction to Knowledge and Practice* (Chicago and London: The University of Chicago Press, 1990), Rawcliffe, C., *Medicine and Society in Later Medieval England* (London: Sandpiper, 1999) and Getz, F., *Medicine in the English Middle Ages* (Princeton, N.J.: Princeton University Press, 1998). A good current study of how the extant (mostly theoretical) evidence about medieval medicine translates into practical health care is Demaitre, L., *Medieval Medicine: The Art of Healing, from Head to Toe* (Santa Barbara, CA: Praeger, 2013). It has more of an English focus than Siraisi's work and mainly examines mainstream medicine. A good starting point for Anglo-Saxon medicine is Cameron, M.L., *Anglo-Saxon Medicine*, (Cambridge: Cambridge University Press, 1993).

Some manuals of remedies have been recorded and tend to be called 'popular' by scholars. The best collection of these is Hunt, T., *Popular Medicine in Thirteenth-Century England: Introduction and Texts*, (Cambridge: Wolfeboro, N. H.; D. S. Brewer, 1990). While they are still at the more learned end of the spectrum, they do help us learn about the wider understanding of treatment. A study containing untranslated examples of original Anglo-Norman texts can be found in Hunt, T., *Anglo-Norman Medicine*, volumes 1–2, (Cambridge: D.S. Brewer, 1994–7). Translated excerpts can be found in Wallis, F., (ed.) *Medieval Medicine. A Reader* (Toronto: University of Toronto Press, 2010).

It is important to keep in mind that most writing about the Middle Ages focusses on the male world, due to the nature of surviving sources. Medicine is an exception, as there has been a great deal of excellent research into this field. The chief scholar in the field of women's health is Monica Green. She has many specialised studies, but a good introductory one is Green, M., *Women's Healthcare in the Medieval West* (Farnham: Ashgate, 2000). For Jewish manuscripts in this field see Barkai, R., *A History of Jewish Gynaecological Texts in the Middle Ages* (Leiden-Boston-Köln: 1998).

Another equally important thing to keep in mind is that popular assumptions (that people in the Middle Ages were uneducated, lacked personal hygiene) can interfere with an understanding of all medieval matters of the mind. These assumptions are especially prevalent in the fields of science and medicine, though they extend to many other areas of medieval life. There is work on all these fields that clearly shows how far these assumptions are from medieval reality. For instance, a recent study on the history of personal hygiene is Smith, V., *Clean. A History of Personal Hygiene and Purity* (Oxford: Oxford University Press, 2007) and a key new work on public health and sanitation is Rawcliffe, C., *Urban Bodies: Communal Health in Late Medieval English Towns and Cities* (Woodbridge: The Boydell Press, 2013). There is a simpler approach than reaching for the specialist treatises first, however, as there is a website (part of the ORB, an excellent resource on the Middle Ages) edited by Stephen J. Harris and Bryon L. Grigsby that has brief essays on some of the most problematic modern misperceptions: http://the-orb.net/non_spec/missteps/misindex.html.

Technology is quite separate from science much of the time and medieval technology has been much less studied. The seminal study in the Middle Ages is White Lynn, Jr., *Medieval Technology and Social Change* (Oxford: Oxford University Press, 1962). It is, however, dated. Scholarly articles examining specific technologies and innovations are thus the most useful resource. A study of some of the uses of new technology in medieval life can be found in Wigelsworth, J. R., *Science and Technology in Medieval European Life* (Westport, CT: Greenwood Press, 2006). Though old, Moorhouse, S., 'Medieval distilling-apparatus of glass and pottery', *Medieval Archaeology* 16 (1972), 79–121 is still the starting point for distillation equipment terminology and English finds.

For technology used by craftspeople, an overview of specific crafts will give some indication. General overviews can seldom demonstrate first use of a given technology. The more specific the study, however, the better the understanding of the technological state of that craft (and the technology level in society as a whole). Studies in this field date very quickly as archaeologists uncover more information. For instance, Gimpel, J., *The Medieval Machine* (New York: Holt, 1976) was an important study in its time, but is not reliable anymore.

Useful references for scientific instruments are Turner, A.J., *Of Time and Measurement: Studies in the History of Horology and Fine Technology* (Aldershot and Brookfield: Ashgate, 1993) and Turner, A. J., *The Time Museum Catalogues: Vol. 1, Time Measuring Instruments, Part 1, Astrolabes, Astrolabe Related Instruments* (Rockford: The Museum, 1985).

12 Written and Spoken Words: Languages and Their Literature

Polyglottal societies are fundamentally different to monoglottal societies. They each operate uniquely and, for the Middle Ages, we only have the written record, which means we do not have a complete picture of language use. Rothwell, W., 'The role of French in thirteenth century England', *Bulletin of the John Rylands University Library of Manchester* 58:2 (1976), 445–66 is useful as a start. A good discussion of the use of written texts in the Middle Ages is Coleman, J., *Public Reading and the Reading Public in Late Medieval England and France* (Cambridge: Cambridge University Press, 2005). A useful study of memory and how it operated within medieval culture (one which offers significant insights into the nature of story in medieval culture) is Carruthers, M., *The Book of Memory. A Study of Memory in Medieval Culture* (Cambridge: Cambridge University Press, 1990). Past this, the best approach is to seek books on specific subjects that used a specific language. Literature, for instance, and the law, are both good entries into how various languages found their niches in England.

For the influence of French language and culture on English literature see also Calin, W., *The French Tradition and the Literature of Medieval England* (Toronto: University of Toronto Press, 1994). The standard guide to the language is Kibler, W. W., *An Introduction to Old French*, (New York: MLA, 1984). A more detailed overview can be found in Zink, M., *Medieval French Literature: An Introduction*, (Binghamton: Medieval and Renaissance Texts & Studies, 1995). The importance of Anglo-Norman is studied by Legge, M. D., *Anglo-Norman Literature and its Background* (Westport, CT: Greenwood Press, 1967).

An outstanding introduction to England's Latin literature in the Middle Ages is Rigg, A. G., *A History of Anglo-Latin Literature 1066–1422* (Cambridge: Cambridge University Press, 1992). A more recent overview is Hexter, R. J. and D. Townsend (eds.), *The Oxford Handbook of Medieval Latin Literature. Oxford Handbooks* (Oxford; New York: Oxford University Press, 2012).

For an overview of English literature, see Treharne, E., and G. Walker (eds.), *The Oxford Handbook of Medieval Literature in English* (Oxford: Oxford University Press, 2010) and in Scanlon, Larry, (ed.), *The Cambridge Companion to Medieval English Literature, 1100–1500* (Cambridge: Cambridge University Press, 2009). The standard overview of Middle English texts is Severs, J. et al., *A Manual of the Writings in Middle English, 1050–1500* volumes 1–26 (Hartford: The Connecticut Academy of Arts and Sciences, 1967–2005).

For an interpretation of the function of 'non-polite' literature, see Ziolkowski, J. M. (ed.), *Obscenity: Social Control and Artistic Creation in the European Middle Ages*, (Leiden: Brill, 1998).

For samples of medieval texts in translation, see Black, J., *The Broadview Anthology of British Literature. The Medieval Period* (Toronto: Broadview Press, 2006).

Key subjects and their treatment in the literature of the various medieval languages are described in Lindahl C., et al., (eds.), *Medieval Folklore: An encyclopedia of Myths, Legends, Tales, Beliefs, and Customs* (Santa Barbara, CA: ABC-Clio, 2000). A useful further study is Gurevich, A., *Medieval Popular Culture: Problems of Belief and Perception* (Cambridge: Cambridge University Press, 1988). The best general resource or starting point on Arthurian literature in the Middle Ages is Lacy, N. J., *The New Arthurian Encyclopedia* (New York and London: Garland Publishing, 1996) while Kreuger, R., *The Cambridge Companion to Medieval Romance* (New York: Cambridge University Press, 2002) provides a good introduction to the romance genre.

REED (Records of Early English Drama), based in Toronto, not only spearheads the work about early drama but maintains a good internet portal for those who wish to explore it: www.reed.utoronto.ca/med-em.html.

There are significant issues in understanding Jewish English culture through literature, as there are very, very few surviving sources. An introduction to those surviving sources is provided by Skinner, P. (ed.), *Jews in Medieval Britain: Historical, Literary, and Archaeological Perspectives* (Woodbridge, Suffolk: The Boydell Press, 2003). The best (although dated) overview of Jewish literature (including Hebrew) in the Middle Ages is Zinberg, I., *A History of Jewish Literature* (New York: Ktav Publishing House, 1972–7).

13 Clothes Make the Man: Clothing and Fashion

As discussed in the text, information concerning clothes and fashion and even accessories is surprisingly scanty. Work using archaeological finds and art and mentions in written works gradually round out our knowledge, but it remains incomplete. Clothing specialists work across national boundaries a great deal as there are next to no garment fragments surviving. This is why, in this part, more sources not from England have been given. Information can be found in unexpected places: one of the few mentions for underpants, for instance, was pointed out to us by Elizabeth Chadwick in a fabliau in Brians, P., *Bawdy Tales from the Courts of Medieval France*, (New York: Harper and Row, 1972), 82–9.

Crowfoot, E., F. Pritchard, and K. Staniland, *Textiles and Clothing c. 1150 – c. 1450* (London: HMSO, 1992) is a good place to start at looking at archaeological textiles from England, including fragments of clothes, woven bands and other small items. Kania, K., *Kleidung im Mittelalter. Materialien – Konstruktion – Nähtechnik. Ein Handbuch* (Köln: Böhlau Verlag, 2010) features a catalogue with almost all known medieval garments (German book with English summary), while Østergård, E., *Woven into the Earth. Textiles from Norse Greenland* (Aarhus: Aarhus University Press, 2004) is a publication about finds from Greenland after our period, but shows impressive details of tailoring and stitching work. Geijer, A., *A History of Textile Art* (Leeds: Sotheby Parke Bernet/Pasold Research Fund, 1982) is a good way for an overview about textile history. For references regarding basic terminology, a few good choices are listed in the 'Crafts' section of this bibliography.

Though mostly later than our period, the values of textiles and their economic importance are treated in many works by Munro, such as Munro, J. H., *Textiles, Towns and Trade. Essays in the Economic History of Late-Medieval England and the Low Countries* (Aldershot: Variorum, 1994). He also published an extensive bibliography about this topic: Munro, J. H., *A Bibliography of European Textiles, c. 1100–1750*, available at www.economics.utoronto.ca/wwwfiles/archives/munro5/ETextBib.htm.

A useful discussion of dress as display is Lachaud, F., 'Dress and Social Status in England before the Sumptuary Laws,' in Coss, P., and M. Keen (eds.), *Heraldry, Pageantry, and Social Display in Medieval England* (Martlesham: Boydell Press, 2002), 105–23.

The standard book about embroidery is Christie, A. G., *English Mediaeval Embroidery* (Oxford: Clarendon Press, 1938). References to woven bands are spread over many books and papers. Spies, N., *Ecclesiastical Pomp and Aristocratic Circumstance. A Thousand Years of Brocaded Tabletwoven Bands* (Jarretsville, Maryland: Arelate Studio, 2000) gives a good impression of the splendour of brocaded tablet-woven bands. Peter Collingwood has treated many different textile techniques in his many books, including narrow wares, and the definitive guides to loopbraiding are Speiser, N., *The Manual of Braiding* (Basel: self-published, 1988; Speiser, N., *Old English Pattern Books for Loop Braiding* (Arboldswil: self-published, 2000).

The classic book about nalebinding is Hansen, E. H., *Nålebinding: Definition and Description* (London: IAP, 1990). Examples for socks worked in nalebinding, as well as many other interesting textile finds, are in Walton Rogers, P., *Textile Production at 16–22 Coppergate* (York: Council for British Archaeology, 1997).

Dyeing is a very complex topic. A standard reference for dyeing is Cardon, D., *Natural Dyes. Sources, Tradition, Technology and Science* (London: Archetype Publications, 2007). Manuals on natural dyeing and indigo dyeing abound again these days: Sandberg, G., *Indigo Textiles: Technique and History* (London: Black, 1989) is an example. For other examples about dyeing literature regarding archaeological finds, see for instance Hall, A. R., *Evidence of Dyeplants from Viking York and Medieval Beverley* (Edinburgh: National Museum of Scotland, 1983) or Taylor, G. W., 'Detection and identification of dyes on Anglo-Scandinavian textiles', *Studies in Conservation* 28, no. 4 (1983), 153–60.

Silk fabrics were especially important as a status symbol; introductions to this topic are Woodward Wendelken, R., 'Wefts and worms: the spread of sericulture and silk weaving in the West before 1300', *Medieval Clothes and Textiles* 10 (2014), 59–77, and Lewis May, F., *Silk Textiles of Spain. Eighth to Fifteenth Century* (New York: Hispanic Society of America, 1957).

The most important source of information about dress accessories is archaeology. While accessories are mentioned in literature and appear in art, the amount of data from archaeology makes detailed interpretation possible. It enables works such as Standley, E. R., *Trinkets and Charms: The Use, Meaning and Significance of Later Medieval and Early Post-Medieval Dress Accessories* (Durham: Durham University, 2010). To gain an overview of the many varieties of dress accessories, archaeological catalogues are again useful. Most of these list finds from a specific place or area. Dress accessories from London are published in Egan, G. and F. Pritchard, *Dress Accessories c. 1150 – c. 1450* (London: HMSO, 1991). Finds from York are published in Ottaway, P. and N. Rogers, *Craft, Industry and Everyday Life: Finds from Medieval York* (York: Council for British Archaeology, 2002); the earlier Anglo-Saxon finds are published in Mainman, A. J. and N. S. Rogers, *Craft, Industry and Everyday Life: Finds from Anglo-Scandinavian York* (York: Council for British Archaeology, 2000).

Finally, with Britain's rather large community of metal detector users, there are also collector's catalogues available. Examples of this are the 'Detector Finds' series by Gordon Bailey, Whitehead, R., *Buckles, 1250–1800* (Witham: Greenlight, 2003), Mills, N., *Medieval Artefacts* (Witham: Greenlight, 1999), and Read, B., *Hooked-Clasps & Eyes: A Classification & Catalogue of Sharp- or Blunt-Hooked Clasps & Miscellaneous Objects with Hooks, Eyes, Loops, Rings or Toggles* (Langport: Portcullis Pub., 2008). As an online source for an overview, the Portable Antiquities scheme collects registrations of finds by the public in Britain: www.finds.org.uk.

Shoes, another important part of dress, are more often preserved than textiles, and they have been studied extensively. For specifically English finds, see for example Grew, F. and M. de Neergaard, *Shoes and Pattens. Medieval Finds from Excavations in London Part 2* (London: HMSO, 2001); Mould, Q., I. Carlisle and

E. A. Cameron, *Craft, Industry and Everyday Life: Leather and Leatherworking in Anglo-Scandinavian and Medieval York* (York: Council for British Archaeology, 2003). For a wider overview, see Goubitz, O., C. van Driel-Murray, and W. Groenman-Van Waateringe, *Stepping Through Time* (Zwolle: Stichting Promotie Archeologie, 2001).

14 Everybody Needs to Eat: Food and Drink

Research into food and drink is a wonderful mixture of glamorous and detailed ... and untrustworthy. Part of the problem is that many popular assumptions colour this work. There are, however, several reliable and cautious historians who can be turned to. Even when reading their work, the nature of the evidence must be considered. It is important to note that the vast majority of our sources on this subject (including recipes and descriptions of great households) are from the fourteenth century or later. Evidence is far more reliable for later in our period than earlier, but scholars are often able to give no more than suggestions for any of it. In reading a book such as Henisch, B., *The Medieval Cook* (Martlesham, Suffolk: Boydell Press, 2013), it's important to find out what the author is citing and the period and place it comes from. Generalisations lead to a reinforcement of assumptions about the period rather than an accurate understanding of foodways in the Middle Ages.

Some of the sources are literary, medical or household accounts. There are, however, some cookbooks still extant. For a brief discussion of surviving English cookbooks and a useful introduction see Hieatt, C. B., 'Listing and Analysing the Medieval English Culinary Collections: A Project and its Problems' in Lambert, C. (ed.) *Du manuscrit à la table.* (Paris/Montréal: Champion-Slatkine/Les Presses de l'Université de Montréal, 1992). In the same volume, there is a listing of manuscripts known at that time to contain recipes (pp. 317–63).

There are some areas where we know extremely little. Peasant food, for instance, is one of these areas, although our knowledge of foodstuffs available expands as the work of archaeologists gets fed into the work of food historians. Also, very little work has been done specifically on Jewish food in medieval England. The best general introduction to Jewish food in Western Europe in the Middle Ages is: Cooper, J., *Eat and Be Satisfied. A Social History of Jewish Food.* (Northvale: Jason Aronson Inc, 1993), 17–37 (for an overview of the dietary laws) and 79–145. For a more general view of aspects of eating and food storage see: Castano, J. et al. *The Jews of Europe in the Middle Ages.* (Berlin: Hatje Cantz Publishers, 2005). Hagen, A., *Anglo-Saxon Food and Drink: Production, Processing, Distribution and Consumption.* (Ely, Cambs: Anglo-Saxon Books, 2006) is the best introductory book on the earlier part of our period. It is, however, dating as new research increases our understanding.

The more accessible modern cookbooks promising to recreate medieval dishes generally use modern ingredients and methods and are mainly based on manuscripts from after our period. There is no book that recreates the precise recipes of our period, for the same reason that we cannot be certain about the feel and drape of cloth: ingredients have changed and medieval recipes do not give exact ingredients. One of the better of these modern-medieval cookbooks is Hieatt, C. E., B. Hosington and S. Butler, *Pleyn Delit: Medieval Cookery for Modern Cooks* (Toronto: University of Toronto Press, 1996). Another source for reconstructed recipes, also providing links to sources and other material (though again generally later than the thirteenth century), is www.medievalcookery.com.

15 Making Money: Medieval Economy

What was England like economically just before 1066? Sawyer, P., *The Wealth of Anglo-Saxon England* (Oxford: Oxford University Press, 2013) presents a good picture of England's economy at that moment and in the lead up to it. This is just one of a number of books that describe medieval economies. Unfortunately, the range of approaches they take is quite broad. A useful starting place for a practical understanding of this complex scholarly situation is Nightingale, P., *A Medieval Mercantile Community. The Grocers' Company & the Politics & Trade of London 1000–1485*, (New Haven, CT: Yale University Press, 1995), which deals with broad issues of economy and social history. For those who need an introduction to the field, Bolton, J., 'What is Money? What is a Money Economy? When did a Money Economy Emerge in Medieval England?' in Wood, D. (ed.), *Medieval Money Matters* (Oxford: Oxbow Books, 2004), 1–15 is helpful. Following that, there are several key works that explore money further: Spufford, P., *Money and its Use in Medieval Europe* (Cambridge: Cambridge University Press, 1993); Spufford, P. et al., *Handbook of Medieval Exchange* (London: Boydell and Brewer, 1986) and Allen, M. R., *Mints and Money in Medieval England* (Cambridge: Cambridge University Press, 2012).

For an introduction specifically to the English economy see Bolton, J. L., *The Medieval English Economy 1150–1500* (London: Dent, 1988); Postan, M. M., *The Medieval Economy and Society: An Economic History of Britain in the Middle Ages* (London: Penguin Books, 1993); Wood, D., *Medieval Economic Thought* (Cambridge, UK; New York: Cambridge University Press, 2002).

The best place to start thinking about the medieval economy, however, is with something concrete such as Allen, M., 'The Volume of the English Currency, *c.* 973–1158,' in Cook, B. and G. Williams (eds.), *Coinage and History in the North Sea World c. 500–1200*, (Leiden: Brill, 2006), 487–523. It is important to keep in mind that economic changes within the Middle Ages were rather extreme. By the later Middle Ages, this resulted in some remarkable changes. See Dyer, C., *Standards of Living in the Later Middle Ages: Social Change in England c. 1200–1520* (Cambridge : Cambridge Univ. Press, 1998).

A helpful book in understanding how economic changes apply specifically to our period is Fryde, E. B., *Studies in Medieval Trade and Finance* (London: Hambledon Press, 1983). Of the economic impact of the diverse crafts, that of the textile industry is currently the best understood. See, for example, Bridbury, A.

R., *Medieval English Clothmaking. An Economic Survey* (London: Heinemann Educational Books, 1982), Lloyd, T. H., *Alien Merchants in England in the High Middle Ages* (Brighton: Harvester Press, 1982) in addition to Munro's works mentioned in the textile section.

The complexity of the economy meant that banking and trade not only had their place, but had their own problems. The stereotype of Jewish moneylenders was alive in the Middle Ages and did not reflect the complex reality. For an introduction to this subject see Shatzmiller, J., *Shylock Reconsidered: Jews, Moneylending, and Medieval Society* (Berkeley: Univ. of California Press, 1990).

For discussion of the rural economy see Thirsk, J., *The Rural Economy of England: Collected Essays* (London: Hambledon Press, 1984). An interesting study of how animal husbandry operated in this economy is Biddick, K., *The Other Economy: Pastoral Husbandry on a Medieval Estate* (Berkeley u.a.: University of California Press, 1989).

Hunt, E. S. and J. M. Murray, *A History of Business in Medieval Europe, 1200–1550* (Cambridge: Cambridge Univ. Press, 2005) is a useful general introduction to this subject.

For learning more about fairs, see Moore, E.W., *The Fairs of Medieval England: An Introductory Study* (Toronto: Pontifical Institute of Mediaeval Studies, 1985) and also (for a wider perspective) Masschaele, J., *Peasants, Merchants, and Markets. Inland Trade in Medieval England, 1150–1350* (London: Macmillan Press, 1997).

16 Getting There and Back: Travel and Transport

People on the move as part of their everyday lives included merchants, messengers and the nobility. The best single book on travel in the Middle Ages is Ohler, N., *The Medieval Traveller* (Woodbridge: Boydell Press, 2010). For the travel experience of specific groups, however, there are other studies. For instance, a good introduction to pilgrims and pilgrimage in the Middle Ages is Davidson, L. K. and M. Dunn-Wood, *Pilgrimage in the Middle Ages: A Research Guide* (New York: Garland, 1993). An outstanding study of the most popular pilgrim route is Candy, J., *The Archaeology of Pilgrimage on the Camino de Santiago de Compostella. A Landscape Perspective* (Oxford: Archaeopress, 2009). For an understanding of how and why women undertook pilgrimages see Hopper, S., *Mothers, Mystics and Merrymakers. Medieval Women Pilgrims* (Phoenix Mill: Sutton Publishing, 2006).

For material on what a given traveller might discover on a given route, archaeological reports and overviews are particularly useful. A book on medieval roads, for instance, is Hindle, B. P., *Medieval Roads* (Aylesbury: Shire Publications, 1989). Much has been published about bridges, for example the York Bridge accounts, Harrison, D. F., *The Bridges of Medieval England: Transport and Society, 400–1800* (Oxford: Clarendon Press, 2007), Wilson, B., F. Mee and P. V. Addyman, *'The Fairest Arch in England': Old Ouse Bridge, York, and Its Buildings; The Pictorial Evidence* (York: York Archaeological Trust, 2002), and Cook, M.,

Medieval Bridges (Princes Risborough, Buckinghamshire: Shire Publications Ltd., 1998).

For ships and their contexts, see Friel, I., *The Good Ship: Ships, Shipbuilding and Technology in England 1200–1520* (Washington, DC: Johns Hopkins Press, 1995). A general good introduction into the archaeological study of ships is Marsden, P., *Book of Ships and Shipwrecks* (London: B.T. Batsford/English Heritage, 1997), and a study of the relationship of ships with one quite specific port is Marsden, Peter, *Ships of the Port of London. Twelfth to Seventeen Centuries AD* (London: English Heritage, 1993).

The tools for travel are very well studied indeed. Information about astrolabes and their fellow instruments can be found in studies of technology and in museum catalogues. The most useful reference is one of the latter: Ward, F. A. B., *A Catalogue of European Scientific Instruments in the Department of Medieval and Later Antiquities of the British Museum* (London: British Museum, 1981).

17 How Many Leagues to Babylon?: Measuring Things

There are several excellent reference books for basic measurements and measuring systems. They include: Connor, R. D. and Science Museum, *The Weights and Measures of England* (London: Her Majesty's Stationery Office, 1987); Zupko, R. E., *A dictionary of Weights and Measures for the British Isles: The Middle Ages to the Twentieth Century* (Philadelphia: American Philosophical Society, 1985). An archaeological example is Shortt, H., 'A thirteenth-century "steelyard" balance from Huish', *Wiltshire Archaeol Natur Hist Mag* 63 (1968), 66–71.

A good overview of the calendar is Cosman, M. P., *Medieval Holidays and Festivals* (New York: Scribner, 1981) while a useful reference book for calendar and custom is Weiser, F.X., *Handbook of Christian Feasts and Customs* (Mahwah, NJ: Paulist Press, 1963). Actual calendars were incorporated into Books of Hours. A good study of how many of these books were used is Scott-Stokes, Charity, *Women's Books of Hours in Medieval England* (Cambridge: D.S. Brewer, 2006).

Regarding time measurements, Cheney's book on dates is again a useful reference, but the standard guide to this subject is Poole, R. L., *Medieval Reckonings of Time. Helps for Students in History*, v.3 (London: Society for promoting Christian knowledge, 1921). Moreover, there are tools available to help writers calculate the dates they require. A good one online is the medieval calendar calculator at www. wallandbinkley.com/mcc/. It allows for the changes between the medieval calendar and our own.

For more about how festivals might be celebrated, see Clopper L. M., *Drama, Play, and Game, English Festive Culture in the Medieval and Early Modern Period* (Chicago, IL: University of Chicago Press, 2001).

For the Jewish calendar and festivals, modern introductions to Judaism (such as Donin, H., *To Be a Jew: A Guide to Jewish Observance in Contemporary Life*, (New York, NY: Basic Books 1991) are useful thanks to the continuity in Orthodox Jewish practice since the Middle Ages.

Besides the obvious differences between travel now and travel in the Middle Ages as explained in the chapter on travel, there are some less obvious ones that can be researched very straightforwardly. Between the early Middle Ages and the fifteenth century, mapping was quite different to what it is now. This is one reason why a reading list of medieval maps is not the same as a reading list that introduces where people are likely to travel to: the two were not quite as entwined as they are today. A good approach to understanding these differences is to examine what purposes maps served in the Middle Ages. A useful introductory book for this is Lilley, K. D. (ed.), *Mapping Medieval Geographies: Geographical Encounters in the Latin West and Beyond, 300–1600* (Cambridge: Cambridge University Press, 2013). It examines where people of the Middle Ages were likely to gain their geographical understanding, including what information certain medieval maps contain and why.

This book was written over a long period of time, and not all topics have recent overviews, so this list gives older literature as well as new. We have done our best to check everything and to provide reliable sources, but of course we cannot guarantee that that we are on top of current research for every topic covered or mentioned here.

When you open these doors and explore the Middle Ages for yourself, keep in mind that scholars can make errors or have hidden misconceptions. You will have to form your own picture and your own understanding. If we have provided a solid foundation and helped you get started with this, our book has fulfilled its purpose, and we wish you success in your further research.

List of Illustrations

26. Harley 4951 f. 298v. British Library, Catalogue of Illuminated Manuscripts
27. Stadt Schlüsselfeld, photo Petra Mytzka
28. Katrin Kania
29. IG Wolf, photo Sonja Natus
30. IG Wolf, photo Sonja Natus
31. Museum of London Archaeology
32. Arundel 157 f. 6v. British Library, Catalogue of Illuminated Manuscripts
33. Nikolaus Hofbauer
34. Nikolaus Hofbauer
35. UPenn LJS 252. Rare Book & Manuscript Library University of Pennsylvania, http://dla.library.upenn.edu/dla/medren/
36. Ms. Ludwig XII 5. J. Paul Getty Museum, Los Angeles, digital image courtesy of the Getty's Open Content Program
37. Sloane 2030 ff. 125v-126. British Library, Catalogue of Illuminated Manuscripts
38. Additional 5474 f. 144. British Library, Catalogue of Illuminated Manuscripts
39. Harley 4751 f. 6v. British Library, Catalogue of Illuminated Manuscripts
40. MS Add. 38663 fol. 1. British Library, Catalogue of Illuminated Manuscripts
41. Katrin Kania
42. Nikolaus Hofbauer
43. Stefan von der Heide
44. LIN-640A55. Portable Antiquities Scheme, www.finds.org.uk
45. Arche Warder, largest centre for rare breeds in Europe, photo Lisa Iwon
46. Rare Breeds Survival Trust
47. Gillian Polack
48. Middelaldercentret (Medieval Centre, Denmark), www.middelaldercentret.dk, photo David Lazenby
49. Middelaldercentret (Medieval Centre, Denmark), www.middelaldercentret.dk, photo David Lazenby
50. Interessensgemeinschaft 14. Jahrhundert in Wien, photo Christina Curreli
51. LIN-D6D1D8. Portable Antiquities Scheme, www.finds.org.uk
52. Royal 13 A XI f. 33v. British Library, Catalogue of Illuminated Manuscripts
53. Harley 2772 f. 70v. British Library, Catalogue of Illuminated Manuscripts

The pictures in this book show both original sources such as manuscript pages and archaeological finds as well as replicas, reconstructions and interpretations done by archaeologists and Living History people. Reconstructions can give a very good impression of how things may have looked that sources alone will not provide, but they can also convey wrong impressions. We have tried hard to select pictures that will give a good and accurate impression. However, all modern reconstructions are our interpretation of the sources we have, and we ask you to keep that in mind.

The finds from www.finds.org.uk are reproduced under the CC BY 2.0 license, manuscript Images from the British Library are under a CC0 1.0 Public Domain license.

Index